Lully Studies

The historical importance of composer Jean-Baptiste Lully has long
been recognized. Regarded as the founder of French opera, as the
embodiment of French Baroque musical style and a key figure in the
development of court ballet, he enjoys growing popular and scholarly
interest. This volume presents the best recent research on Lully's life,
his work, and his influence. Eleven essays by American and European
scholars address a wide range of topics including Lully's genealogy,
the *tragédie lyrique*, Lully's Palais Royal theatre, the collaboration
with Molière, the transmission of Lully's work away from the Ile-de-
France, and a heretofore unexplored link with Marcel Proust.
Illustrated with musical examples and photographs, the volume also
contains surprising archival discoveries about the composer's early
life in Tuscany and new information about his manuscript sources. It
will interest all those involved in the music of Lully and his time,
whether musicologists, historians, performers, or listeners.

JOHN HAJDU HEYER is Professor of Music and Dean of the College
of Arts and Communication at the University of Wisconsin,
Whitewater. He is editor of *Jean-Baptiste Lully and the Music of the
French Baroque* (Cambridge University Press, 1989). His scholarly
work also includes critical editions of music by Lully and Gilles.

Lully Studies

Lully Studies

EDITED BY JOHN HAJDU HEYER

CAMBRIDGE
UNIVERSITY PRESS

PUBLISHED BY THE PRESS SYNDICATE OF THE UNIVERSITY OF CAMBRIDGE
The Pitt Building, Trumpington Street, Cambridge, United Kingdom

CAMBRIDGE UNIVERSITY PRESS
The Edinburgh Building, Cambridge CB2 2RU, UK   www.cup.cam.ac.uk
40 West 20th Street, New York, NY 10011–4211, USA   www.cup.org
10 Stamford Road, Oakleigh, Melbourne 3166, Australia
Ruiz de Alarcón 13, 28014 Madrid, Spain

First published 2000

Printed in the United Kingdom at the University Press, Cambridge

Typeface Adobe Minion 10.25/14pt   *System* QuarkXpress™ [SE]

A catalogue record for this book is available from the British Library

Library of Congress cataloguing in publication data

Lully studies / edited by John Hajdu Heyer.
        p.   cm.
Includes bibliographical references (p.   ) and index.
ISBN 0 521 62183 6 (hardback)
1. Lully, Jean Baptiste, 1632–1687.   2. Lully, Jean-Baptiste, 1632–1687 – Criticism and
interpretation.   I. Heyer, John Hajdu.
ML410.L95 L96   2000
780′.92–dc21   00-020313

ISBN 0 521 62183 6 hardback

Contents

List of plates [viii]
Foreword by James R. Anthony [ix]
Preface [xvii]

1   Lully's Tuscan family [1]
JÉRÔME DE LA GORCE

2   Lully plays deaf: rereading the evidence on his privilege [15]
PATRICIA RANUM

3   The phrase structures of Lully's dance music [32]
REBECCA HARRIS-WARRICK

4   Quinault's libretto for *Isis*: new directions for the *tragédie lyrique* [57]
BUFORD NORMAN

5   The articulation of Lully's dramatic dialogue [72]
LOIS ROSOW

6   The Amsterdam editions of Lully's music: a bibliographical scrutiny with commentary [100]
CARL B. SCHMIDT

7   "Pourquoi toujours des bergers?" Molière, Lully, and the pastoral *divertissement* [166]
JOHN S. POWELL

8   The presentation of Lully's *Alceste* at the Strasbourg Académie de Musique [199]
CATHERINE CESSAC

9   Walking through Lully's opera theatre in the Palais Royal [216]
BARBARA COEYMAN

10   Gluck and Lully [243]
HERBERT SCHNEIDER

11   Jules Ecorcheville's genealogical study of the Lully family and its influence on Marcel Proust [272]
MANUEL COUVREUR

List of works cited [289]
Index [299]

Plates

3.1   Choreography from *Recüeil de Dances contenant un tres grand nombres des meillieures Entrées De Ballet De Mr. Pecourt*... (Paris: Feuillet, 1704) [38]

8.1   Brossard's score of *Alceste. ou le Triomphe d'alcide. mis en musique par m^r de Lully* in Brossard's own hand. F-Pn Vm^2 12bis [204]

9.1   Israel Silvestre, Palais Royal, exterior, *c.* 1675 [227]

9.2   Carlo Vigarani, Palais Royal, floor plan, *c.* 1674. Stockholm, Nationalmuseum, CC175 [230]

9.3   Carlo Vigarani, Palais Royal, elevation, *c.* 1674. Stockholm, Nationalmuseum, CC176 [231]

9.4   Anonymous, stage candles. Stockholm, Nationalmuseum, THC 614 [235]

9.5   Carlo Vigarani, stage decor, *Thésée*, Act V. Stockholm, Nationalmuseum, THC 662 [236]

9.6   Jean Berain, stage decor, unidentified. Stockholm, Nationalmuseum, THC 606 [238]

9.7   Jean Berain, stage decor, *Hésione*, 1701. Stockholm, Nationalmuseum, THC 688 [240]

9.8   Anonymous. Palais Royal, stage machinery. Stockholm, Nationalmuseum, CC186 [241]

Foreword by James R. Anthony

As we welcome another collection of Lully essays, the fourth to appear in the past decade,[1] we must ponder the fact that among those composers who define an epoch, Lully continues today to be more admired and more scrutinized than performed. The *Œuvres complètes* begun by Henry Prunières almost seventy years ago remains incomplete, and there are few if any available performing editions of Lully's dramatic and religious music. Such neglect surely would have amazed the author of the Lully obituary, found in the *Mercure galant* of March 1687, who wrote: "The world wide acclaim accorded M^r [de Lully] will not let you ignore his death."[2] In *Les hommes illustres qui ont paru en France pendant ce siècle*, Charles Perrault tells us "Lully had composed pieces of music which have delighted all of France for a long time and which passed beyond the boundaries [of France] to foreign lands."[3] We know for a fact that between 1677 and 1725 Lully's operas were performed outside of France in Holland (The Hague, Amsterdam), in Belgium (Brussels, Antwerp, Ghent), in Germany (Wolfenbüttel, Regensburg, Ansbach, Darmstadt, Hamburg, Stuttgart, Bonn), in Italy (Modena, Rome) and in England (London),[4] surely a remarkable geographic spread considering the relative lack of mobility of opera during that time.

There is hope that Lully's fortunes may improve as we enter the twenty-first century. A newly formed international committee has begun preparation of the *Œuvres complètes* under the direction of Jérôme de La Gorce and Herbert Schneider – this after years of frustration (the first Lully Works committee met at Berkeley in 1977). There have been recent staged

1 These are: HeyerL, Heidelberg87, and Sèvres98. See p. 289 below for full citations.
2 "Le bruit que Mr a fait dans le monde ne vous aura pas laissé ignorer sa mort."
3 "Lully avoit composé des pièces de Musique qui en fait pendant un très longtemps les délices de toute la France, & qui on passé chez tous les Estranges" (Paris, 1696), 85–86.
4 See SchmidtG, 183–211.

and concert performances of *Atys, Amadis, Armide, Isis, Phaëton, Roland,* and *Acis et Galathée.* The staying power of a Lully opera is impressive when it is performed with some knowledge of performance practices and with some attempt to replicate what we know about Baroque staging, dance, and gesture. Since 1987, the production of *Atys* by Les Arts Florissants under the direction of William Christie has been performed more than seventy times for enthusiastic audiences in Paris, Florence, Montpellier, and Brooklyn. The Lully discography continues to grow; presently there are even two different compact disc recordings of *Alceste.*

Writings about Lully and his works date from the lifetime of the composer and increased after his death in 1687. Several are merely anecdotal. Many by aestheticians are preoccupied with the validity of the Quinault *livret* (libretto) seen as tragedy, for as the Abbé Mably wrote: "An excellent Poem is absolutely necessary for the long range success of an Opera. The Music, all by itself, can only give it passing vogue as a novelty."[5] Charles Perrault was chief among those who supported what Antoine-Louis Le Brun labeled a "tragédie irregulière." Perrault clearly saw the fallacy of comparing opera with ancient tragedy: "Opera or *Pièces de machines,* not having been invented at the time of Horace, can hardly be subjected to laws made at that time . . . Nothing is less bearable in a Comedy than to resolve the intrigue by a miracle or by the arrival of a god in a machine; and nothing is more beautiful in the Opera than these kinds of miracles and appearances of Divinities when there is some basis for introducing them."[6] Perrault's spirited defense of Lully and Quinault's *Alceste* provoked an answer from Racine in the preface to his *Iphigénie* of 1674, which in turn elicited a

5 "La bonté du Poème est absolument necessaire pour assurer un succès constant à un opéra. La Musique toute seule ne peut lui donner qu'une vogue passagère dans sa nouveauté." *Lettre à Madame la Marquise de P. sur l'opéra* (Paris, 1741), 6.

6 "Les Opéra ou Pièces de Machines, qui n'estant point en usage du temps d'Horace, ne peuvent estre sujjettes aux lois en ont esté faites de ce-temps-là . . . Rien n'est moins supportable dans une Comédie que de dénouer l'Intrigue par un miracle, ou par l'arrivée d'un Dieu dans une machine; et rien n'est plus beau dans les Opéra que ces sortes de miracles & d'apparition de Divinitez quand il y a quel-que fondement de les introduire." *Critique de l'opéra, ou Examen de la tragédie intitulée Alceste, ou le Triomphe d'Alcide* (Paris, 1674), 69–70.

response from Perrault.[7] These exchanges between Perrault and Racine may be viewed as an opening volley in what became the "Quarrel of the Ancients and the Moderns."

There are relatively few attempts in the seventeenth century to analyze Lully's music *qua* music, that is, without reference to its text. One such example is the two-page appreciation of Lully found in Charles Perrault's *Les hommes illustres . . .* where it would seem that an inordinate amount of space in the short article is allotted to an analysis or, better, to an observation of Lully's skill in composing bass and inner parts for five-part instrumental "pièces de violon":

> Before him [Lully], only the *Dessus* in the *Pièces de Violon* was considered: the *Basse* and the middle parts consisted only of a simple accompaniment and heavy counterpoint, which the performers themselves most often composed as they heard the *Dessus*, there being nothing easier to accomplish than such a Composition. But M. Lully made all the *Parties* sing together as agreeably as the *Dessus*; he introduced some totally new *mouvemens* there, which up to this time were almost completely unknown by our Masters.[8]

The term *mouvemens* was used in the seventeenth century to mean tempo. Antoine Furetière wrote in his *Dictionnaire universel* of 1690: "It is the tempo (*mouvement*) that differentiates the courante and the sarabande from gavottes, bourrées, chaconnes, etc."[9] One is tempted to conjecture that Perrault's "totally new tempos" may have been referring to the *airs de*

---

7 "Lettre à Monsieur Charpentier de l'Académie Françoise, sur la Préface de l'Iphigénie de Monsieur Racine." This letter as well as the *Critique de l'opéra* and the preface to *Iphigénie* is found in *Philippe Quinault, Alceste suivi de La Querelle d'Alceste. Anciens et Modernes avant 1680*, ed. William Brooks, Buford Norman, and Jeanne Morgan Zarucchi (Paris, 1994).

8 "Avant luy on ne consideroit que le chant du Dessus dans les Pièces de Violon; la Basse & les Parties du milieu n'estoient qu'un simple accompagnement & un gros Contrepoint, que ceux qui jouoient ces Parties composoient le plus souvent comme ils l'entendoient, rien n'estant plus aisé q'une semblable Composition, mais M. Lully a fait chanter toutes les Parties presque aussi agréablement que le Dessus; il y a introduit des fugues admirables, & sur tout des mouvemens tout nouveaux, & jusques-la presque inconnus à tous les Maîtres." Charles Perrault, *Les hommes illustres* (Paris, 1696), vol. I, 85–86.

9 "C'est le mouvement qui fait différer la courante, la sarabande, des gavottes, des bourrées, des chaconnes, etc." vol. II, n.pag.

vitesse that Lully introduced in his court ballets. Michel de Pure, writing in 1668, described the frustration of Lully, who was continually embarrassed by the "stupidity of most of the grands Seigneurs," many of whom appeared quite incapable of mastering the more rapid steps.[10]

Very few eighteenth-century analyses of Lully's music are concerned with harmonic function, voice leading, treatment of dissonance, modulation and the like until we reach Rameau's famous analysis of the recitative "Enfin il est en ma puissance" from *Armide*. Joel Lester has brought to light one remarkable exception: an anonymous English manuscript that contains a detailed harmonic and melodic analysis of Lully's *Proserpine* (1680).[11] "As an extant dissection of a contemporaneous work by a major composer from this period, this analysis is unique" (Lester, p. 42).

In spite of gross inadequacies, the publication in the 1880s of eleven Lully operas "reduced for piano and voice" under the general title *Chefs d'œuvre classique de l'opéra français* contributed much to a revival of interest in the life and works of Lully.

Nuitter and Thoinan's *Les origines de l'opéra français* (1886) documents the creation of French opera and so serves as background for all subsequent studies. It was followed in 1891 by *Lully, homme d'affaires, propriétaire et musicien* by Emile Radet, who was one of the first scholars to make use of archival research. From the turn of the century to the First World War there was a proliferation of Lully studies by such notable scholars as Romain Rolland, Lionel de La Laurencie, Jules Ecorcheville, and Henry Prunières. The work of these important "lullistes" is admirably summarized by Manuel Couvreur in these pages.

In her contribution to Cambridge's first collection of Lully essays (*Jean-Baptiste Lully and the Music of the French Baroque*, 1989), Catherine Massip wrote: "In the field of Lully scholarship, there yet remains an important area to be investigated – that of stylistic analysis." Five of the essays found in this second collection may be loosely grouped under the rubric "stylistic analysis." They are by Lois Rosow, Rebecca Harris-Warrick, Buford Norman, John Powell, and Herbert Schneider. With one exception, the remaining essays may be grouped under two subjects: biography (Manuel

10 *Idée des spectacles anciens et nouveaux* (Paris, 1668), 248.
11 "An Analysis of Lully from circa 1700," *Music Theory Spectrum* 16 (Spring 1994), 41–61.

Couvreur, Jérôme de La Gorce, and Patricia Ranum) and reception (Carl Schmidt and Catherine Cessac). Barbara Coeyman's contribution creates its own category: the physical layout of the Académie Royale de Musique where Lully's operas were first performed in Paris. Her startling thesis, that Lully may have considered this theatre with all its limitations as only temporary, seems borne out by the facts. She takes us on a guided tour. One wonders what the price of tickets was during Lully's tenure. Was it "double that of any other entertainment," as reported by Riccoboni in the next century?[12]

Typically, most studies of musical characterization in the operas by Lully have emphasized his use of affective melodic intervals and dissonant harmonies to express deep feelings. As early as 1659 in a letter to Archbishop Girolamo della Rovera, Perrin recognized the unique capability of operatic ensembles to "say the same thing at the same time" or to express "diverse sentiments at the same time"[13] as, for instance, in the "divergent duos" so labeled by Masson. These duos occur very rarely in Lully's work. (One example is found in the duo "Voyez couler mes larmes" in Act IV, scene 4 of *Proserpine*.)

The essays of Lois Rosow and Rebecca Harris-Warrick give us new and original insights. Rosow examines the procedures used by Lully to organize his dialogue scenes. These procedures vary greatly from scene to scene and give evidence of the composer's understanding of how the relationship between poetry and music affects dramatic flow. Harris-Warrick argues that the dramatic context of Lully's operatic dances as well as the text of associated vocal pieces may have imposed a particular structure on the music itself, often resulting in irregular phrase groupings.

Buford Norman views Lully and Quinault's *Isis*, the "opéra des musiciens", as offering an alternative to the linear plot development found at its best in *Atys*. *Isis* presents a new concept of the *tragédie lyrique*: a concept that can accommodate a series of *divertissements* to expose the suffering of the nymph Io. John Powell gives us a wide-ranging and systematic study of the use of the pastoral in the comedy ballets and court *divertissements* by Lully.

12 *Reflexions upon Declamation: or the Art of Speaking in Publick; with an Historical and Critical Account of the Theatres in Europe* (London, 1741, anon. trans. from French original), 153.
13 The letter is found in Louis Auld, *The Lyric Art of Pierre Perrin. Founder of French Opera* (Henryville, NY, 1986), vol. I, 104.

In so doing, he answers Monsieur Jordain's plaint, "Pourquoi toujours des bergers?" Herbert Schneider examines the writings of Gluck's contemporaries for their treatment of the *tragédie lyrique* as a genre.

Jérôme de La Gorce, with the sure hand of a seasoned archivist, fills in the gaps found in earlier Lully biographies. He reasons, for example, that Lully's claim on his marriage contract to have been the son of "Laurent de Lully, gentil-homme florentin" may have caused the breach between father and son. Patricia Ranum sees the musicians and writers connected to the powerful House of Orléans as a "phalanx" with which Lully was forced to do battle. We learn that because of the Orléans network, Charpentier was able to circumvent Lully's restrictive privileges and compose ten chamber operas in the 1690s.

We learn from Carl Schmidt that about sixty editions of Lully's music were printed by eight Dutch publishers between 1682 and the late 1720s. Surprisingly, four Amsterdam editions of extracts from Lully's *tragédies lyriques* pre-date any Paris publications. Of interest is the fact that Estienne Roger's editions of *Ouvertures avec tous les airs à jouer* are scored in the Italian manner, that is, for *dessus* I, *dessus* II, *taille* and *basse*, rather than the five-part scoring "à la française" (*dessus, haute-contre, taille, quinte,* and *basse*).

From Catherine Cessac we learn that Sébastien de Brossard arranged extracts from Lully's *Alceste* for a performance in Strasbourg – probably at the Académie de Musique founded by Brossard in 1688. Brossard's autograph in the Bibliothèque Nationale dates from about 1691–95 and, Cessac believes, may be based on a Philidor autograph that is found today at the Bibliothèque municipale de Versailles. Like the editors of the Amsterdam collections of *Ouvertures avec tous les airs à jouer,* Brossard modernized his *Alceste* arrangements by employing the Italian *a*4 scoring rather than the five-part scoring "à la française." It is safe to assume that gradual change from *a*5 to *a*4 scoring with the elimination of the *partie de la quinte* was practiced as early as the last decade of the seventeenth century.

The essays in this volume range through the large period from Lully's Tuscan ancestors to the time of Marcel Proust. Even so, there remains much more to be done to shed light on the Lully canon. We have not yet fully met the challenge of librettist Pierre-Charles Roy, who in 1749 despaired that Quinault, unlike Corneille, left no word concerning the genre that he "invented and perfected." We have only begun to "tear from Quinault his secret and to . . . *décomposer* all his operas in order to examine their inner workings, to reconstruct the play . . . to appreciate the adroitness of his expositions, always fashioned within the plot, always condensed (because sung Tragedy does not have the conveniences of declaimed Tragedy); to be conscious of the liaisons between the *divertissement* and the plot, and to be conscious of his particular skill in deriving an interesting situation from a decorative element."[14] There needs to be a systematic analysis of Lully's harmonic procedures. Lois Rosow's innovative study of text and music in Lully's scene structure opens a new direction of research. The study of verse schemes in the *livrets* of Quinault, once the exclusive territory of the drama historian, has caught the attention of music scholars in recent years. It is fast becoming another tool in the stylistic analysis of Lully's music. We need to learn more about Lully's use of orchestral color and the dance in the service of musical characterization. The various functions of the *divertissement* need re-examination. Lastly, perhaps it is time to undertake a critical examination of Lecerf de la Viéville's monumental *Comparison de la musique italienne et de la musique françoise*, which has served so long as a principal source for Lully studies. In addition to Lully's live-in page, Brunet, who else supplied Lecerf with information? Can we verify, for example, that "grotesque anecdote" (Zaslaw) that has Lully fatally injuring himself by wounding his toe while conducting his Te Deum at the church of the Feuillents? The *Mercure de France* mentions no such event in its description of the performance. Were the death bed scenes ("j'en avois une seconde copie") genuine or rather a Lecerf fantasy? In any case, it is reasonably certain that the next generation of Lully studies will, *mirabile dictu*, have the new *œuvres complètes* as a point of departure for further research.

JAMES R. ANTHONY

14 "Il faut arracher à Quinault même son secret . . . décomposer tous ses Opéra, en examiner les ressorts, en développer le jeu . . . apprécier l'adresse de ses expositions toujours tournées en action, toujours serrées (car la Tragédie chantée n'a pas les commodités de la Tragédie declamée), sentir les liaisons des divertissements à l'intrigue, a l'habilété singulière de tirer d'une décoration une situation intéressante." "Lettres sur l'opéra," in *Lettres sur quelques écrits de ce tems*, vol. II (Geneva, 1749), 7–22, 16 (reprint Geneva, 1966).

Preface

This volume contributes to the momentum of research on the music of Jean-Baptiste Lully that has continued to advance in the decade since the publication of *Jean-Baptiste Lully and the Music of the French Baroque* by this press in 1989. Recent Lully scholarship, summarized by James R. Anthony in his foreword, has resulted in several collections of essays and in the issuing of the first volume of previously unpublished works, the motets (*Quare fremuerunt gentes*, LWV 67; *Notus in Judaea Deus*, LWV 77/17; and *Exaudiat te Dominus*, LWV 77/15 issued by The Broude Trust, 1996 as series IV, volume V of *Jean-Baptiste Lully: The Collected Works*) to complement the partial *Œuvres Complètes* prepared under the direction of Henry Prunières in the early part of the twentieth century. Accelerating activity now promises to bring us closer to a completed collected works in the next decade. While several of the studies in this volume, most notably that of Carl Schmidt, continue the important study of the sources of Lully's works that yet must be completed, the majority of essays here offer historical studies, beginning with Jérôme de La Gorce's surprising discoveries in the archives of Tuscany, and concluding with Manuel Couvreur's investigation into Lully matters at the turn of the last century. The broader readership should find these essays both informative and enlightening with respect to this important, yet recondite master.

The following libraries have kindly granted permission for the reproduction of plates and other material: Bibliothèque Nationale de France, Paris; Nationalmuseum, Stockholm; Archivio di Stato, Florence; the Musée Carnavalet, Paris; the Bibliothèque Musée de l'Opéra, Paris; and the Archives Nationales, Paris.

The Fonds National de la Recherche Scientifique of Brussels has supported Manuel Couvreur's work for this volume. Jérôme de La Gorce is supported in his capacity as *directeur de recherche au Centre national de la recherche scientifique (CNRS)* of France. I want to express my gratitude to the University of Wisconsin, Whitewater, and to former Chancellor Gaylon

Greenhill in particular, for support in preparation of the volume, and to the following individuals who have contributed to the completion of this volume: to Carl B. Schmidt, Lois Rosow, and Rebecca Harris-Warrick for advice and counsel; to Foster Jones for the initial translation work of the articles prepared in French; to Buford Norman, Sherwood Dudley, Lucy Carolan, Mary Kay Gamel, Sandra Heyer, and C. Thomas Ault for assistance clarifying certain points regarding the translations from the French; to David Heyer for the preparation of the music examples; to George Ferencz and Sandra Heyer for assistance in reading the manuscript; to Mary Whittall for her translation of Herbert Schneider's article from the German; and most certainly not least, to James R. Anthony, who brought to my attention details that otherwise might have been overlooked .

JOHN HAJDU HEYER

Note on the text

Sources in the footnotes that appear more than once are cited in abbreviated form; explanations and full details are supplied in the List of Works Cited on pp. 289–298 below. Library references throughout the book follow the *RISM* sigla.

1   Lully's Tuscan family

JÉRÔME DE LA GORCE

When Henry Prunières undertook his new edition of Lully's work, he discussed the composer's origins in the "notice historique" of the first volume devoted to the ballets. He wrote: "What is known for certain about Lully's youth takes just a few lines."[1] Then, making reference to research that he had published in several articles between 1909 and 1912,[2] he listed the important milestones: the marriage of the musician's parents and his baptism. Since then musicologists and biographers have been content to recite these few facts – important to be sure, but quite insufficient for this great figure. In fact many documents conveying more extensive information are still in Florence today. They were unearthed in several archives during a series of research visits I made to this famous Tuscan city.[3]

The composer's father, Lorenzo di Maldo Lulli, accurately identified by Prunières, first attracted my attention. It was already known that after marrying a miller's daughter Lorenzo practiced that trade in Florence in the Ognissanti quarter, not far from the Arno, where several gristmills were then

---

1 "Ce qu'on sait de certain sur la jeunesse de Lully tient en peu de lignes." Jean-Baptiste Lully, *Les Ballets*, vol. I (Paris, Edition de la Revue Musicale, 1931), xiii.
2 Specifically PrunièresJ, 234–242, PrunièresF, 57–61, and Henry Prunières, "Recherches sur les années de jeunesse de J.-B. Lully," *Rivista Musicale Italiana* 17 (1910), 646–654. The circumstances under which Lully left Florence, mentioned in these studies, are reviewed in my book on the life and work of the composer (forthcoming, Paris, Fayard).
3 My research in Florence was assisted by several individuals to whom I wish to express appreciation: Dottoressa Cotta, Curator of the Archivio di Stato; Dottoressa de Gramatica of the Sovraintendenza ai Beni culturali of Florence; Luca Faldi of the Archivio della Curia arcivescovile of Florence; Professor Sara Mamone of the University of Florence; her students Silvia Castelli and Maria Alberti, who assisted with several archival sources; Dottoressa Ludovica Sebregondi, specialist in the religious orders; and Gino Corti for his help at the Archivio di Stato. Special thanks are due my colleague and friend Marie-Thérèse Bouquet-Boyer, to whom I owe the transcription of several archival sources, including those found in the appendices published here for the first time.

1

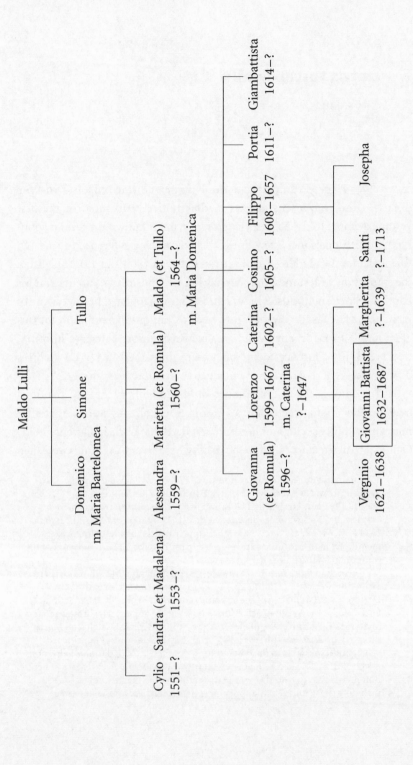

located on both banks of the river. Was he from one of the families of the Grand Duchy's capital who followed the same vocation? A fruitless search for reference to his parents and his birth in the registers of the Baptistery led to the certain conclusion that he must have been born outside the city. A notarial deed from 1640 listing the possessions he held in common with his two brothers, Cosimo and Filippo, and his cousin, Giovanni, guided this investigation.[4] Land that they must have inherited from their parents consisted of a forest of chestnut trees situated at Campestri near Vicchio.

Campestri, a charming hamlet, overlooks the valley of the Sieve from a height of 450 meters, in the Mugello region about thirty-five kilometers north of Florence. The area gave birth to artists as illustrious as Giotto and Fra Angelico. This part of Tuscany, not yet overrun with tourists, has scarcely changed for several centuries. Small farms are scattered throughout the landscape around the little church of San Romolo and the Villa Roti, the only patrician building. At the top of the hill above the village are numerous chestnut trees, providing one of the specialties of the Mugello. Some archival resources concerning the modest church have been preserved, including a regrettably incomplete account of marriages and funerals between 1567 and 1812.[5]

Among the references to the Lulli family appears an entry for December 3, 1581, recording the marriage of "Vettorio Lulli del popolo di S^to Romulo" with a girl of the same parish named Francesca. A little later there is mention of the burial of Lucretia di Cresci Lulli on July 3, 1636, only a few years after the birth of the famous composer. Indeed, some members of the family must never have left Campestri.

The Lulli family was large. We know this through the records of a valuable baptismal register from San Cresci in Valcava,[6] where all the newborn infants of Campestri were brought several kilometers to receive their first sacrament in this venerable place. Thanks to this fairly complete document covering the period from 1549 to 1639, a genealogical tree of Lully's Tuscan family can now be traced. First, we find the record concerning his father,

---

4 Archivio di Stato, Notarile moderno protocolli 14146, December 2, 1640 (see Appendix 1, p. 11 below).

5 Florence, Archivio della Curia arcivescovile, S. Romolo a Campestri, matrimoni e morti, n° 296.

6 *Ibid.*, n° 2136.

Lorenzo, son of Maldo Lulli and Maria Domenica. Lorenzo was born on December 15, 1599, at six o'clock in the evening and was baptized the next day. He was the eldest of at least four boys. His brothers Cosimo and Filippo were born after the turn of the century in 1605 and 1608, respectively. A third brother, named Giambattista (like the future composer), died before 1640. The other given names, like Lorenzo's, were not chosen at random: they are those of the illustrious Medicis, the sovereigns of Tuscany, also natives of the Mugello. Lorenzo's sister, three years older than he, was graced with the name Giovanna "et Romula," a probable reference to the family birthplace of Campestri.

The registry of San Cresci conveys other information of equal importance. In addition to the 1564 baptismal record of Lorenzo's father, "Maldo et Tullo," we find entries for his aunts and uncles. References to their relatives allow us to go back two more generations to a second Maldo Lulli, whose birth may have occurred in the *quattrocento*. Unfortunately, these fascinating details are not accompanied by any reference to the occupations of Lully's ancestors in the Mugello. Nevertheless, the existing village, the holdings of the Campestri family, and the association Lorenzo had with Florence until the end of his life indicate that in all likelihood they were peasants who lived off the land.

It is probably thanks to the produce from the forest at Campestri that Lorenzo Lulli first met then married Caterina del Sera, a miller's daughter. Among the witnesses at their wedding we first find a baker, Jacopo Papini,[7] to whom millers supplied wheat and chestnut flour, even flour ground from the highest quality chestnuts, the *marroni*. Through this business Lorenzo would have had the opportunity to meet Caterina. In the month of October 1619, at scarcely twenty years of age, he was engaged to marry her. He was then already living in Florence in the quarter of "San Pancratio."[8]

Following the wedding Lorenzo set up household near the church of San Salvatore di Ognissanti, probably with his father-in-law, Gabriello del Sera. The baptismal record of his oldest son, Verginio, dated Thursday, April 1, 1621,[9] attests to this change of domicile while indicating that the

---

7 Marriage act of February 17, 1620, cited by PrunièresF, 59.
8 The church of San Pancrazio is situated in the present via della Spada.
9 Florence, Archivio dell'Opera di S. Maria del Fiore (Opera del Duomo), battesimi, maschi, 1620/21.

boy's godmother, Maria, was the daughter of a gardener. The personal relationships remained within a humble social class. Their modest status did not prevent millers from contributing financially to the religious confraternities of Florence. Indeed, in 1624 Gabriello appears in the accounts of the "Compagnia del terzo Ordine," "gathered" at the church of San Salvatore.[10] Four years later, on May 7, 1628, it is Lorenzo Lulli's turn to be mentioned when he is recorded as a "mugnaio" (miller).[11]

When Giovanni Battista was born on November 29, 1632, his father was already practicing the miller's trade. According to a notarial deed of 1640, he was already living at this date in the "via di Borgo Ognissanti," a major artery running parallel to the Arno.[12] Indeed, the document specified that he had been living there with his brother Filippo since the first of May 1632. Giovanni Battista would have been born not in a mill, as people have too often reported, but in a house in the via Borgo Ognissanti, probably the one where his grandfather Gabriello died in 1636. Two extant death certificates permit us to situate it even more precisely in this part of the city. In one case the deceased was a "mugnaio in Ogni Santi,"[13] and in the other a "mugnaio del popolo di S. Lucia."[14] The indication of the two churches should not be interpreted as an error. Both are linked by the via Borgo Ognissanti. Gabriello's home, like that of his son-in-law and grandson, would thus be situated between the two churches in the most populated section of the street, next to the old city gate.

One finds the same uncertainty in other documents relating to dates in Lully's youth. His baptismal record[15] indicates the parish of Santa Lucia, but it is at the church of San Salvatore di Ognissanti that several of the closest family members were buried several years later: his brother, Verginio, on June 13, 1638, and his sister, Margherita, in October 1639.[16] At

10 Archivio di Stato, Compagnie religiose soppresse da Pietro Leopoldo 2071.
11 *Ibid.*
12 See Appendix 1, p. 11 below.
13 Archivio di Stato, Arte di Medici e Speziali 258, August 26, 1636.
14 Florence, Archivio della Curia arcivescovile, S. Salvatore in Ognissanti, morti, August 26, 1636.
15 Florence, Archivio dell'Opera di S. Maria del Fiore (Opera del Duomo), battesimi, maschi, 1632/33. Cited in PrunièresJ, 235.
16 Florence, Archivio della Curia arcivescovile, S. Salvatore in Ognissanti, morti, June 13, 1638 and October 1639.

the early age of seven, Giovanni Battista became the only one of his parents' children to remain in the father's household.

This state of affairs allowed for greater care over his education. By that time, Lorenzo Lulli had already achieved a fairly comfortable life; in addition to the revenue he realized from the forest at Campestri, he managed other business ventures. He operated at least one gristmill, probably that of his recently deceased father-in-law. Lorenzo's brother, Filippo, was asked to pay him twelve *lire* a month for his board and lodging. In one of his ledgers Lorenzo mentioned what his brother owed him, crediting him in 1640 with 126 *scudi* – that is, six years' room and board.[17] This was a large sum of money to advance at that time, even to a close member of the family. In this context, the education offered to Giovanni Battista would not have been neglected. Certainly he was taught to write at an early age; his earliest autograph signatures[18] show perfect mastery of a calligraphic style more common in Italy than in France.

We know neither where he was educated nor who taught him. According to Lecerf de la Viéville de Fresneuse "it is certain" that he had a "Cordelier"[19] as his first music teacher. The Cordeliers (Franciscans) were common in Florence, established for several centuries at Santa Croce to the east of the city, but also to the west as well, at the Ognissanti in fact, where they were called the "Zoccolanti." The populace around the church of San Salvatore supported several confraternities including that of the "Terzo Ordine," in which Lorenzo Lulli played an active role. In 1643, when the eleven-year-old Giovanni Battista was receiving his early musical education, Lorenzo was not content just to pay a tithe to this congregation, which perpetuated the memory of its namesake, Saint Louis of France. He took it upon himself to organize a special collection.[20] His religious devotion and financial acumen must have allowed him to hold an increasingly important position in this religious community.

17 See Appendix 1.
18 The first known signature of the composer appears at the end of his marriage contract (Paris, Archives nationales, Minutier central, XLVI-85). It it reproduced in the catalogue of the exhibition, *Lully, Musicien Soleil* (Versailles, Domaine de Madame Elisabeth, 1987), 32.
19 LecerfC, 183.
20 Archivio di Stato, Compagnie religiose soppresse da Pietro Leopoldo 2071, October 25, 1643.

Such an ascent may have been facilitated by the state of his fortune, to which a second marriage may have contributed. In 1647, one year after the departure of Giovanni Battista for France, Caterina died. The register of deaths of the church of the Ognissanti indeed mentions that at this date, March 5, "Caterina di Lorenzo Luli" (sic) was interred in the sanctuary.[21] Having been widowed, the miller lost no time in marrying Alessandra, the daughter of Domenico Campani, on August 2, 1648.[22] This second wife evidently was much younger than he, for she lived until 1693.[23] This difference in age may have led some to believe that she was Giovanni Battista's sister.[24] Today we know that Alessandra remained Lorenzo's wife until the end of his life and that she brought to the marriage a handsome dowry valued at 200 *scudi*,[25] but there is no evidence in the presently known documents that the marriage produced any children.

The first will and testament of Lorenzo, drawn up on May 19, 1655, is clear on this point.[26] It specifies that only one son from his marriage with Caterina survived and that he thereafter had no further descendants. The document in which he recorded his last wishes is impassioned: Giovanni Battista is mentioned three times. Lorenzo made him his sole inheritor, leaving him his worldly goods and all his "outstanding claims, accounts and notes of all kinds present and future." Should the beneficiary die childless, the inheritance would pass to Alessandra and, upon her death, to Lorenzo's brothers, Cosimo and Filippo. The miller also named an executor of his will: an oat merchant named Giovanni Battista di Vicenzo Zampettini, who conducted business on the "Piazza del grano" in Florence.

Nor were the religious institutions of the town forgotten. In addition to the charities of the cathedral of Santa Maria del Fiore, to which Lorenzo appropriately made a financial contribution to validate the notarial forms, he made bequests to several Franciscan confraternities with the request that

---

21 Florence, Archivio della Curia arcivescovile, S. Salvatore in Ognissanti, morti, March 5, 1647.
22 *Ibid.*, matrimoni, August 2, 1648.
23 *Ibid.*, morti, March 24, 1693.
24 PrunièresL, 61.
25 From the second will of Lorenzo Lulli. Florence, Archivio di Stato, Notarile moderno protocolli 14151, July 1, 1666.
26 Archivio di Stato, Notarile moderno protocolli 14150, May 19, 1655 (see Appendix 2, p. 12 below).

they celebrate masses for the salvation of his soul. Along with the confraternity "del Terzo Ordine," the "Compagnia di Santa Maria Maddalena e Francesco" related to the church of Santa Croce is mentioned.

In this regard Lorenzo was very active. First, as of 1650, he was a "camerlingo" (chamberlain),[27] with functions which he fulfilled two years later in the former congregation[28] and which consisted of managing the current financial accounts. This was already a clear sign of confidence. From 1659 until 1663 he would occupy a much more prestigious post: that of "proveditore" (steward or purchaser). His role was no longer limited to that of a financial manager but henceforth permitted him to participate in making important decisions. He kept the books on outstanding debts and claims, overseeing expenses including those for fabrics and candles from Venice. Moreover, the institution he served enjoyed a reputation of great prestige in Florence, having been founded by Lorenzo the Magnificent at the close of the fifteenth century.[29] In his will Lorenzo Lulli asked to be interred upon his death in the cloister of Santa Croce, the seat of the "venerable" confraternity. His request was subsequently carried out on April 19, 1667.[30] Lorenzo's brother Filippo had the same right of interment, probably thanks to Lorenzo's intervention, for Filippo died ten years before him in 1657.[31]

Lorenzo's declining health may have prompted him to prepare another will on July 1, 1666, just nine months before his death.[32] From this point on he left 10 *scudi* to each of the children of the late Filippo, the same sum to his brother Cosimo and 500 *scudi* to his wife Alessandra, including 400 to thank her for having been a good spouse. But for Giovanni Battista, by then absent for twenty years, nothing was provided. The name of his only surviving son does not even appear in the document.

How can this omission be explained? It certainly appears that there was a marked change in attitude on Lorenzo's part regarding the son whom

---

27 *Ibid.*, Compagnie religiose soppresse da Pietro Leopoldo 1402, February 26, 1650.
28 *Ibid.*, 2066, October 13, 1652.
29 Ludovica Sebregondi, "Lorenzo de Medici confratello illustre," *Archivio Storico italiano, Studi su Lorenzo dei Medici e il secolo XV* 150/552 (April–June 1992), 319–341.
30 Archivio di Stato, Arte di Medici e Speziali 259, April 19, 1667.
31 *Ibid.*, December 12, 1657.
32 Archivio di Stato, Notarile moderno protocolli 14151, July 1, 1666.

he had identified in 1655 as his principal heir. One event may have contributed to this. Between the times of the two wills, in 1662 when his marriage contract was drawn up, the composer claimed that he was "the son of Laurent de Lully, a Florentine gentleman."[33] Indeed, at that time in Florence, there was a respected family of that name. The Ceramelli papers preserved in the Archivio di Stato[34] include reference to a member named Lorenzo, according to indications in 1666 and 1668. Did Giovanni Battista know of this? Did he hope in this way to deceive informers likely to investigate his origins? The deception, it appears, was quickly exposed in France, and probably also in the Tuscan capital, where it may have come to the attention of the miller, who increasingly frequented the well-born society of the town.

Lorenzo, moreover, may have been disappointed by his son's attitude. There is no evidence that they exchanged letters after their separation in 1646, nor does it appear that the king of France's favorite musician ever sought to send any of his earnings to his father or even to learn news of him. A letter from the famous castrato Atto Melani,[35] sent to the grand duke of Tuscany, for whom he had become a secret agent, allows us to surmise. In this document dated March 31, 1687, just after the composer's death, Melani asked if Lulli still had "sisters or relatives" in Italy and "if it is true" that Lully had refused help to the father to whom there remained the only child. Such ingratitude would thus have justified the writing of Lorenzo Lulli's second will and testament in 1666.

Lorenzo's widow Alessandra also had her last testament recorded twice. In a first will, dated July 9, 1687,[36] she bequeathed 10 ducats each to several of her nephews, whose names are mentioned: Michele, Giovanni, and Santi Lulli. She also expressed a wish to be interred at the church of San Salvatore and she lived until the end of her life in the via Borgo Ognissanti,[37] probably in the house where Giovanni Battista was born.

33 Paris, Archives nationales, Minutier central, XLVI-85, July 14, 1662.
34 Archivio di Stato, Ceramelli Papieri 2833 (Lulli). I gratefully thank Professor Warren Kirkendale for having drawn my attention to the genealogical papers conserved in the Archivio di Stato.
35 Archivio di Stato, Mediceo 4802.
36 Ibid., Notarile moderno protocolli 17165, July 9, 1687.
37 After indications of the domicile in the second will: Archivio di Stato, Notarile moderno protocolli 20597, March 17, 1693.

The Archivio di Stato also holds the final will and testament of Santi Lulli.[38] This son of Filippo, whom Alessandra wished to reward, had been ordained as a priest. In a notarial document of April 12, 1713, he mentioned another member of his family: his sister Josepha, by then the widow of Antonio Feraci. His most ardent concern, however, remained his desire to be interred at the Compagnia della Maddalena, "like his brothers of the confraternity," with his father and his uncle.

What conclusions can we draw from this research conducted in the archives of Florence? The discovery of these documents permits us to verify the modest origins of the composer which he, upon arriving in France, tried to conceal. We knew he was the son of a miller. Now, the baptismal register of San Cresci permits us to glimpse the rural roots of his father's family, thus revealing even humbler beginnings. Though imprecise, the remarks of Lecerf de la Viéville de Fresneuse become significant when he asserts: "Lulli was of Florence, apparently a peasant of the region."[39]

This situation, from which the musician must have suffered during his career, should not however obscure another fact hitherto unnoticed: the remarkable social ascent of Lorenzo Lulli. The latter succeeded in becoming wealthy himself and in rising in Florentine society, preoccupations which were certainly common in the capital of the grand Duchy, but which he augmented with exceptional personal qualities. Like Giovanni Battista, he revealed himself to be remarkably gifted in business. One senses also that he was motivated by an uncommon character, rigorous and headstrong, which was stimulated by exceptional energy. He nonetheless remained no less committed to deep religious feelings. The role he played in several Franciscan confraternities gives proof of this and permits one to advance the hypothesis maintained by Lecerf de la Viéville that the young Lully must have been initiated into music by a "Cordelier." Research into the brotherhood of these orders, known for the education that they offered to young people, especially those of the "Compagnia del Sagramento" situated close to the church of San Salvatore,[40] has unfortunately afforded no further evidence on this subject.

38 *Ibid.*, 23060, April 12, 1713.
39 Le CerfC, 182.
40 Archivio di Stato, Compagnie religiose soppresse da Pietro Leopoldo 1761 and 1762.

It is a pity that no other writing of the seventeenth century has been found in Florence concerning the education of the composer. Despite the undeniable renown that he experienced during his lifetime throughout Europe, it seems that no one has ever delved into this period of his life. To be sure, he left early to make his career in France. In his native city, so brimming with art and history, he provoked little interest. In Tuscany, however, his name has not completely disappeared. In Campestri, on the façade of the church of San Romolo, a plaque listing the parishioners killed during the First World War bears the name of Raffaello Lulli, probably a descendant of one of the famous musician's cousins. This connection has probably never occurred to the inhabitants of the village in the Mugello. Was it forgetfulness, indifference or ignorance? Indeed, is Lully himself not in some measure responsible for this situation? Did his desire to obscure his family origins not lead him to break the links that united him with his father, to the point of proving himself prodigal toward him and depriving himself of his inheritance? Because of his attitude, he may have been the first victim of his own weaknesses in Italy as well as in France, thereby tarnishing the image that he left to posterity.

Appendix 1

In Dei nomine Amen. Anno Domini nostri Jesu Christi ab eius salutifera Incarnatione millesimo sexcentesimo quadragesimo Indicione octava die vero secunda mensis decembris Urbano summo Pontifice, et serenissimo Ferdinando 2do Hetrurie Magno Duce Dominante. Actum Florentiae in Domo incliti Laurentii de Lullis sita in [?] omnium sanctorum ubi dicitur in via di Borgo ognissanti presentibus ibidem Johanne Antonio quondam Bartolomei de Cambinis, et Victorio quondam Marci de Giorgis testibus.

Publicamente apparisca e sia noto qualmente constituiti personalmente d'avanti a me notaio infrascritto e testimoni soprascritti, Cosimo e Filippo fratelli e figlioli di Malbo Lulli fiorentini, non per forza, inganno o paura, ma di loro certa scienzia, e libera voluntà in ogni miglior modo fecero generali fine, quietanza, e patto perpetuo di più non domandare salvo quanto di sotto si dirà, a Lorenzo di Malbo Lulli loro fratello carnale al presente mugnaio in Firenze presente, e per se et suoi heredi e successori ricevente, e stipulante, e domandante la detta fine generale in tutto e per tutto, e di tutto quello, che per ragione, attione, debito, obligatione e

11

contratto, e di tutte quelle cose alle quali il detto Lorenzo insino ad hora in qualsisia modo fussi tenuto alli detti suoi fratelli, ò poteva tenere, ò in futuro fussi obligato per qualsisia causa pensata, ò impensata insino a questo presente giorno, e la presente fine li detti Cosimo e Filippo fecero perché si chiamano dal detto Lorenzo loro fratello carnale bene satisfatti, taciti, et contenti, renonciando all'eccettione della non numerata pecunia, la quale fine volsero estendersi, et havere luogo ancora alle cose non conosciute, e non pensate / ne intese liberando, et assolvendo il detto Lorenzo loro fratello per l'aquiliana stipulazione, et inoltre il detto Lorenzo Lulli per il presente instromento confessò havere appresso di sé altre masseritie notate in un suo libro segnato A: con carta pecora bianca debitori e creditori, e ricordi, aspettanti dette masseritie al detto Filippo suo fratello, quale disse tenerle per renderglene ad ogni suo piacimento, et voluntà del medesimo Filippo, et in oltre il medesimo Filippo confessò esser stato in casa del detto Lorenzo agli alimenti di vitto à ragione di lire dodici il mese convenute fra di loro dal dì primo di maggio 1632 in quà che sono [scudi] venti e lire quattro l'anno, e cosi sareberro anni otto e mesi sette; ma perchè sono d'accordo fra di loro, che detto Filippo sià stato fuori per un'anno il detto tempo si riducé à anni sette, e mesi sette e a detto conto sareberro sino al presente [scudi] 156 alla detta ragione, ma perchè nel presente instromento il detto Lorenzo confessò, e confessa, che a detto conto il detto Filippo gl'ha pagato [scudi] trenta di [grossi] 7. attalché li detti due fratelli, convengano d'accordo che detto Filippo resti debitore del detto Lorenzo di [scudi] centoventisei di [grossi] 7 come sopra sino al presente, et convennero ancora di seguitare così aventi alla detta ragione di [scudi] 20 e [grossi] 4. l'anno fin'a che il medesimo Filippo starà in casa agl'alimenti con detto Lorenzo suo fratello; et inoltre li detti tre fratelli confessano, et asserino [= asseriscono] havere, et possedere un pezzo di marroneto, che è livellario à comune et per indiviso con [beni] di Giovanni Lulli cugino delli detti fratelli posto detto marroneto nel posto di Campestri potestaria di Vichio, dichiarano infra di loro, che del frutto, che si ritorrà annualmente del detto marroneto, ciaschuno dei detti fratelli sia obligato tener' conto della sua terza parte da parte, ò sieno marroni, ò sià ritratto di quelli, e così concordano li detti tre fratelli come sopra, la qual fine, e tutte le cose sopradette le dette parte promessero attendere, et osservare sub pena dupli etc. que pena etc. qua pena etc. pro quibus obligaverunt etc. renunciaverunt etc. quibus guarantigiaverunt etc. Rogantes etc.

Appendix 2

In Dei nomine Amen. Anno Domini nostri Jesu Christi ab eius salutifera incarnatione millesimo sexcentesimo quinquagesimo quinto Indicione octava die

verò decima nona mensis Maii Alessandro septimo summo Pontifice et serenissimo
Ferdinando 2do Hetrurie Magno Duce dominante. Actum Florentiæ in sacrario
Reverendorum Patrum sancti Francisci omnium sanctorum, presentibus ibidem
infrascriptis testibus ore proprio infrascripti testatoris vocatis habitis atque rogatis
videlicet infrascripti testatoris vocatis habitis atque rogatis videlicet Reverendo
Patre fratre Innocentio de Florentia, Rev.do Patre fratre Josepho de Florentia,
Revd.do Patre fratre Antonio de Aquila, Rev.do Patre fratre Nicolao de Cortona,
Rev.do Patre fratre Petro de Florentia, Rev.do Patre fratre Onofrio de Urbe, et fratre
[Mario] de Florentia omnibus fratribus in dicto convento. Non essendo cosa piu
certa che la morte ne piu incerta dell'hora di quella, et essendo cosa da huomo savio
il pensare a morire di qui è che Lorenzo di Maldo Lulli mugnaio in Firenze, sano per
la divina gratia di mente, senso, vista, intelletto, di voluntà e di corpo, volendo
disporre delle sue faculttà, e sustanze, a ciò che dopo sua morte non naschino
scandali et massime per salute dell'anima sua fece et procurò di fare questo presente
suo ultimo nuncupativo testamento, che si dice senza scritti in [??] ogni altro
miglior modo vi è; In prima con ogni humiltà di cuore raccomando et raccomanda
l'anima sua all'omnipotente Dio, et alla sua gloriosa et sempre Vergine Madre
Maria, et al serafico Padre San Francesco, e a tutta la celestiale Corte del paradiso, e
quando quella si separerà dal corpo, elesse la sepoltura del suo cadavere nella
venerabile compagnia di Santa Maria Maddalena della città di Firenze posta
ne'chiostri di Santa Croce con quella spesa di mortorio che parrà alli infrascritti
suoi heredi ò suoi esecutorii. Per ragione di legato lassò all'opera di Santa Maria del
Fiore la solita tassa di [grossi] 3.10 per la validità del presente testamento, et 2do
gl'ordini. Et il detto testatore confessò havere havuto e ricevuto dall'Alessandra di
Domenico Campani sua dilettissima moglie scudi dugento di [grossi] 7 per scudo
per la sua dote perciò per ragione di legato gli lassò la detta sua dote in detta
somma, et inoltre a detta dote gli lassò altri [scudi] cento in ogni miglior modo, Et
lassò per ragione di legato et per l'amor di Dio e per remedio / dell' anima sua alla
veneranda compagnia del 3^{zo} ordine di San Francesco di ognissanti scudi cinque di
[grossi] 7 per scudo da darseli dopo la morte del detto testatore, acciò con quelli gli
faccino dire tante messe et [officio] per l'anima sua in detto luogo per una volta
tanto; Et per ragione di legato et per l'amor di Dio lassò et legò alla venerabile
Compagnia della Maddalena ne chiostri di S. Croce scudi cinque di [grossi] 7 per
una volta tanto, acciò li fratelli di quella gli faccino celebrare un officio e messa da
morti per l'anima di detto testatore. In tutti gl'altri suoi beni mobili, semoventi,
crediti, ragioni et attioni di qualunque sorte tanto presenti, che futuri per suoi
heredi universali instituití fece et esser volse e di sua propria bocca nominò Gio.
Batta [=Giovanni Battista] suo figliolo nato di lui e della Caterina di Gabbriello di
Simone della Seta sua prima moglie defunta e tutti gl'altri figlioli da nascere di lui e
della detta Alessandra al presente sua seconda moglie tanto maschi che femine
ciaschuno per rata e portione se n'haverà, con dichiaratione che non havendo altri
figlioli che detto Gio. Batta e che al tempo della morte del detto testatore il detto

Gio. Batta fussi morto senza figli né maschi né femine, all'hora et in tal caso sostituì sua herede universale la detta Alessandra sua moglie sendo viva et non essendo viva sostituì in detta sua heredità Cosimo e Filippo fratelli carnali del detto testatore ciaschuno di loro per la metà e li loro figlioli maschi sen'haverano, et non havendo le loro figliole femine. Esecutore del presente testamento, et ultima voluntà, elesse nominò et deputò Gio. Batta di Vincenzo [Zampettini] biadaiolo alla piazza del grano, e li [Messeri?] Cosimo e Filippo fratelli carnali del detto testatore ciaschuno di loro insieme et da parte, come à loro parrà, dandoli ampla autorità solita darsi a simili esecutori testamentarii. Et hunc dicit, et asseruit dictus testator esse et esse velle suum ultimum testamentum et suam ultimam voluntatem, quam et quod prevalere voluit omnibus aliis testamentis, codicillis, et donationibus causa mortis et quibuscumque ultimis voluntatibus per eum hactemus factis et si jure etc. cassan etc. non obstantibus etc. rogans etc.

2 Lully plays deaf:
rereading the evidence on his privilege

PATRICIA RANUM

The tale of how Jean-Baptiste Lully snatched the operatic *privilège* from Pierre Perrin and Robert Cambert in 1672 has been reconstructed by the historians of French music. Yet there is something troubling about the melodrama they sketch. We see the creators of French opera pirouette, make aggressive gestures, bow in despair or crow over their successes like puppets in a Punch and Judy show. When the curtains open, a Perrin, a Cambert, a Molière, a Charpentier, a Guichard each waves his arms, in a simulacrum of writing verse or directing musicians. At that point Lully, armed with the long baton with which he beats time at the opera, ferociously attacks each artist, much as Don Quixote charged the windmills, striving blindly to beat them into submission.

Various explanations for Lully's behavior have been proposed. Some suggest that Lully was an aggressive, egotistic, and quite sadistic man who took pleasure in breaking his competitors. Others portray him as merely defending his privilege, just as the king's first physician defended his primacy or the Ballards defended their monopoly over music printing. Still others reduce Lully's actions to personal feuds, first with Molière, next with Charpentier, then with Guichard. Each of these explanations surely contains a grain of truth. But why did Lully feel so threatened? Was it simply his personality? Or did he see a threat lurking out there that we have missed?

The evidence suggests that Lully's behavior was prompted by a concerted threat that he continually parried but could never completely deflect. That is to say, although Lully became the royal *surintendant* of music in 1661 and received the opera privilege in 1672, he was continually tested by a group of musicians and writers who were linked by ties of blood, marriage, and service to the House of Orléans. Despite Lully's position at court – and

15

despite his privilege – these artists went about their work on Lully's horizon, and sometimes dared to show their wares at court. Lully found himself in a position where he had to, as the saying went, *faire l'oreille sourde*, that is, "play deaf" and continue about his business as if unaware of the sounds these artists were making. These artists constituted a permanent threat, for they were, so to speak, "powered" by the king's closest relatives: to be precise, they benefited first from the protection of Louis XIV's uncle Gaston d'Orléans, and later from that of Louis's brother, Philippe d'Orléans, and his first cousin Elisabeth d'Orléans, Duchess of Guise.

This chapter will present the affective and protective ties that welded the members of this group into a phalanx with which Lully periodically did battle. Then, with the focus on Marc-Antoine Charpentier, it will investigate the role that these protégés of the House of Orléans played in the emergence of French opera. It will allude only in passing to the performances of the first French operas, the back-biting among the individuals involved and their financial incompetence or greed, for that tale has been told by Nuitter and Thoinan, Couvreur, and La Gorce.[1]

The core of these affective and protective ties was already in place by 1659, when Pierre Perrin and Robert Cambert's *Pastorale d'Issy* created a sensation. By the late 1640s[2] Perrin had entered the service of "Monsieur" – the name traditionally given to the head of the House of Orléans, who at the time was young Louis XIV's uncle Gaston, Duke of Orléans. Monsieur retired to Blois in 1652, in disgrace, but he maintained his Parisian household. At the Luxembourg Palace, Perrin served as the absent duke's *introducteur des ambassadeurs* ("introducer of ambassadors"), a position that involved seeing to protocol and greeting foreign dignitaries. While carrying out his duties in the Orléans household, he played a role in the intense negotiations with the House of Savoy and with the Medicis of Florence that culminated in the marriages to two of Gaston's four daughters. In short, the post was not the sinecure that historians have thought. These negotiations, and Perrin's pivotal position in the chain of communication between Louis XIV and Mazarin in Paris, Gaston's agent in Turin and Gaston in Blois, shed light on why the archbishop of Turin happened to be in Paris, *c.* 1658, talking with Perrin and Cambert about operas and singers. "You know the

1 Charles Nuitter and Ernest Thoinan, *Les Origines de l'opéra français* (Paris: Plon, 1886); CouvreurL; La GorceO.
2 Nuitter and Thoinan, *Les Origines*, 4–23, and especially 12.

principal [singers]," Perrin would write him in 1659. "As for the music, you know also the composer, and the concerts he performed for you ... do not permit you to doubt his ability."[3] This letter about the *Pastorale d'Issy*, shows that, although Lully had declared the French language unsuitable for opera, one of Gaston's most cosmopolitan household officers was proud to have demonstrated that it was feasible to write operas in French – and was asserting this in the context of a broader debate over the merits of music at the French court and at the court of Turin. This helps explain why, in his poem of May 10, 1659,[4] Loret touted the *Pastorale* as an Orléanist project: "The author of this pastorale / Belongs to His Royal Highness / Monseigneur the Duke of Orleans."[5] A few days after the first performance, the exiled Gaston appeared in Paris, ostensibly, it would seem, to honor Perrin by attending the command performance of the *Pastorale* before the court at Vincennes, but also with the vain hope of convincing Louis XIV to wed one of his daughters.[6]

Upon Gaston's death in 1660, his widow and daughters (among them Elisabeth, the future "Madame de Guise") hastened to Paris and the Luxembourg Palace. Madame d'Orléans and her daughters probably saw little of Perrin, who was in and out of prison for debt, but they consented to maintain the existing associations with the Parisian families who had "belonged" to Monsieur – among them some "friends"[7] of Marc-Antoine

3 "Vous en connoissez les principaux acteurs ... Pour la musique, vous en connoissez aussi L'Autheur, et les concerts qu'il vous a fait entendre ... ne vous permettent pas de douter de sa capacité."
4 Also quoted by Nuitter and Thoinan, *Les Origines*, 43–45.
5 "L'auteur de cette Pastorale / Est à Son Altesse Royale / Monseigneur le Duc d'Orléans."
6 His daughter's memoirs place Gaston in Paris from May 15 to *c.* May 30, 1659, *Mémoires de Mlle de Montpensier*, ed. A. Chéruel (Paris: Charpentier, 1859) vol. III, 367, 374. He declined an invitation to a *fête* on May 18 at the country house of a royal minister (p. 372), pleading age and health. But had Gaston been willing to humiliate the imprisoned Perrin by declining an invitation to the performance at Vincennes, would he have dared irritate Mazarin and Louis XIV at such a crucial moment in the marriage negotiations? Of course, one cannot rule out the possibility that the outcast duke was slighted by Mazarin and the king (as in vol. III, 276–278) and was not invited.
7 In many cases the "friends" who sign a wedding contract prove to be cousins of in-laws, employees in the household where the bride or groom works, or (but far less often) personal friends in today's sense of the word. On friendship, see Maurice Aymard, "Friends and Neighbors," *A History of Private Life, vol. III: Passions of the Renaissance*, ed. Roger Chartier (Cambridge, Mass.: Belknap Press, 1989), 447–491, especially 449–450 and 452–453.

Charpentier and his sisters. Thus, in 1662, the wedding contract of orphaned Elisabeth Charpentier, Marc-Antoine's sister, was signed by several people who, like Perrin, would have described themselves as "belonging" to the House of Orléans. Since these friends can be presumed to have contributed to the bride's dowry, at least one of the Charpentier children was rescued from a loss of social dignity by the protective network that revolved around the Luxembourg Palace. The presence of these influential people at this wedding should come as no surprise, for two of the orphan's cousins served the House of Orléans.[8] Through their craftsmen ancestors, the Charpentiers were linked to Molière's immediate family by cousinships that they described as "friendship." This friendship stretched across time and space, from Meaux, the provincial city that Marc-Antoine's father left *c.* 1620, to the Halles of Paris, where, in 1651, Marc-Antoine's cousin Gilles signed the marriage contract of Madeleine Pocquelin, Molière's sister, and André Boudet, the grandson of an artisan from Meaux.[9]

When Gilles Charpentier married in 1654, the family became linked to Henri Guichard (a future target of Lully's enmity), this time through ties

8 For this wedding, see Patricia M. Ranum, "1662: Marc-Antoine Charpentier et les siens," *Bulletin . . . Charpentier* 2 (1990), 9–11. Another Orléanist guest, Elisabeth Grymaudet, has subsequently been identified: her brother René was Gaston's *lieutenant général* at Blois, F-Pn, mss. Carrés d'Hozier, 314, fols. 100, 134. The Charpentier cousins serving Gaston were Jacques Havé de Saint-Aubin, husband of Marthe Croyer (Archives nationales, Minutier central (henceforth abbreviated as "A.N., M.C."), XXXIX, 109, foundation, March 15, 1664), who had been a *gentilhomme ordinaire* in the household of the late Monsieur; and Gilles Guichard de la Bressondière (a relationship to Henri Guichard is probable but has not been proved), who had married David Croyer's cousin and who was the *écuyer* (equerry) of Gaston's eldest daughter, the Grande Mademoiselle.
9 For Gilles Charpentier, the "secrétaire de M. de Saint-Luc," see Ranum, "1662," 7, 9; and Jean-François Viel, "Les Charpentier avant Charpentier," *Bulletin . . . Charpentier* 7 (1992), 68 and 12. The original of the Pocquelin–Boudet marriage contract, January 14, 1651 – quoted in Elizabeth Maxfield-Miller and Madeleine Jurgens, *Cent Ans de recherches sur Molière* (Paris: Imprimerie nationale, 1963), 614 – is in private hands, so the signature of the groom's "friend" (whose name is rendered as "*H.* Charpentier, secrétaire de M. de Saint-Luc") cannot be compared with that of Gilles, who appears to have been the only Charpentier to serve as Saint-Luc's secretary. Cousinship probably linked Denis Charpentier and Geneviève Soudain (Marc-Antoine's great-grandparents) to the descendants of Samuel Charpentier and his wife Agnès Soudain, their contemporaries at Meaux. Even if one supposes that Samuel was not a blood relative of Pasquier Charpentier (who was Gilles's grandfather and the husband of Geneviève Soudain's daughter by her first marriage), notarial acts show that both couples owned land in the tiny village of Neufmoûtier, Archives départementales, Seine-et-Marne, 142E 44, September 27, 1645, signed by

of guardianship.[10] René Mignon, the bride's guardian, was present that day. Four years later Mignon signed Guichard's wedding contract. (If Mignon described himself as young Mme Guichard's "friend," it was because his son was engaged to marry the girl's sister.) Since a blood relative was usually appointed as the guardian of a minor, one can quite safely assert that, in 1658, young Mme Gilles Charpentier became what notarial acts would call either the "cousin" or the "friend" of Mme Guichard – the designation "cousin" generally referring to blood ties, while "friend" often denotes the cousin of an in-law or the in-law of an in-law.

With Henri Guichard we return to the household of Gaston d'Orléans. At the time of his death in 1641, Henri's father was Gaston's valet. Although Henri lost both parents before his eleventh birthday, the boy doubtlessly remained within the orbit of the House of Orléans, for several of his close relatives were in Monsieur's service.[11] By 1670, Henri had

Pasquier's heirs, versus 80E 5 1, December 8, 1621 and 147E 23, February 10, 1637, for Samuel's heirs. The latter act was signed by Nicolle Charpentier, whose marriage contract with Jean Boudet bears the signature of Abraham Blanchet, one of Pasquier Charpentier's sons-in-law, who stated that he was a cousin of the groom, 141E 37, June 29, 1611. According to 150E 42, October 27, 1656, Jean Boudet was the brother of Molière's brother-in-law, André Boudet. These documents, and others too numerous to cite here, suggest why Gilles Charpentier would attend the Boudet–Pocquelin marriage in 1651 and, for want of a better term, identify himself as the groom's "friend."

10 For Gilles Charpentier's marriage to Françoise Liger, see A.N., M. C., LIX, 112, February 10, 1654; for her guardian René Mignon, "intendant of M. de Châteauneuf," see Gilles's inventory, LVII, 187, May 8, 1696, titre 3; and for Mignon's relationship to the Guichard-Le Vau couple, see LIV, 578, marriage of Henri Guichard and Jeanne Le Vau, January 27, 1658, and marriage of Louise Le Vau and Jacques Mignon, January 29, 1658, where René is identified as the "intendant of M. de Châteauneuf." For an idea of the extra-Orléans protection available to Henri Guichard and Gilles Charpentier (and through him, Marc-Antoine), thanks to the Mignons, see LXXV, 164, marriage of Gertrude Mignon, René's niece, February 7, 1673: the act is signed by the powerful royal minister, Michel Le Tellier and his son, Louvois, and by Colbert de Villecerf and Colbert de Saint-Pouanges, the cousins of the "Great Colbert."

11 The marriage contract of Henri's parents, Nicolas Guichard and Françoise Guyard, A.N., M.C., VI, 446B, June 5, 1633, is signed by a cousin, Louis Le Grand, first valet and secretary of the *menus plaisirs* of Gaston d'Orléans. For Nicolas's will and inventory (he himself was Gaston's valet) see VI, 462, May 9 and May 29, 1641; for Françoise Guyard's second marriage, VI, 462, June 3, 1641; and for her will and inventory, VI, 490, April 19 and May 5, 1645. For Henry's wedding of January 27, 1658, see LIV, 578, where his paternal cousin, Le Grand, has retained these titles, despite Monsieur's exile. For more on Guichard's life, see Nuitter and Thoinan, *Les Origines*, especially 198–206 and 321–331.

himself become a servant of the House of Orléans: he was a *gentilhomme ordinaire* ("gentleman in ordinary") to Gaston's nephew and successor, Philippe d'Orléans, Louis XIV's brother.

Robert Cambert may be the only member of this cohort of opera-creators who did not "belong" to the House of Orléans prior to 1670. Or was this son of a Parisian sword-furbisher Marc-Antoine Charpentier's distant cousin, through the Croyers of Meaux? This possibility cannot be ruled out, for one of Robert Cambert's cousins was named Croyer and lived on the rue d'Arnetal where Charpentier's more affluent Croyer cousins were renting out all or part of a house they owned.[12] Because it was widespread practice to rent one's portion of an inherited property to the descendants of that common ancestor who occupied the other part, the hypothesis that Robert Cambert and Marc-Antoine Charpentier were related is less far-fetched than it might seem.

By the time Giovanni Battista Lulli reached France in the mid-1640s, a network of friendships, cousinships, and guardianships linked Pierre Perrin, Robert Cambert, Marc-Antoine Charpentier, Henri Guichard, and Molière, and this network could potentially appeal to the House of Orléans for protection. That is not to suggest that these five individuals necessarily knew one another prior to 1670. Still, Lully can scarcely have been unaware that his principal rivals belonged to the Orléans: he himself had once belonged to them, for his first position in France had involved teaching Italian to the Grande Mademoiselle, Gaston's eldest daughter, during the very years when the Guichards and the "friends" and cousins of the Charpentier family were, like Lully, the honored servants of Monsieur or his daughter.[13] Nor should we imagine that the Orléans paid undue attention to the members of this network. Great nobles usually waited for one of *leurs gens*, "their people," to approach them with a petition to help a needy relative or friend, and would respond with a letter of recommendation, a purse with a few gold coins or perhaps a position in their household. Indeed, this sort of network served less a regular economic function than a protective

---

12 According to A.N., M.C., 61, March 24, 1610, David and Roland Croyer owned a house on the rue d'Arnetal; and XXXV, 77, fol. 311, shows that David's widow, Jeanne Charpentier, still owned and rented out that "corps d'hotel" (the main part of a large private house) on June 12, 1618. The act involving Cambert's cousin, Baltasard Croyer, A.N., Y 160, fol. 439, November 30, 1619, lists his heirs, who include Jacques Croyer, living on rue d'Arnetal.

13 *Mémoires de Montpensier*, vol. III, 347.

one: it was, so to speak, a safety net to which one could appeal in last resort, when other financial or professional possibilities had failed.

Marc-Antoine Charpentier's career, like Henri Guichard's, exemplifies how such a network functioned. When Charpentier's father died leaving four orphans, high-ranking Orléans householders protected his sister. The person who protected Marc-Antoine between 1662 and 1669 has not been identified, but there is a strong chance that this protector also belonged to the Orléans. For when the young musician returned from Rome, he entered the service of Elisabeth d'Orléans, Gaston's third daughter, who had wed the young duke of Guise in 1667 and was now creating a Paris-based court with strong Italianate leanings.

Charpentier's return to Paris coincided with rehearsals of Perrin and Cambert's *Ariane*, soon replaced by their *Pomone*. At the rehearsals for *Pomone* in June 1670, François Bellinzani, a native of Mantua, appears on the scene. Bellinzani's importance to the birth of French opera tends to be overlooked. As one of Jean-Baptiste Colbert's principal assistants, he was in a position to speak to the minister on Perrin and Cambert's behalf. Indeed, as the resident for Savoy astutely observed, "Sieur Bellinzani . . . is superintendent of commerce, and he has Colbert totally under his thumb."[14] When, in 1676, Bellinzani's daughter wed Michel Ferrand, whose parents and sister were "friends" of Marc-Antoine Charpentier's elder sister, Etiennette, the Mantuan became a potential spokesman to Colbert on behalf of Charpentier and his friends. Indeed, does Bellinzani's presence in Colbert's circle help explain why, c. 1679, Charpentier used some of Colbert's personal paper for his own copies of some of his earliest compositions for the Dauphin's chapel?[15] We shall meet Bellinzani again.

14   "Le sieur Bellinzani . . . est surintendant du commerce et gouverne tout à fait M. Colbert."
15   For the rehearsal, see Nuitter and Thoinan, *Les Origines*, 134, 137. For Bellinzani's power over Colbert, see Thomas-François Chabod de Saint-Maurice, *Lettres sur la Cour de Louis XIV*, ed. J. Lemoine (Paris: Calman Levy, 1910), vol. II, 63. The affective ties between Etiennette Charpentier and the Ferrands (whom the Grande Mademoiselle, *Mémoires de Montpensier*, vol. II, 122, called "our very good friends") will be presented in a forthcoming article. In 1683, after Colbert's death, Bellinzani was disgraced for peculation. Since publication of my *Vers une Chronologie des œuvres de Marc-Antoine Charpentier* (Baltimore: the author, 1995), I have discovered that the watermark of paper 6 shows Colbert's arms. (A notice about this paper appears in "Jean-Baptiste Colbert: un protecteur de Marc-Antoine Charpentier?" *Bulletin Charpentier* 14 (1997), 22–23.)

Perrin's skills as a poet were proving a disappointment: in April 1671, the audience greeted his libretto for *Pomone* with cat-calls and guffaws. Philippe d'Orléans nonetheless made a public show of support for Perrin by attending several performances. His brother the king, on the other hand, did not deign to appear.[16] By mid-1671, Colbert had also come to see that Perrin lacked the managerial skills to run the "académie d'opéra": the following June the poet was once again imprisoned for debt. At that point, Bellinzani stepped in to arbitrate Perrin's dispute with Sourdéac and Champeron. Anxiety clearly was mounting in Colbert's circle. By August, Perrin had turned over his privilege to Sablières, the intendant of the music of Philippe d'Orléans. This meant that the future of French opera had unexpectedly been placed in the hands of a man who belonged to the king's brother, in contrast with Perrin, who had been more or less marginalized by Gaston's death in 1660 and by Philippe's failure to absorb him into his household, and who therefore was beholden to the minister and the monarch. Then, in November, Sablières and Guichard produced an "opéra en musique" entitled *Les Amours de Diane et d'Endymion* (reworked and performed in 1672 as *Le Triomphe de l'Amour*), to rejoice over Monsieur's marriage. Louis XIV insisted that this opera, which starred Monsieur's and Perrin's combined ensembles, be performed at Versailles. Shortly afterward, Perrin, Sablières, and Guichard agreed to split the privilege three ways.

When they learned of this agreement, some of Louis XIV's house-holders may have viewed it as a threat. Would Sablières and Guichard be able to wear two hats, simultaneously managing the académie d'opéra for the glory of the king, and composing operas and pastorales for the glory of the House of Orléans? Would the new genre die in the hands of these relatively inexperienced gentlemen of Philippe's court? (And was the king slightly jealous of the way his brother's protégés were insidiously gaining control of what was supposed to be a royal project?)[17]

The spring of 1672 brought a stand-off: two different teams of operatic impresarios claimed the privilege. In February, Sablières and Guichard

16 Nuitter and Thoinan, *Les Origines*, 168.
17 Louis is presented as jealous of his brother's successes in Nancy Nichols Barker, *Brother to the Sun King, Philippe, Duke of Orléans* (Baltimore: Johns Hopkins University Press, 1989), for example, 164–165.

(and, in name at least, the imprisoned Perrin) invoked their privilege when performing *Le Triomphe de l'Amour* for the king at Saint-Germain; and, in Paris, Sourdéac and Champeron produced an opera, *Les Peines et les plaisirs de l'Amour*, with music by Cambert. "Divide and conquer," the saying goes. The holders of the privilege having become irrevocably divided and disputatious, Lully (obeying Colbert's orders) convinced Perrin to surrender his privilege, thereby returning opera to the control of the royal administration in March 1672.[18] The rest is history.

Molière's protests are also history, but his reasons for choosing Charpentier as Lully's replacement merit a closer look. The ties of "friendship" between the Pocquelins and Gilles Charpentier may suffice to explain why Marc-Antoine Charpentier was engaged in the spring of 1672 to provide new music for *La Comtesse d'Escarbagnas* and *Le Mariage forcé*; but these ties scarcely explain why Molière broke his word to Dassoucy in August 1672 and asked Charpentier to write the music for *Le Malade imaginaire*. Dassoucy asserts that Molière yielded to the pressure of goddesses, heroines, and irritated virgins: "In the actors' world there are always heroines and goddesses to whom one must burn incense, but . . . how could I pacify so many irritated virgins?"[19] In the parlance of the day, these words do not denote the actresses who played such roles on the stage: Dassoucy's contemporaries primarily used these metaphors when discussing princesses – and the principal French princesses in 1672 were Philippe's wife and adolescent daughter, Gaston's two daughters (Mme de Guise and the Grande Mademoiselle), and the aging Mlle de Guise (not only Charpentier's other protectress but Gaston's sister-in-law).[20] That these Highnesses were so eager to foist their protégé upon Molière appears linked

18 As Nuitter and Thoinan have shown, *Les Origines*, 227.
19 "Parmy les commediens il y a toujours des Heroinnes et des Deesses qu'il faut encenser, mais comment pourrois-je, pacifier tant de Vierges irritées?" Charles Coypeau, called Dassoucy, *Les Rimes redoublées* (Paris, 1671), F-Pn, Rés. 1936, 124.
20 For example, Mlle de Guise was called a "heroine" by the *Mercure Galant*, September 1678, 70, and Loret's *Muze Galante* of April 1657 describes her as having been born into a "heroic family of demi-gods." In June 1665, Robinet, another verse gazetteer, called Philippe d'Orléans's first wife a "great heroine," a "goddess." After the Grande Mademoiselle's participation in a battle during the Fronde, she herself and her contemporaries described her as a "heroine," *Mémoires de Montpensier*, vol. II, 197.

23

to the duke of Guise's death in July 1671. Their household music had been silenced during this period of mourning, and Mme de Guise was preparing to move to the Luxembourg Palace and spend a good part of each year at court. Once the Guise princesses had extended their protection to Charpentier, they could not abandon him. They had to find a new and prestigious outlet for his talents, and Molière's theatre clearly met their standards.

Fate, of course, decreed otherwise: six months later, Molière was dead and the theatre only remained solvent thanks to a loan of 14,000 *livres* from André Boudet, Gilles Charpentier's "friend."[21] Then Lully began systematically reducing the number of musicians who could participate in a theatrical performance. Charpentier nonetheless worked with the troupe until 1686, as it struggled to preserve a modicum of music in its performances. That too is history, and the sequence of events has been narrated by Hitchcock and Cessac.[22]

One is nonetheless tempted to speculate about what would have happened if Molière had lived a decade longer. Would the House of Orléans have rekindled the protection it had given Molière early in his career, thereby limiting Lully's devastation of theatrical music? The playwright surely realized that preferring Charpentier to Dassoucy in 1672 would give him a crucial advantage in the skirmishes with Lully that were looming on the horizon. Not only could Charpentier turn to the House of Orléans, he could have brought the entire troupe under its wing. Indeed, is that not the message that Philippe d'Orléans was sending on March 5, 1673, when he, Madame, and their entourage attended the first performance of *Le Malade imaginaire* after Molière's death? (Louis XIV had declined to attend the opening performance of the play.)

For the rest of the decade, Lully progressively strangled music in spoken plays. Yet despite the fact that his privilege of March 1672 forbade "all persons ... to organize the performance of any piece that is completely sung, whether in French verse or in other languages, without the written permission of the said Sieur Lully, on pain of a fine of ten thousand *livres* and confiscation of the theatre, the machines, the decorations, the costumes, and

21 *Le Registre de la Grange*, ed. B. and G. Young (Paris: Droz, 1947), vol. I, 147.
22 H. Wiley Hitchcock, "Marc-Antoine Charpentier and the Comédie-Française," *JAMS* 24 (1971), 255–281; CessacCf, 53–107.

other items,"[23] Lully seems to have allowed the Orléans protégés to go about their operatic and oratorical programming unperturbed. For example, Lully apparently did nothing to stop the *tragédies chantées*, the "sung tragedies" that were held at Sieur Filz's academy in September 1673. The impetus behind these performances clearly was Bellinzani, whose son was one of the students performing side by side with several of Perrin's former singers.[24] In a word, Lully seems to have preferred to play deaf and ignore the fact that Colbert's loyal servitor was treading on his privileged turf.

Nor can one imagine that Philippe d'Orléans and Elisabeth d'Orléans (or Mlle de Guise, the duke of Richelieu, or the unidentified patrons who commissioned chamber operas from Charpentier between 1676 and 1687) would humble themselves and petition Lully for written permission to sponsor such an event. Their position in the realm and their power at court was so superior to the general category of opera-writers and opera-producers against whom Lully's privilege was directed that these great nobles could do as they wished, as long as they took care not to upstage the king, and made sure that the entertainments they sponsored would extol either the glory of the monarch or, as Louis sank into devotion, the glory of God. Thus, from 1675 to 1687, Mme de Guise and Mlle de Guise seem not to have been troubled by Lully, although they sponsored a spate of chamber operas and elaborate Latin oratorios that technically infringed upon his monopoly over all "poetic" works that were entirely sung, in *any* language whatsoever.

Lully strove to make his monopoly increasingly specific. By April 30, 1673, he had reduced to two the number of singers, and to six the number of "violins" that could participate in a theatrical performance. Let us however note in passing that the cast of the opera in which the Bellinzanis were involved the following September included four professional singers, plus an unspecified number of students. Indeed, if Lully attempted to have his restrictions extended to chamber operas performed in princely homes or at court, he clearly failed. Charpentier's autograph manuscripts include

---

23 "toutes personnes . . . de faire chanter aucune pièce entière de musique soit en vers françois, ou autres langues, sans la permission par escrit du dit sieur Lully, à peine de dix mille livres d'amendes et de confiscation des Théâtres, machines, décorations, habits et autres choses."

24 Nuitter and Thoinan, *Les Origines*, 164.

secular works for nine, ten, even thirteen singers, accompanied sometimes by two treble instruments and continuo, but sometimes by an orchestra of strings and wind instruments. It is also clear that Charpentier was permitted to disregard certain clauses of the royal decrees. For example, in the privilege granted Lully in 1672, the king stipulated that Lully was forbidden "to use for his operas any musicians who are in our pay."[25] Yet Charpentier was allowed to use royal musicians in one of his operas: the score of *La Descente d'Orphée aux enfers* (H. 488) shows Antoine and Pierre Pièche performing with the Guise ensemble.

During the decade 1676–86, various musical performances described as "operas" were performed for the Orléans. Some of these works were created by Guichard and Sablières for performance at Monsieur's country house at Saint-Cloud; others were written by Charpentier for entertainments that Mme de Guise offered visitors to the Luxembourg Palace, or that she prepared for performance at Versailles, before her kingly cousin.

Charpentier's *Petite pastorale* (H. 479) was performed at Saint-Cloud, in 1676. This pastorale either was *the* "opera" sung after the baptism of Monsieur's two children on September 5, in the presence of Louis XIV, or else served as the prologue for a longer work by Guichard and Sablières. Monsieur's reasons for including Charpentier in the festivities are clear: the godmothers of these royal children were Elisabeth d'Orléans and her sister, the grand duchess of Tuscany. Although it does not name the composer or composers, the *Gazette de France* for October 1676 (p. 728) recounts how the illustrious guests "were entertained with an opera ... which had been prepared with all possible magnificence"[26] – doubtless thanks to the efforts of Guichard, who normally was entrusted with the decorations for Monsieur's fêtes. Charpentier's pastorale can only have been written for this event. It specifically mentions entertaining the king; it alludes to the recent military campaign during which Philippe d'Orléans had played an important role; and, by incorporating an air with lyrics by Jean de La Fontaine, it pays a compliment to Mme de Guise's late mother, who had protected the poet.[27]

25 "se servir pour l'exécution des dites pièces [de musique] des musiciens qui sont à nos gages."
26 "eurent ensuite le divertissement de l'Opera ... qui avoit esté preparé avec toute la magnificence."
27 For a tableau of how La Fontaine moved from one protective network to another,

This was not the only time Charpentier's music was performed at Saint-Cloud. When the *Mercure Galant* for May 1682[28] praised the Dauphin's musicians, who had replaced the royal musicians during a fête that Monsieur had prepared for the court, it was sending a veiled compliment not only to the young prince's composer, Charpentier, but to the House of Orléans.

Not until the 1680s did Charpentier begin to produce a spate of chamber operas for the expanded Guise ensemble. Each work followed rapidly on the heels of its predecessor, most of them observing a chronology that corresponds to the presence at court of Elisabeth d'Orléans.[29] The series begins with *Les Plaisirs de Versailles* (H. 480), written for the *fête des appartements* that the king offered his court during the fall of 1682. Then, in mid-1684, "pastorales," "idylls," and "operas" began to flow from Charpentier's pen. First came *Actéon: Pastorale en musique* (H. 481), performed twice in 1684 under changed circumstances that remain mysterious. Although this work is supposedly "pastorale," the overture is described as introducing an "opera." Next came two Christmas pastorales in French (H. 482, H. 483) and *La Dispute des bergers* (H. 484), all performed by the Guise singers but apparently commissioned by some of Their Highnesses' friends. These works were followed by *La Feste de Ruel* (H. 485), commissioned by the duke of Richelieu for September 1685, the centenary of Cardinal Richelieu's birth.

With the spring of 1685, Elisabeth d'Orléans found herself caught up in the trend: Charpentier's *La Couronne de fleurs* (H. 486), written for the Guise ensemble, was promptly followed by *Les Arts florissants: Opéra* (H 487), and *La Descente d'Orphée aux enfers* (H. 488) – the latter an opera in all but name that was performed by the fourteen Guise singers, the

see Marc Fumaroli, *Le Poète et le roi: Jean de La Fontaine en son siècle* (Paris: Fallois, 1997), including 255–259 for Gaston d'Orléans and his wife.

28   *Mercure*, 175–190.

29   For the chronology of Charpentier's works, see Ranum, *Vers une Chronologie*. Between 1670 and 1687, the compositions in the notebooks with arabic numerals are made to measure for the Guises, while those in notebooks with roman numerals clearly were outside commissions. That several opera-like works were written for the Guise musicians but were subsequently copied into the "roman" notebooks suggests that friends of the Guises obtained the princesses' permission to hire both Charpentier and the Guise musicians. These privileged friends have not yet been identified.

Guise instrumentalists and at least two royal musicians. After this came a hiatus, followed by *L'Idyle sur le retour de la santé du Roi* (H. 489) of January 1687, with which Mme de Guise rejoiced over her cousin's recovery from a life-threatening illness. A few weeks later, Lully succumbed to gangrene; and, by a strange coincidence, Charpentier ceased writing chamber operas.

In sum, in 1682, with patent disregard for Lully's privilege, Elisabeth d'Orléans first brought the Guise musicians and their composer to Lully's own turf, to perform before the king an opera-like *divertissement* that was entirely sung. Her gesture apparently encouraged other ambitious, high-ranking courtiers, who soon invited Charpentier to prepare opera-like works for performance at their country estates, their apartments at court, or their mansions in Paris. This flowering of opera-like works between September 1683 and late 1685 coincides with the growing irritation with Lully's monopoly and his near disgrace, both sketched by La Gorce.[30] Did Mme de Guise's friends at court seek out Charpentier, rather than another composer, because they knew that the weakened Lully would not dare invoke his privilege? Indeed, did Charpentier start a trend? That is to say, after July 1685 Dangeau cites several chamber operas by other composers: Elisabeth Jacquet de La Guerre (the sister of a Guise musician) in July 1685, and Delalande (his "opera," *Le Ballet de la jeunesse*) in February 1686.

Although Lully had managed to throttle Charpentier and his actor associates, he clearly was unwilling to challenge the musical entertainments that the great nobles considered theirs by right of birth. In addition, to invoke his monopoly against Charpentier would mean making a public show of ingratitude toward the House of Guise, which had brought Lully to France, and toward the Grande Mademoiselle, who had been his first protectress. Any one who incurred the Grande Mademoiselle's displeasure risked being placed in a verbal thumbscrew, while the strong-willed princess vented her spleen.

Is there any evidence that the members of the House of Orléans actually considered themselves the protectors of Perrin, Cambert, Guichard,

30 La GorceO, 71–74.

Charpentier? Or were these great nobles simply enjoying these artists' creative efforts, with little thought for the personal well-being of the men who had devoted their lives to them? There can be no doubt that the Orléans were personally committed to these artists: they not only promoted the careers of their protégés, they cared for their close relatives as well. If Pierre Perrin eventually was freed from jail, it was because Elisabeth d'Orléans paid his debts.[31] If Cambert was welcomed at the court of Charles II, it was because Philippe d'Orléans had maintained the ties with his English brother-in-law (also his first cousin) that had been forged prior to the death of the first Madame in 1671. Indeed, the evidence suggests that Cambert did not emigrate to London in a fit of despair to escape Lully's monopoly; he had been offered the opportunity to be England's Lully.[32]

In 1675, when Lully accused Henri Guichard of plotting to poison him, Monsieur convinced the king to order an investigation by the courts, "so that the truth can be distinguished from the lies."[33] Guichard was eventually acquitted. At that point, Philippe d'Orléans continued his protection for the Cambert family, whisking Guichard away from the emotionally charged climate of Paris to a sinecure far from the detested Lully. Guichard, Cambert's daughter Marie-Anne, and her husband, Michel Farinel, were incorporated into the household of Philippe's daughter, who was about to marry the king of Spain and set off for Madrid.[34]

Philippe d'Orléans and his son likewise ensured the well-being of several Charpentiers. Circa 1693, Marc-Antoine was appointed to teach composition to Monsieur's talented adolescent son, the Duke of Chartres. Chartres showed his gratitude in 1698 by pressuring the canons of the

---

31 A.N., M.C., XXIX, 216, élargissement, August 27, 1672: she supplied the requisite 300 *livres*.

32 See the convincing evidence unearthed by Nuitter and Thoinan, *Les Origines*, 301–309, and the more general context set forth by Marie-Claude Canova-Green, *La Politique-spectacle au Grand Siècle: les rapports franco-anglais*, Biblio 17 (Paris–Seattle–Tübingen: Papers on French Seventeenth Century Literature, 1993), especially 110–114 and 186–187, which discuss Cambert.

33 "afin que l'on pût connoistre la vérité d'avec l'imposture."

34 For Lully and Guichard's lawsuit, see Nuitter and Thoinan, *Les Origines*, 324–331, and La GorceO, 56–59. For the household musicians of Mademoiselle d'Orléans, see Marcelle Benoit, "Les Musiciens françois de Marie-Louis d'Orléans, reine d'Espagne," *Revue Musicale* 226 (1955), 48–60.

Sainte-Chapelle to name Charpentier as their *maitre de chapelle*. The grati-
tude that father and son felt toward Marc-Antoine probably explains why
Gilles Charpentier's sons, René and Jean-Baptiste, were, in 1696, respec-
tively the "almoner of His Royal Highness Monsieur" and an "officer of His
Royal Highness Monsieur"; and why Jean-Baptiste's son, Jean-Baptiste-
Thomas Charpentier, succeeded his uncle.[35]

In conclusion, instead of viewing royal patronage as a single and somewhat
monolithic source of creativity in the realm, historians should examine the
role played by rivalry – rivalry between the households of the great nobles,
as well as rivalry between the creative individuals who were linked to these
households and who sometimes had to fight for survival. In Lully's case, a
picture begins to emerge that helps us understand why he defended his
operatic privilege so ferociously. He saw himself surrounded by potentially threatening "windmills" whose powerful arms seemed poised to
sweep down and overthrow him, should he become complacent – or
should he misstep, as he did in 1685, and teeter on the brink of disgrace.[36]

35 For Marc-Antoine and the Duke of Chartres, see CessacCf, 377–379. For the sons
   and grandson of Gilles, see A.N., M.C., LVII, 187, inventory, May 9, 1696; and
   A.N., Y 14062, scellé, January 4, 1734, where the grandson is called the "almoner
   of the duke of Orléans," which probably should be interpreted as meaning that
   he had been in the service of Chartres, who succeeded his father as duke of
   Orléans in 1701 and who died in 1723.
36 Forming about them what the French called a *cabale* (a "clique"), powerful
   individuals would sometimes embark upon a *cabale* (an "intrigue") whose aim
   was to destroy an artist who had presented a negative image of them or who
   espoused a cause with which they did not agree. One of the more devastating of
   these *cabales* coalesced around Mme de Bouillon in 1677 and attacked Jean
   Racine's *Phèdre*, causing the playwright to give up the theatre: René Jasinski, *Vers
   le Vrai Racine* (Paris: A. Colin, 1958), vol. II, chapter 19, especially 437, 441–445.
   Lully's librettist, Philippe Quinault, fell victim to a similar *cabale* the same year:
   his libretto for *Isis* was seen as insulting the royal mistress, Mme de Montespan
   (La GorceO, 61–63, and CouvreurL, 373–377). Interestingly enough, Quinault's
   temporary disgrace prompted numerous chamber operas (La GorceO, 62), just
   as Lully's disgrace of the mid-1680s seems to have given rise to a succession of
   operas by Charpentier. (Should the way Charpentier's colleagues at the *Mercure
   Galant* touted the "opera" he composed for Rians in the February 1678 issue,
   131–132, be seen as a jab at Lully, who was unable to present an opera that year
   owing to Quinault's disgrace?) Not even the overt protection of the House of
   Orléans – joined this time by Louis XIV and the Dauphin – sufficed to keep
   Charpentier's *Médée* (1693) from falling victim to what Brossard called a
   "cabale," CessacCf, 380, 382, 384, 404.

No wonder Lully swatted right and left, aiming at the vulnerable targets but playing deaf to the music being made by others. He knew he was powerless to silence entirely the musicians and the poets who worked for the heroes, the heroines, the virgins, and the goddesses of the houses of Guise and Orléans.

3   The phrase structures of Lully's dance music

REBECCA HARRIS-WARRICK

Common perception holds that Baroque dance music is metrically regular, based on four- or eight-bar phrases. The familiar dance pieces of J. S. Bach, for example, generally conform to this model. However, the model does not accurately describe the compositional practices of Jean-Baptiste Lully, the man credited with raising French dance music to such heights that it was imitated all over Europe. Only a small proportion of Lully's dance music – roughly a quarter of his binary dance pieces – is based on consistent four- or eight-bar phrases; the rest is irregular in a variety of ways. Given that Lully composed virtually all his dance music for actual dancing in ballets or operas, not as suites for listening, we know that his music was – by definition – danceable. Is it therefore possible to explain the construction of Lully's dances on extrinsic grounds? Could factors such as the dramatic context, the text of associated vocal pieces, or the choreography be responsible for imposing structures on the music? Or are we looking at the question the wrong way around: could it be that our perceptions regarding the norms of dance music require revision?

This study will draw upon dance music from Lully's thirteen completed *tragédies en musique*, composed between 1673 and 1686. There are generally about fifteen dances in a Lully opera. (This number includes pieces in binary or rondeau form plus chaconnes and passacailles, but not the through-composed instrumental pieces labeled "prélude" or "ritour-nelle" that may sometimes accompany action or dance.[1]) Of these fifteen,

1   Préludes and ritournelles often serve as entrance music for one or more of the solo singers. Some of the through-composed instrumental pieces, however, accompany more vigorous action, such as the tempest in Act I, scene 8 of *Alceste* (LWV 50/34), variously called the "Entrée des Aquilons" or "Les Vents" in the sources, of which the libretto gives the following description: "les Acquilons excitent une tempeste, qui agite les Vaisseaux qui s'efforcent de poursuivre Licomede."

32

Example 3.1

Phaéton, Menuet. Troupe d'Astrée dansante

approximately one third to one half bear generic designations such as "menuet" or "gigue" in the score:[2] the others are called simply "Air" or "Entrée." The dances in both categories are assigned to specific characters within the opera, thus are not neutral in content. Each category will be examined in turn.

Let us start by getting a sense of the variety of phrase structures Lully used for a single dance type, the menuet.

(1) Example 3.1 shows a simple piece from *Phaéton* (LWV 61/6), one that seems a classic menuet in the clarity of its structure.[3] Each eight-bar strain breaks down neatly into two parallel four-bar phrases. (The vertical slashes above the staff have been added to mark the phrase breaks.) Moreover, the dominant rhythm – short, long, long, short, going over two bars – is the rhythm of the earliest known menuet step.[4]

2 Although in her "Inventory of the Dances of Jean-Baptiste Lully," *RMFC* 9 (1969), 21, Meredith Ellis [Little] estimates that "pieces with specific dance titles" probably constitute "eighty per cent of the dance music," this figure cannot be supported by the evidence she herself presents in this article. First, very few of the dances in the ballets have generic titles. By her count, there are only two (both bourrées) in the *Ballet des Arts* of 1663, yet this ballet has twenty dances, which means that only 10 percent of them have "specific dance titles"; this low percentage is not exceptional in the ballets. In the operas the percentage of generic dances is considerably higher, yet even by Little's own evidence the figure does not begin to approach 80 percent. For example, she lists five dances from *Proserpine* with generic titles, but this opera has fourteen dances in all. Similarly, only five out of the sixteen dances in *Psyché* are generic types.

3 Unless noted otherwise, musical examples have been taken from the scores published in Paris by Christophe Ballard the year of the opera's premiere. The headings for the examples also come from these scores.

4 See n. 10 below.

Example 3.2

Armide, Menuet. Hautbois

(2) Example 3.2 comes from *Armide* (LWV 71/14). It, too, manifests symmetrical phrases within each strain. In the first section the units are three bars long, on which basis one might be tempted to classify the piece as a "menuet de Poitou."[5] But in the second section the two melodically parallel eight-bar phrases are made up of four-bar units. (It is perhaps worth pointing out that this menuet is the second of a pair, the first of which has eight bars divided four-plus-four in the first strain, and twelve bars divided six-plus-six in the second.)

(3) Example 3.3 shows two consecutive menuets from *Roland* (LWV 65/4 and 65/5). The first has consistent five-bar phrases that are melodically parallel within each strain.

The second menuet has six bars in the first strain, and eight in the second, neither of which breaks down easily into sub-units. Cadential motion in the bass of bars 3 and 10 is overridden by the insistent repetition

---

5 Some of the pieces so designated in seventeenth-century sources for dance music (e.g., the anthologies made by Philidor *l'aîné* of music played for balls at court) do have three-bar phrases; however, many other pieces labeled "menuet de Poitou" are square or show varied construction. The origins of the menuet – one hypothesis being that it grew out of the branle de Poitou – have not yet been satisfactorily resolved.

Example 3.3
(a) *Roland*, Première Entrée. Menuet

(b) *Roland*, Menuet

in the melody of a triadic figure that confounds any attempts to hear either strain as divided neatly in the middle.

(4) In Example 3.4, from *Alceste* (LWV 50/9), the number of measures alone is surprising for a menuet: nine in the first strain, eleven in the second.[6] The first strain is particularly ambiguous in its internal structure: a melodic figure that is almost parallel to the opening appears in bar 5, but the harmony makes the first three – not the first four – measures a unit. The first

---

6 This musical example has been drawn from the edition of *Alceste* in LullyOC. No scores of *Alceste* were published during Lully's lifetime.

Example 3.4

Alceste, Menuet

strain could almost be scanned as a group of three bars, plus one, plus another three with a two-bar cadential figure. The second strain can be heard more easily in groupings of three, four, and four measures.

These examples belie the common perception of the menuet as inherently "square." Moreover, they do not exhaust the possible phrase structures found among Lully's operatic menuets; variety is more in evidence than consistency. Only approximately one quarter falls into four-bar phrases throughout; a few others also have a consistent phrase structure, but one built on either three-bar or five-bar groups. A slightly larger number mixes four- and six-bar phrases in various patterns, while the remaining menuets all have unique groupings that involve phrase lengths of both odd and even numbers of measures.[7]

---

7   Establishing a count of the number of dances Lully wrote in any given genre is problematic. The biggest impediment is the state of the sources, both printed and manuscript, which do not assign dance types in a consistent manner. In her dissertation, "The Dances of J. B. Lully" (Stanford University, 1967) and in the article drawn from it (see n. 2), Meredith Ellis [Little] provided a listing, with incipits of all the generic dances in Lully's oeuvre (she excluded "airs" and "entrées") that allowed her to arrive at a total of 268 dances, among which 92 were menuets. This number is, however, probably too high, in that many of the attributions as to dance type were derived not from the primary Lully materials, but from secondary sources such as suite arrangements, often far removed

Moreover, the menuet is hardly unique in its structural variety. Others among the dance types Lully used – the gavotte, for example, and a dance such as the gigue to a still greater extent – also defy stereotypes about the square phrasing commonly attributed to dance music. Not even the march is reliably regular: the processional that brings on the priests preparing for a sacrifice in the third act of *Cadmus et Hermione* (LWV 49/42) has seven measures in the first strain, nine in the second; the trumpet march accompanying the arrival of "La Gloire" in the prologue of *Alceste* (LWV 50/4) has a rondeau structure whose refrain consists of two five-bar phrases.

Because Lully composed almost all his dance music for the stage, explanations for this pervasive irregularity may be sought in the dramatic context within which the dances function. Three inter-related areas will be examined in turn: choreography, the texts that are often sung in close association with the dance pieces, and the roles the dancers occupy.

Choreography

There are fifty-two surviving choreographies in Feuillet notation set to music by Lully. (For one example, see Plate 3.1.)[8] Each of them is through-choreographed to its own tune; this means that although the music repeats, every strain of the choreography has its own steps and figures. Unfortunately, none of these choreographies is likely to date from Lully's lifetime. The ones most suited to the present purposes, eleven dances known to have been performed at the Paris Opéra, can all be dated to revivals of Lully's works from between 1698 and 1710, not to the original productions.[9] However, given that the choreographer of these dances, Guillaume Pécour, trained under Lully and danced in many of his

temporally and geographically from Lully's circle. Given the ambiguities even within the primary sources, I have found it prudent in my own attempt to tabulate Lully's dance types to avoid specific counts and to view proportions as approximate.

8 For a catalogue of the 330 or so known choreographies in Feuillet notation, see Meredith E. Little and Carol G. Marsh, *La Danse Noble: An Inventory of Dances and Sources* (Williamstown, New York, Nabburg: Broude Brothers Limited, 1992), henceforth LMC.

9 See Rebecca Harris-Warrick, "Contexts for Choreographies: Notated Dances Set to the Music of Jean-Baptiste Lully," Heidelberg87, 433–456.

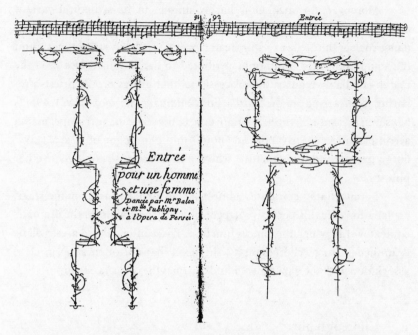

Plate 3.1   From *Recüeil de Dances contenant un tres grand nombres des meillieures Entrées De Ballet De Mr. Pecourt...* (Paris: Feuillet, 1704). This choreography, set to the "Second Air des Jeux Junoniens" from Act I of *Persée*, probably dates from the revival of the opera at the Académie Royale de Musique in 1703. [LMC 4480]

productions, their style is probably similar to that of Lully's day. Thus Pécour's dances, and others from the same period, offer potentially valuable evidence as to how dance and music worked together in this repertoire.

The earliest datable menuet choreography comes from 1688, the year after Lully's death; it is preserved in a different system of notation invented by Jean Favier.[10] Like most of the eighteenth-century menuets preserved in

10   This menuet comes from *Le Mariage de la Grosse Cathos*, a comic *mascarade* composed by André Danican Philidor *l'aîné*. Its music survives along with choreography for all the dances by Jean Favier *l'aîné*. A facsimile and discussion of the manuscript may be found in Rebecca Harris-Warrick and Carol G. Marsh, *Musical Theatre at the Court of Louis XIV: "Le Mariage de la Grosse Cathos"* (Cambridge: Cambridge University Press, 1994); regarding the menuet, see esp. 53–54 and 144–148. Because Favier notation is rhythmically precise, it is

Feuillet notation, this choreography is based on a repeating step-unit that goes over six beats; that is, one menuet step requires two bars of music. The step alone would thus suggest at the very least that menuet phrases should come in multiples of two measures, and, in fact, *all* of the surviving menuet choreographies are set to music that not only has an even number of measures, but that usually has four-bar phrase lengths.

The examples above show, however, that Lully's menuets often do not follow this pattern. The question then becomes how to make sense of a two-bar step and a three- or five-bar phrase. Perhaps Pierre Beauchamps, Lully's choreographer at the Opéra, allowed the dance step to get "out of sync" with the music, waiting for repetitions of strains to make odd numbers even and set everything aright.[11] This hypothesis, however, seems improbable. First, all forty-five menuet choreographies surviving in Feuillet notation[12] adhere

---

possible to be certain that the rhythm of his step was quarter note, half note, half note, quarter note.

The menuet was exceptional in the period in that it was generally built around a small number of repeating step-units, whereas most other dances were through-choreographed and used a more varied step vocabulary. Two basic menuet steps are described in chapter 21 of Pierre Rameau's *Maître à danser* (Paris, 1725; trans. Cyril W. Beaumont [London, 1931]); these are somewhat different in execution and timing from Favier's step, although like his, they occupy two bars of music.

11 Meredith E. Little proposes this possibility in the article "Minuet," *NG*, vol. XII, 355: "Ex. 1, from the [Lully] 'Menuet des Thébains' (*Entr'acte d'Œdipe*, 1664), shows a five-bar minuet strain, which, though unorthodox, would not necessarily preclude social dancing, since with the repeat an even number of bars would result." Little is also willing to accept the "tension [that] may have arisen from the lack of coincidence between music and dance" (p. 354) in the eighteenth-century ballroom menuet, which is based on floor patterns requiring multiples of twelve measures of music, whereas most surviving eighteenth-century menuet music is constructed in eight- or sixteen-bar phrases. Julia Sutton has taken issue with this latter conclusion; see "The Minuet: An Elegant Phoenix," *Dance Chronicle* 8 (1985), 119–152, esp. n. 11. Little does acknowledge that "theatrical dancing in general was more elaborate and virtuoso than contemporary social dancing, permitting and even encouraging considerable freedom in the accompanying musical structures" (p. 355); she does not, however, discuss how the choreography for such free structures might have worked. In his article "Structures métriques du menuet au XVIIe et au début du XVIIIe siècle," *Revue de musicologie* 78 (1992), 27–65, Herbert Schneider discusses another possible example of music–dance disparity – this one on the level of the step – the frequent appearance of hemiola in menuet music from this period.

12 For a list see LMC, 160.

REBECCA HARRIS-WARRICK

closely to the phrase structure of the music, whether it be in four-, eight-, or twelve-bar phrases, as does the single menuet in Favier notation. It seems very unlikely that seventeenth-century menuets would have systematically transgressed what seems to have been such a fundamental principle of choreographic construction in the period. Second, menuets choreographed for the theatre do not restrict themselves to the three or four variants on menuet steps found in ballroom dances. They frequently incorporate some of the numerous step-units that occupy only one bar of music; instead of pairing such steps to make a two-bar unit, a skilled choreographer could easily build a dance phrase containing an odd number of measures.[13]

A gavotte for a solo woman set by Pécour for the 1708 revival of *Atys* (LMC 4520) shows that musical asymmetries pose no problems for the choreographer. The five-bar refrain of this rondeau has two phrases whose beginnings are parallel, but with the second phrase a measure longer than the first (see Example 3.5).[14] Pécour's choreography sets the refrain differently each time it occurs, but always in a way that respects the musical structure. Since in a dance such as a gavotte the individual step-units each occupy one bar of the music, there are no choreographic requirements for phrases of any particular length. Pécour's choreographic phrases, defined through judicious step choices combined with changes in the dancer's spatial orientation, make visible the phrase structure Lully composed into the music.[15]

13 One theatrical example is the "Menuet à deux" danced at the Opéra in 1702 by Mr Dumoulin *l'aîné* and Mlle Victoire in the *Ballet des Fragments de Lully* (LMC 5540), which intersperses menuet steps with steps such as the *coupé* that require only a single measure of music. In this case, where the music is very square, such steps are paired with another step occupying only one measure, but had there been a three-bar phrase, it would have been perfectly possible to add only one such step to a two-bar menuet step. In fact, in some of Lully's menuets with five-bar phrases the music itself suggests a possible choice of steps. In Example 3.3a, for instance, bars 2–4 of each melodic phrase outline the rhythm of the Favier menuet step (see note 10 above); the choreographer might perhaps have set this music with a one-measure step followed by two menuet steps in Favier rhythm, thus yielding five measures of dance.
14 The source for this example is the reduced score engraved by Baussen and published in Paris in 1709; although Ballard published a full score in 1689, no score of *Atys* was published during Lully's lifetime.
15 The relationship between choreography and music is much more complicated than my brief remarks here suggest. The few music/dance analyses done to date have tended to focus on steps, especially in regard to their rhythm. See in this regard Meredith Ellis [Little], "The Contribution of Dance Steps to Musical Analysis and Performance: 'La Bourgogne,'" *JAMS* 23 (1975), 112–124. More

40

Example 3.5

Atys, Gavotte en Rondeau. Air pour la Suite de Flore

In the case of a choreography such as this one, created thirty years after the opera premiered, the music clearly came first, the dance second. But in 1676, when *Atys* was composed, could Lully's choreographer Beauchamps have had a particular set of movements in mind for which he requested five measures of music from the composer? This kind of chicken-or-egg question is difficult to answer. Lully's apprenticeship in dance composition took place within a tradition of court ballets in which the choreographers and composers were often the same people.[16] In the middle

recently Carol Pharo has been examining the gestures that constitute cadences in dance; see "Musical form and dance form: the role of cadential formulae in early eighteenth-century choreographies," *Proceedings of the Society of Dance History Scholars Twentieth Annual Conference* (June 1997), 305–310. Other factors, such as spatial orientation or the figures of the dance, also influence perception of what constitutes a dance phrase. For work that analyzes more than the steps, see Jennifer Thorp and Ken Pierce, "Taste and Ingenuity: Three English Chaconnes of the Early Eighteenth Century," *Historical Dance* 3 (1995), 3–16; Judith Schwartz, "The Passacaille in Lully's *Armide*; Phrase Structure in the Choreography and the Music," *EM* 26 (1998), 300–320; and Carol G. Marsh, "Regular and Irregular Figures: Symmetry in Baroque Dance Choreographies," paper presented at the annual conference of the Society of Dance History Scholars, Barnard College, New York City, June 1997.

16 See Henry Prunières, *Le ballet de cour en France avant Benserade et Lully* (Paris: Henri Laurens, 1914), 208–210. Regarding Beauchamps himself as composer, see

of the seventeenth century the roles of choreographer and composer began to separate, and by the 1670s when Lully began composing operas, the two roles seem distinct, even if some people still had talents in both areas. Anecdotes about Lully's compositional practices emphasize the importance of his working relationship with his librettist, Quinault, but do not mention Beauchamps at all as part of the initial creative process.[17] On the other hand, Lully himself is reported to have choreographed some of his own dance pieces,[18] in which case it is possible that he composed with specific choreographic movements or phrasings in mind. One anecdote about his own choreographic effort does, however, suggest that Lully wrote the music first: according to the Abbé Dubos, Lully had to choreograph some of his own dances, for example, the chaconne in *Cadmus et Hermione* (LWV 49/22) because Beauchamps "did not relish the character of this air."[19]

This inconclusive evidence notwithstanding, one can draw some useful inferences from the surviving choreographies, both those in Feuillet notation and the ones Favier notated in 1688, all of which adhere to the same basic principles of construction. In most instances one step-unit of the dance requires one measure of music. There are two categories of exceptions to this general rule: menuet steps and their variants, which require two bars of 3/4 music (or of 3/8 music, for a passepied); and certain dances in a

Footnote 16 (*cont.*)
 Régine Astier, "When Fiddlers Danced to Their Own Tunes," *The Marriage of Music and Dance*, papers from a conference held at The Guildhall School of Music and Drama, August 9–11, 1991 (London: National Early Music Association, 1992) and George Houle (ed.), "*Le Ballet des Fâcheux*": *Beauchamp's Music for Molière's Comedy* (Bloomington and Indianapolis: Indiana University Press, 1991).
17 See LecerfC, vol. II, 212–224; see in particular the passage cited in n. 23 below regarding the composition of the divertissements.
18 LecerfC, vol. II, 228–229: "Lulli se mêloit de la danse presque autant que du reste. *Une partie du Ballet des fêtes de l'Amour a & [sic] de Bachus avoit été composée* par lui, *l'autre par Desbrosses*. Et Lulli eût presque autant de part aux Ballets des Opera suivans, que *Beauchamp*. Il réformoit les Entrées, imaginoit des pas d'expression & qui convinssent au sujet; & quand il en étoit besoin, il se mettoit à danser devant ses Danseurs, pour leur faire comprendre plûtôt ses idées."
19 Jean-Baptiste Dubos, *Réflexions critiques sur la poésie et sur la peinture* (Paris, 1719); trans. Th. Nugent, *Critical Reflections on Poetry, Painting, and Music*, 5th edn. (London, 1748), vol. III, 128.

slow tempo in which there are two step-units per measure. (The only generic dance type in this category is the loure, whose 6/4 measures were treated choreographically as two measures of 3/4; the other such dances are theatrical *entrées*.) The enormous step vocabulary of Baroque dance, apparent to anyone who flips through the pages of Feuillet's *Chorégraphie*, was combined by choreographers in a myriad of inventive combinations. Moreover, the steps could be adapted to either duple or triple meter – and they could easily be set into phrases of three bars, four bars, five bars, or any length whatsoever. Although it is true that the ballroom dances in particular operate within a range of norms both in terms of steps and floor patterns, even there such norms were flexible, not rigid. Of the nine ballroom dances published by Feuillet in 1700 in conjunction with his book *Chorégraphie* (all choreographed by Pécour to specific pieces of music), six of them have consistent four- or eight-bar phrases, but three intersperse phrases of five or seven bars.[20] Thus it can be inferred that irregular phrase structures were not viewed as problematic even for amateur dancers, let alone for the professionals who danced on the stage of the Paris Opéra.

The question of priority – of whether the music or the choreography came first in Lully's operas – may not ultimately matter very much. Whether Lully and Beauchamps collaborated from the start or whether one responded to a framework set by the other, each could easily have adapted to the other's requirements; the conventions within which they worked gave them aesthetic choices, not fixed templates. It is clear from the variety in Lully's music that not even the menuet, the simplest dance of its day from a movement perspective, had a choreographic pattern so inflexible as to impose a reproducible structure on the music. It is high time to discard the myth that dance steps force composers into a metrical straitjacket.

---

20 These three are the "Rigaudon des Vaisseaux" (LMC 7400), which has two consecutive rigaudons, the first with a phrase structure of 8 // 12 (6+6), the second 8 (4+4) // 12 (7+5); "La Conty" (LMC 2220), a vénitienne (forlana) in rondeau form whose C section has 10 bars (4 +6) but is otherwise square; and "La Mariée" (LMC 5360), whose quirky phrase structure (14 [4+5+5] // 12 [7+5]) was apparently no impediment to making it one of the most popular ballroom dances of the eighteenth century (it was published for the last time in 1765; see Rebecca Harris-Warrick, "La Mariée: The History of a French Court Dance," HeyerL, 239–258).

Example 3.6
Bellérophon, Menuet

Pourquoi n'avoir pas le cœur tendre?	a	8+
Rien n'est si doux que d'aimer.	b	7
Peut-on aisément s'en défendre?	a	8+
Non, non, non, l'amour doit tout charmer.	b	9

Text

If choreography does not offer a mechanistic explanation for the phrase structures of the dance, might the structure of the sung texts have had an influence? The dance pieces in Lully's *divertissements* almost always form part of a multi-movement musical structure. Often a dance is performed more than once in alternation with a vocal piece that is either sung to the same music or to music very similar in character. Example 3.6, a menuet from *Bellérophon* (LWV 57/7), belongs to the first category: first the piece is played entirely by instruments, during which time the dancers participate; next a shepherd sings the first verse, set to the same music as the dance; then comes a repeat of the instrumental dance and finally the second verse.[21] Each verse of the song has four lines of text, rhymed a b a b. The a lines have eight syllables plus a mute "e" (a so-called "feminine" rhyme), the b lines seven and nine respectively with a masculine rhyme.

---

21 The general pattern in Lully's divertissements was to alternate singing and dancing, not to have the two occur simultaneously, even when the vocal numbers are structurally identical to the dances. Choruses sometimes did incorporate dancing, but only within a limited set of conventions. For further discussion, see this author's "Recovering the Lullian Divertissement," *Dance and Music in French Baroque Theatre: Sources and Interpretations* (London: Institute of Advanced Musicological Studies, King's College London, 1998), 55–80.

Lully set the text syllabically and gave each line its own phrase of music. The first three lines are all set to three-bar phrases, but at the start of the fourth line the word "non" is repeated twice, with each repetition receiving an entire measure of music. This makes the answer to the question of the previous line – essentially, "Is it possible to ward off love?" – a much more emphatic "No," but it also extends the phrase from three to five bars. This extension looks very much like a musical, not a textually driven choice: Lully could have avoided the text repetition and written a three-bar phrase, which would have trimmed this line to seven syllables, like its rhyming pair. (It is possible – or even likely – that Quinault conceived of the line with seven, rather than nine syllables. Although varied line lengths are not at all rare in his dance songs, word repetition is.) But even with the text repetition Lully could have set the nine syllables to a three-measure phrase, had he so desired. Quinault's verses did not impose this phrase structure; Lully opted for the irregularity.

Although in vocal settings such as Lully's that are largely syllabic the length of a line of verse does bear some connection to the length of the phrase, the number of syllables in a line does not fix that length in advance. The example from *Bellérophon* draws three-bar phrases from both seven- and eight-syllable lines. Another vocal menuet, "Amants, aimez vos chaines / Vos soins et vos soupirs" from *Cadmus et Hermione* (LWV 49/56), arrives at three-bar phrases from shorter, six-syllable lines. A choral menuet from *Thésée*, "L'amour plaît malgré ses peines" (LWV 51/67), has seven-syllable lines and four-bar phrases throughout. It is not my intention to reopen the complicated issue of the relationship between the internal structure of a line of verse and its musical setting, about which much has already been written, primarily regarding patterns of textual and musical stress within the phrase.[22] Here the question is rather whether the length of a line of verse in any sense predetermines the number of measures to which it is set within a given meter. Whereas it can be observed in Lully's dance songs that certain line lengths lend themselves to particular types of musical treatment, there

---

22 See, for example, David Tunley, "The Union of Words and Music in Seventeenth-century French Song – The Long and the Short of It," *Australian Journal of French Studies* 21 (1984), 281–307; Patricia Ranum, "Les 'Caractères' des danses françaises," *RMFC* 23 (1985), 45–70; and the same author's "Audible Rhetoric and Mute Rhetoric: The Seventeenth-century French Sarabande," *EM* 14 (1986), 22–39.

is nonetheless too much variety to posit a formulaic relationship between number of syllables and phrase length.

The argument made in the above two paragraphs may, however, be moot: if anecdotal evidence from Lecerf de la Viéville and Charles Perrault is to be believed, in the *divertissements* Lully reversed his usual practice of setting text Quinault gave him, by instead writing the dance songs first, then asking Quinault to fit words to them.[23] In giving the music priority over the words in this kind of piece, Lully was apparently adhering to time-honored practices, ones that he inherited from the ballet de cour and that lasted for decades after him.[24] Thus if the music of the divertissements did, in fact, precede the text, then the phrase structure of the dance songs cannot be attributed to the poetry.

One may nonetheless wish to compare the phrase structures between Lully's instrumental dances and the binary vocal pieces with which they are paired – and this especially when the two back-to-back pieces are not musically identical – to see whether there are noteworthy differences in construction. In most such cases the two pieces share key, meter, surface rhythms, and general affect, but do not have identical structures. One might expect in such pairings that the vocal piece would show greater freedom in its phrase structures than the purely instrumental dance – certainly Lully's vocal writing is noted for its metric flexibility – but such is not the case. One finds square and irregular phrasings among both the dances and the paired vocal numbers, in roughly the same proportions. Moreover, the dance is not

<hr/>

23 "C'est ainsi que se composoit par Quinaut & par Lulli le corps de l'Opera, dont les paroles étoient faites les premieres. Au contraire, pour les divertissemens, Lulli faisoit les airs d'abord, à sa commodité & en son particulier. Il y falloit des paroles. Afin qu'elles fussent justes, Lulli faisoit un canevas de vers, & il en faisoit aussi pour quelques airs de mouvement. Il apliquoit lui-même à ces airs de mouvement & à ces divertissemens, des vers, dont le mérite principal étoit de quadrer en perfection à la musique, & il envoyoit cette brochure à Quinaut, qui ajustoit les siens dessus." LecerfC, vol. II, 218–219. See also Charles Perrault, *Les hommes illustres* (Paris, 1696), vol. I, 173: "Ce qui le [Lully] charmoit encore davantage, c'est que Mr. Quinault avoit le talent de faire des paroles sur les airs de danse dont il embellissoit les Opera, qui y convenoient aussi bien et souvent mieux que si elles avoient esté composées les premiéres."
24 Herbert Schneider has traced the practice of the "canevas," a metrical pattern set by the composer to which the poet had to conform, from the early ballet de cour into the nineteenth century. See his article "Canevas als Terminus der lyrischen Dichtung," *Archiv für Musikwissenschaft* 42 (1985), 87–101.

infrequently *less* regular than the paired vocal air. In *Roland*, for example, an instrumental gavotte with three-bar phrases in the first strain and four- and six-bar phrases in the second is followed by a binary choral gavotte that has four-bar phrases throughout (LWV 65/12 and 65/13; see Example 3.7). A similarly square vocal air sung by Straton in the last act of *Alceste* ("A quoi bon," LWV 50/83) follows a duple-meter dance for shepherds with a phrase structure of nine measures (divided four-plus-five) in the first strain and seventeen (divided nine-plus-eight) in the second (LWV 50/82). Once again no template is in evidence; the medium of performance – vocal as opposed to instrumental – does not appear to influence Lully's choice of phrase structures within the divertissements.

Dramatic context

What, then, of the dramatic context? Does phrase structure correlate either with the kinds of characters dancing or with the dramatic situation? Could it be, for instance, that Lully deliberately manipulated phrase structures as an aspect of his musical characterization?

First let us recall how Lully employs dance in his operas. Dancers are minor characters: members of the populace, nymphs and shepherds, allegorical characters such as Pleasures, or the followers of a major singing character. Thus in the prologue to *Phaéton*, the god Saturn has a group of followers, some of whom sing, others of whom dance. In a sense, dancers are double cast with the members of the chorus who, at the Paris Opéra, did not move; the dancers were, in effect, their bodies. Since the chorus remained motionless around the perimeter of the stage, the dancers sometimes engaged in pantomime in their stead. The most famous such example is the scene in *Isis* (IV/1) showing the people who live in frozen climes, shivering with cold, which reportedly used not a single recognizable dance step.[25] However, in many more scenes the dancers participate in celebrations in which they are to be perceived as actually dancing. In fact, festivities provided one of the possible frameworks within which dance could be dramatically justified.[26] In the

---

25 Dubos, *Critical Reflections*, vol. III, 186–187.
26 Regarding the French concern with dramatic verisimilitude, which extended to the use of dance, see Catherine Kintzler, *Poétique de l'opéra français de Corneille à Rousseau* (Paris: Minerve, 1991).

Example 3.7

(a) *Roland*, Gavotte

(b) Une Fée chante ce qui suit, et les Chœurs des Genies et des Fées luy respondent.

fourth act of *Atys*, the river god Sangar celebrates the imminent wedding of his daughter with a group of fellow deities. "Let us sing and dance," he declares ("Que l'on chante, que l'on danse"), and his followers obey.

All of the dances shown in Examples 3.1–6 come from the prologues to various operas. Tradition demanded that the prologue present an allegorical paean to the greatness of Louis XIV, usually in the form of festivities in honor of the unnamed "hero." The very square menuet from *Phaéton* in Example 3.1 is performed by the companions of the goddess Astrée in conjunction with a duet in celebration of love. It clearly represents dance, not action, and equally clearly it is celebratory.

But so are *all* the menuets discussed so far. The immediate setting and the names of the characters may differ, but the contexts are all similar. In *Alceste* (Example 3.4) the dancers are river gods "who demonstrate their joy by their dancing." In *Roland* (Example 3.3) they are spirits and fairies, in *Bellérophon* (Example 3.6) shepherds, in *Armide* (Example 3.2) the followers of Glory and Wisdom celebrating the concord the two divinities share in their admiration of the hero. In every case the reigning affect is joy, and nothing suggests that Lully automatically assigns five-bar phrases to shepherds or nine- and eleven-bar phrases to river gods. On the contrary, the same set of characters may perform back-to-back dances with completely different metrical structures, as Example 3.3 from *Roland* shows. In celebratory scenes the affect may be predictable, but the phrase structure of the dances is not.

Dances entitled "Air" or "Entrée"

Thus far I have considered only dances bearing generic designations in the sources (menuets, gavottes, etc.); these account for approximately one third to one half of the dances in any opera and tend to be used in celebratory contexts when the dance is to be read as "real." Dances identified in the scores simply as "Air" or "Entrée" (sometimes followed by the role of the characters dancing) have a wider range of expressive functions, from the celebratory through the dramatic to the outright pantomimic; these are even less likely than the generic dances to show metrical regularity. Whereas about a third of the pieces identified as generic dance types are constructed in four-bar phrases – with roughly another 30 percent either having phrases

Example 3.8
Phaéton, Entrée des Furies

with even numbers of measures other than multiples of four (as in Example 3.3b above) or having a consistent phrase structure of an odd number of bars (Example 3.3a) – only about 15 percent of the airs and entrées have consistent four-bar phrases, with pieces in an even number of bars (but not multiples of four) constituting another 15 percent. The remaining two thirds either have phrase lengths that vary within a single piece, or are constructed so as to avoid clearly defining a phrase until the end of a strain.

Example 3.8, the "Entrée des Furies" from the third act of *Phaéton* (LWV 61/50), has the rushing sixteenth notes Lully typically assigns to furies, demons, and other nasty characters. The two parts of this piece have seven and eleven measures respectively. In the first strain although Lully sets up similar patterns in bars 1 and 3, he does not make bars 2 and 4 parallel and pushes toward the cadence in bar 6, which then is extended by a one-bar flourish. In the second strain Lully temporarily shifts the metrical emphasis from the downbeat to beat 3 via the cadence on E in bar 10, although he restores the emphasis via the cadence to A major on the downbeat of bar 12. However, the effect of this cadence is minimized by the forward motion in both treble and bass, and Lully does not provide a real point of repose until the end of the strain.

This piece comes from the end of the spectrum of Lully dances that was probably close to mime. The music accompanied not only movement by the dancers, but a scenic transformation. The stage directions in the *livret* read: "The doors of the temple open, and this place, which had formerly appeared magnificent, turns into a frightful abyss that vomits flames and from which emerge furies and terrifying phantoms who overturn and break the offerings and who threaten and chase away the assembled people."[27] The irregularities in this piece could easily be attributed to its dramatic context.

However, many of the metrical features of the "Entrée des Furies" – uneven numbers of measures in each strain, avoidance of internal cadences or a lessening of their effect through continued forward motion – may also appear in dances of a completely different character. Take, for example, the divertissement known as the "Jeux Junoniens" from Act I of *Persée*. In this scene Cassiope tries to appease the anger of Juno by offering her a dance contest performed by young couples about to get married. Because an air of both competition and uncertainty hangs over this scene, the two dance pieces that make up the contest do not have the celebratory qualities of the dances found in prologues. However, there can be no doubt that they represent real dances, not mime. Moreover, this is supposed to be dance at its best, a true test of skill.

The first dance, labeled "Second Air" in the score (the "Premier Air" provides entry music for the characters in the divertissement) has eleven bars in the first strain, twenty-nine in the second (see Example 3.9a). For ears conditioned to expect antecedent/consequent phrases, the first four bars, with a feminine cadence to the tonic in first inversion, might set up expectations for a consequent phrase of four bars ending with another feminine cadence to the dominant. But Lully does not provide a sense of repose at the

27 "Les Portes du Temple s'ouvrent, & ce lieu qui avoit parû magnifique, n'est plus qu'un gouffre effroyable qui vomit des flames, & d'où sortent des Furies & des Fantosmes terribles, qui renversent & brisent les offrandes, & qui menacent & escartent l'Assemblée."

Example 3.9

(a) *Persée*, Second Air [des Jeux Junoniens]

end of four bars; rather he keeps the motion going in both the treble and bass leading toward bar 6, where despite the half cadence in the bass, the melody continues to provide forward momentum. The first strain is thus heard as an eleven-bar unit, with no real stopping point until the double bar.

The second strain has a clear cadence to the mediant in bar 20, which gives the phrase nine measures. A return to the tonic occurs six measures

Example 3.9 (*cont.*)

(b) *Persée*, Troisieme Air

later, at bar 26. In both places the moment of repose is only an eighth-note. The next phrase encompasses the remainder of the strain up to the final cadence, fourteen measures in all. (This long-winded quality is much more frequent in entrées than in generic dances; in the latter the phrase structure may be irregular, but the phrases are much shorter than the nine-plus-six-plus-fourteen groupings found here.)

The "Troisième Air" (Example 3.9b) initially appears more like what one expects of a dance: the first strain is eight bars long, divided into two four-bar phrases, and the quarter-note upbeat gives the piece the character of a bourrée, which, in fact, the dance is called in some sources. However, in bar 4 at the start of the second phrase Lully switches to a more gavotte-like anacrusis of two beats and varies the rhythmic pattern in the melody. The second strain opens in a straightforward way with two four-bar phrases that cadence to the mediant in bar 16. However the cadence provides not a moment of repose but a point of departure for a new melodic figure that passes through a half cadence on D three bars later, reaching the final cadence after another three bars. This telescoping gives the second strain fourteen rather than sixteen measures. (The overlap that occurs at bar 16 and that poses problems for scanning the phrases – should bar 16 be counted as the eighth measure of the phrase that is ending or the first of the new one? – is typical of Lully's dance music. Another typical feature of this piece is that the first strain is relatively square, while the second introduces metrical irregularities.)

Choreographies by Pécour survive for these two dances, dating from the revival of *Persée* in 1703 (see Plate 3.1, p. 38 above, for the two A sections of the "Second Air"). Both are for a man and a woman and draw upon the intricate and technically demanding step vocabulary typical of theatrical entrées. Both demonstrate not only that irregular and varied metrical structures pose no impediment to choreography, but also that such structures are perfectly compatible with dances in the noble style.[28] Lully did not compose these two pieces for grotesque or comic characters, but as representatives of the art of dance. The art they exhibit is subtle and varied, not restricted to predictable, square phrases.

Although Lully's dance pieces manifest notable structural similarities between the music for two such different sets of characters – frightful furies on the one hand, and amorous dance contestants on the other – they nonetheless exhibit a few general trends regarding how phrase structure relates to musical characterization. Demons, furies, and other threatening creatures move to irregular, long-winded phrases; their music becomes regular only if, as in Act II of *Amadis*, they are disguised as something benign (shepherds, in this case). Similarly, characters engaged in some kind of miming dance, either serious or grotesque (e.g., *forgerons*, *sacrificateurs*, or *sorciers*) generally get irregular phrases, although this pattern is not absolute: the famous *trembleurs* in *Isis*, for example, have music built on four-bar phrases, with one five-bar phrase added. Pastoral characters –

---

28 LMC 4480 and 3080, published by Feuillet in a collection of theatrical choreographies by Pécour, *Recüeil de dances* (Paris, 1704). Pécour's choreography pays more attention to the major points of articulation provided by the ends of strains than to internal cadences, but, not surprisingly, has a clearer internal phrase structure in the "Troisième Air," where the cadences are clearly marked in the music, than in the "Second Air," where melodic momentum minimizes the effect of the cadences.

shepherds, nymphs, *driades, silvains,* and the like – have dances in both irregular and regular phrasings, although both types of phrase tend to adhere to short, well-defined units. Celebratory characters, whether humans or divinities, have a fairly high proportion of dances that are either square or reasonably regular – that is, dances that either have a regular number of odd-numbered phrases or that only once or twice deviate from a basically four-bar pattern. But the "hedging" adverbs in the previous sentence show how unstable this category is: even here pieces built on consistent four-bar phrases are simply not the norm.[29]

Are there, then, only weak correlations to be found in Lully's dance music between dramatic context and musical expression? There are, in fact, many such connections, but they reside in the inter-workings of all the parameters of a piece: harmony, melody, rhythm, tempo, key, and orchestration, as well as in phrase structure. Dances for nymphs are *not* the same as dances for demons. If, however, I have artificially narrowed my focus to a single aspect of Lully's style, it is to demonstrate that commonly held notions about the inherent "squareness" of dance music simply do not apply to this repertoire. Lully definitely had ideas about musical characterization – the strong association between woodwind instruments and pastoral settings is only one example – but he did not have a simple metrical template for dance pieces. His music is too varied and too supple to support the idea that he heard four- and eight-bar phrases as the norm for dance music and only deviated from them in pursuit of specific expressive goals. Nor was Lully alone in this flexible approach to the construction of dances; seventeenth-century dance music in general exhibits a much freer approach to phrase structures than does the dance music of the eighteenth

---

29 It is interesting in this regard to look at another body of theatrical dances, those found in Gregorio Lambranzi's *Neue und curieuse theatralische Tantz-Schul* (Nuremberg, 1716; reprint New York: Dance Horizons, 1966). The book includes a few dances in the noble style, but most are comic or burlesque, often for *commedia dell'arte* characters. The elegantly dressed couple dancing a sarabande moves to simple, square phrases, but so do ridiculous old women scratching where they itch or Mezzetin and his wife. On the other hand, the Swiss soldier performing fancy maneuvers with his pike has three seven-bar phrases and Scaramuzza (*sic*) performs his antics to phrases of eleven and fifteen bars. But in this collection the tunes with irregular phrase lengths actually occupy a smaller proportion of the total than in Lully's works, their comic intent notwithstanding.

century, one that embraces irregularity and sees square phrasing as only one possibility among many. The notion that stretching a four-bar phrase into six represents a deliberate distortion of an underlying dance pattern may be tenable in regard to a Haydn minuet, but not to one by Lully.

But if Lully's dances frequently sound irregular to the ear, they undoubtedly appeared very symmetrical to the eye. A look at the choreographic notation of the "Second Air" from *Persée* (Plate 3.1) reveals that the two dancers always move in mirror image to each other and that they trace their paths relative to an invisible axis of symmetry that bisects the stage. It is beyond the scope of this paper to explore the implications of this juxtaposition, or the myriad other possible intersections between movement and music. This image may, however, serve to remind us that dance music operates in conjunction with the visual and the kinetic. A study of the phrase structures of Lully's dances needs to take these intersecting systems into account.

The phrase structures of Lully's dances are not exceptional for his period. Dance in the seventeenth century was a sophisticated, varied, and highly developed art; it did not impose restrictions on a composer's imagination. It is time to look at this rich repertoire of music as Lully wrote it, not through the lens of preconceptions.

4 Quinault's libretto for *Isis*: new directions for the *tragédie lyrique*

BUFORD NORMAN

Isis opened on January 5, 1677 – the same week as Racine's *Phèdre* (January 1) – at Saint-Germain-en-Laye, where it had less success with the court than had Quinault and Lully's earlier operas. Some spectators found fault with certain characters, such as the Fury Erinnis, who wasn't cruel enough,[1] while some of the earlier commentators found it too "savant" and not natural enough.[2] Louis XIV was not completely happy with the new work either, especially in comparison with the preceding Quinault–Lully opera, *Atys*, which he liked so much that it came to be known as "l'opéra du roi." Furthermore, he can hardly have enjoyed the gossip about Mme de Montespan/Junon and Mme de Ludres/Io,[3] nor would he have been very pleased with the inevitable associations between himself and Quinault's Jupiter, who was tricked by Junon into giving up his new favorite, unable to protect her from the ensuing persecution, and finally forced to admit the errors of his ways.[4] He asked Lully to make some changes, which delayed the Paris premiere until August 1677.

A summary of the plot of *Isis* can be found in the Appendix, p. 71 below. An earlier version of parts of this essay was read at the 1995 meeting of the Society for Interdisciplinary Seventeenth-Century French Studies (SE17) and will be published in *Cahiers du Dix-Septième*.

1 See ParfaictH. This work was probably written in collaboration with his brother François.

2 LecerfC, vol. I, 89.

3 I do not have the space to go into the complex issue of what the choice of the myth of *Isis* owes to the notorious jealousy of Mme de Montespan and her persecution of Mme de Ludres. Quinault's libretto was written well before Mme de Ludres's return to favor in early 1677 and Mme de Montespan's terrible vengeance. See GrosQ, 119–121; BeaussantL, 583–592; and Primi-Visconti, 33, 35, 103–106.

4 See CouvreurL, 377 and Saint-MardR, who criticized the role of Jupiter: "Quelle

Either Lully made some important changes, or the work was not as bad as the court thought, since it ran continuously from August until the Easter closing in March of 1678.[5] On the other hand, it is the only Quinault-Lully opera not to be revived in the seventeenth century, and it had the least number of revivals in the eighteenth century of any of their works. Lully's numerous enemies certainly contributed to the mitigated success of *Isis*. His near monopoly on the musical theatre angered many of his rivals, and his remarkable ascent from kitchen boy to royal favorite had made many people jealous. Although La Fontaine certainly exaggerated somewhat in writing, in "Le Florentin" (1674), that

> ... the whole human race,
> Humble and grand, in their prayers,
> Say evening and morning:
> "Lord, whose uncommon mercy has always been granted us,
> Save us from the Florentine,"[6]

there was probably a concerted effort by Lully's enemies to keep *Isis* from being a success at Saint-Germain-en-Laye in early 1677.[7] La Fontaine, whose libretto *Daphné* had been refused by Lully in 1674, contributed his poem to Niert's "Sur l'opéra" to the effort, deploring the success of opera at the expense of the *air de cour* and of a separation between tragedy, ballet, and song.

However, neither royal displeasure nor jealous rivals can explain the relative lack of success of *Isis* at the Académie Royale after 1678. Audiences and critics alike continued to admire the music – *Isis* became known as "l'opéra des musiciens" – and to enjoy excerpts from the work, such as the

Footnote 4 (*cont.*)
figure fait-là Jupiter? Et lui qui avoit tant d'autorité, ne devoit-il pas en prendre un peu sur sa femme, & laisser moins souffrir cette malheureuse Isis, qu'il aimoit tant?" (What kind of figure does Jupiter cut here? He who had such great authority, shouldn't he lord it over his wife a little, and ease the suffering of this unfortunate Isis, whom he loved so much?), 31.

5 Isis shared the stage with *Cadmus et Hermione*, *Alceste*, *Atys*, and perhaps *Thésée*, in September 1677 and with all four in the first months of 1678, after the performances of these same operas at court.

6 "... tout le genre humain, / Petits et grands, dans leurs prières, / Disent le soir et le matin: / 'Seigneur, par vos bontés pour nous si singulières, / Délivrez-nous du Florentin.'"

7 LaGorceO, 61.

"chœur des trembleurs" (IV, 1) and the "plainte d'Io" (V, 1), but complete performances were rare. In the eighteenth century, Rémond de Saint-Mard found Quinault's libretto "ridicule"[8] and La Harpe, while he admired many passages from *Isis*, said that the last two acts "languish on account of the uniformity of a situation that is sustained too long"[9] and that this manner of tormenting Io "seems to have been created only for the sake of scenic effects" (p. 154).[10] Parfaict wrote that "one does not feel in the play this interest which should be the soul of all works written for the theatre."[11] Parfaict did not blame Quinault, however; rather, he sympathized with him "to have been obliged to accept an intractable, sterile subject and to flesh it out with episodic scenes."[12]

Parfaict is assuming – perhaps incorrectly – that Quinault had little or no role in the choice of his subject and that he and Lully were trying to write another opera that, like *Atys*, could be compared favorably to Racinian tragedy. Such comparisons were inevitable in France in the 1670s. Quinault had been one of the most successful playwrights of the 1650s and 1660s, but his concept of tragedy was under attack by Boileau, Racine, and other "Ancients" who preferred simpler, more unified plots in which love was less a positive emotion that bound two noble characters together and united them at the end than a source of unresolvable conflicts that led the main characters to suffering, soul-searching, and recognition. This is of course a dangerously sweeping generalization, since Racine had just written *Mithridate* (1673) and *Iphigénie* (1674), in which a young couple is united at the end and in which glory and love are not necessarily incompatible. Still,

8 Saint-MardR, 31.
9 "languissent par l'uniformité d'une situation trop prolongée."
10 "semble n'avoir été imaginée que pour des effets de décoration." The discussion of Quinault is in volume VII of his *Lycée, ou Cours de littérature ancienne et moderne* (1799–1805), 18 vols. (Paris, Pourrat, 1835), Part 2, Book 1, chapter 8, 154. See also GrosQ, 753, n. 2. Gros says that La Harpe found *Isis* lacking in "pathétique," but the discussion of *Isis* in the editions I have been able to consult contains nothing comparably specific. La Harpe does say that only in *Roland* and *Armide* does Quinault attain the "sublime des grands sentiments" (p. 164) and that Armide's is the only role with passions that approach those of tragedy (p. 167).
11 "on ne sent point dans [l]a pièce cet intérèt qui doit être l'âme de tous les ouvrages de Théâtre."
12 "d'avoir été obligé de traiter un fond ingrat et stérile, dont il a été contraint de remplir les vides de scènes épisodiques" (ParfaictH, 37).

at least since the "querelle d'Alceste" in 1674,[13] Quinault had been criticized not only for the exaggerated *tendresse* with which he portrayed his young lovers, but also for taking too many liberties with his classical sources, for including secondary – and often comic – action, and for interrupting the inexorable march toward denouement with *divertissements*.

Literary and musical historians have always tried to find development and improvement as the career of an author or composer unfolds. *Phèdre*, Racine's last profane tragedy, is universally considered his masterpiece, and for many commentators on the Quinault–Lully operas, *Atys* is a clear improvement over their first three collaborations (four, counting *Les Fêtes de l'Amour et de Bacchus*), since it shows a tendency toward a Racinian conception of tragedy. The plot is tightly constructed, there is no subplot involving minor characters, the divine Cybèle behaves very much like a mortal, Atys and Sangaride resist their passion before giving in to it and then suffer the consequences. In fact, *Atys* can be compared to *Phèdre* in many ways, as a jealous and powerful woman takes revenge on the man who spurns her love and later comes to regret her hasty decision.

The problem with such a view of the Quinault–Lully operas – in addition to imposing a rather simplistic and anachronistic concept of "progress" on the creative process – is that *Atys* is only the fourth of their eleven *tragédies lyriques*. Having succeeded in creating an opera that could be compared favorably in many ways to spoken tragedy, they might be expected to continue in this noble vein, reaching their crowning achievement with *Armide*, which features another powerful female who cannot have the man she loves. However, one can by no stretch of the imagination see *Isis* as a step in this direction. Rather, *Isis* moves the Quinault–Lully collaboration in a new direction – we have a *tragédie lyrique* that is extremely *lyrique* but far from *tragique*. In addition, it does not develop one of the standard elements that one finds in all of Racine's tragedies from *Alexandre* to *Phèdre* and in Quinault and Lully's first four operas – after Hiérax is turned into a bird of prey in Act III, scene 7, there is no character who can be said to be truly in love. Nor do we ever have a

---

13   See Philippe Quinault, *Alceste, suivi de La Querelle d'Alceste*, ed. William Brooks, Buford Norman, and Jeanne Morgan Zarucchi, *Textes Littéraires Français 451* (Geneva: Droz, 1994).

united couple threatened by rivals in love, since the love – not very strong, apparently – between Hiérax and Io is a thing of the past before the opera begins. Audiences expected to find a loving couple at the beginning and to follow their trials and tribulations to the end, but they hardly found it in *Isis*.

Isis is also unusual in that:

1 Hiérax, who at first appears to be the male lead, does not appear in the second act and disappears near the end of the third;
2 The fourth act does little to advance the plot, but is devoted to a series of scenes featuring divinities and strange peoples;
3 The last act resolves very little, other than the quarrel between Jupiter and Junon. There is no real-life solution for Io, who becomes a goddess.

Why would Quinault and Lully write a *tragédie lyrique* that places little emphasis on the development of a standard plot and on realistic, individual psychological portraits, and this one year after *Atys*, the closest thing they wrote to a "regular" tragedy, which had precisely the more expected emphasis that I just mentioned? Almost every critic who has dealt with *Isis* in some detail has struggled with the same question:

> *Atys* came at the end of an evolution that was characterized by progress in the areas of the dramatic and of the human. *Isis* will constitute a drastic change of direction. Quinault and Lully abandon the path that was taking their genre toward a more strictly dramatic form. Did they realize the futility of trying to make opera a double of tragedy, enhanced by song and dance?[14]

> If he were to continue in the path he had begun to follow with *Atys*, Quinault would be forced to move away from his original conception of the *tragédie lyrique*. *Atys*, as an opera libretto, is a sober work. The spectacular plays a much less important part than in the preceding libretti, and if there is still a relatively large number of dances, the role of machinery is strictly limited: action tends to be decidedly more interior, interest to be concentrated on the plot, attention to be directed to characters and feelings. In *Isis*, on the contrary, action once more becomes exterior; the spectacular

14 "Atys venait au terme d'une évolution caractérisée par le progrès du dramatique et de l'humain. Isis marquera un violent coup de barre. Quinault et Lully abandonnent la voie qui menait leur genre à une forme plus strictement dramatique. Ont-ils compris la vanité de faire de l'opéra une doublure de la tragédie additionnée de chant et de danse?" (GirdlestoneT, 77).

regains its preponderant role, dances become more numerous and the sets and costumes are more sumptuous than ever.[15]

After the progressive concentration of the *tragédie lyrique* and the constant joint effort of Quinault and Lully to move closer to tragedy – and with *Atys* they both succeed, given the nature of the type of theatre they offer – here suddenly is a work without true dramatic force, without pretension to have any, without unity of action, with a return to a light tone and even to the comic. A regression? Or a diversion? Did the two authors think that the excessive rigor of *Atys* might make their theatre seem too forbidding? Or tire their audiences?[16]

The most obvious answer to these questions is that Quinault and Lully wanted to try a new approach to the *tragédie lyrique*. *Isis* has many qualities that make it effective theatre, and one can attribute its mitigated success less to any weaknesses the work might have than to its experimental nature, to Quinault and Lully's obvious decision to give a larger role to spectacle[17] and to the music and dance that were so popular with their audiences. This they did, but hardly at the expense of unity, structure or drama.

Instead of a love interest or traditional unity of action, Quinault used the theme of liberty as one means to give unity to his libretto. Io's suffering, which dominates the final acts of the opera, can best be understood in the context of the restrictions that are placed on her freedom and on that of

15 "A persévérer dans la voie où il s'engageait avec *Atys*, Quinault devait être amené à s'éloigner de sa conception première de la tragédie lyrique. Atys, en tant que livret d'opéra, est une œuvre sobre. Le spectacle y tient une place beaucoup moins importante que dans les livrets précédents, et si les danses y sont encore relativement nombreuses, la part des machines est strictement limitée: l'action, très nettement, tend à s'intérioriser, l'intérêt à se concentrer sur l'intrigue, l'attention à s'attacher aux personnages et aux sentiments. Dans *Isis*, au contraire, l'action s'extériorise de nouveau; le spectacle reprend une place prépondérante, les danses sont plus nombreuses et la mise en scène est plus somptueuse que jamais" (GrosQ, 607).

16 "Après le resserrement progressif de la tragédie lyrique, l'effort constant et conjoint de Quinault et de Lully pour se rapprocher de la tragédie – et ils y parviennent, l'un et l'autre, dans *Atys*, compte tenu de la nature du spectacle qu'ils proposent – voici tout à coup une œuvre sans force proprement dramatique, sans volonté d'en avoir, sans unité d'action, avec un retour au ton léger et même au comique. Une régression? Ou une diversion? Les deux auteurs ont-il pensé que l'excès de rigueur d'*Atys* risquait de durcir leur théâtre? Ou de lasser leur public?" (BeaussantL, 579).

17 As Girdlestone points out (GirdlestoneT, 80), there are eight different sets and eight appearances of divinities.

62

most of the other characters. Io apparently made a free choice to enter into a relationship with Hiérax: "My vows have been sworn, my heart has made a choice."[18] Pirante says that her father approves of the match but emphasizes Io's preference, not her father's wishes:

> The daughter of Inachus openly prefers you
> To a thousand other suitors who are jealous of your fate;
> You have the accord of her father.[19]

Jupiter's attentions do not of course force her to change her choice, but it is as if Jupiter represents a force that cannot be resisted:

> He is a suitor whom one dares not scorn;
> And it is difficult to refuse
> The glorious empire of the greatest of hearts.[20]

She sincerely tries to stick to her choice of Hiérax, but she seems trapped in a hopeless situation, doomed to lose Hiérax, to be abandoned by Jupiter and punished by Junon. Once the gods begin to intervene in human affairs, there is no more freedom for mortals.

Examples of characters who limit the freedom of other characters can be found throughout the libretto. Jupiter is of course the most powerful of the gods, but even he cannot simply impose his will; as Junon says,

> To his almighty power everything must yield;
> But since he has decided to use trickery as his only weapon,
> Jupiter he may be, he is still less clever than I.[21]

There are certain conventions that even Jupiter must obey. He does not simply abduct Io, as Pluton will do in *Proserpine*, nor does he openly flaunt his new passion. Similarly, Junon has the power to imprison and punish Io for as long as she likes, but her "courroux fatal" and "injuste fureur" finally must give way to "une juste pitié" (V, 3: 869, 881, 868). It is not just that her jealousy and anger cause her to impose excessive punishment on a relatively

18 "Mes vœux sont engagés, mon cœur a fait un choix" (I, 5: 165).
19 "La fille d'Inachus hautement vous préfère / A mille autres amants de votre sort jaloux; / Vous avez l'aveu de son père" (I, 2: 29–31).
20 "C'est un amant qu'on n'ose mépriser; / Et du plus grand des cœurs le glorieux empire / Est difficile à refuser" (I, 4: 135–137).
21 "Sous sa toute-puissance il faut que tout fléchisse, / Mais puisqu'il ne prétend s'armer que d'artifice, / Tout Jupiter qu'il est, il est moins fort que moi" (II, 5: 330–331).

innocent victim, since she is powerless to punish Jupiter except through artifice and emotional blackmail; there are also "laws" of the theatre that govern her behavior as well as that of Jupiter and the other characters.[22] The audience would become bored if there were too many scenes portraying Io's sufferings and would feel such injustice that to continue them would go against the principles of *vraisemblance* and *bienséance*. Similarly, it would be unheard of for the opera to end with Jupiter still unable to impose his will; the normal balance of power must be reestablished in the end.

There are numerous other examples of characters with limited freedom, such as Mercure and Iris ("Jupiter et Junon nous occupent sans cesse"; II, 4: 277), Argus, who puts his duty to Junon above brotherly love (III, 2; 487–488), or the Fury Erinnis, who executes Junon's orders without question. Most important, however, for the thematic unity of the opera, is the example of Syrinx, who is pursued by Pan in the same way that Io is by Jupiter. This episode, among its other functions (I will return to it toward the end of this chapter), serves as another example of a man forcing his attentions on a woman while making explicit the theme of freedom that was more indirectly present in the first two acts. The word *liberté* occurs eighteen times in Act III, and even more often when one counts all the repetitions in the score, serving as a sort of refrain for Syrinx and her nymphs.[23] It is introduced, however, by Argus and Hiérax (III, 2: 514), thus linking Hiérax's desire to be free of his love for Io to Syrinx's desire to be free from any amorous engagement. At the same time, the theme of liberty becomes linked to imprisonment and forced suffering, as Io is first locked up (end of III, 1) and then forced to undergo a series of punishments (IV, 1–V, 1). Finally, the last scene brings us back to the theme of freedom of choice, as Jupiter and Junon decide to put their quarrel aside.

Isis is thus much more than a collection of episodes designed to provide opportunities for spectacle and dance. Is it, however, effective drama? If one takes the definition of a dictionary such as the *Nouveau Petit*

22 Catherine Kintzler, *Poétique de l'opéra français de Corneille à Rousseau* (Paris: Minerve, 1991), 287–91.
23 "Liberté" occurs twenty times in *Isis*, which represents 37 percent of the fifty-three occurrences in Quinault's eleven libretti; the other two occurrences are in Hiérax's speech at the beginning of the first act. A similar repetition of "liberté" by the chorus is found in the first act of *Thésée* which also features – like *Isis* – an innocent female character who suffers at the hands of a jealous woman.

Robert (1994), "That which is capable of moving, of keeping the spectator keenly interested, in the theatre"[24] there would be no problem; after all, we all know that "the principal rule is to please and to touch"[25] i.e., keep interested ("intéresser") and move ("émouvoir"). However, one finds in all too many critical works the idea that nothing is worthy of interesting the spectator, of moving him/her, except the linear development of a well-constructed plot. For example, Joseph Kerman, whose *Opera as Drama* has interested a large number of people and moved many of them to fairly emotional reactions, both denies that the dramatic has a necessary link to plot and talks about plot all the time. He bases his concept of the dramatic on the reactions of the characters in a play or opera, rather than on those of the spectators: "What is essentially at issue is the response of the persons in the play to the elements of the action."[26] As a result, how these characters react and interreact, which is all too often the same thing as how the plot works out, is considered more important than the effects these characters have on the emotions of the spectators.

To take another example, closer to the time of Quinault and Lully, Charles Perrault, in his *Critique d'Alceste*, devoted most of his small book to "la conduite du sujet," in spite of having promised near the beginning to discuss versification and music. It is clear from this defensive strategy, as well as from most of the criticisms of *Alceste* in Racine's Preface to *Iphigénie* (1674), that opera's detractors could not argue that the new *tragédie lyrique* did not please or move their audiences; their best bet was to criticize it because its plot did not always meet the standards of Racinian tragedy, especially in terms of *vraisemblance*.

Quinault and Lully seem to have wanted to have it both ways. They had showed that they could write a near-Racinian tragedy with *Atys*, which could hardly be criticized for the working out of its tightly knit plot. Then, with *Isis*, they seem to have decided to pay considerably less attention to plot and to a narrow definition of the dramatic. In agreeing to take the myth of Io as his subject, Quinault obviously realized that the resulting opera would

24 "Qui est susceptible d'émouvoir, d'intéresser vivement le spectateur, au Théâtre."
25 "la principale règle est de plaire et de toucher" (Racine, *Bérénice*, Preface).
26 Joseph Kerman, *Opera as Drama* (Berkeley: University of California Press, 1988), 5.

have a form quite different from that of *Atys*, that it would represent an experiment with a different concept of the *tragédie lyrique*. This concept involves a structure that can accommodate a series of *divertissements*, that can bring the audience to recognize and feel the emotions, the suffering of Io – and to think about what caused them – as much through these *divertissements* as through the unfolding of the plot. At the same time, this concept represents what one could call an apotheosis of *divertissement*, an apology for the power of music, dance, and spectacle to move audiences even if they are not caught up in a tightly woven plot. Girdlestone seems to have understood this, though he did not seem to appreciate its advantages: "We are in the presence of an esthetic that aims to produce emotion and which shows little interest either in action or in structure. There will be juxtapositions of emotional states, not linear advance."[27] He is exaggerating of course, especially about the structure of *Isis*, which has a strong thematic unity that makes the representation of the emotions of Io and the other characters more than just "juxtapositions of emotional states." When seen from the point of view of *divertissement* and dance, it also has a very carefully elaborated structure. One way of seeing this structure is as follows:

Act I: Jupiter descends to Earth, after a quarrel between Io and Hiérax. He pursues Io.

Act II: Junon's nymphs await Io. She arrives, but cannot stay (Junon will have put her under lock and key by the beginning of the next act).

Act III: Actors replace the gods and stage an opera within the opera, a work that demonstrates the power of opera.

Act IV: The Fates are waiting for Io. She arrives, asks them for death, but must continue her torments.

Act V: Jupiter descends to Earth again, after a quarrel with Junon. Io is no longer pursued or punished but immortalized as Isis.

In this ABCBA structure, Jupiter's pain-causing intervention (Act I) and his moment of self-mastery (Act V) frame the sufferings of Io, who is pursued by Jupiter before becoming a member of Junon's court (Act II) and by Junon before becoming a goddess (Act IV). Act III, which could seem a

27 "Nous sommes en présence d'une esthétique qui vise à produire l'émotion et qui ne se soucie ni d'action ni de structure. Il y aura juxtaposition d'états d'âme, non d'avance linéaire." Beaussant says *Isis* "se présente comme une mosaïque" (takes on the appearance of a mosaic) (BeaussantL, 583). His comment is in the context of how easy it is to excerpt scenes from the opera.

digression, functions as a variation on these themes of intervention, self-control, freedom, pursuit, and transformation.

The best example of Girdlestone's "juxtapositions of emotional states" as a means of evoking intense emotional response is the fourth act, where Io, as in Ovid and Aeschylus, goes from Scythian cold to the burning forges of the Chalybes[28] to the den of the Fates (Parques). What a series of opportunities for the composer, choreographer, and stage designer, what a series of reactions on the part of the spectator! Pity for Io, of course, and anger at Junon and Erinnis, but also fear, uneasiness in the face of the arbitrariness of Destiny and of the Fates, frustration at the refusal or inability of Jupiter to end Io's suffering, disorientation caused by the unfamiliarity of all these exotic settings, or simply cold and heat. Does one really have to regret, as Girdlestone did, that the emotional and the spectacular come to the fore here, at the expense of a notion of the dramatic that is little more than linear plot development? Does one really have to regret that, at least during part of this fourth act, the spectator is as interested in the unusual characters that surround Io as in the heroine herself?[29] Io's fate and the working out of the plot are hardly forgotten while Quinault and Lully dwell on the variety and intensity of her suffering. In the long run, however, Io is less important than what the spectator feels and learns. Is the goal of the theatre not to please, to touch, to instruct? This fourth act does it all, asking questions about liberty, human suffering, fate, justice, and power, both domestic and political, while at the same time offering just what the public loved: spectacle, music, and especially dance. Why, I hear Quinault and Lully asking themselves, should this kind of opera not be as effective and as successful as *Atys*, which was truly a *tragédie en musique*? In other words, just how independent of traditional theatrical forms can, or should, opera be?

I see evidence that this question is more than rhetorical in the great *divertissement* of the third act of *Isis*, where Mercury and a group of *sylvains*

---

28 The Chalybes, who lived in the Black Sea region, were known for their iron mines and forges.

29 Related to the theme of liberty are those of rivalry (among gods, lovers, or politicians), self-control, and compromise that one finds in *Isis* as well as in classical sources that treat the story of Io, such as the *Prometheus Bound* of Aeschylus. Quinault and Lully will continue to develop these themes in works such as *Proserpine* (rivalry and compromise among gods), *Phaéton* (rivalry among heroes), *Roland* and *Armide* (self-control).

put Argus to sleep by staging, and especially by singing and dancing, the story of Pan and Syrinx. One could say that Quinault was just following Ovid, or that Lully was glad to have an occasion for another *sommeil* (slumber scene), after the huge success of the one in *Atys* the year before, but I prefer to think they had more artistic reasons for developing this scene – easily the longest in Quinault's libretti – to such an extent.[30]

Io, Syrinx, and pipe-like instruments are already associated in Aeschylus' *Prometheus Bound*, although Syrinx does not appear as a character. Io enters, pursued by the gadfly and bemoaning her fate, and Aeschylus gives her these beautiful – in Mazon's edition at least – lines: "Et sur mes pas le roseau sonore à la gaine de cire fait entendre son assoupissante chanson" (II. 574–575).[31] In the *Metamorphoses*, Mercury, disguised as a shepherd, meets Argus, makes some pan pipes (also called syrinx), and begins to play. Argus is charmed and invites the stranger to sit down; then, "Whiling the time away with conversation / And soothing little melodies, and Argus / Has a hard fight with drowsiness."[32] Argus does not go to sleep, however, and asks Mercury to tell him the history of the pan pipes, which had just been invented. Mercury begins the story of Pan and Syrinx, but Argus goes to sleep well before the end. It is music that charms Argus and makes him sleepy, but it is the tale of Pan and Syrinx that closes the hundred eyes. It was fairly easy for a few flutes to close the two eyes of the mortal Atys, especially when they were playing by order of the powerful goddess Cybèle, but considerably more difficult in the case of Argus. One can infer that, to please Louis XIV and to amuse his court, instrumental music is not enough; one requires poetry, staging, music, and dance, i.e., the *tragédie lyrique*.

The only example in Quinault's libretti of a play within a play, his version of Pan and Syrinx (scenes 3–6, lines 515–681) is a true miniature opera, complete with a prologue where Mercury promises a "spectacle

---

30 Scene 6 contains 135 of the 918 lines of *Isis*, which is 15 percent of the total. The three preceding scenes can also be considered part of the *divertissement*, which brings the total to 166 lines. The only other scene in Quinault's libretti with more than 100 lines is IV, 4 of *Thésée*, which contains 113.

31 "And as I walk, the sonorous reed in its waxen sheath brings forth its slumberous song." See Paul Mazon, Introduction to *Prométhée enchaîné. Eschyle*. (Paris: Belles Lettres, 1966), lines 574–575.

32 From Humphrey's translation of the *Metamorphoses* (Bloomington: Indiana University Press, 1955), 24:1.

touchant."[33] According to Quinault's stage directions, "Argus commence à s'assoupir" as he listens to the "concert de flûtes" played on the reeds that once were Syrinx. If flutes have the place of honor at the end of this miniature opera, one of the reasons is certainly that pipe-like instruments made from reeds take us back to the origins of music and of opera. They are among the first musical instruments, the ones that helped the Greeks create the emotional effects that the creators of opera at the beginning of the seventeenth century in Italy wanted to imitate. More specifically, the aulos – often confused with the flute – led the chorus in Greek tragedy,[34] and the flute is associated with the pastoral, a genre in great favor earlier in the century and that played an important role in the development of opera.

We thus have a reflection on the origins of opera, but especially on its power – it is only at the end of a *representation*, where music, words, and dance have played the major role,[35] that the flutes that *accompany* the representation succeed in putting Argus to sleep. Furthermore, this reflection is found in the Quinault–Lully opera that "strays" the farthest from the conception of theatre that stresses the unfolding of the plot and the psychological development of a love conflict. It is as if they said to themselves: "In *Atys*, we gambled on drama and won; we created a *tragédie lyrique* that can hold its own with spoken tragedy. We reduced the spectacular to a minimum, had the goddess Cybèle interact with the other characters as if she were a mortal, put music and dance at the service of plot. Now, let us try something different, even the opposite: plot at the service of music and dance." Gros had more or less the same view of *Isis*:

33 "MERCURE déguisé en Berger, parlant à Argus: De la Nymphe Syrinx Pan chérit la mémoire, / Il en regrette encor la perte chaque jour: / Pour célébrer une fête à sa gloire, / Ce Dieu lui-même assemble ici sa cour; / Il veut que du malheur de son fidèle amour / Un spectacle touchant représente l'histoire" (III, 4: 524–529). One could compare these lines to lines 114–117 of Quinault's Prologue to *Persée*, where La Vertu suggests bringing the eponymous hero back to life, i.e., representing his story.

34 The *Oxford Companion to Musical Instruments* describes the aulos as "a reed instrument and particularly the pair of slender pipes played together by one musician." It adds that "[i]t is for poetic euphony that in later literature 'aulos' has generally been translated 'flute' rather than 'pipe.'"

35 The first thing Argus and Hiérax say when they see the nymphs approaching in III, 3 is "Quelles danses, quels chants, et quelle nouveauté!" (What dances, what songs, what a novelty!).

While in *Atys* opera, without abandoning any of its unique features, moved nearer to tragedy and tended toward a concept of theatre that was more dramatic and more sober, more strictly tragic; while with *Atys* opera tended to be more interior, it moved, with *Isis*, toward a concept infinitely more free and more whimsical, where the exterior elements, sets and costumes, dances and machines began once more to invade action and to reserve for themselves, within this action, an excessive role.[36]

Excessive? Perhaps. The work was, if not a failure, not a great success. Still, the contemporary criticisms that have come down to us involve the music or the characters, not the general conception of the work. The opera is not really flawed, just different. To quote Gros again, "the plot is no longer anything but a pretext within the overall action, *Isis* is one of the best of Quinault's libretti; *Isis* is a work of art; but *Isis* opened the door to excess."[37] The excesses that Gros mentions are those of the *opéras-ballets* of the early eighteenth century, many of which were hardly more than a string of dances with very tenuous links among them. Perhaps Quinault and Lully saw this danger; at any rate, they would not write another opera – and they would write six more together – that gave so much importance to dance and to spectacle. The *tragédie lyrique* remains, after all, *tragédie*, inspired by Greek tragedy. On the other hand, music and dance are essential parts of the *tragédie lyrique*, and one can understand that the creators of a new type of theatre would want to see how far one could tip the drama/spectacle scales toward spectacle. The result is a unique work, hardly deserving of the neglect it has known. Could its critics be like Hiérax at the beginning of Act I, overly eager to criticize a beautiful creature who has been unfaithful to their idea of how things should be and too ashamed to admit that they really like *Isis*? If they listened to it more carefully, they too might say "Hélas! malgré moi je soupire!" (I, 1: 6).[38]

---

36 "Tandis que dans *Atys* l'opéra, sans rien abandonner de ce qui lui était propre, se rapprochait de la tragédie et tendait vers une conception plus dramatique et plus sobre, vers une conception plus proprement tragique; tandis qu'avec *Atys* l'opéra s'intériorisait, il s'orientait, avec *Isis*, vers une conception infiniment plus libre et plus fantaisiste, où les éléments extérieurs, la mise en scene, les danses et les machines, tendaient de nouveau à envahir l'action et à réserver, dans cette action, une part excessive" (GrosQ, 614).

37 "l'intrigue n'est plus qu'un prétexte dans l'action, *Isis* est l'un des meilleurs livrets de Quinault; *Isis* est une œuvre d'art; mais *Isis* ouvrait la porte à un excès" (GrosQ, 614).

38 "Alas! in spite of myself I sigh!"

QUINAULT'S LIBRETTO FOR *ISIS*

Appendix

Philippe Quinault, *Isis*
Plot summary

Quinault followed Ovid's version of the myth in the *Metamorphoses* fairly closely. Jupiter is trying to seduce Io, a beautiful nymph who is engaged to Hiérax but who is beginning to doubt that she will be able to resist "le Maître des dieux." Junon finds out about her husband's latest escapade and cleverly chooses Io to be the new nymph that Jupiter has promised her as a sort of divine lady-in-waiting. Hiérax is at first distraught, then jealous, then angry, but neither he nor Jupiter can do anything, and the second act, as well as what one could call the first section of the opera, closes with a kind of double *divertissement*, as Junon's other nymphs wait for Io and then welcome her, to the tune of "Que c'est un plaisir charmant / D'être jeune et belle!"

As the third act opens, however, young and beautiful Io is not in the gardens of Hébé but in a "solitaire séjour," where Junon has placed her under the guard of hundred-eyed Argus. Mercury tries to free her and succeeds in putting Argus to sleep with a dramatization of the story of Pan and Syrinx, but the even more watchful Hiérax warns Junon, who appears and turns Io over to the Fury Erinnis. In the fourth act, Io undergoes a series of torments: first "l'endroit le plus glacé de la Scythie" (IV, 1–2, with the famous "chœur des trembleurs"), then the heat of the forges of the Chalybes, then the den of the Fates.

The fifth act finally brings the reconciliation of Junon and Jupiter, as the latter decides, like Alcide in *Alceste*, that "il faut que je commence / A me vaincre en ce jour" (V, 3: 884–885). An apotheosis with all the divinities of Olympus concludes the opera.

5 The articulation of Lully's dramatic dialogue

LOIS ROSOW

According to Jean-Philippe Rameau, "Lully pensoit en grand": Lully thought on a large scale.[1] Rameau referred in particular to the long-range tonal unity in the famous recitative monologue from *Armide*, but his remark may be applied to Lully's operatic style in general. On the one hand, it is a short-breathed style, combining miniature closed forms, both vocal and instrumental, with recitative that makes frequent cadences and frequent returns to a principal key. On the other hand, the short vocal and instrumental units are like the variegated plantings of a formal French garden, artfully arranged to make a larger picture.[2] Scholars who have discussed Lully's scene-building techniques have focused mainly on his clever use of recurring elements (such as choral refrains), as well as his use of patterns of scoring (such as the alternation of vocal music with a series of related instrumental interjections), along with the resulting tonal architecture. They have written evocatively of the dramatic effect of such designs.[3] This chapter will concentrate on a different aspect of Lully's patterning: his manner of giving large-scale shape

1 Jean-Philippe Rameau, *Observations sur notre instinct pour la musique* (Paris, 1754; reprint New York: Broude Brothers, 1967), 78.
2 I am indebted to Graeme Boone for the elegant image of the formal garden, along with a number of other helpful suggestions for this article. I also thank Tim Carter for raising provocative questions in response to the oral version of this paper, read at a meeting of the Society for Seventeenth-Century Music, Rochester, New York, 1994.
3 Especially Herbert Schneider, "Strukturen der Szenen und Akte in Lullys Opern," in Heidelberg87, 77–98. Also AnthonyJ, 31–40, and Raphaëlle Legrand, "Persée de Lully et Quinault: orientations pour l'analyse dramaturgique d'une tragédie en musique," *Analyse musicale* 27 (1992), 9–14. An approach emphasizing continuously unfolding tonal motion may be found in Jean Duron, "L'Instinct de M. de Lully," in *La Tragédie lyrique*, ed. anon. (Paris: Cicero Editeurs and Théâtre des Champs-Elysées, 1991), 65–119 (especially 99–118). The treatment of scene structure in Joyce Newman, *Jean-Baptiste Lully and His Tragédies-Lyriques* (Ann Arbor: UMI Research Press, 1979) cannot be recommended. An excellent survey of the stylistic elements in Lully's operas may be found in Caroline Wood, *Music and Drama in the Tragédie en musique*,

to dialogue scenes by introducing points of articulation of varying strength – musical punctuation marks and paragraph indicators that complement the poetry and highlight the progression of the drama. It will also consider ways in which ambiguity – between declamatory and songful melody, between closed form and through-composition – serves as a component of Lully's scene-building technique. This study thus aims to formulate an improved model for understanding the structure of dialogue scenes devoted entirely (apart from the introductory *ritournelle* or *prélude*) to music for vocal soloists.

The model is best introduced by way of an extended presentation of a single example. The following discussion will concentrate on Act V, scene 1 of *Armide* (1686), while turning briefly to other examples along the way. The excerpt from the libretto found in Table 5.1 is annotated to show number of syllables per line and rhyme scheme; the plus sign is adopted here to indicate feminine rhyme. (The keys of all perfect authentic cadences, and selected half-cadences, are shown as well. The music will be discussed presently.)[4] In considering the *vers libres* (lines of varied length) used throughout Philippe Quinault's libretti, it is useful to keep in mind that a mixture of line lengths had long been favored for song lyrics, including songs occurring in dramatic contexts. One recalls Pierre Perrin's assertion, made in 1659, that in a pastoral dialogue to be set to music, lyrical poetic lines (*vers lyriques*) are preferable to the steady alexandrines of spoken drama because short lines, with their frequent caesuras and rhymes, better suit the singing voice and provide the variety demanded by music.[5]

As Table 5.1 shows, Quinault used rhyme to link groups of lines together. Each group has two rhyme-endings, one masculine and the other

1673–1715: Jean-Baptiste Lully and His Successors (New York and London: Garland, 1996).

4 Transcribed from *Armide, tragédie en musique representée par l'Académie royalle de musique* (Paris: Christophe Ballard, 1686), 43–46. Original spellings are retained throughout. The translation is loosely based on that in the liner notes for Harmonia mundi France, HMC 901456–57 (1993). Regarding the various kinds of rhyme in French poetry, see Jacques Barzun, *An Essay on French Verse for Readers of English Poetry* (New York, 1991), 25–43.

5 Pierre Perrin, "Lettre écrite à Monseigneur l'Archevesque de Turin," in Becker, 109–110; English trans. in Louis E. Auld, *The Lyric Art of Pierre Perrin, Founder of French Opera* (Henryville, Ottawa, Binningen: Institute of Medieval Music, 1986), vol. I, 107–108. By "vers lyriques" Perrin meant song poetry. Similar uses of this adjective in the eighteenth century include "poème lyrique" (libretto), "théâtre lyrique" (opera) – and, of course, "tragédie lyrique," a term dating from well after Lully's lifetime.

Table 5.1. *Armide*, Act V, scene 1

Syllables	Rhyme	Text	Cadences	Arch-form
		[Ritournelle]	c	
8	a	Ren: Armide, vous m'allez quitter!	V of c	
12	a	Arm: J'ay besoin des Enfers, je vay les consulter;		
8+	b	Mon Art veut de la Solitude.		
12+	b	L'amour que j'ay pour vous cause l'inquiétude,		
8	a	Dont mon cœur se sent agitter.	c	
8	a	Ren: Armide, vous m'allez quitter!	V of c	
8+	c	Arm: Voyez en quels lieux je vous laisse.	Eb	*4 individual lines*
8	d	Ren: Puis-je rien voir que vos appas?		
8+	c	Arm: Les plaisirs vous suivront sans cesse.	G	
8	d	Ren: En est-il où vous n'estes pas?	V of c	
12+	e	Arm: Un noir pressentiment me trouble et me tourmente,		*quatrain*
12	f	Il m'annonce un malheur que je veux prévenir;		
8+	e	Et plus notre bonheur m'enchante, } [twice]	Eb, c	
8	f	Plus je crains de le voir finir.		
12+	g	Ren: D'une vaine terreur pouvez-vous estre atteinte,	G	*2 couplets*
12	h	Vous qui faites trembler le ténébreux Séjour?		
10	h	Arm: Vous m'aprenez à connoistre l'Amour,	C (Picardy third)	
10+	g	L'Amour m'aprend à connoistre la crainte.		

12	i	Vous brusliez pour la Gloire avant que de m'aimer,	G	*first of 2 central airs*
12+	j	Vous la cherchiez par tout d'une ardeur sans esgale:		
7+	j	La Gloire est une Rivale		
7	i	Qui doit toûjours m'allarmer. } [twice]	d, C	
8+	k	Ren: Que j'estois insensé de croire		*second of 2 central airs*
10+	k	Qu'un vain Laurier donné par la Victoire,		
10	l	De tous les biens fut le plus précieux! } } [twice]	G, G	
8+	k	Tout l'esclat dont brille la Gloire		
8	l	Vaut-t'il un regard de vos yeux? } [twice]	d, C	
10+	m	*Est-t'il un bien si charmant et si rare	Eb	*return of c minor* *2 couplets*
12	n	Que celuy dont l'Amour veut combler mon espoir?		
12+	m	Arm: La severe Raison & le Devoir barbare		
10	n	Sur les Heros n'ont que trop de pouvoir.	c	
12+	o	Ren: J'en suis plus amoureux plus la Raison m'esclaire.		*quatrain*
12	n	Vous aimer, belle Armide, est mon premier devoir,		
8+	o	Je fais ma gloire de vous plaire,		
8	n	Et tout mon bonheur de vous voir. } [twice]	c, c	
12+	p	Arm: Que sous d'aimables loix mon ame est asservie!		*4 individual lines*
12	q	Ren: Qu'il m'est doux de vous voir partager ma langueur!		
12	q	Arm: Qu'il m'est doux d'enchainer un si fameux Vainqueur!		
8+	p	Ren: Que mes fers sont dignes d'envie!	G	
8+	p	Ensemble: Aimons-nous, tout nous y convie.		*Arch-form ends.*
8	q	Ah! Si vous aviez la rigueur		
6	q	De m'oster votre Cœur,		
6+	p	Vous m'osteriez la vie. } [twice]	Eb, c	

Table 5.1 (*cont.*)

Syllables	Rhyme	Text	Cadences
8	h	Ren: Non, je perdray plustost le jour	E♭
6+	r	Que d'esteindre ma flame.	
8+	r	Arm: Non, rien ne peut changer mon ame.	G
8	h	Ren: Non, je perdray plustost le jour,	
12	h	Que de me desgager d'un si charmant Amour.	c
8	h	Ensemble: Non, je perdray plustost le jour	B♭
6+	r	Que d'esteindre ma flame.	
8+	r	Non, rien ne peut changer mon ame. [twice]	G, (C), f
8	h	Non, je perdray plutost le jour	
12	h	Que de me desgager d'un si charmant amour. [twice]	E♭, c
8+	s	Arm: ∗Tesmoins de nostre amour extréme,	∗ g minor introduced
12	t	Vous, qui suivez mes loix dans ce Séjour heureux,	
12	t	Jusques à mon retour, par d'agréables Jeux,	
8+	s	Occupez le Heros que j'aime.	g

Translation: (Ren) Armide, you are going to leave me! (Arm) I need advice from the Underworld, I go to consult it. My art requires solitude. The love I feel for you causes the distress that agitates my heart. (Ren) Armide, you are going to leave me! (Arm) But look at this place where I leave you. (Ren) Can I see anything but your charms? (Arm) Pleasures will incessantly follow you. (Ren) Are there any where you are not? (Arm) A dark foreboding disturbs and torments me; it tells me of a misfortune I wish to forestall, and the more our happiness enchants me, the more I fear to see it end. (Ren) Can you be moved by an idle fear, you who shake the haunts of the night? (Arm) You teach me to know Love, Love teaches me to know Fear. Glory was your passion before you loved me; you sought it everywhere with matchless ardor. Glory is a rival that should always frighten me. (Ren) How mad I was to think that a vain laurel crown bestowed by Victory was the most precious of prizes! Is all the radiance with which Glory shines worth one look from your eyes? Is there a prize as lovely and as rare as that with which Love rewards my hopes? (Arm) Relentless Reason and inhuman Duty have all too strong a grip on heroes' hearts. (Ren) The more Reason enlightens me, the more I love them. To love you, fair Armide, is my first duty, my glory is to please you, and all my happiness is to see you. (Arm) To what amiable laws my soul is subject! (Ren) How sweet it is to me to see you share my yearning! (Arm) How sweet it is to me to hold captive so famed a conqueror! (Ren) How worthy of envy are my chains! (Together) Come let us love, everything enjoins us to it. Ah! If you were so cruel as to take your heart away from me, you would take away my life. (Ren) No, I would rather lose my life than extinguish my passion. (Arm) No, nothing can change my soul. (Ren) No, I would rather lose my life than disengage myself from such a charming love. (Together) No, I would rather lose my life than extinguish my passion. No, nothing can change my soul. No, I would rather lose my life than disengage myself from such a charming love. (Arm) Witnesses to our great love, you, who observe my laws in this happy place, until my return, with agreeable diversions entertain the hero I love.

feminine. The groups vary in the number of lines they contain, though the quatrain is apparently normative. The groups also vary in how the lines are divided between the participating characters; the presence of a loosely structured arch-form, with alternation of characters making mirror images, shows that the variation is unlikely to be random. Within each rhymed group the line lengths (normally two) form some sort of pattern – for instance, alexandrines and octosyllables in loose alternation or in pairs – and that pattern is usually independent of the pattern of linking rhymes. (The pattern made by masculine and feminine endings, on the other hand, is necessarily tied directly to the rhyme scheme.) These are supple, flexible organizing devices, not rigid ones, and they are remarkably effective in giving large-scale shape to a scene. We shall see that Lully's articulation of the music complements the irregular patterning introduced by Quinault.

This scene is populated by two characters, the sorceress Armide and the knight Renaud (Armida and Rinaldo from Torquato Tasso's *Gerusalemme liberata*); the setting is Armide's enchanted palace. Renaud – who appears here "unarmed and adorned with garlands of flowers," according to the libretto – has been placed under a spell by Armide so that he will love her; he has forgotten all about his duty as a crusader and lives only for her. She is uneasy, for she knows that Renaud's colleagues are searching for him in order to break the spell, and she is well aware that she has a powerful rival for Renaud's affections: la Gloire ("Glory"). If released from her magic, Renaud will surely return to his *gloire* – that is, his duties as a warrior in the Crusade. In this scene Renaud confronts Armide as she prepares to leave in order to "consult the Underworld."

The entr'acte connecting Acts IV and V, during which the scenery changes, is in C major. It is followed by a brief *ritournelle*, during which Armide and Renaud make their entrances. (See Example 5.3, pp. 95–99 below, for a score of the entire scene.[6]) Laden with affective harmonies, the *ritournelle* establishes the sensuous mood of scene 1 as well as its principal key, C minor. The dialogue then begins. As is typical of Lully's recitative, the melody varies from a formulaic singsong, as in Armide's first cadential

6 *Armide, tragédie mise en musique par Monsieur de Lully* (Paris: Christophe Ballard, 1686), 211–220. A facsimile edition and a critical edition of *Armide* are both in preparation, for Pendragon and Olms respectively; the former will contain the score cited here and the libretto cited in n. 4.

phrase ("L'amour . . . agiter"), to moments of true songfulness, such as Renaud's opening arpeggiation. The span between these extremes is very small.

The dialogue begins with Renaud's repeated whimper, prefigured in the first phrase of the *ritournelle*: "Armide, vous m'allez quitter!" Recurring bits of poetry in Quinault's librettos – whether a hemistich, a line (*vers*), or a couplet – are invariably set by Lully to recurring music, typically strongly cadential music. In the opening recitative dialogue of *Alceste*, for instance, Alcide's emphatic response to a series of questions, "J'aurai beau me presser, je partirai trop tard," is memorable the first time precisely because it makes a strong perfect authentic cadence, a firm arrival in the home key of the scene, C major. We cannot help but remember this hemistich when we hear it again two dozen lines later, set to the same music: "Je te l'avois bien dit, je partiray trop tard." The recurring cadence both shapes the scene and drives home the character's frame of mind.[7]

In the scene from *Armide*, on the other hand, the recurring line has the character of an antecedent. Despite the exclamation point in the libretto, Renaud's expression of disbelief comes across as a question: "Armide, are you going to leave me?" It is Armide's role to respond firmly each time with an authentic cadence. Her first response comprises a quatrain of poetry, concluding firmly in the principal key. With her second response the poetry moves to a new set of linked rhymes and a new quatrain structure (four octo-syllables, alternating between the characters), and the music begins to mod-ulate tonally. Here Renaud continues to ask questions – rhetorical ones now – and Armide's declarative (though evasive) answers continue to make the cadences. Soon enough (in yet another quatrain) she gets to the point: she is afraid that their happiness is finished. While the cadences up to this moment have provided emphasis, they have signaled very little closure. Here Lully increases the degree of emphasis by introducing closure as well: the couplet "Et plus notre bonheur m'enchante, / Plus je crains de le voir finir" is sung twice (mm. 29–34), the first time making a cadence in a secondary key (the relative major) and the second time returning firmly to the principal key.

This conventional closing formula, Lully's favorite, is borrowed straight from Italian models. It is associated with the so-called "extended

---

7 See the score, ed. Henry Prunières, in LullyOC, "les Opéras," vol. II, 47–54.

Example 5.1

Luigi Rossi, *Orfeo*, excerpt from Act I, scene 2

binary" form – ABb, "B" and "b" having the same words but different music – a ubiquitous structure in mid-seventeenth-century Italian operas and cantatas.[8] Example 5.1, an excerpt from Luigi Rossi's *Orfeo* (which had its premiere at the French court in 1647), shows a short speech (six lines of poetry) by Euridice; it occurs immediately after the florid conclusion of an

8 The relationship was first pointed out in James Anthony, "Lully's Airs – French or Italian?" *The Musical Times* 128 (1987), 126–129. (I adopt the scheme ABb rather than ABB´ to avoid the implication that the "B" sections are similar in pitch content.) For a discussion of the similarity of Lully's recitative to that of Venetian opera, see Claude Palisca, "The Recitative of Lully's *Alceste*: French Declamation or Italian Melody?" *Biblio* 17 (Paris–Seattle–Tübingen: Papers on French Seventeenth-Century Literature, 1986), 19–34; reprint in Palisca, *Studies in the History of Italian Music and Music Theory* (Oxford: Clarendon Press, 1994), pp. 491–507. It is unfortunate that Palisca's examples show melody only; the difference between the two styles resides principally in the bass lines. See Lois Rosow, "Lully," *The New Grove Dictionary of Opera*, ed. Stanley Sadie (London: Macmillan, 1992), vol. III, 84–86.

aria in G minor for Orfeo.[9] Euridice's remarks begin in recitative but culmi-
nate in a lilting triple-meter arioso conclusion; the last line of text ("Altro
Cielo...") occurs twice, the first time with a cadence in a secondary key (the
dominant minor) and the second time with a cadence in tonic. In this particular case the beginning of the extended binary pattern is ambiguous. On
the one hand, the shift from recitative to lilting arioso is impossible to miss,
and the arioso has the customary effect of heightened emotion. On the
other, the triple-meter portion of Euridice's speech does not stand alone as
a syntactical unit; only when taken together with its preceding recitative
does the arioso conclusion round out a tonally unified passage. In any case,
the conventional "Bb" conclusion (further emphasized by a melismatic
extension of the final phrase) is heard here as very strong punctuation, both
insisting on that final line of poetry and letting the listener know that a
musical paragraph has ended.

Lully's ways of using the extended binary pattern often have a pecu-
liarly French flavor. Let us return to Armide's quatrain beginning "Un noir
pressentiment" – a pair of alexandrines followed by a pair of octosyllables,
the pairs linked by rhyme – which, as we have seen, ends with the "Bb"
closing formula. The librettist has provided the quatrain not only with an
emphatic ending, in which Armide comes to the point about her fears, but
with a powerful opening as well: "noir" is the first adjective in the scene, and
it is in the strong position, preceding the noun.[10] It would not be surprising
to encounter the beginning of a musically regular closed form here. Yet
while this quatrain (which follows a questioning half-cadence for Renaud,
m. 25) does indeed start in C minor, the key in which it will end, there is little
in the music that might lead the listener to believe that a closed form is

9   From Act I, scene 2. Transcribed (with added capitalization and punctuation)
    from Rome, Biblioteca apostolica vaticana, Chigi Q.V.58, fols. 27v–28r.
    Translation: (Euridice) "And yet, ah no, I do not feel, other than from your lovely
    gaze, any contentment enter my soul. If Love wishes to make our hearts happy,
    there is no heaven other than your eyes."
10 I owe the observation concerning "noir" to Rebecca Gottlieb (unpublished
    seminar presentation, Cornell University, 1984). (It might be added that the
    word order also avoids an infelicitous juxtaposition of accented syllables: "un
    pres-sen-ti-ment noir.") Gottlieb's analysis of character development in this
    scene, based on numerous poetic details, has contributed greatly to my reading
    of the scene's structure. I am grateful to the Society for the Humanities at
    Cornell for the fellowship I held that year.

beginning. The syllabic setting, choice of note values, degree of melodic lyricism, and fast-moving bass line continue as in the preceding recitative dialogue, without significant change; the beginning of the first phrase is tonally weak; and though the march-like tune of the first phrase invites a metrically regular performance, the varied musical anapests and shifting meters associated with Lullian recitative quickly return. In short, one perceives the beginning of this ABb pattern only in retrospect; like Rossi's it is an ambiguous beginning, but for entirely different reasons. In any case, within this context – a context in which the range between the most melodious and most declamatory moments is much smaller than Rossi's – the "Bb" closing formula makes an entirely solid paragraph ending, as capable of closing off the preceding recitative as was the florid ending of Rossi's arioso passage.

Yet Lully and his librettist extend the paragraph, with one more rhetorical question by Renaud and a still more powerful answer by Armide (their couplets linked by rhyme and related keys): now the principal weight of Armide's utterance falls on the word "fear": "la crainte." Here Lully makes a different kind of articulation, one based not on concluding repetition but on strong contrast with what follows. The cadence on "crainte" (m. 42) introduces a Picardy third, announcing a change from C minor to C major. The rhythm changes from the gentle metrical alternation and moderate tempo associated with this style of recitative, in which many syllables are set to eighth-notes and sixteenth-notes, to the stricter beat and livelier tempo of an air in triple meter, in which syllables are rarely set to anything smaller than quarter-notes and eighth-notes.[11] The melodious lilt of Lully's triple-meter airs reminds us of Rossi's or Cavalli's triple-meter arioso passages, and of course the relationship is no coincidence.[12]

11 Duple-meter airs are less obviously different in tempo from the preceding recitative; a bar of duple meter within a phrase of recitative is likely to have the same dotted-quarter-plus-eighth-note pattern as found in a duple-meter air. Yet Lully has ways of making sure the beginning of a duple-meter air stands in clear relief – for instance, by relying on quadruple and triple meter for the final bars of recitative preceding the air, changing to duple only in the cadential bar. The notation implies a change of character, if not of tempo. See Lois Rosow, "The Metrical Notation of Lully's Recitative," in Heidelberg87, 405–422, especially 410.

12 Any discussion of structural elements in Lully's dialogues must eventually face terminological embarrassment: Lully himself did not place genre labels on passages of vocal music. Our sense of what he might have referred to as an "air" in opera derives largely from the labeling practices of the next generation. See,

The strong contrast at "crainte" is effective because what follows is the emotional heart of the scene: two adjacent speeches – four lines for Armide and five for Renaud, set apart from their surroundings and each other by rhyme – presenting the lovers' conflicting notions of la Gloire as Armide's rival. Each begins in some type of past tense ("brusliez" and "cherchiez"; "j'estois" and "fût") and concludes in present tense;[13] in this way the poetry both draws attention to the parallel nature of these passages and invites musical settings in binary form. (The parallel passages also stand at the center of a loosely structured arch-form, as mentioned earlier. See Table 5.1.) Lully does indeed set this pair of speeches as unambiguous closed forms (mm. 43–58, 59–83). Armide's air, as we have just seen, is set apart musically from what precedes it by mode, meter, tempo, and character; it is set off from what follows by the "Bb" closing formula of the extended binary form. Renaud's response is encased in its own frame by the direct repetition of the "A" portion as well as the by-now expected varied repetition of "B." The two airs have musical parallels as well as poetic ones: both are in C major and lilting triple meter; they have the same key plan; and their initial pitch accents (quite strong in both cases) occur on rhyming words, "Gloire"

for instance, the "air" labels in André Cardinal Destouches's *Amadis de Grèce*, 3rd edn. (Paris, 1712; reprint Farnborough, Hants.: Gregg Press, 1967), 53, 120, 209, 210, 212; the labels in the third edition reflect exactly those in the first edition (Paris: Christophe Ballard, 1699). Moreover, as others have pointed out, eighteenth-century "air" labels are sparse and often inconsistent; defining "air" for Destouches, Campra, or Rameau is itself a problematic task. For purposes of this essay, "air" refers to a small song in one of several miniature closed forms (most often ABb or AABb, less often ternary or rondeau), but it is understood that formal ambiguities, such as those mentioned above regarding "Un noir pressentiment," make many passages difficult to classify. One caveat: it should be kept in mind that Lully grew up in the era of the *air de cour*. For his generation the unmodified word "air" referred to a piece of chamber music, usually in strophic or ternary form, that fluctuated gently between duple and triple meter according to the stresses in the poetry, and that combined syllabic text-setting with delicate ornamentation. A song that maintained a steady beat, on the other hand, might be called an "air de mouvement" (literally, "air in tempo"); or it might be named by some other word altogether, such as "chanson." Under the circumstances, we should not assume that Lully's conception of an operatic "air" necessarily included the requirement of metrical regularity. The term "air de mouvement" is used – but without definition – in Bénigne de Bacilly, *L'art de bien chanter* (Paris, 1679; reprint Geneva: Minkoff, 1971), 89; it is defined in Sebastien de Brossard, *Dictionnaire de musique* (Paris: Ballard, 1703), n.pag., s.v. "Motto"; it remained in use in the era of Rameau's operas.

13 This is another of Rebecca Gottlieb's observations.

and "croire" (Armide's "Gloire" occurring at a poetic caesura, not a line-ending). Renaud having completed his air – with yet another rhetorical question, incidentally – the third of the tonic triad is immediately flatted, and C minor returns (m. 84). Major mode, along with the only unambiguous fully closed forms in the entire passage, thus highlights a central idea of the drama.[14]

But the return to C minor is not accompanied by a return to metrical irregularity or to the melodic singsong associated with recitative. Instead, Lully prolongs the heightened emotional intensity of the airs by maintaining the Italianate triple meter and regular melodic structure;[15] in addition, he ensures that the ensuing eight lines are heard as an unbroken group by avoiding any strong articulation at the next C minor cadence ("trop de pouvoir"). After one more worried exchange – Renaud's final rhetorical question and a reply from Armide that introduces "reason" and "duty" to the discussion – Renaud finally abandons his questions and declares expansively, in a repeated cadential phrase (repeated note-for-note, not varied tonally as in the "Bb" formula), that his *gloire* is to please Armide and his "entire happiness" is to see her. At that climactic moment (m. 115) the discussion gives way to an exchange of joyous and sensuous exclamations of love, which twice come together in duets.[16] In the duets (for which the meter changes to quadruple), particularly in the second, an outpouring of music overtakes recitation; nevertheless, even here the setting is entirely syllabic, and Lully is characteristically careful to make poetic and musical

14 The space shown in the libretto transcription (Table 5.1), separating Renaud's air from his next line even though there is no change of speaker, is found in the *libretto* of 1686. An analogous space marks the beginning of Armide's air (occurring here at a page break). Since we lack earlier sources, there is no way to know whether the spaces were present in Quinault's handwritten draft or were introduced only after Lully had decided on the musical setting.

15 This is not to suggest that the singer makes no expressive break at the end of the air. A description by Louis Racine (1692–1763) is evocative: "Lorsqu'au commencement du cinquième acte Renaud chante: 'Armide, vous m'allez quitter,' on entend un homme amolli par la volupté; il relève sa voix à ces mots: 'Que j'étois insensé de croire / Qu'un vain laurier, etc.' et retombe dans les tons de tendresse, en disant: 'Vaut-il un regard de vos yeux?'" Louis Racine, *Réflexions sur la poésie*, in *Œuvres complètes* (Paris, 1808; reprint Geneva: Slatkine, 1969), vol. II, 252. See below regarding expression marks in an eighteenth-century part that support Racine's description.

16 Those who like to describe operatic love scenes according to sexual metaphors should have no trouble embellishing my language slightly here.

accents coincide. Quinault perhaps invited this greater emphasis on music at the expense of declamation by avoiding alexandrines in favor of short lines in this portion of the scene; he certainly invited it by introducing concluding ensembles.

The gentle shifting meters and melodic singsong of recitative, abandoned at that C major cadence on "crainte" that preceded the central airs, return only near the very end of the scene, after the final duet. Here Armide turns her attention away from Renaud and addresses the demons who serve her. Lully indicates the change by modulating definitively away from C minor, the principal key of the scene being completed, to G minor, the key of the *divertissement* to follow (mm. 163–164). This sort of definitive modulation, by means of a brief stepwise descent in the bass that was known in the eighteenth century as a "chute,"[17] is a cliché of the genre but an evocative one: just as Quinault took care to elide this scene to the next, keeping Renaud on stage as Armide exits and the troupe of disguised demons enters,[18] so Lully linked their principal tonics in this familiar gesture. It is interesting that the G minor quatrain, the last one before Armide's exit, is the only group of lines in the entire scene in which the pattern of line lengths and the rhyme scheme are perfectly aligned with each other.

The preceding description mentions a number of procedures used by Lully to give musical shape to this particular scene, such as articulating (or not articulating) beginnings and endings in various ways, using structural elements to highlight parallelism between adjacent passages, and prolonging metrical and melodic regularity, apparently as a way of maintaining a certain level of expressive intensity. In examining the use of these and other organizational procedures throughout Lully's operas, one is struck by the high degree of variety among scenes: the order and relative importance of

17 See Raphaëlle Legrand, "Ricercar sopra fa la mi: préludes de basse et articulation des scènes dans l'opéra français de Lully à Rameau," in *D'un opéra l'autre: hommage à Jean Mongrédien*, ed. Jean Gribenski, Marie-Claire Mussat, and Herbert Schneider (Paris: Presse de l'Université de Paris-Sorbonne, 1996), 211–214. The terms "chute" and "chute de basse" appear occasionally in eighteenth-century musical sources; Legrand suggests "prélude d'articulation."

18 Regarding the rule of elision of scenes, see Jacques Schérer, *La dramaturgie classique en France* (Paris: Nizet, n.d.), 266–284. (This book first appeared in 1950. There have been several undated reissues.)

LOIS ROSOW

structural events varies considerably from one scene to another. Under the circumstances, the listener needs whatever guidance the poetry and music might provide in order to perceive the dramatic shape of a particular scene. Viewed in this light, the lack of a sharply defined beginning for Armide's "Un noir pressentiment" (in the scene described above) serves a purpose: by de-emphasizing this quatrain as a salient moment, Lully focuses greater attention on the two airs that form the dramatic core of the scene.[19] Still, the poetically and rhythmically strong beginning of this quatrain, along with its tonal unity and the poetic and tonal strength of the closing formula, give it an undeniable independent identity, one perceived better in retrospect than at the moment the opening line is heard. The structural ambiguity of such a passage enriches the scene, simultaneously focusing the listener's attention on the passage and on its broader context. That ambiguity is an essential component of Lully's (and Quinault's) scene-building technique.

Context has a good deal to do with our perception of such a passage. If, for instance, "Un noir pressentiment" occurred within a series of airs – all in the same key, each set to four or five lines of poetry, but not necessarily all in the same meter or form – we would probably hear it simply as an unambiguous item in the series. The formal ambiguity of this passage has as much to do with its surroundings as with its own internal characteristics.[20] Thanks in part to their contexts, many passages in Lully's operas seem to begin as recitative then gradually redefine themselves, becoming "songs" by the time they end, with no strong line of demarcation. These include not only extended binary passages with ambiguous beginnings, but also duets in which the voices gradually entwine and finally come together.[21] In addi-

19 "Vous brusliez pour la Gloire" and "Que j'estois insensé de croire" are included in the table of "airs à chanter" accompanying the score of *Armide* engraved by Henri de Baussen (Paris, 1710; reissued by Ballard in 1713, 1718, 1725), but "Un noir pressentiment" is not mentioned there. The excerpts named in the table include extended passages of recitative as well as songlike pieces; Baussen's aim was to serve the needs of amateur singers, not to define a genre. Indeed, his table underscores the varied and often vague usage of the word "air" at the time; surely the appropriate translation for the heading would be something very general, such as "passages to sing."

20 Regarding the effect of context on the perception of vague categories, see Diana Raffman, "Vagueness without Paradox," *The Philosophical Review* 103 (1994), 41–74.

21 See, for instance, the duet between Alceste and the dying Admète in *Alceste*, Act II, scene 8, LullyOC, "les Opéras," vol. II, 165–171. This sort of duet has its

tion to context, familiarity with such a passage (or lack thereof) affects our perception of it: do we hear the music purely diachronically, or understand the beginning of the passage according to our prior knowledge of where it is going? Seventeenth- and eighteenth-century French audiences included many individuals who went to see the same opera over and over; many also enjoyed playing or singing favorite excerpts at home. The three stages of listening described by Edward Cone – initial diachronic hearing, study and appreciation of the score, and diachronic hearing affected by prior study of the score – can, with a few modifications to suit cultural differences, be applied to early audiences as well as to ourselves.[22]

Performers, of course, have a particular responsibility in this regard. They clearly know where the passage is going, but they must also present the music – and the drama – in the order in which it unfolds. In a style as subtle as this, the singer's manner of delivering certain phrases can strongly affect the listener's perception of form. Consider, for example, "Admète avoit mon cœur," an extended binary passage in *Alceste*, Act II, scene 2, which is surrounded by recitative of the most formulaic type over a slow-moving bass.[23] Since the beginning of "Admète avoit mon cœur" serves as a foil for the anguished outpouring of its repeated closing lines, Lully minimizes the impact of the first few bars. The repeated notes and extremely limited range of the opening phrase suggest declamation of the simplest sort. The rhythmic values are those of recitative, and the meter shifts between quadruple and triple. Finally, Lully mitigates the feeling that something new is starting by introducing faster harmonic rhythm during the drive to the cadence in the preceding phrase of recitative, then maintaining it as "Admète avoit mon cœur" begins. On the other hand, the conjunct melody of the opening few bars, supported by affective harmonies in the continuo, is not at all like

stylistic roots in the *air de cour* in dialogue form; an example (by Lully's father-in-law) may be seen in Michel Lambert, *Les airs corrigez de nouveau de plusieurs fautes de graveure* (Paris, 1666; reprint Geneva: Minkoff, 1983), 80–82.
22 Edward T. Cone, "Three Ways of Reading a Detective Story – or a Brahms Intermezzo," in *Music: A View from Delft: Selected Essays*, ed. Robert P. Morgan (Chicago and London: University of Chicago Press, 1989), 77–93. See Jérôme de La Gorce, "L'Opéra et son public au temps de Louis XIV," *Bulletin de la Société de l'histoire de Paris et de l'Ile-de-France* 108 (1981), 27–46; reprint in *The Garland Library of the History of Western Music*, ed. Ellen Rosand (New York: Garland, 1986), vol. XI, 143–162.
23 LullyOC, "les Opéras," vol. II, 119–120.

the arpeggiated formulaic singsong that precedes it; the occasional written-out *agrément* supports this difference. Which side of the equation the audience perceives more clearly depends entirely on the singer's approach – whether she delivers her first few measures as relatively perfunctory declamation, or introduces a sensuously lyrical delivery starting with the first mention of Admète's name.

Even metrically unified passages might be susceptible to multiple interpretations. While Lully evidently saw no need to place explicit performance instructions or genre labels in his scores, by the mid-eighteenth century composers and editors preparing materials for the Paris Opéra, as well as Paris Opéra singers who marked their parts, had adopted (along with occasional "air" labels) the cautionary sign "mesuré," indicating performance to a strict, regular beat. It was used for through-composed passages as well as *airs de mouvement* in closed forms.[24] Like "air," the label "mesuré" appears inconsistently; it is not at all unusual to see the same passage unlabeled in one part, marked "air" in another, and marked "mesuré" in a third. A part for Renaud copied for the 1764 production of *Armide*, then annotated by a performer, provides a good illustration of the use of "mesuré": in Act V, scene 1 (see the score in Example 5.3 below), "Que j'estois insensé de croire" (m. 59) is marked "gracieux et mesuré"; the second instance of "Vaut-il un regard de vos yeux" (m. 81) is marked "tendrement"; "Est-il un bien si charmant et si rare" (m. 84) is marked "mesuré"; and "J'en suis plus amoureux" (m. 99) is marked "avec une tendresse vive."[25]

At first glance the "mesuré" markings in singers' parts might seem uninformative; after all, one can easily see regularity in the metrical notation

24 See n. 11 above regarding the term *air de mouvement*. The perplexing term "récitatif mesuré," as understood by the mid-eighteenth-century aesthetician Pierre Estève, apparently included formally closed *airs de mouvement* only, not through-composed "mesuré" passages. See Charles Dill, "Eighteenth-Century Models of French Recitative," *Journal of the Royal Musical Association* 120 (1995), 232–250 – an important article, reexamining the standard terminology for classifying types of vocal settings in French Baroque opera, as first outlined by Paul-Marie Masson in 1930, from the point of view of the political agendas and aesthetic values reflected in the eighteenth-century sources.

25 Paris, Bibliothèque de l'Opéra, Mat.18.[27(80). See Rosow, 480, regarding the dating of the part. The scene contains numerous other expression marks as well. In consulting these late parts, we should recall that, according to anecdotal evidence, vocal passages were presented at a much slower tempo in the mid-eighteenth century than during Lully's era.

itself. Still, in at least one intriguing case involving Lully's music, different phrases of a through-composed passage are annotated "mesuré" and "récitatif" respectively; the entire passage is in duple meter and has a fast-moving contrapuntal bass line.[26] The juxtaposition of these annotations, probably made at the same time and dating from the 1760s, demonstrates that music notated in a regular meter might nonetheless be performed as free declamation. The "récitatif" phrase represents a climactic moment in the poetry; the change in delivery evidently expressed that climax. Turn-of-the-century aestheticians Lecerf de la Viéville and Grimarest both point to this phrase as a fine example of expressive recitative; thus, it was probably performed as free declamation in their day as well as the 1760s, metrically unified notation notwithstanding.[27]

The flexibility of Lully's scene structure surely starts with Quinault's poetry. The typical passage of dramatic dialogue unfolds as an undifferentiated series of *vers libres*, a mixture of alexandrines, decasyllables, octosyllables, and occasional shorter lines, whose patterning does almost nothing to demand any particular musical structure. Recurring lines, to be set by Lully as cadential refrains, constitute the principal exception; these might be widely spaced (see the discussion of the opening dialogue in *Alceste*, above) or close together, as in a ternary-form air. (In ternary-form and rondeau-form airs, the episodes between refrains are normally indistinguishable from recitative.) There are no song types akin to the arias of seventeenth-century Venetian opera, with strophic form and a markedly different type of poetic line from that of the surrounding recitative. (Lully's operas do include strophic airs, but they belong to the *divertissements* and prologues, not to the dramatic dialogue. Their poetic structures are quite variable.)

26 The end of *Armide*, Act I, scene 2; see the facsimiles of score and part in Lois Rosow, "French Baroque Recitative as an Expression of Tragic Declamation," *EM* 11 (1983), illus. 2 and 3 on p. 470, as well as discussion on p. 472.
27 LecerfC, vol. II, 197, and Jean-Léonor Le Gallois, sieur de Grimarest, *Traité du récitatif* (Paris: Le Fèvre and Ribou, 1707), 208–209. Later aestheticians, such as Jean-Philippe Rameau and Toussaint Rémond de Saint-Mard, discuss this phrase as well. Its text is "Le Vainqueur de Renaud, si quelqu'un le peut estre, / Sera digne de moy"; the fascination centered on Lully's setting of the parenthetical phrase in its center. In view of its celebrity, surely Pierre Estève had this phrase in mind when he chose this scene to exemplify "récitatif simple"; compare Dill, "Eighteenth-Century Models," 242.

Quinault's principal means of suggesting groupings is rhyme; as we have seen, this device is used flexibly, though the quatrain is the normative group. Lully could theoretically set any rhymed group as either air or recitative. In practice, of course, Quinault guided his choices; for instance, the adjacent central passages in Act V, scene 1 of *Armide*, as suggested above, are structured poetically in a way that invites musical setting as airs in binary form.[28] Still, there is enormous flexibility in this system. Perhaps the only relevant formal convention strong enough to be truly predictable is that of the "maxim air" (a term invented by Paul-Marie Masson): a short rhymed group, perhaps four to six lines, sung by a confidant and ending with an aphorism will – invariably, it seems – be set as an air in some sort of binary form; the aphorism is the repeated "B" section of text. In Act I, scene 1 of *Armide*, for instance, Phénice sings, "Pourquoi voulez-vous songer / A ce qui peut vous déplaire? / Il est plus seur de se vanger / Par l'oubly que par la colère" ("[*AA*:] Why do you wish to dream about something that can only displease you? [*Bb*:] One can better get revenge by forgetting than by getting angry").[29]

Quinault's rhyme schemes give shape not only to airs but to passages of recitative as well. While the resultant patterning often seems unremarkable, there are moments when this method of organization has powerfully suggestive results. Act II, scene 2 of *Atys* begins with the lines shown in Table 5.2;[30] the initial speech at first appears to unfold entirely in alexandrines, heroic poetry that befits the rank of the goddess Cybèle. While punctuation, complemented by Lully's placement of perfect authentic cadences, shows organization in quatrains, the initial *rimes croisées* (a b a b) unite the first eight lines. The first hint of an irregularity is the altered rhyme scheme at the

28 I have explored some ways a librettist might have guided a composer in "Structure and Expression in the *scènes* of Rameau's *Hippolyte et Aricie*," *Cambridge Opera Journal* 10 (1998), 259–273.

29 The tendency for basses to sing so-called "doubled continuo" airs when they are deceived as lovers – observed by Patricia Howard, "Lully and the Ironic Convention," *Cambridge Opera Journal* 1 (1989), 45–59 – is less consistently applied than the maxim-air convention. For instance, in *Armide* Ubalde sings doubled continuo airs not when he is a deceived lover (Act IV, scene 4) but when his colleague is the deceived lover and he is the protector (Act IV, scene 3).

30 Source for Table 5.2 is the *Recueil général des opéra*, vol. I (Paris, 1703; reprint Geneva: Slatkine, 1971), 397; source for Example 5.2 is *Atys, tragédie mise en musique par Monsieur de Lully* (Paris: Christophe Ballard, 1689), 129–130.

Table 5.2. Atys, *beginning of Act II, scene 2*

Syllables	Rhyme	Text	Cadences
		[Prélude]	G
12+	a	Cybèle: Je veux joindre en ces lieux la gloire & l'abondance,	
12	b	D'un Sacrificateur je veux faire le choix,	
12+	a	Et le Roy de Phrygie auroit la preference,	
12	b	Si je voulois choisir entre les plus grands Roys.	D
12+	a	Le puissant Dieu des flots vous donna la naissance,	
12	b	Un Peuple renommé s'est mis sous vôtre loy;	
12+	a	Vous avez, sans mes soins, d'ailleurs trop de puissance:	
12	b	Je veux faire un bonheur qui ne soit dû qu'à moy.	G
12+	c	Vous estimez Atys, & c'est avec justice:	
12+	c	Je prétens que mon choix à vos vœux soit propice,	
8	d	C'est Atys que je veux choisir.	
12	d	Célénus: J'aime Atys, & je voi sa gloire avec plaisir.	G
8+	e	Je suis Roy, Neptune est mon pere,	
12	f	J'épouse une beauté qui va combler mes vœux:	
8+	e	Le souhait qui me reste à faire,	
12	f	C'est de voir mon Amy parfaitement heureux.	D

Translation: (Cybèle) I wish to join here glory and abundance; I wish to choose a Sacrificer; and the king of Phrygia would be preferred if I wanted to choose among the greatest kings. The powerful god of the sea was your father, a renowned nation submitted to your rule; you have acquired, without my help, great power. I want to bestow happiness that comes from me alone. You hold Atys in high esteem, and justly so. I believe my choice will suit your wishes. It is Atys whom I wish to choose. (Célénus) I love Atys, and I am pleased to see him honored. I am king, Neptune is my father, I am marrying a beauty who will fulfill my desires; what is left for me to wish is to see my friend completely happy.

Example 5.2

Atys, excerpt from Act II, scene 2

beginning of the third quatrain – new sounds and a change to rhymed couplets – but perhaps this is too subtle a gesture to make an impression. The irregularity that follows, however, cannot be missed: Cybèle breaks off, almost nervously, after only three lines, and the third is an octosyllable instead of the expected alexandrine. Presumably feeling guilty about her secret and inappropriate love for Atys, the goddess offers her announcement in a tone of supplication; she wants Célénus's approval. He gives it, his first line completing her unfinished rhyme ("choi*sir*," "plai*sir*"). Lully's music complements the poetic gesture (see Example 5.2). After the regular musical anapests of Cybèle's preceding alexandrine, the unexpected quarter-note and rest at the beginning of her octosyllable not only accent Atys's name but throw weight on the meaningful word "veux" ("want"). Moreover, Cybèle breaks off on a half-cadence; it is Célénus's response that makes the full cadence. In addition, Lully displaces the central accent in Célénus's first hemistich; it occurs not on the poetic caesura, "voy," but on "A*tys*."

The virtual lack of contrasting structural elements in Quinault's poetry lends itself to the absence of strong differentiation between song and declamation in this style. Indeed, Lully's music remains attentive to poetic detail and the needs of prosodic declamation at all times, even during closed forms and even when regular meter prevails. In the opening couplet of Armide's air shown on p. 96 (Example 5.3, mm. 43–50), for instance, hemiola places particular insistence on Armide's perception of Renaud's desire for glory:

m'ai-mer, Vous la cher-chiez par-tout d'u-ne ar-deur

As one expects, metrical stress – whether effected by barline or by hemiola –
coincides with the fixed accents (sixth and twelfth syllables) and mobile
accents (normally one per hemistich) of each of the two alexandrines:
"Vous brusliez pour la Gloire avant que de m'aimer, / Vous la cherchiez
partout d'une ardeur sans esgale." In effect, the hemiola creates an extra
accent ("la" as well as "cherchiez" and "partout") in the third hemistich.

The ambiguous relationship between air and recitative in this genre,
alluded to several times in the foregoing discussion, is of course well known.
As Blainville wrote in 1754, "Our recitative sings too much, or our airs not
enough."[31] (His pejorative tone reflects the date of his comment and need not
concern us here.) While Blainville draws our attention to the musical surface –
the nature of melody and bass line – the stylistic ambiguity involves dramatic
function as well. The functional aspect deserves our attention here, for it
contributes significantly to the flexibility inherent in Lully's scene-building
technique. The airs in Lully's dialogues, thanks to their brevity and formal
simplicity (and despite their modest internal repetitions), involve almost no
Italianate suspension of time; thus, an emotionally charged conversation
often takes place in a series of airs. Adjacent airs are typically all in the same
key; whether they are otherwise musically parallel (such as the pair in the
scene from *Armide* presented above) or contrast with each other in form,
meter, and texture is determined by the needs of the drama. A good example of
a conversation composed of contrasting airs is the unusually long series (six
airs in a row) in Act II, scene 2 of *Amadis*.[32] In more than one scholarly commentary on the intermingling of airs with recitative, it has been suggested that
Quinault wrote the poetry for airs only after Lully had written the music.[33] In

31 "Notre Récitatif chante trop, ou nos Airs pas assez." BlainvilleE, 52. See also
    James Anthony, "The Musical Structure of Lully's Operatic Airs," in
    Heidelberg87, 65–76.
32 *Amadis*, ed. Henry Prunières, in LullyOC, "les Opéras," vol. III, 81–86.
33 Catherine Kintzler, "Essai de définition du récitatif: le chaînon manquant,"
    "*Recherches*" sur la musique française classique 24 (1986), 138, and *Poétique de
    l'opéra français de Corneille à Rousseau* (Paris: Minerve, 1991), 392 (citing
    Etienne Gros in each case); and CouvreurL, 314.

view of the way the airs are integrated into conversations, such a compositional chronology is inconceivable. The misunderstanding results from a misreading of Lecerf de la Viéville, whose comment concerns the dance songs and other airs in the *divertissements* and prologues, not the airs in dramatic dialogue.[34]

Moreover, the relative dramatic weight of recitative and air is variable. Weighty ideas and heightened emotion are as likely to appear in recitative as in airs. In the first scene of Act I of *Armide*, for instance, the protagonist's two confidants express their simplistic reassurances primarily in airs (one of them Phénice's maxim air, "Pourquoi voulez-vous songer," quoted above), while the emotional weight of the scene rests squarely on Armide's two principal passages of recitative. The only generalization that may safely be made regarding the dramatic function of airs is that each expresses a single emotional state, whether fraught with important meaning (as in the pair for Armide and Renaud in the scene examined above) or relatively frivolous (as in so many of the airs sung by confidants). It is telling that both Grimarest, who insisted that musical regularity was incompatible with the expression of passion, and Lecerf de la Viéville, who characterized the thoughts expressed in an *air de mouvement* as "livelier" and "more passionate" than those in the rest of the discourse, referred to the Lullian style of opera. They evidently had different scenes in mind.[35]

In short, the structure of Lully's dialogue scenes, while highly conven-

34 See Herbert Schneider, "'Canevas' als Terminus der lyrischen Dichtung," *Archiv für Musikwissenschaft* 42 (1985), 87–101, especially p. 91. The air from *Roland* based on a *timbre* from the era of Cardinal Mazarin, quoted by Couvreur (citing Monique Rollin), belongs to the prologue of that opera.

35 Grimarest, *Traité du récitatif*, 196–197: "Il faut établir pour principe, que la passion ne saurait être exprimée que par les accens, par la prononciation, et par les gestes qui lui sont propres. Or il est impossible, en conservant les règles de la musique, de donner à la passion ce que je viens de dire; il n'y a que la seule déclamation qui puisse le faire. Donc toute passion assujettie aux intervalles et aux mesures de la musique perd de sa force." LecerfC, vol. I, 60: "Un personnage qui dit quelque chose de plus vif, de plus emporté que le reste de son discours, qui est pris de quelque saillie, qui a tout d'un coup quelque redoublement de passion: quitte le train ordinaire du récitatif. Il prend un ton d'un mouvement vîte & piqué, & qui est marqué encore par l'accompagnement de deux violons, & il exprime ainsi ce qu'il sent, il fait sentir aux autres d'une maniere vive sans être outrée: sans sortir des régles, sans bizarrerie: puis quand l'emportement est calmé, il retourne au récitatif ordinaire pour le quitter encore à la première saillie." The *air de mouvement* in Lecerf's hypothetical scene is evidently for a bass since it is a doubled continuo air in trio-sonata texture.

tional, is also highly flexible. As a result of the supple structure of Quinault's poetry, along with the fluid relationship between recitative and air (from both structural and functional points of view), Lully had both the latitude to shape his scenes in a variety of ways and a special responsibility to help his audience perceive the shape of each scene as it unfolded. Thanks to the subtle means used to differentiate structural elements, by both poet and composer, the simplest expedients – repeating an introductory phrase or changing mode, for instance – could make the difference between articulating a salient moment and allowing that moment to be subsumed into relative continuity. Through clever placement of cadences of varying strength, closing formulas, clear beginnings and ambiguous beginnings, and recurring elements, Lully ensured that his listeners experienced a hierarchy of points of articulation, one that closely complemented the drama. As a scene unfolds, the music breathes with the poetry – and we as listeners breathe with both.

Example 5.3
Armide, Act V, scene 1 (Renaud's part, originally in alto clef, sounds an octave lower than written)

Example 5.3 (*cont.*)

Example 5.3 (*cont.*)

Example 5.3 (*cont.*)

98

Example 5.3 (*cont.*)

6 The Amsterdam editions of Lully's music: a bibliographical scrutiny with commentary
(for H. Wiley Hitchcock)

CARL B. SCHMIDT

Historians do not doubt that the splendor, pomp, and brilliance of life at the court of Louis XIV was envied and imitated by his contemporaries with sufficient means and power. Louis's chosen designation as "Le Roi Soleil" provided the appropriate metaphor. Just as the sun gives light and life to everything it touches, so Louis's influence extended throughout Europe in matters political, commercial, and artistic. Political influence was often exerted through the king's many military campaigns (including three against the Dutch Republic between 1672 and 1713), Versailles provided a splendid repository for furnishings (including porcelains, tapestries, furniture, paintings, glassware, clocks, and other *objets d'art*) executed by French craftsmen, and artists in the broadest sense (including Molière, Corneille, Racine, Quinault, Lully, and numerous others) had their works widely disseminated outside the king's realm.

A version of this paper was read at Hunter College on October 9, 1993 at a meeting of the American Musicological Society honoring the seventieth birthday of H. Wiley Hitchcock. Research was made possible, in part, by a grant from the Division of Research Programs of the National Endowment for the Humanities, an independent federal agency. The author is particularly grateful to Rebecca Harris-Warrick for her most helpful comments on an earlier draft of this study and to all the librarians in whose collections Amsterdam editions of Lully's music can be found. Their hospitality during personal study of the materials and their generosity in supplying microfilms or information is most appreciated. In particular, deepest thanks are extended to Catherine Massip and François Lesure of the Bibliothèque Nationale (Paris) and to Albert Cohen and Anne Witherell of the Lully Archive at Stanford University. Finally, Buford Norman graciously refined several of the lengthier English translations of French texts contained in the main body of the text and generously clarified several points.

Given Louis's proclivity for choosing military options, why was French artistic influence so dominant in some of the very places where political enmity was the strongest? In the case of territories to the northeast of Paris, the Northern Netherlands (or Republic of the Seven United Provinces) and the Southern Netherlands, Louis's battles were fought mostly in the latter, and the Dutch welcomed an influx of French immigrants (particularly Huguenots) following the revocation of the Edict of Nantes in 1685. Furthermore, ties were established between the Dutch and the United Kingdom when Prince William of Orange became William III, King of England in 1689. The succession of wars involving Louis XIV and his northern neighbors neither stemmed the flow of foreign artists to Amsterdam nor retarded the rise of that city as a center of music publishing. The growing prosperity of the Northern Netherlanders during the waning years of the seventeenth century created a climate in which the arts could be appreciated, and music in particular became a factor in the daily lives of bourgeois society. The appetite for music by Jean-Baptiste Lully evident in the Northern Netherlands provides us with an ideal opportunity to view an important aspect of the *rayonnement* of French culture.

Fundamental work by James Anthony and Herbert Schneider published during the 1980s has led to a significant reawakening of interest in the music of Jean-Baptiste Lully.[1] Following their lead, scholars have been addressing the many issues needing clarification if we are to understand Lully's music and to place it in its proper historical and sociological contexts. Schneider's thematic catalogue has documented the wealth of printed and manuscript Lully sources, and his study of the reception of Lully's music in France has shown how widely Lully's works were known and appreciated in his adopted country.[2] Schneider has also established that Lully's music was performed and published in various French cities outside the Ile-de-France orbit of Saint-Germain-en-Laye, Paris, Versailles; it has been demonstrated that Lully's music was performed and published beyond French borders in places such as the two Dutch Republics. Notable among the cities which harbored Lully activity are Brussels, where Lully *tragédies lyriques* were performed between 1682 and 1741 (but none of his

1 See AnthonyF, AnthonyJ, SchneiderC, and SchneiderR.
2 See also SchmidtN for additions and GustafsonLL for cross-references and corrections to SchneiderC.

music is known to have been published),[3] and Amsterdam, where various of
his stage works were performed between 1687 and 1723. Dozens of Lully
scores and parts (as well as collections of poetry intended to be sung to
tunes from Lully's stage works) were also published in Amsterdam.[4] It is
especially important that four Amsterdam editions of excerpts from Lully's
tragédies lyriques, including those for *Cadmus et Hermione*, *Alceste*, *Atys*,
and *Psyché* predate the publication of any of their music in Paris. Although
preliminary study has been made of the music contained in some of these
Amsterdam sources, no comprehensive list of Amsterdam prints has yet
been published, nor have the locations of copies beyond those cited in
RISM been reported.[5] The present study will discuss the extent and scope of
these publications (the first of which were printed when Lully was still
alive), the reasons why they found a willing public in the north, and the relationships between printers who issued the volumes. Finally, the bibliographical scrutiny that forms the basis of this article describes all known
Dutch printed editions of Lully's music except parodies. Included for each
edition are a diplomatic transcription of the title page, a description of the
score or parts, a list of the contents given according to Schneider's LWV
(Lully Werke Verzeichnis) numbers, the location of all known exemplars,
and appropriate bibliographical references.

Background

In France special privileges granted to Lully and the Ballard family
strictly regulated the publication of Lully's music. Lully, by legal agreement

3 See SchmidtG for a detailed assessment of the spread of Lully's *tragédies lyriques*
   to the provinces and to other European cities; La GorceA for a study of Lully
   performances in Rouen; and La GorceC for a discussion of French influence on
   opera in Hamburg and The Hague.
4 For a summary of Dutch parodies see SchneiderP and SchneiderR. For
   discussion of a recently discovered collection see SchmidtP.
5 See SchneiderA for a study of the instrumental suites found among these
   editions and SchneiderF for a summary of the issue of instrumental suites in the
   period between Lully and Rameau. SchneiderF, 172–173 also includes a very
   useful list of French and Dutch publications of chamber trios from Du Mont
   (1657) through François Couperin (1726). Schneider's cogent description of
   how Lully's five-part texture was reduced to four parts need not be duplicated
   here. For information about early reductions of Lully's music into trios see
   Ranum.

with Christophe Ballard and the librettist Jean-Philippe Quinault, exercised tight control over the publication of his *tragédies lyriques* in France during the last decade of his life.[6] The regular printing of full scores of Lully's larger stage works in France was delayed until 1679 when Christophe Ballard issued *Bellérophon*. Thereafter, at least one major work was published yearly in Paris until Lully's death in 1687.[7] Jérôme de La Gorce has documented that Lully further exerted control over productions of his music throughout France; performances could not legally be given without the purchase of a privilege obtainable only from the composer.[8] However, no record exists that any printed musical edition of a Lully work was ever issued in the French provinces during Lully's lifetime. In spite of strict controls, some works such as the early ballets and *comédies-ballets* remained unpublished at Lully's death after which their fate proved much more difficult to control.

Immediately following Lully's death an interesting phenomenon took place, which has been discussed by Patricia Ranum in several articles about the musical establishment of Mademoiselle de Guise. She has written: "During the early 1690s, a unique phenomenon was observable throughout France. Instead of being discarded in favor of the latest compositions, the late Lully's works were fast becoming what would be called 'classics.' ... This history might have been brief without the *curieux* and the elite who first decided to collect the Surintendant's works and who slowly assembled bits and pieces of unpublished ballets and operas."[9] It should be emphasized that in France Lully's music – generally available only in expensive folio-sized books and commercially produced manuscripts, or privately copied manuscripts – remained largely the domain of the aristocratic class.

Beyond French borders restrictions on the publication and performance of Lully's music were largely ignored. The most sustained activity

6 The best summary of Lully's legal arrangements with printers is found in Rosow, vol. I, 8–13. Louis XIV's printing privilege for Lully is reprinted in Becker, 124–126.
7 Christophe Ballard's 1677 printing of *Isis* in partbooks actually began the major publications. Except for the motets of 1684 (*RISM* A/I, L 2929) this is Ballard's only major Lully publication in partbooks.
8 See La GorceA.
9 See Ranum, 323–324. Other articles by Ranum on Etienne Loulié and the musical establishment of Mademoiselle de Guise can be found in various issues of *RMFC*.

took place in Amsterdam where, although only a modest number of stage works were performed, Quinault's *livrets* for Lully's *tragédies* were reprinted almost two hundred times, and dozens of Lully parts and scores issued. The latter include full or reduced scores of stage works, collections of vocal and/or instrumental excerpts, and a large number of parodies in which new words (often vulgar) were set to Lully's tunes. Before we examine the scope of this music, let us consider further why such interest in Lully existed in the Northern Netherlands.

Throughout the late seventeenth and early eighteenth centuries the Dutch showed a growing interest in French culture, particularly in the repertoire of the Académie Royale de Musique and that of such great playwrights as Molière, Corneille, and Racine.[10] Bourgeois society developed an appetite for Lully's tunes and for arrangements of his music which, when made into suites, became what Schneider has referred to as the Dutch *Gebrauchsmusik* of the time serving also as pedagogical repertory for learning to play instruments such as the violin or flute. Vocal excerpts served a similar function for singers. Anthologies were generally published in small format, sold in wrappers or in modest paper bindings, and comparatively inexpensive. With the exception of full scores, which followed Parisian exemplars very closely, most Amsterdam editions of excerpts were newly arranged and ordered either by the publishers themselves, or by musicians in their employ.

Dutch interest in Lully's music, which had less to do with aristocratic heritage than with the emerging middle class, first flowered during the 1680s and reached its zenith in the first decade of the eighteenth century.[11] The Dutch printer Antoine Pointel in the previously unstudied preface to his 1688 wordbook entitled *Recueil des airs des chansons, et des endroits les plus passionnez de tous les opera* (*Collection of airs and songs, and the most moving moments from all the operas*), published in Amsterdam, alluded to this interest. Although Pointel's intent was to explain the usefulness of a pocket-sized edition of words for famous airs, his preface implies a widespread Dutch predilection for imported stage music.

> In the intention that I have contributed, as far as possible, to music's perfection, and to the noble passion that one has to sing opera, I thought

10 About Molière, see Guibert.
11 For two overviews of Lully's influence in the Dutch Republics, see Noske and RaschD.

that this collection will be useful. There are few people who take pleasure in music who do not know various *airs* and many *chansons* from the operas ... I hope soon to publish all the music of the *airs*, *chansons*, and most beautiful moments contained in this collection. This book, however, will not lose its usefulness because after having mastered the notes of an *air*, one can try one's hand at singing the words without looking at the music, thus gradually learning to sing by memory.[12]

Before discussing Amsterdam editions of Lully's music, a few words about the plethora of reprinted *livrets* for Lully's stage works is justified because statistically they are by far the most numerous. From 1680 until 1753 Dutch printers reprinted *livrets* for Lully's stage works either as single volumes, in *recueils factices*,[13] or in collected literary editions. The vast majority, not intended to accompany performances, slavishly reproduce Paris texts, often replete with names of performers and/or dates for Parisian performances. A few Dutch translations or French versions published in Amsterdam in quarto format accompanied performances, or were intended to. In some cases these *livrets* included texts for new prologues and all expunged references to French performers. Table 6.1 clarifies the extent of Dutch printings of *livrets* for a sample of Lully stage works. But our primary focus must return to Lully's music.

Pointel, whose preface is quoted above, was neither the first nor the sole printer to introduce Lully's music to Holland. He was, in fact, but one of a group of printers who labored to produce publications devoted to instrumental and/or vocal excerpts, reduced scores (*partitions réduites*), or full scores (*partitions générales*) of Lully's music. Some, like Estienne Roger, are relatively well known and have been the object of considerable bibliographic

---

12 The "AVERTISSEMENT" on [3–4] reads: "DAns le dessein que j'ai de contribuer, autant qu[']il m'est possible, à la perfection de la musique; & à la noble passion qu'on a de chanter les Opera, j'ai cru ce Recueil, seroit de quelque utilité. il y a peu de personnes qui se plaisent á la musique, qui ne sachent divers Airs & plusieurs Chansons des Opera ... J'espere de donner bien tôt en musique tous les airs, toutes les chansons & tous les beaux endroits contenus dans ce Recueil: Mais ce Livret ne perdra pas néanmoins son utilité car aprés avoir appris un air sur les notes, on pourra s'exercer á chanter les paroles sans voir la musique, & s'habituér ainsi peu à peu à chanter par coeur." For a full description of this volume see SchmidtC. The only known exemplar is in F-Pa (Ro. 1405).
13 A volume made up of discrete editions, each one with its own title page, to which has been added a general title page.

Table 6.1. *Statistical table of* livrets *for Lully* tragédies lyriques *published in The Netherlands*[a]

	Place of publication				
Title	Amsterdam[b]	The Hague	Paris/ Antwerp[c]	Brussels	Galanbrun
Cadmus et Hermione	11	1	3	0	1
Alceste	13	1	1	1	1
Thésée	15	1	1	2	1
Atys	17	2	2	1	1
Isis	13	0	2	0	1
Psyché	13	0	1	0	1
Bellérophon	13	0	2	1	1
Proserpine	14	0	2	0	1
Persée	13	0	2	1	1
Phaéton	15	0	2	0	1
Amadis	13	1	3	4	1
Roland	10	2	2	2	1
Armide	12	0	3	3	0
Acis et Galatée	9	0	1	2	0
Achille et Polixène	8	0	1	0	0
Total	189	8	28	17	12 (254)

[a] Includes *livrets* contained in collected literary editions (CLE). Information about Dutch reprints of Molière's *comédie-ballets*, for many of which Lully provided the music, is contained in Guibert.
[b] Includes all *livrets* published in Amsterdam or thought to have been published there.
[c] "Imprimée à Paris et on les vend à Anvers."

Table 6.2. *Printers of Lully's music in Holland*

Printer	Dates	Dates of known Lully printing activity
Jean Philip Heus	late 17th century	1682–85
Antoine Pointel	1660–1702	1687–1700
Jean Stichter	late 17th century	late 17th century
Pieter Blaeu	1637–1706	1690–91
Joan Blaeu	1650–1712	1690–91
Amédée Le Chevalier	c. 1650–1720	1690–92
Estienne Roger	1664/65–1722	1697?–c. 1715
Pierre Mortier	1661–1711	1710–11 Mortier died February 18)
Michel Charles Le Cène	1683/84–1743	After 1711 (works reprinted from Mortier's plates) – later 1720s?

work, while others, like Jean Stichter, the brothers Blaeu, and Amédée Le Chevalier, have received far less attention.[14] These men, who printed or engraved the scores and parts that form the basis for our study, are listed in Table 6.2. They will be considered in the order they first began issuing Lully's music, with emphasis placed on both their interrelationships and the specific nature of their importance.

Jean Philip Heus

In 1682, five years before Lully's death at the age of fifty-four, Jean Philip Heus became the first Dutch music printer to test the Lully market with a publication of musical excerpts from *Cadmus et Hermione*. We do not know the size of Heus's press runs, but exemplars today are of the

---

14 Thomas Walker summarized the interrelationships of some of these printers during 1980, in advance of the writings of Anthony or Schneider (see Walker). Although Walker's focus was on a spurious Pointel edition of Arcangelo Corelli, he made significant reference to Amsterdam editions of Lully published by the very printers under consideration in this article. I am indebted to Walker's work, which provided the spark for my own investigation.

utmost rarity.[15] Because the score of *Cadmus* was not published in France until 1719, this was both the earliest printing of music from Lully's first *tragédie lyrique* and the first foreign printed or engraved edition ever known to precede its French counterpart.[16] *Cadmus* was followed by editions of excerpts from *Persée, Phaéton, Amadis,* and *Roland* respectively. The last four of these editions had the distinction of being issued in the years the *tragédies lyriques* were premiered in France. Heus's first four publications (each issued in a set of four oblong quarto part books) were entitled *Ouverture avec tous les airs [de violon] de l'opéra.* ... The remaining book of *Airs à tous chanter* for *Roland* was published in score. The only other known Heus publications are of music by Pascal Collasse entitled *Les Airs de la tragédie de Thétis et Pélée* (Amsterdam, 1684),[17] and an edition of twelve trio sonatas by Giovanni Battista Vitali published in 1684.[18]

Unfortunately, Heus is a publisher about whom virtually nothing significant is known. Neither his birth nor death date has been ascertained, and we lack even rudimentary information about his relationship to other Dutch or French printers. Yet Heus's few Lully editions are important because they form the models in content and format for later editions by Pointel and Roger. Occasionally, as will be demonstrated below, Roger even borrowed music directly from Heus's editions. Heus's editions, unlike most Lully editions issued in Amsterdam except some by Pointel, are graced with decorative engraved title pages. The title page for *Cadmus,* for example, shows four musicians surrounding a vignette of Cadmus slaying the chimera. Heus engraved rather than printed the music, and each page is relatively packed with notes. His editions contain few errors of pitch, duration, or rubric when compared to later Ballard editions, with only an occasional incorrect passage covered by a *collette*. The edition of *Cadmus,* however, incorporates three unusual features. First, Heus included an *air* for La Nuit

15 A full list and description of Heus's Lully publications, and of those by the other publishers under consideration in this article, are given in the appendix, pp. 128–165 below.
16 Manuscript copies of Lully's works were sold openly in the French marketplace during the composer's lifetime and for more than fifty years thereafter. Various French music dealers, including Henri Foucault and the Ballard family, advertised the sale of Lully works in manuscript as well as printed copy.
17 See *RISM* A/I, C 3395 (copy in GB-Lbl).
18 See Kleerkooper, 257–258, who cites an advertisement for this print dated July 22, 1684.

and a Chœur des Cariens from the ballet *Le Triomphe de l'Amour* (1681: see LWV 59/43 and 45 respectively) without revealing their new source. Second, he included three minuets whose Lullian paternity is highly doubtful. These same minuets as well as the *air* for La Nuit also occur in a Roger edition published at the opening of the eighteenth century.[19] Finally, the music engraving was apparently done by two different engravers. Pages 1–10 contain six staves per page and are in a more refined hand. Pages 11–14 contain seven staves per page (for no demonstrable reason) and are in a bolder hand.

By publishing excerpts from *Persée, Phaéton, Amadis,* and *Roland* each in the same year they were created and published in Paris, Heus aligned himself with the many Amsterdam *contrafaisseurs* of *livrets* by Quinault for Lully's *tragédies lyriques*. Heus, like Abraham Wolfgang and the others who printed *livrets*, was particularly important for getting Lully's music into Dutch hands expediently. What his precise relationship was with his immediate successor, Antoine Pointel, is presently unknown. It would not be surprising if Pointel knew Heus personally and perhaps even worked for him; but for now this remains conjecture.

Antoine Pointel

Our basic knowledge about most Dutch printers who followed Heus has been greatly enhanced by the meticulous archival research of Isabelle van Eeghen.[20] Her lengthy study of Dutch printers and booksellers from 1680–1725 informs us that Antoine Pointel (June 5, 1660–November 7, 1702) was the son of the shoemaker Michael Pointel and of Marie Herveau. Antoine had three sisters – Anne, Judith, and Susana – the first of whom married Nicolas Derosier, who will be discussed in greater detail below. In his mid-twenties, Antoine Pointel opened a bookshop in Amsterdam (from 1689 on advertised as "Inde Roose-boom, op Cingel, schuyns over den Doele, by 't Konings-pleyn"), and between 1687 and 1700 he published numerous Lully works in addition to music of Colasse, Louis Grabu, Robert de Visée, Derosier, and others. Pointel's inventory maintained the French

---

19 See Roger 7 in the appendix, p. 156 below: the three minuets are not known to occur in *Cadmus* or any other Lully work.
20 Concerning Pointel see Eeghen, 4, 48–49.

CARL B. SCHMIDT

emphasis found in Heus's extant works; he is known to have published only one collection of Italian airs around 1690.[21] Unlike his successor Estienne Roger, who published a variety of books, he devoted himself exclusively to the publication of music or works related to music.

Altogether, music by Lully is contained in eighteen extant Pointel editions and is thought to be contained in eight others presently known only from seventeenth-century advertisements and secondary sources. Pointel published music from eleven of Lully's fourteen *tragédies lyriques* plus five works in other genres (*Les Fêtes de l'Amour et de Bacchus, Le Temple de la Paix, Le Triomphe de l'Amour, Acis et Galatée*, and *La grotte de Versailles* plus *La Mascarade*). Of the *tragédies lyriques* excluded by Pointel – *Thésée, Isis,* and *Bellérophon* – only *Thésée* failed to appear in at least one Amsterdam edition.[22] The vast majority of Pointel's editions are of excerpts from Lully's works. Continuing the pattern established by Heus, Pointel published collections of *ouvertures* and *airs* as well as *Airs à chanter.* To these he added a series of five volumes entitled *Les simphonies à 4. avec les airs et triots[sic] de . . .* and two more of miscellaneous dances or contre-dances containing only isolated excerpts by Lully.[23] His anomalous 1689 publication of *Achille et Polyxène* in a *partition générale* will be discussed separately below.

Some Pointel editions, like all of Heus's known editions, were engraved, although he also used movable type. Here the Dutch printers followed the more progressive tendencies of French printers, a few of whom turned to engraving in the later years of the seventeenth century. Christophe Ballard, however, who held the French royal privilege to publish Lully's music, did so exclusively from movable type until 1708.[24] Christophe Ballard

---

21 See in particular the 1689 catalogue transcribed in Walker, 397–398 and the undated catalogue bound in Pointel 19. A full list of Pointel's Lully editions (as well as the catalogue in Pointel 19) appears in the appendix, pp. 133–145 below. A copy of the *Airs Italiens* may be found in F-Pn (Vm⁷ 12): see LesureC, 658.

22 A few numbers did appear in the trio volumes published by Blaeu, Roger, and Mortier, but no more extensive excerpts were published.

23 Unfortunately, only one set of *dessus* parts for this series can be located. See Pointel 4, 11, 12, 16, and 18 respectively. All of them share the same decorative border on their title pages.

24 His handsome large folio editions of Lully *partitions générales* retained a printing process handed down from father to son since the mid-sixteenth century, a process Christophe steadfastly maintained until his death in 1715. He even attempted to defend his exclusive right by bringing a suit against Jean-Marie Leclair and others for obtaining privileges in 1713 to publish engraved

and his son Jean-Baptiste-Christophe Ballard continued to print Lully *partitions générales* from movable type for several decades into the eighteenth century even though Henri de Baussen was retained to engrave many Lully *tragédies lyriques* in *partitions réduites* that were then issued beginning in 1708.[25] Pointel apparently had the opposite problem from the Ballards. His engraved editions seem to have posed fewer technical problems (although they are only of mediocre technical quality), but his attempt to publish *Achille et Polyxène* in a typeset *partition générale* and *Proserpine* in a short score (both 1689) gave him difficulty.

In the "AUIS DU LIBRAIRE" from his edition of *Achille* Pointel remarks that he faced two special obstacles in reprinting operas first published in Paris: (1) "The lack of music appropriate for these publications" and (2) "The difficulty of their correction."[26] The first obstacle may have been a mere publisher's smoke-screen, for the majority of Lully's scores had already been published in *partitions générales* and those that had not were probably available in manuscript copies even if their wider commercial availability had to await the last decade of the century. The second obstacle would appear obscure were it not for the fact that Pointel went on to explain that a Monsieur Derosier (actually Pointel's brother-in-law) had invented "a type of music [font] suitable for my plans."[27] Further on, Pointel tells us that Derosier had created "Notes with a slightly larger typeface in order to

editions (see PogueB, 86). Ballard's privilege, it was ruled, applied only to printing from movable type and the way was then cleared for a host of publishers to break the Ballard monopoly on French music publishing. The fact is, however, that engraved editions appeared in France as early as 1660 when Michel Lambert (Lully's father-in-law) had his *Airs* engraved by Richer and published by Charles de Sercy (see *RISM* A/I, L 382); for a facsimile of the title page see Fraenkel, no. 110.

25 De Baussen's editions, which were frequently reprinted from the original plates by Christophe Ballard himself or by Jean-Baptiste Christophe Ballard after Christophe's death, include: *Alceste* (1708: *RISM* A/I, L 2936), *Atys* (1708: *RISM* A/I, L 2962), *Phaéton* (1709: *RISM* A/I, L 3003), *Roland* (1709: *RISM* A/I, L 3028), *Armide* (1710: *RISM* A/I, L 2955), *Persée* (1710: *RISM* A/I, L 2993), *Amadis* (1711: *RISM* A/I, L 2946), *Thésée* (1711: *RISM* A/I, L 3038). The Ballard firm never engraved a single *partition générale* of a Lully *tragédie lyrique*. AnthonyP, no. 62 indicates that de Baussen engraved Campra's *Alcine* in 1705, three years before his first Lully edition.

26 (1) "le manque de Musique propre pour ces Ouvrages" and (2) "la difficulté de la Correction." The entire "AUIS" is transcribed in the appendix under Pointel 1b, p. 134 below.

27 "une sorte de Musique convenable à mon projet . . ."

save performers from difficulty . . ."[28] Clearly then, it must have been Derosier who designed the type used in this edition of *Achille* and who most likely solved the technical problems involved in production.[29] When compared to Christophe Ballard's edition of *Achille* (Paris, 1687), however, Pointel's edition does not fare well. Ballard's large folio (*c.* 37 × 25 cm) contains 354 pages of music while Pointel's (only *c.* 24.5 × 20.5 cm) contains 324 pages of music.[30] The quality and layout of Ballard's edition are vastly superior to those of Pointel, which are crowded and more difficult to read. Even though Ballard's edition contains dozens of technical errors (which are frequently the object of manuscript corrections in extant copies), errors that Pointel generally corrected, Ballard's is still the more elegant edition. Only by including a "Table des airs à chanter & à jouer" did Pointel improve on Ballard's work. Such tables became particularly popular during the early eighteenth century and were included by the Ballards in numerous later editions of Lully's *tragédies lyriques*.[31] Finally, it should be noted that the prefatory materials in Pointel's edition exist in two states, one of which (Pointel 1b) is a corrected version of the other (Pointel 1a).

Pointel may also have struggled with production problems in his 1689 edition of *LES AIRS DE LA TRAGÉDIE DE PROSERPINE*.[32] This publication, which contains thirty-one excerpts arranged in the original order of the *tragédie lyrique*, was issued in two editions. One edition uses diamond-shaped notes and generally smaller type (Edition 1: see GB-Lbl Hirsch III.

28 "Nottes dont l'oeil soit un peu plus gros, afin d'épargner de la peine à ceux qui chantent en Concert . . ."
29 Derosier's career as a guitarist and composer is summarized by Strizich, but his relationship with Dutch printers and Pointel in particular has not previously been mentioned. Derosier apparently also had a business relationship with the printer Jean Stichter. According to the title page, Stichter's edition of Lully's *Le Temple de la Paix* (see Stichter 1) was "*Imprimé chez* Jean Stichter, *dans le Kalver-straat,* pour Nicolas de Rosier." Derosier also invented a system of guitar notation used by Pointel. See the note transcribed under Pointel 19 in the appendix, p. 142 below. Derosier wrote twelve ouvertures (Op. 5; The Hague, 1688), Psalm 150 for voice and basso continuo (Amsterdam, 1688), *Les princeps de la guitarre* (Amsterdam, 1688; reprint Bologna, Forni, 1975), and *Les nouveaux principes de la guitarre* (Paris: Christophe Ballard, 1699).
30 The Ballard edition omits page numbers 80–81, so the actual total is two less.
31 The exemplars at US-BE (M1500.C.653A2 Case X and M1500.C652A2 cop. 2 Case X) both exhibit such manuscript corrections.
32 See Pointel 17a and 17b in the appendix, pp. 140–141 below.

908), while the other uses lozenge-shaped notes and generally larger type (Edition 2: see GB-Lbl A.409.(1.)). The former edition gives only part one of the anthology, whereas the latter also includes part two. Although a comparison of the actual music for part one shows the two editions to be nearly identical, the A.409 (1.) copy contains fewer figures for the *basse-continue* and new line divisions for several pages. Did Pointel first publish the diamond-note edition of part one and then, after Derosier's invention, reissue the volume using the new type?

Pointel's importance in producing Lully editions should not be underestimated. Building on the idea introduced by Heus, Pointel established an impressive catalogue of Lully editions including both vocal and instrumental excerpts and one *partition générale*. He even included Lully's music in two miscellaneous collections of dance music published in 1688 and 1700 respectively.[33] The majority of his collections retain the order of numbers found in the original Lully scores, as opposed to groupings into suites by key. Finally, Pointel obviously intended his editions to appeal to a broader public than did his predecessor Jean Philip Heus. Five of his editions include the ungrammatical English statement "Fit for to sing and to playd uppon all sorts of Instruments" in addition to their normal French titles.[34] There is no direct evidence that Pointel's publications were sold in England, but it appears that he was courting an English-speaking clientele.[35] It will be shown later that Roger's editions were widely sold throughout Europe. A sixth edition, that of the *AIRS DE DANSES ANGLOISES, HOLLANDOISES, ET FRANÇOISES* (1700), states on its title page that the dances were gathered by Pointel but published in Paris by Christophe Ballard.[36] The precise nature of the Ballard/Pointel connection is presently unknown.

---

33 See Pointel 25 and 26 in the appendix, pp. 144–145 below.
34 See Pointel 9, 13, 14, 17, and 23 in the appendix, pp. 137, 138–139, 140–141, and 143 below.
35 At least we know from annotations in his own "Catalogue des livres de musique ... qui sont dans le Cabinet de Sr. Sébastien de Brossard" (F-Pn) that Brossard owned the copy of Pointel 13 now at F-Pn (Rés. Vm Crlt 241). We also know, according to a catalogue of Amédée Le Chevalier's editions found at the end of Jacque de Gouy's *Airs à quatre parties sur la paraphrase des pseaumes* (Amsterdam, 1791: see *RISM* A/I, G 3219), that Le Chevalier sold copies of music printed by Pointel. See Vanhulst.
36 See Ballard/Pointel 26 in the appendix, pp. 144–145 below.

Jean Stichter

Among the Dutch printers of Lully's music, Jean Stichter had the smallest involvement of any. His sole publication was a *RECUEIL. De tous les Airs a Jouer sur le Violon & sur la Flute DE L'OPERA D'ARMIDE* printed for Nicolas Derosier. Stichter came from a family of printers with Antwerp connections, but his father maintained a shop in Amsterdam. According to a note in one of his earliest publications, his shop was "in de Kalverstraat bij de Kapel in den ouden bergh Calvarien." "Kalverstraat" is the same street named by Pointel, whose involvement with Derosier has already been discussed. We know very little about Stichter, but he was one of the first Dutch printers and publishers to announce (in 1686) that he sold music "printed in a newly invented way." Unfortunately, Stichter is only briefly mentioned in Eeghen's study and we must rely on the sketch provided by Goovaerts over a century ago.[37] Stichter published several liturgical books with plainchant during the early 1690s, including a Graduale and an Antiphonarium, and his presses were active from *c.* 1675 to *c.* 1700. His edition of excerpts from *Armide* is similar in every respect to those issued by Pointel and in spite of the fact that the title page carries no date, it was probably printed in the late 1680s or early 1690s. Derosier, for whom the volume was printed, was actively involved in Pointel's business at this same time, and although his death date is unknown, he can be documented only until the end of the seventeenth century.[38]

Pieter and Joan Blaeu and Amédée Le Chevalier

The brothers Blaeu must be considered together with Amédée Le Chevalier (*c.* 1650–1720) because Pieter (1637–1706) and Joan (1650–1712) actually printed books edited and arranged by Le Chevalier until 1692 when Le Chevalier began to print his own books.[39] It seems that Le Chevalier came

37 See Goovaerts, 137–138 and Poole/Krummel, 249. A brief notice about Stichter is given in Kleerkooper, 1501. Leuven, 63–64 gives the dates for Johannes Stichter as 1637 +/– 1705.
38 See Stichter 1 in the appendix, p. 000 below.
39 See Eeghen, vol. III, 22–27 for a detailed discussion of the Blaeus' printing and selling activities, as well as titles of some of the non-musical volumes they published. Joan and Pieter belonged to a distinguished family of printers known for publishing splendid atlases and numerous other fine books. Pieter is further known to have had a strong tie with Antonio Magliabechi (librarian of the Biblioteca Medicea Laurenziana in Florence) and to the Florentine Court. Veen

114

to Amsterdam in the 1680s as a musician, and on December 1, 1689 he was granted a fifteen-year privilege to publish music. Le Chevalier's main importance rests in being the first to publish Lully's trios in anthologies and in continuing to publish Italian works for Dutch consumption. His first publication, entitled *LES TRIO DES OPERA DE MONSIEUR DE LULLY, Mis en ordre pour les concerts* (vol. I 1690, vol. II 1691), was financed by the Amsterdam merchant Daniel Robethon, who agreed to pay for an edition of 1,000 copies, and printed by the Blaeu brothers.[40] Volume one of the anthology contains a lengthy "AVIS AU LECTEUR" signed by Le Chevalier in which he explains various principles behind the edition: (1) he has chosen trios because they are "the most sought-after pieces and the least difficult to perform";[41] (2) he has transposed the clefs "de la haute contre, de la Taille, & du Bas desus" into a single clef that is better understood in Holland by those learning to play the flute or violin; (3) he has taken care "to group pieces together by mode in order to avoid moving from one mode to another which commonly interrupts performances."[42] In closing his "AVIS" Le Chevalier promised to use more elegant type in the future than he was able to use in this, his first edition.

Le Chevalier's other publication printed by Blaeu to include music by Lully, a collection of Italian arias dated 1691, is similar in scope to Pointel's *Airs Italiens* thought to have been published *c.* 1690.[43] Pointel's collection

describes P. Blaeu as a "roving agent of the business, traveling tirelessly through Europe to sell and to buy books and to seek assistance in completing the plans launched by his father." See Veen, 133 and passim. Concerning Le Chevalier see Eeghen, vol. III, 202–203 and Vlam. Various of Eeghen's findings about Le Chevalier are summarized in English by Vanhulst. Their accounts are the basis for the background given here.

40 See Blaeu 1a and 1b in the appendix, pp. 145–151 below. Le Chevalier's claim that the trios are by Lully is not completely true. Lully wrote the clear majority, but small groups were composed by Collasse (from *Thétis et Pélée* of 1689 and *Achille et Polyxène* of 1688 [portions not by Lully himself]) and by Louis and Jean-Louis de Lully (from their *Zéphire et Flore* of 1688). Concerning the agreement between Le Chevalier and Robethon (dated July 24, 1690), see ScheurleerA.

41 "les pieces les plus recherchées, & les moins dificiles à executer."

42 "de mettre tous les tons de suite afin d'eviter l'interruption qui se fait pour entrer d'un ton à un autre, & qui trouble ordinairement les concerts."

43 For more *Airs italiens*, see the collection gathered by François Fossard and André Danican Philidor *l'aîné* (Paris: Pierre Ballard, 1695: copy in F-V MSK 1a [see *RISM* B/I, 1595[5]]). The fact that this collection of thirteen arias includes one by Lully led the author to check Le Chevalier's publication for possible Lully inclusions.

contains twenty short arias, not one of which has yet been attributed to
either a composer or a larger work from which it was taken (if in fact these
arias belong to longer compositions such as operas), whereas Blaeu's somewhat longer *SCELTA* contains twenty-five excerpts. Again, like Pointel, Le
Chevalier omits the composer's names, but with this collection we have
been more fortunate in recognizing three arias, all with Italian texts, that
come from Lully's *Le Bourgeois gentilhomme*. Of the remaining twenty-two
arias, I have been able to identify only three, from Antonio Cesti's opera *Il
Tito*, first performed in Venice during 1666.[44] As with many Venetian
operas, the libretto was printed in 1666 for its premiere performance and
also for various revivals, but until now no music is known to have been published during the seventeenth century. In the hope that someone may identify the remaining pieces, a full list of textual incipits appears in the
bibliographical scrutiny.[45]

Le Chevalier's last known publication to include music by Lully, a
partition réduite of thirty-six excerpts from *Bellérophon*, was issued in 1692,
without the assistance of P. & J. Blaeu. This engraved edition, preceded by a
full-page coat of arms, is quite handsome and represents an artistic advance

44 Concerning *Il Tito*, see SchmidtE.
45 See Blaeu 2, pp. 151–153 below. The author is grateful to Lowell Lindgren for
    checking incipits from this volume through his extensive files of cantatas and
    opera excerpts, even though no further identifications have resulted. Aside from
    the publications discussed here, only three other Blaeu/Le Chevalier
    collaborations are known. In 1691 they published the following works: a set of
    parts for Charles Rosier's *Pièces choisies à la manière italienne . . .* (see *RISM* A/I,
    R 2653); a single volume entitled *Recueil d'airs nouveaux, serieux et à boire, de
    différents autheurs . . .* (see *RISM* B/I, 16913); and another single volume entitled
    *Airs à quatre parties sur la paraphrases des Pseaumes de Messire Antoine Godeau,
    composez par Monsieur Jacques de Gouy* (see *RISM* A/I, G 3219). An
    advertisement dated December 27, 1691, reprinted in Eeghen, vol. III, 203,
    mentions most of Le Chevalier's known musical activity through that date:
    "Amadeus le Chevalier, continueert in 't publicq te verkopen nieuwe Airs, 't welk
    hij belooft heeft alle drie maenden uit te geven. Van Dubuyson, van Cousset,
    Bausse en andre voorname meesters; hij verkoopt ook de Trios van de Operaes
    van Mons. de Lully in 6 partie, voor de fluytjes, violen en eenige andere
    instrumenten; sij sijn ook bequaem voor de liefhebbers van 't singen. Item een
    gedeelte getrokken uit de beste Italiaense Operaes, met eene stem en twee
    instrumenten. De Simphonie van Charles Rosiers, voor de fluyte of violons in 3
    partije; de psalmen van Godeau, in 4 partie, en seer ligte wijse om de muzyk te
    leeren; dit alles wert verkogt op de Pijpe-markt, naast het Schilt van Vrankrijk,
    en in den Haeg bij de Broeders van Dolle, in de Pote."

over the editions produced with the Blaeus. Since no reduced score of *Bellérophon* had been issued in either Paris or Amsterdam, Le Chevalier (whose preface to *Les Trio* makes clear that he could arrange music himself) may have made the reduction.[46] The music, presented in LWV order, is not altered in any way and therefore requires no particular comment.

After *Bellérophon*, Le Chevalier must have turned to activities unrelated to publishing Lully. Very little is known about his career after 1692 except that he spent some time as a printer in Ghent around 1698 before returning to Holland in 1702.[47] Following a promising beginning which included issuing the first anthology of Lully trios, the mantle was passed to Estienne Roger, who wore it proudly in the waning years of the seventeenth and early years of the eighteenth century.

Estienne Roger

Estienne Roger (1664/65–1722) is the only Amsterdam printer of Lully's music whose Lully output did not make up a large percentage of the firm's total publications. The most prolific and important publisher of those under consideration in this study (his complete catalogue numbers over five hundred works), Roger issued numerous histories, grammars, and other works in addition to an impressive list of music publications.[48] Although he printed approximately twenty Lully editions (about 4 percent of his total output), the musical portion of his vast catalogue was dominated by works of composers such as Corelli, Torelli, Veracini, Albicastro, and Albinoni.[49]

---

46 The first Amsterdam edition was by Roger, *c.* 1700–01. The Parisian *partition réduite* by Christophe Ballard was not issued until 1714.

47 For example, he published a series of *Recueils d'airs nouveaux, serieux et à boire, de différents autheurs* beginning in 1692. See *RISM* B/I, 1692[4], 1692[5], 1692[6], and 1692[7].

48 See Koole for general information about Roger's activities as a printer.

49 The most succinct overview of Roger's musical output occurs in an advertisement inserted in Roger's 1714 edition of *Les Victoires de l'Amour ou histoires de Zaïde* (see LesureE, 37). LesureB contains the most detailed account of Roger's musical editions, including reproductions of period catalogues listing his music and transcriptions of advertisements that appeared in seventeenth- and eighteenth-century periodicals. Hortschansky provides new information about Roger's earlier musical publications, revising some of Lesure's dates, and listing a few of Roger's non-musical offerings. Eeghen, vol. II, 58–72 cites sixteen of Roger's joint editions with de Lorme.

CARL B. SCHMIDT

Moreover, Roger's editions were highly prized among musicians of the eighteenth century. No less a commentator than Sir John Hawkins, writing in 1776 of Estienne Roger and Michel Charles Le Cène, "two booksellers of Amsterdam," noted that "These persons were the greatest publishers of music in Europe; and as they greatly improved the method of printing music on copper plates, are entitled to particular notice."[50]

Roger, a French Protestant, had emigrated to Amsterdam from Caen in Normandy with his family after the Edict of Nantes was revoked in 1685.[51] Once in Amsterdam, he entered the printing business as an apprentice to Antoine Pointel (for three and a half years) and then to Jean-Louis de Lorme (for one year) between 1691 and 1695. From Pointel he must have gained considerable experience with music engraving and from de Lorme experience with the non-music book trade.[52] Roger, already mentioned as a "marchand" in 1691, is listed in the 1695 rolls of the association of booksellers, printers, and binders.[53] His career as a publisher commenced in 1696, when he printed a number of books jointly with de Lorme, and he worked independently from 1697 for about twenty-five years. Roger had two daughters: Jeanne (1701–22), to whom he willed his business – using her name on title pages after September 1716 – and Françoise (1694–1723), who married Michel Charles Le Cène in 1716.[54] Unfortunately, as Jeanne died on December 10, 1722, she survived her father by only a few short

50 See Hawkins, vol. II, 800. Roger North also spoke highly of "Stephen Rogers in Holland," whose music was "wonderfull fair." See Poole/Krummel, 249. On 253 they note the following about Roger's method of engraving: "It seems that Roger engraved his vertical folios on large plates (278 mm deep × 516 mm wide for example) with two pages to view, to provide a fold down the middle; his oblong music is usually printed on a single plate to a page ..."
51 See PogueR, 99. Most of the documentary material given by Pogue is found in Eeghen, vol. IV, 68–75. See also Kleerkooper, 639–640 and LesureB, 9–30.
52 According to information found in Eeghen, vol. I, 60ff., de Lorme frequently corresponded with Christophe Ballard in Paris.
53 PogueR, 99.
54 Jeanne's birthdate, given as 1692 in PogueR, 99, is actually May 13, 1701 (see LesureB, 10). Lesure also gives a summary of Roger's will: "l'editeur stipule que jusqu'à la majorité de sa fille Jeanne les planches de cuivre du fonds d'édition resteraient leur propriété commune et qu'elles ne pourraient être utilisées par ses exécuteurs testamentaires, à l'exception des planches des opéras de Lully, *Cadmus, Proserpine* et *Alceste*, et des planches des œuvres qui avaient été gravées deux fois, dont les doubles pouvaient être vendus pour être fondus ou pouvaient être utilisés pour de nouvelles planches après avoir été rendus inutilisables."

118

months, and the business was then left to a Roger employee named Gerrit Drinkman (Françoise having been previously cut out of Jeanne's will). Drinkman ran the firm for several months before his own death and the business was finally bought in mid-1723 by Le Cène, who successfully ran it for another twenty years. Le Cène's Lully activities will be discussed in greater detail below.

Roger's Lully catalogue rivals that of his mentor Pointel; together they far exceed the scope and number of Lully pieces published by all the other Dutch printers. His engraved editions include excerpts from twelve of the fourteen *tragédies lyriques* (lacking only *Achille et Polyxène* and *Thésée* – which never appeared in Holland), three works in other genres (*Acis et Galatée*, *Le Temple de la Paix*, and *Le Triomphe de l'Amour*), plus two volumes of trios predominantly devoted to Lully, and two volumes of suites for various instruments including lute, violin, flute, and *basse-continue*.[55] The first of these two volumes of suites contains only isolated pieces by Lully and the second volume is known only from advertisements (see Roger 18 and 19 respectively). Most of the Roger volumes are entitled *Ouverture avec tous les airs à jouer de l'opéra . . .*, and contain between eighteen and thirty-three excerpts. Those excerpts, originally scored for the normal five-part French string ensembles, have been reduced to four parts: dessus, second dessus, taille, and basse.[56] Only one Roger edition, *Le Temple de la Paix* (Roger 15), is arranged in LWV order.[57] All the others are presented as suites suitable for concert use by small ensembles.

Apparently Roger harbored great aspirations as a publisher of Lully's music. Marc Pincherle drew attention to correspondence between Jean-Louis de Lorme in Amsterdam and Christophe Ballard in Paris dating from 1707 and 1708 during which de Lorme told Ballard (August 8, 1707):

> I have seen M Roger, who still seems unhappy to me; I won't go into whether he has cause since this is none of my business. He showed me tools from which to have music type molds made and he claims that by the end of the year he will have a font of the most beautiful type there is in the world and

---

55 We exclude discussion of Roger 20, *De Musyk Schouwtoneel*, about which virtually nothing is presently known.

56 The process of editing and reducing Lully's scores is thoroughly discussed in SchneiderA.

57 Only LWV 69/14 and 69/18 are reversed.

[that he intends] to publish the works of M Lully more beautifully and more accurately than the editions you [Ballard] issue. We shall see what will become of it . . .[58]

De Lorme wrote to Ballard again on August 29, 1707 about Roger and on January 12, 1708 sent Ballard a catalogue of Roger's publications via Lille. For his part, Ballard seems not to have responded to de Lorme's last letter and in one of February 2, 1708 de Lorme showed impatience before indicating that Roger was preoccupied because of a dispute with Pierre Mortier concerning Mortier's "piracy" of his editions.[59] Precisely what Ballard's interest was in this intrigue cannot be determined because none of Ballard's responses to de Lorme have survived, but Ballard was probably sought out by Roger to be his agent. De Lorme appears to have acted as a go-between, but the final act in this relationship between four men – de Lorme, Ballard, Roger, and Mortier – must await our introduction of Mortier. In any event, Roger apparently never published any of Lully's works from new type in corrected editions and the issue only resurfaced during his controversy with Mortier.

Even if Roger's later Lully plans never materialized, his commitment to Lully's music was clearly established by his early publications. Roger was the last Dutch printer to publish anthologies of Lully's works, and his musical publications were disseminated throughout Europe to a degree unparalleled at the time. As early as 1706 he had agents in Cologne and London, and by 1716 his foreign legion had been enlarged to include Rotterdam, Berlin, Liège, Leipzig, Halle, Brussels, Utrecht, and Hamburg.[60]

58 See Pincherle, 88 (and note that he clearly expresses his debt to Eeghen for having found the letters from which he quotes "dans les archives de l'église wallonne [Waalse Kerk] d'Amsterdam"). The original French, printed by Pincherle, reads: "J'ay vu Mr. Roger, qui me paroit toujours malcontant, je n'entre point s'il a raison, ce ne sont pas là mes affaires, il m'a montré des instruments pour faire faire des matrisses de musique et il prétend avoir à la fin de cette année une fonte des plus belles qui soient dans le monde et de faire les opéra de Mr. Lully plus beaux et plus correctes que l'édition que vous en faites, nous verrons ce qui en sera." Eeghen, vol. V, 382 notes that de Lorme printed five volumes of André Dacier's translations of Horace for Ballard.

59 See Pincherle, 88–89. Summaries of these letters are also given in Eeghen, vol. I, 60–61.

60 See Pincherle, 83 and 87, who based his information on the following statements recovered from Roger catalogues: (1706) "Catalogue des livres de Musique nouvellement imprimés à Amsterdam chez Estienne Roger, Marchand Libraire,

One of his London agents, for example, was the famous John Walsh (i); the same gentleman with whom Roger had had a significant disagreement in 1700.[61] Roger advertised his stock widely, not only printing separate catalogues that he inserted in books he sold between 1698 and 1716, but also in London and Amsterdam journals. His successor Le Cène continued to advertise and sell Roger's editions until his own death in 1743.

Pierre Mortier

Prior to Eeghen's work, relatively little was known about Pierre Mortier (1661–1711) or the family to which he belonged.[62] Eeghen gathered a wealth of information about Mortier's non-musical publications, establishing that between 1685 and 1711 Mortier published numerous books in French on diverse subjects plus a modicum of works in Latin, Italian, Spanish, and Dutch. Mortier's musical output, like Roger's, was strong in contemporary Italian music; works of Corelli, Albinoni, Torelli, Marini, and others grace his catalogue. He also published music by French composers including Chambonnières and Lully, French treatises or musical dictionaries by Sébastien de Brossard and others, and even English duos by H. Purcell and J. Eccles. Mortier is known to have sought out and opened up a market for his books in Leipzig.[63]

Mortier's known involvement with Lully's music as a publisher, however, came only at the end of his life. It is inextricably linked to the controversy, first signaled in de Lorme's February 2, 1708 letter to Christophe Ballard in Paris with the words: "but I will tell you confidentially that he [Roger] is at war with Mortier, the bookseller from here [Amsterdam], and it is he [Mortier] who is counterfeiting his [Roger's] music, and has corrupted

ou dont il a nombre, avec les prix, et qui se vendent à Londres, chez François et Paul Vaillant, libraires dans le Strand, à Cologne chez Philippe Poner, Facteur de Poste de Liége, demeurant dans le Kloeger-Gas"; and (1716) "à Londres chez Henry Ribotteau, à Berlin chez A. Dussarrat, à Halle chez A. Sellius[,] à Cologne chez P. Poner, à Bruxelles chez Joseph Serstevens Marchands Libraires, et à Hamburg chez Jean Chrestien Schickhardt, fameux Componiste." See also PogueR, 100 and LesureB, 21–22.

61 For a brief summary of Walsh's business arrangement with Roger after 1716, see Kidson *et al.*, 186. See also SmithB, xvi–xvii and LesureB, 12–13.

62 See Eeghen, vol. III, 256–265. Eeghen uses the Dutch spelling "Pieter" Mortier.

63 See Laeven, 185–197.

the workers of M Roger."[64] Ten years after Pincherle wrote about the Roger/Mortier controversy, François Lesure thoroughly reevaluated the evidence in his well-known article "Estienne Roger et Pierre Mortier: Un épisode de la guerre des contrefaçons à Amsterdam," adding new documents unknown to Pincherle. Most important was Lesure's discovery of a gazette entitled *Nouvelles de la République des Lettres* that became Mortier's property in June of 1708 and that he used as an organ for his own publicity.[65] By January 1709 Mortier advertised the following intention: ". . . [to print] the operas of the late M de Lully and those of other authors. In four weeks *l'Europe galante* [music by André Campra]. The printing will surpass in beauty any music that has ever been seen before, great expense having been spent in order to create a printing establishment with all types of music books."[66] Then, in August of the same year, Mortier published a catalogue that issued the following challenge: "The public and principally musical amateurs are informed that the aforementioned Mortier is working to correct the majority of editions of Italian and French music, and that he is having them (it) engraved with such beauty and accuracy that none have ever been seen which are so handsome or precise. The aforementioned Mortier also advises that he sells this music for two thirds cheaper than it is sold by other booksellers."[67]

---

64 The French text was first cited by Pincherle, 89, but our discussion is based on the slightly different reading in Eeghen, vol. I, 61: "Je vous diray entre nous qu'il est en guerre avec Mortier, libraire d'icy, et luy contrefait sa musique, lequel a debouchées les ouvriers a monsieur Roger."

65 See LesureE. Our discussion is based on information contained in Lesure's article.

66 See LesureE, 38: "les opéras de feu Mr. de Lully et ceux des autres auteurs. Dans quatre semaines *l'Europe galante*. L'impression surpassera en beauté tout ce qu'on a jamais vu en musique, ayant fait de grandes dépenses pour établir une imprimerie de toutes sortes de livres en musique." Anthony discusses the Campra edition, giving a diplomatic transcription of its title page on which Mortier claims that his firm "vend toutes sortes de Musique, les plus belles & Correctes qu'il y ait du Monde. Et il donnera toutes les Operas de Mr. Lully, de la même Grandeur & Beauté que cet Ouvrage." Anthony also prints a translated excerpt from Mortier's dedication to his niece, Agata Amelia Cocquis, in which it is stated: "I dedicate this work to you. It is the first that I have brought out which is worthy of your study . . . I hope to publish all the most beautiful pieces of music and principally those by Monsieur de Lully. I will present these to you after they are printed." See AnthonyP, 57–58.

67 See LesureE, 39: "On avertit le Public et principalement les Amateurs de Musique, que ledit Mortier fait travailler à la correction de la plus grande partie

Further on, Mortier spoke of correcting more than six hundred mistakes in five *opere* by Corelli and of all the elegant refinements he had made to the headings, spacing, and other technical and aesthetic aspects of these editions. As Lesure points out, Roger wasted no time responding to what he considered to be a boastful challenge to both his editorial policies and his skills as a publisher. He addressed the issue of Mortier's counterfeit editions in an essay and catalogue inserted in his edition of Rapin's *Œuvres diverses* (1710).[68] Roger confronted Mortier (who is not mentioned by name) in uncompromising terms: "Estienne Roger, shopkeeper and bookseller in Amsterdam, who sells the most accurate music that has ever been published, also sells it cheaper than anyone else. You are going to see proof of these two truths at the end of this advertisement, where the price of music that has been counterfeited is marked and also the price that he [Roger] sells it for, and through a comparison of corrections that he [Roger] engraved with those that have been counterfeited . . ."[69] In effect, Roger, thoroughly disgusted that Mortier had pirated approximately seventy of his editions, stated his willingness to meet Mortier's lower price if the potential buyer could provide written documentation.

Apparently, Mortier did not technically keep his promise to publish Lully's music in elegant corrected editions until 1711, the last year of his life.[70] Aside from a reprint of Lully trios (publication date unknown), Mortier issued *Phaéton* and *Roland* in handsome *partitions générales*, both dated 1711, and an undated "Nouvelle édition" of *Persée* in a *partition réduite*.[71]

---

de la Musique Italienne et Françoise, et qu'il la fait graver avec tant de beauté et d'exactitude qu'on n'en a jamais eu de si belle ni de si correcte. Ledit Mortier avertit aussi qu'il vendra ladite Musique les deux tiers à meilleur marché qu'elle ne se vend chez les autres Libraires." Lesure prints the entire French text for this 1709 catalogue as well as that for a later catalogue inserted in the sixth edition of Brossard's *Dictionnaire*.

68 The original French text for this catalogue is given in LesureE, 40–44.
69 See LesureE, 40: "Estienne Roger, marchand libraire à Amsterdam, qui vend la Musique la plus correcte qui se soit jamais imprimée, la vend aussi à meilleur marché que qui que ce soit. L'on va voir des preuves de ces deux vérités dans la suitte de cet Avertissement, en y marquant le prix qu'on vend la Musique qu'on lui a contrefait, et le prix qu'il la vend, et en comparant la correction des ouvrages qu'il grave à celle des ouvrages qu'on lui contrefait."
70 Our only reason for caution is that we do not know the precise date when Mortier reissued Blaeu's two volumes of trios.
71 See Mortier 1–3 in the appendix, pp. 162–164 below.

Because Mortier died in February of 1711, he must already have completed major production work on the three Lully *tragédies lyriques* during 1710. His two *partitions générales* are the first such Dutch editions of Lully since Pointel's *Achille et Polyxène* in 1689 and the only non-Parisian full scores issued except for Le Cène's restrikes from Mortier's engraved plates. James Anthony, who examined Mortier's claim about the aesthetics and accuracy of his editions by comparing Mortier's editions of *L'Europe galante* with the known Parisian editions, states that it is "the most beautifully printed of all the editions of this opera-ballet," that "Mortier, if indeed he was responsible for the preparation of the edition, took pains to correct some of the errors found in Ballard III [Paris: Christophe Ballard, 1699]," and that "there is some evidence of carelessness, not uncommon at this time, in Mortier's figuring of the continuo."[72] Our comparison of Mortier's Lully editions with those of Ballard (either printed or in de Baussen's engraved versions) confirms Anthony's findings.

A comparison of Mortier's edition of *Phaéton* with the Paris *partition générale* (Christophe Ballard, 1683) reveals that Mortier (1) incorporated most of the manuscript penned corrections found in many Ballard scores; (2) followed Ballard's page layout, but numbered the pages consecutively (1–273); (3) added an engraved illustration and verbal description of a stage set to the beginning of the prologue and each act (the engravings printed on especially thick paper); (4) omitted the dedicatory "Au Roy" found in the Paris editions, but added a "CATALOGUE *Des Livres de Musique qui se trouvent Chez Ledit* MORTIER" on the verso of the title page; (5) changed Ballard's "t" sign designating ornaments to a "+" sign and added a brace to the left margin of each page.[73] The added engravings and verbal descriptions of stage sets are the same as those found in de Baussen's 1709 edition (see *RISM* A/I, L 3003). A comparison of Mortier's edition of *Roland* with Ballard's 1686 Parisian publication reveals most of the same points except that Mortier did not include engravings of sets. Rather, he used decorative engravings at the end of each act. He was also far less consis-

72 See AnthonyP, 57–58.
73 Rosow, vol. I, 29–44 contains information concerning Ballard's practice of correcting errors in his printed scores. We have compared Mortier's edition with two copies of the Ballard edition found in F-Pn (Vm² 68 and Vm² 68A).

tent in correcting errors found in the Ballard score of *Roland* than in his edition of *Phaéton*.[74]

Finally, we can offer a few observations concerning Mortier's undated *partition réduite* of *Persée*. Here the yardstick of comparison must be de Baussen's engraved *partition réduite* (Paris, 1710: *RISM* A/I, L 2993). Although accused by Roger as a pirate of his editions, Mortier did not copy any of Roger's Lully editions, nor did he copy de Baussen's 1710 edition of *Persée*. To begin with, the formats used are entirely different; Mortier's is an oblong quarto ([2] + 384 pp.) and de Baussen's an upright folio ([2] + 229 pp.). Moreover, the reductions themselves are considerably different. The chorus "Heureuse intelligence" (LWV 60/12), for example, is reduced to four parts by de Baussen, but given in six parts by Mortier. Mortier also provides fewer figures in the *basse-continue*.

In spite of the severe rivalry between Roger and his contemporary Mortier, each made a significant contribution to the life of Lully's music in the waning years of the seventeenth or the dawn of the eighteenth century. Ethics aside, and we do know that Mortier directly copied Blaeu's two volumes of trios, Mortier's Lully editions are elegantly engraved and should be taken into account because of the corrections they contain. Their availability well into the eighteenth century was assured because Le Cène, to whom we now turn, reprinted them. Perhaps Roger had the last word when, upon Mortier's death in 1711, he purchased his stock and plates from his widow. Subsequently Roger had his revenge by publishing some of Mortier's editions under his own name but with the annotation "Le même livre beaucoup mieux gravé et nouvellement corrigé par Estienne Roger sur l'impression de Mortier"![75]

Michel Charles Le Cène

Michel Charles Le Cène (1683/84–1743), a native of Honfleur, enters the sphere of our study in 1716 when, at age thirty-two, he married

74 In Mortier's defense it should be stressed that a survey of more than twenty exemplars of Ballard's edition reveals considerable discrepancy in the manuscript correction of errors. Mortier even became confused in some places, correcting the text in one voice but leaving it uncorrected in another. Space here precludes any more detailed discussion of this phenomenon.

75 See LesureB, 20 for a similar statement on an edition of Froberger's keyboard works.

Françoise Roger.[76] Pincherle was able to document that on February 18, 1717 Le Cène was received as a "bourgeois d'Amsterdam" and that on May 31 he was welcomed by the brotherhood of booksellers, printers, and bookbinders. Le Cène's activities from 1717 to 1723 include the publication of several non-music books (his address is given by the *Gazette* as "dans le Nes a Amsterdam"), but there is little documentation and we cannot say if he had any hand in Roger's business, now carried on in part by Roger's daughter Jeanne.[77] His major significance is as the owner of the firm after Jeanne's death and ownership had passed through Gerrit Drinkman (see the details given above in our discussion of Roger). Le Cène actually acquired the business from Drinkman's widow and on June 15, 1723 the *Gazette d'Amsterdam* announced, "Michel-Charles Le Cène, Amsterdam bookseller, on the Cingle, opposite the Drie Koningstraat, advises the public, and particularly amateur music lovers, that he is continuing the business of the late M Estienne Roger, his father-in-law, which had been interrupted since his death."[78] After buying the business, Le Cène added nearly one hundred editions to Roger's catalogue and continued reprinting editions to replenish inventory. Reprints were listed under the joint names Estienne Roger & Le Cène, while new additions to the catalogue carried only his own name.[79]

As owner of the firm, Le Cène reprinted three of the four known Mortier editions of Lully's music including *Phaéton* and *Roland* in *partitions*

76 Concerning Le Cène see Pincherle, 86ff. and Eeghen, vol. III, 198–202. According to Swift, 270–271, Le Cène had spent his childhood in Holland, having arrived there with his parents, who had fled France in 1685. He was in business in London with Jacob [James] Moetjens by September 1711, but returned to Amsterdam in 1716. Le Cène maintained a tie with London, however, because Moetjens married his daughter Elizabeth on April 22, 1717. Ultimately James Moetjens, the one son produced by this marriage, acted as heir for Le Cène upon his decease in 1743.

77 The 1721 Le Cène edition of Gherardi's *Le Théâtre italien* (which contains music), is listed by Goovaerts, 460, no. 1028. Koole, cols. 629–630, states that Le Cène was active in the Roger firm between 1717 and 1721, but offers no conclusive proof.

78 See Eeghen, vol. III, 199: "Michel-Charles le Cene, libraire à Amsterdam, sur le Cingle, vis-à-vis le Drie Koningstraat donne avis au public, et particulierement aux amateurs de musique, qu'il continue le commerce de feu Sr. Etienne Roger, son beau-pere, qui avoit été interrompu depuis son décès." Eeghen also prints a slightly later announcement in Dutch from August 22, 1723.

79 See PogueR, 99.

générales and *Persée* in a *partition réduite.* Aside from the inclusion of a newly engraved frontispiece (signed "*Deur f*") in his edition of *Persée,* the musical portions are identical to those published by Mortier. Because none of these editions contains a plate number of the sort initially used by Roger and then continued by Le Cène, we are unable to suggest a *terminus ad quem* for the reprints. And, for whatever reason, Le Cène chose not to reissue Mortier's edition of *Les trios des opéra,* which was already a reprint of an edition by Blaeu. When Le Cène died in 1743, the remaining stock was purchased by G. J. de la Coste and it is not known how much Lully, if any, remained as inventory. His death also severed the last vestigial link with a great Dutch tradition of printing Lully's music.

Conclusions

During the more than forty years between the first Amsterdam publication of Lully's *Cadmus et Hermione* by Jean Philip Heus in 1682 and the last ones of *Persée, Phaéton,* and *Roland* reprinted by Michel Charles Le Cène sometime in the late 1720s, approximately sixty Lully editions were issued by eight Dutch publishers. Contained in volumes ranging from oblong quarto books of instrumental or vocal excerpts to elegant large-folio *partitions générales,* this extensive repertory composed by one of the brightest stars in Louis XIV's galaxy helped satisfy the Dutch appetite for French music and culture. Dutch arrangers and publishers made much of Lully's music available to a more diverse group of consumers by printing excerpts and often by simplifying the instrumental scoring. They also made the music suitable as chamber music by grouping numbers into suites.

However, we have demonstrated that Amsterdam printers were not always followers, but sometimes leaders. Heus, for example, issued the first printed excerpts of music for four of Lully's *tragédies lyriques,* Le Chevalier contributed a collection of Lully trios that even Ballard imitated in Paris, Mortier published *partitions générales* that corrected some errors found in Ballard editions, and the Dutch in general led the way by moving from printing to engraving. These Amsterdam editions deserve our scrutiny not only for the relationship they have to other French printed or engraved editions, but because they reflect the extent to which Lully's music was a dominant force on the European musical scene. The bibliographical information about these editions, previously available only in the diverse works of Pincherle, Lesure, Hortschansky, Walker, Schneider, and others, has been reexamined and expanded in this present study. When considered as a repertoire, it has demonstrated clear connections between printers and publications. Now we can hope that scholars and bibliographers will strive to locate editions known only from advertisements and to clarify the still shrouded relationships between Dutch and Parisian printers. Then the important task of evaluating the musical content of those volumes that have not yet been studied carefully, and of making available modern editions or historical facsimiles for a twenty-first-century clientele, can be undertaken. Even now, the extraordinary *rayonnement* of French culture – and Lully's music in particular – in the Northern Netherlands can be seen more clearly.

Appendix: bibliographical scrutiny

The following bibliographical descriptions of Amsterdam prints containing music by Lully are given in chronological order by printer beginning with Jean Philip Heus, the earliest Dutch printer of his music. Within each printer's œuvre we have maintained a chronological ordering where possible or an alphabetical listing when dates are either unknown or problematic. Works known only from secondary literature, but that cannot now be located, are also listed. Each print is described and its content inventoried according to the LWV (*Lully Werke Verzeichnis*) numbers found in SchneiderC. A typical entry may read: LWV 69: 37 (C: "Gigue" 11). In this entry LWV 69 refers to *Le Temple de la Paix* as found in SchneiderC (and the preceding index); 37 refers to the thirty-seventh number in LWV 69; "C" means that the piece has been transposed to "C" from that listed in SchneiderC; and 11 refers to the eleventh piece in the anthology being described. All known copies of each edition have been cited using abbreviations and *RISM* sigla as listed below.

Abbreviations
B	Basse
Bc	Basse-continue
BVn	Basse de violon
Ds	Dessus

128

DsVn   Dessus de violon
HCVn   Haute-contre de violon
LWV   *Lully Werke Verzeichnis* (see SchneiderC)
QVn   Quinte de violon
MS   Manuscript
TaVn   Taille de violon

An asterisk denotes that this particular number is not listed among the sources described in SchneiderC.

RISM sigla

A: Austria
Wn   Vienna, Österreichische Nationalbibliothek, Musiksammlung

B: Belgium
Bc   Brussels, Bibliothèque, Koninklijk Conservatorium
Br   Brussels, Bibliothèque Royale Albert 1er
Lc   Liège, Conservatoire Royale de musique

C: Canada
Lu   London (Ontario), University of Western Ontario, Lawson
                 Memorial Library
Tu   Toronto, University of Toronto, Edward Johnson Music Library

CH: Switzerland
N   Neuchâtel, Bibliothèque Publique et Universitaire
Zjacobi   Zurich, Former Private Library of Edwin Jacobi (now in CH-Zz)
Zz   Zurich, Zentralbibliothek

CS: Czechoslovakia
Pnm   Prague, Národní Muzeum, Hudební Oddělení

D: Germany
Bds   Berlin, Deutsche Staatsbibliothek
Dl   Dresden, Bibliothek und Museum Löbau [in Dlb]
Dlb   Dresden, Sächische Landesbibliothek
FUl   Fulda, Hessische Landesbibliothek
Hs   Hamburg, Staats- und Universitätsbibliothek Carl von Ossietzky
HEms   Heidelberg, Musikwissenschaftliches Seminar der Ruprecht-Karl-
                 Universität
Mbs   Munich, Bayerisches Staatsbibliothek
ROu   Rostock, Wilhelm-Pieck-Universität, Universitätsbibliothek
Sl   Stuttgart, Württembergische Landesbibliothek
W   Wolfenbüttel, Herzog August Bibliothek
ZW   Zweibrücken, Bibliotheca Bipontina

DK: Denmark

Kk   Det Kongelige Bibliotek

F: France

AM	Amiens, Bibliothèque Municipale
BO	Bordeaux, Bibliothèque Municipale
G	Grenoble, Bibliothèque Municipale
LB	Libourne, Bibliothèque Municipale
Nm	Nantes, Bibliothèque Municipale
Pa	Paris, Bibliothèque de l'Arsenal
Pmeyer	Paris, former Private Library of André Meyer
Pn	Paris, Bibliothèque Nationale (musique)
Po	Paris, Bibliothèque Nationale-Musée de l'Opéra
RS	Reims, Bibliothèque Municipale
Sim	Strasbourg, Institut de Musicologie de l'Université
TLm	Toulouse, Bibliothèque Municipale
V	Versailles, Bibliothèque Municipale

GB: Great Britain

DRc	Durham, Cathedral
DRu	Durham, University Library
Lbl	London, British Library
Lcm	London, Royal College of Music
Lgc	London, Gresham College (Guildhall Library)
Ltc	London, Trinity College of Music
Ob	Oxford, Bodleian Library

I: Italy

Bc	Bologna, Civico Museo Bibliografico Musicale
PAc	Parma, Conservatorio di Musica Arrigo Boito

MO: Monaco

Ml'oiseau-lyre Monte Carlo, Private collection of Madame Margarita Hanson. Library of *Editions de l'Oiseau-Lyre* (collected by Louise Hanson-Dyer)

NL: The Netherlands

DHgm	The Hague, Gemeentemuseum
Lu	Leiden, Universiteitsbibliotheek

S: Sweden

N	Norrköping, Stadsbibliotek
Skma	Statens Musiksamlingar (formerly Kungliga Musikaliska Akademiens Bibliothek)
St	Stockholm, Kungliga Teaterns Bibliotek
Uu	Upsala, Universitetsbiblioteket

US: United States of America

BAo'keefe	Baltimore, Private Library of Mr. O'Keefe
BEfelker	Berkeley, Private Library of Mr. Felker
CAl	Cambridge, Eda Kuhn Loeb Music Library, Harvard University
R	Rochester, Sibley Music Library, Eastman School of Music, University of Rochester
Wc	Washington, Library of Congress (Music Division)

USSR: former Union of Soviet Socialist Republics

Mrg	Moscow, Rossiyskaya Gosudarstvennaya Biblioteka (formerly Ml, Lenin Librari)

Editions of Jean Philip Heus containing music of Jean-Baptiste Lully (listed by date of publication)

HEUS 1: TITLE – [Engraved title page of four musicians surrounding a vignette of Cadmus slaying the chimera. DsVn and BVn partbooks are open at the top center showing the beginning of LWV 49/15, and on the base of the scene are inscribed the words] *Ouverture auec tous les airs de L'opera de Cadmus | Fait à paris par Mons.ᵣ Jean Baptiste lully sur Intendant | de la Musique du Roy | Imprime a Amsterdam par J: P: Heus. 1682.*

DATE – 1682

DESCRIPTION – Four parts: Dessus de violon (14 pp.); Havte-Contre [de violon] (8 pp.: wanting last three pp.); [Taille de violon (14 pp.)]; Basse de violon (extant copy incomplete: contains only the last 4 pp. and has a *collette* on the final page)

CONTENTS – Contains twenty-two pieces arranged as suites including **LWV 49:** 1 (1), 4 (17), 5 (15), 8 (12), 10 (2), 14 (16), 15 (3), 22 (19 "Chaconne"), 34 (4), 36 (5 "Air du Prologue"), 42 (9), 44 (10), 47 (11), 51 (7), 54 (13), 55 (14), 56 (d: 6 "Menuet"), 57* (8); **LWV 59:** 43 (18b), 45 (18a); at the end three unidentified "Menuets" are given (20–22)

NOTES – This collection contains two pieces borrowed from *Le Triomphe de l'Amour* (LWV 59). Pages 1–10 of each part appear to be the work of one engraver (six staves/page, more refined hand), with pp. 11–14 that of a different engraver (seven staves/page, bolder hand). The three unidentified "Menuets" also appear in an edition by Estienne Roger (Amsterdam [1702]); see Roger 7.

COPIES – **GB**-Lbl (K.7.c.2.(11.)) [DsVn, TaVn, BVn (which lacks all pieces before no. 18): see *CPM*, XXXVI, p. 374]; **US**-R (M1505.L956) [HCVn only]

BIBLIOGRAPHY – *RISM* A/I, L 2981; SchneiderC, p. 210; SchneiderR, p. 333

HEUS 2: TITLE – [Engraving of four musicians surrounding Perseus, mounted on a horse holding the head of Medusa. Beneath the scene are inscribed the words] *Ouverture auec tous les airs de Violons de L'opera de | Perséé fait á paris par Mons.ᵣ Ian Baptiste lully | Conseiller e. Sur Intendant de la Musique du Roy. | Imprimée a' Amsterdam par Iean Philip Heus 1682*

DATE – 1682

DESCRIPTION – Four parts: Dessus de violon (14 pp.: title page wanting); Haute-contre de violon (no copy located); Taille de violon (16 pp.); Basse de violon (14 pp.: title page wanting)

CONTENTS – Contains twenty-nine pieces arranged as suites including **LWV 60**: 1 (1), 6 (6), 10 (10), 11 (9), 26 (20), 28 (14), 29 (15), 30 (13), 31 (19), 44 (25), 45 (12), 47 (26), 49 (27), 50 (17), 56 (18), 57* (16), 59 (24), 69 (29), 70 (22), 71 (21), 72 (23), 73 (28), 76 (4), 77 (3), 78 (7), 79 (8), 81 (11), 82 (5), 84 (2)

COPIES – **GB**-Lbl (K.7.c.2.(12.)) [DsVn, TaVn, and BVn only: see *CPM*, XXXVI, p. 375]; a copy of what may be this edition was offered for sale by Scientific Library Service, cat. 59, no. 358 with the indication "Arrangement for the 'Haute-Contre.'"

BIBLIOGRAPHY – *RISM* A/I, L 2999; SchneiderC, p. 370; SchneiderR, p. 333

HEUS 3: TITLE – [Engraving with a large border of instruments (resembling the proscenium of a stage) framing Phaéton falling from the sky on his chariot. Below the scene are inscribed the words] Ouverture *avec tous les airs de Violons de* L'opera | *de* Phaeton *fait a' paris par Mons:* Baptist *de* | Lullij *Conseiller Secretaire et sur intendant de la* | *Musique* du Roij. | *Imprimée a' Amsterdam par Iean Philip Heus 1683.* | [signed "*P. Schenck Fcit*" in the lower right corner]

DATE – 1683

DESCRIPTION – Four parts: Dessus de violon (12 pp.: title page wanting); Haute-contre de violon (no copy located); Taille de violon (10 pp.); Basse de violon (12 pp.: title page wanting)

CONTENTS – Contains twenty-nine pieces arranged as suites including **LWV 61**: 1 (1), 2 (4), 6 (17), 7 (18), 8 (5), 14 (2), 15* (3), 23 (7), 25 (6), 27 (8), 29 (16), 37 (9), 40* (15), 41 (13), 47 (27), 48 (20), 50 (28), 52 (19), 53 (25), 55 (26), 57 (10), 58 (11), 59 (12), 61 (14), 66 (23 "Prelude"), 66 (24 "Choeur"), 67 (21), 68 (22), 72 (29)

COPIES – **GB**-Lbl (K.7.c.2.(13.)) TaVn lacks nos. 11–18 [see *CPM*, XXXVI, p. 375]; a copy of one part was listed for sale in Scientific Library Service, cat. 59, no. 359 with the note "Three leaves defective at upper outer corners, with considerable loss of music. Arrangement for the 'Haute-Contre.'"

BIBLIOGRAPHY – *RISM* A/I, L 3011; SchneiderC, p. 389; SchneiderR, p. 331

HEUS 4: TITLE – [Engraved title page of two warriors jousting. On a pillar to the right are inscribed the words] *OUVERTURE* | *avec tous les airs de Violons* | *de L OPERA d AMADIS* | *fait à paris par Mons* | *BAPTISTE de LULLY.* | [signed below by the engraver] *B' Overbeek inv.* | *P. Schenk fecit 1684.* | [and then continuing] *Imprimee à Amsterdam par Iean Philip Heus 1684.*

DATE – 1684

DESCRIPTION – Four parts: Dessus de violon [14 pp.]; Havt-con[t]re [de violon] [12 pp.: lacks title page]; Taille de violon [14 pp.]; Basse de violon [12 pp.: lacks title page]

CONTENTS – Contains twenty-six pieces (numbered 1–25 with the Ouverture not numbered) arranged as suites including **LWV 63:** 1 (not numbered), 4 (1), 5 (2), 10 (21), 11 (19), 12 (20), 22 (7), 23 (8), 24 (9), 26 (14), 29 (3), 33 (18), 34 (4), 36 (5), 41 (12), 42 (11), 46 (6), 48 (15), 49 (16), 50 (17), 55 (22), 57 (23), 58 (24), 59 (25), 60 (13), 67 (10)

NOTES – BVn misnumbers piece 25 as 24. This and the other Heus prints (except Heus 5) measure approximately 167 × 208 mm. According to an advertisement in the 1684 *livret* for *Amadis* ([Amsterdam]: "Suivant la Copie imprimée à Paris"), "Les Curieux sçauront qu'il se vend aussi les Airs, à chanter & à joüer sur les violons, chez Antoine Pointel." This advertisement must refer to Heus's edition.

COPIES – **GB**-Lbl (K.7.c.2.(10.)) [DsVn, TaVn, and BVn only: see *CPM*, XXXVI, p. 371]; **US**-R (M1505.L956) [HCVn only, incorrectly listed in *RISM* A/I as L 2950]

BIBLIOGRAPHY – *RISM* A/I, L 2951; SchneiderC, p. 411; SchneiderR, p. 333

HEUS 5: TITLE – LES AIRS A CHANTER | DE | L'OPERA DU ROLAND, | MISES | EN MUSIQUE, | Par Monsieur de Lully, Escuyer, Conseiller Secretaire du Roy, Maison, Couronne | de France & de ses Finances, & Sur-Intendant de la Musique de sa Majesté. | [design] | Imprimé à Amsterdam, par JEAN PHILIPPE HEUS, Anno 1685.

DATE – 1685

DESCRIPTION – Oblong quarto score: 38 + [1] pp.

CONTENTS – Contains fifteen excerpts arranged in strict LWV order including **LWV 65:** 7, 13–15, 17–19, 23, 26, 33, 61, 64, 72, 74, 80

COPY – **I**-Bc (AA. 211) [see Gasparini, vol. III, p. 314]

BIBLIOGRAPHY – *RISM* A/I, L 3036; SchneiderC, p. 429; SchneiderR, p. 331

Editions by Antoine Pointel containing music by Jean-Baptiste Lully (listed alphabetically by title of composition except for two anthologies [nos. 25 and 26], which are placed at the end)

POINTEL 1a: TITLE EDITION 1 – ACHILLE | ET POLIXENE, | TRAGEDIE. | MISE EN MUSIQUE | *Le premier Acte par Feu MONSIEUR DE LULLY.* | Le Prologue, & les quatres autres Actes | PAR MONSIEUR COLASSE, | *Maistre de la Chapelle du Roy.* | [printer's mark] | *Sur la Copie de Paris.* | [rule] | A AMSTERDAM, | Par ANTOINE POINTEL, dans le Kalver-straet, vis à vis la Chapelle, au Rosier, | ET SE TROUVE, | Chez HENRY DESBORDES, | Marchand Libraire dans le Kalver-straet | M.DC.LXXXVIII.

POINTEL 1b: TITLE EDITION 2 – ACHILLE | ET POLIXENE, | TRAGEDIE. | MISE EN MUSIQUE, | Le premier Acte, | *Par Feu MONSIEUR DE LULLY,* | Le *Prologue, & les quatre autres Actes* | *Par MONSIEUR COLLASSE,* | Maître de la Chapelle du Roi. | [printer's mark] | *Sur la Copie de Paris.* | [rule] | A AMSTERDAM, | Chez ANTOINE POINTEL, dans le Kalver-Straat, vis à vis la Chapelle, au Rosier. | Et se trouve, | Chez HENRI DESBORDES, Marchand Libraire, dans le Kalver-Straat | [rule] | M.DC.LXXXVIII.

DATE – 1688

DESCRIPTION – Score (*partition générale*): [4] + xxxvj + 288 pp.

CONTENTS – Contains a full score of **LWV 74**

NOTE – The "AUIS DU LIBRAIRE" differs somewhat between the two editions, but the music itself is the same. The "AUIS" printed below is the "revised" version found in Edition 2.

AUIS DU LIBRAIRE

IL y a long-temps que j'ay rêvé aux moyens de réimprimer ici les Opéra qu'on publie tous les ans à Paris; Je voulois par-la donner occasion aux Curieux de se satisfaire à peu de frais; mais le manque de Musique propre pour ces Ouvrages, & la difficulté de la Correction, ont été les deux premiers & principaux obstacles qui ont reculé mon dessein: MONSIEUR DEROSIER m'a enfin tiré de cet embarras, par la peine qu'il s'est donné pour inventer une sorte de Musique convenable à mon projet, & s'etant bien même voulu charger de la Correction, Voici, le premier Opéra que je publie par ses soins. Si le célébre MONSIEUR DE LULLY vivoit encore, j'aurois commencé par un de ceux qu'il à achevé avec toute l'approbation des Connoisseurs; J'étois déterminé à commencer par un des premiers qui n'ont jamais été impriméz avec la Musique, mais l'Opéra d'ACHILLE ayant parû, j'ay crû mieux faire d'en entreprendre l'impression; outre la grace de la nouveauté, c'est la premiére production des successeurs de ce grand Homme, & je n'ai par-là aucun engagement à réimprimer les Opéra cii publiez, mais seulement à continuer l'impression de ceux qu'on pourra mettre au jour ci-aprés. Je ne desespére pourtant pas d'entreprendre les Opéra de ce célébre MONSIEUR DE LULLY, suivant que le public sera content de celui-ci, je dois seulement avertir ceux pour qui j'imprime cet Ouvrage, que je tâcherai par l'Industrie de MONSIEUR DEROSIER, d'employer ci-aprés des Nottes dont l'oeil soit un peu plus gros, afin d'épargner de la peine à ceux qui chantent en Concert; La chose seroit bien plus facile, si la nécessité où je me suis renfermé d'épargner la bourse des Curieux, ne gênoit les mesures qu'autrement on pourroit prendre, j'espére pourtant que cela ira de mieux en mieux, & quele public agréera ce coup d'essai; j'ose sur tout me le promettre par l'augmentation d'une Table dont l'usage sera fort considérable, elle est au devant du Prologue, par son aide on verra d'un coup d'oeil tous les Airs à chanter, & à jouer, & on s'épargnera la peine de feüilleter tout l'Ouvrage pour trouver à coup-prez ce qu'on cherche; Il est assez surprenant que dans les Opéra qu'on à publiés jusqu'à present, on n'aye pas songé à soûlager par ces sortes de Tables la peine & l'impatience de ceux qui aiment la Musique.

COPIES – **B**-Bc (26.260), Br (Fétis 2650 B.I.P.) [see Fétis, p. 328, no. 2650]; **C**-Tu (Rare Books and Special Collections: Music F-4 127) [pp. 111–14 and 227–30 lacking and supplied in MS]; **CH**-Zz (Mus Jac D40) [see Puskas, p. 26, no. 98; formerly in **CH**-Zjacobi]; **D**-Hs (M A/1364), HEms (L 326), Mbs (4° Mus. pr. 19);

Dlb (Mus. 1827–F-28); **F-AM** (SA. 4354), Nm (22185), Pn (D. 2286) [see LesureC, p. 130 (this is an exemplar of Edition 2)]; **GB-Lbl** (F.1455.a.) [see *CPM*,XIII, p. 36], Lcm (I.C.28.) [see Husk, p. 97, no. 863]; Lgc (Gresham Mus. 154) [see *GML*, p. 17]; **S-St** (Kungl. teaterns saml. Franska partitur A 27 [now in **S-Skma**]); US-CAl (Mus.640.512.605 [rare book room]) [see Wood, p. 61, no. 365], Wc (M1500.C69A4) [see Sonneck, p. 34 (this is an exemplar of Edition 1)]; Note: F-RS reports it does not own the copy attributed to it in *RISM;* Eitner, VI, p. 244 also listed a copy in the Wagener collection, which can no longer be located
BIBLIOGRAPHY – Goovaerts, p. 430, no. 907; *RISM* A/I, L 2931 and 3384; SchneiderC, p. 495

POINTEL 2*: TITLE – Airs à chanter des operas. Galatée. [= Acis et Galatée] à 1. 2. & 3. voix.
DATE – Before 1689
CONTENTS – Excerpts from **LWV 73**
COPY – None located
BIBLIOGRAPHY – Walker, p. 398 as advertised in *CATALOGUE DES LIVRES DE MUSIQUE, A CHANTER ET A JOUER* (1689)

POINTEL 3*: TITLE – Airs pour les violons ou pour les flûtes. Galatée. [= Acis et Galatée] à 4. parties.
DATE – Before 1689
CONTENTS – Excerpts from **LWV 73**
COPY – None located
BIBLIOGRAPHY – Walker, p. 398 as advertised in *CATALOGUE DES LIVRES DE MUSIQUE, A CHANTER ET A JOUER* (1689)

POINTEL 4: TITLE – [Within a decorative border of instruments and foliage] LES I SIMPHONIES I à 4. I AVEC LES AIRS I *ET TRIOTS,* I D'ALCESTE. I MISE EN MUSIQUE I *Par* Monsieur de LULLY. I [rule] I *DESSUS.* I [printer's mark] I A AMSTERDAM, I Par A. POINTEL.
DATE – [*c.* 1687–1700: SchneiderC, p. 226]
DESCRIPTION – Four parts: Dessus (12 pp.); [Haute-contre], [Taille], [Basse] no copies located
CONTENTS – Contains twenty-three pieces arranged in strict LWV order including **LWV 50:** 1, 4, 9, 11, 14, 15, 26, 28, 29, 31, 32, 34, 36, 41, 43, 61 ("Ronpons"), 68, 69, 72, 81–84
COPY – A-Wn (S.A.79.C.18) [Ds only]
BIBLIOGRAPHY – *RISM* A/I, L 2943; SchneiderC, p. 226; SchneiderR, p. 333

POINTEL 5: TITLE – [Within a decorative border of instruments, foliage, and putti] *Tous Les Airs de Violon* I *de L'Opera D'Amadis* I *Composez par Monsieur* I *de Lullÿ, Escuier,* I *Conseiller Secretaire,* I *du Roÿ. &* I [continuing below in a cartouche] *Imprimé a Amsterdam.* I *par Antoine Pointel.*

DATE – (1687?)

DESCRIPTION – Four parts: Dessus de violon ([2] + 13 pp.; only pp. 1–3 numbered); Hautcontre [sic] de violon ([2] + 12 + [1] pp.); Taille de violon ([2] + 12 + [1] pp.); Basse de violon (not seen). Concerning LWV 63:1, see Notes below

CONTENTS – Contains twenty-two pieces arranged as suites including **LWV 63:** 1 (1), 4 (2), 5 (3), 11 (16), 12 (17), 22 (5), 23 (6), 24 (7), 26 (11), 33 (18), 34 (4), 35 (19), 36 (20), 41 (9), 42 (8), 49 (12), 50 (13), 55 (14), 57 (15), 59 (21), 60 (10), 67 (22)

NOTES – The chaconne (LWV 63/67) is engraved on larger paper in the DsVn and TaVn parts. The TaVn part contains a QVn part for LWV 63/1. Advertised in *Cattalogue, des Livres de Musique, à Chanter et à Joüer* (see Pointel 19) as "*Les Livres de Violons d'Amadis, à 3. 4. 5. et 6. Parties.*" DsVn, p. 2: "*Il se vend aussij le livre des paroles et le livre des Air a chanter.*" The border on the engraved title page is based on the design found in Michel Lambert's *Les Airs du Sieur Lambert. Grauez par Richer* (Paris: Charles de Sercy, 1660). For a facsimile of the Lambert title page, see Fraenkel, no. 110.

COPIES – **CS**-Pnm (XXXIV B 78) [DsVn, TaVn, BVn only]; **GB**-Lbl (K.7.c.2.(9.)) [DsVn, Ta Vn only: see *CPM*, XXXVI, p. 371]; **US**-R (M1505.L956) [HCVn only: purchased from Scientific Library Service, cat. 59, no. 355: see *NUC*, CCCXLV, p. 444]

BIBLIOGRAPHY – *RISM* A/I, L 2952; SchneiderC, p. 411; SchneiderR, p. 333; Walker, p. 398

POINTEL 6: TITLE – Airs à chanter des opera. Amadis. à 1. 2. & 3. voix.
DATE – Before 1689
CONTENTS – Excerpts from **LWV 63**
NOTE – Advertised in *Cattalogue, des Livres de Musique, à Chanter et à Joüer* (see Pointel 19) as "*Le Livre d'Air d'Amadis, augmentez à 1. 2. 3. Voix.*"
COPY – None located
BIBLIOGRAPHY – Walker, p. 398 as advertised in *CATALOGUE DES LIVRES DE MUSIQUE, A CHANTER ET A JOUER* (1689)

POINTEL 7: TITLE – Les airs à chanter des opera. Armide. à 1. 2 & 3. voix.
DATE – Before 1689
CONTENTS – Excerpts from **LWV 71**
COPY – None located
BIBLIOGRAPHY – Walker, p. 398 as advertised in *CATALOGUE DES LIVRES DE MUSIQUE, A CHANTER ET A JOUER* (1689)

POINTEL 8: TITLE – Airs pour les violons ou pour les flûtes d'Armide. à 3. parties
DATE – Before 1689
CONTENTS – Excerpts from **LWV 71**
COPY – None located

BIBLIOGRAPHY – Walker, p. 398 as advertised in *CATALOGUE DES LIVRES DE MUSIQUE, A CHANTER ET A JOUER* (1689)

POINTEL 9: TITLE – LES AIRS, I DE LA I TRAGEDIE I D'ATYS. I *Propres à Chanter & à Joüer sur toutes I sortes d'Instruments.* I Par Monsieur DE LULLY, Sur-Intendant de la I Musique du Roy. I [rule] I THE AIRS, I OF THE I TRAGEDY I OF ATIS. I *Fit for to sing and to playd uppon all sorts I of Instruments.* I By Monsieur DE LULLY, Sur-Intendant I of the Kings Musicke. I [printer's mark] I AMSTERDAM, I [rule] I By ANTHONY POINTEL, *in de Kalver-straat, in de Rozeboom,* I *is alderley gelineert Papier en Musyc te koop.* 1687.

DATE – 1687

DESCRIPTION – Short score (voice and Bc): 59 pp.

CONTENTS – Contains thirty-nine pieces in strict LWV order including **LWV 53:** 6, 7, 10, 16–19, 20*, 21, 24–28, 32, 37, 38, 40, 41, 43, 44, 48, 49, 50, 51, 53, 54, 55, 57, 64, 65, 67, 68, 69, 74–76, 78, 80

COPIES – F-BO (M 651), (M 1700), Pn (Rés. Vm Crlt 239) [see LesureC, p. 405]; I-Bc (AA. 213) [see Gasperini, vol. III, p. 314]; note: F-RS reports it does not own the copy attributed to it in *RISM*

BIBLIOGRAPHY – *RISM* A/I, L 2969; SchneiderC, p. 270; SchneiderR, p. 331; Walker, p. 398

POINTEL 10*: TITLE – Les Airs de l'Opera de Cadmus & d'Ermione, Tragedie. en Musique. Par Monsieur de Lully. sur-Intendant de la Musique du Roy, Rapresentée par l'Academie Roy-alle Propre à chanter & joüer sur toute sorte d'Instruments. A Amsterdam, Par Anthoine Pointel, pour Nicola Derosier, by de Kapel, in de Rooseboom. 1687

DATE – 1687

DESCRIPTION – Score?

CONTENTS – Excerpts from **LWV 49**

COPY – I-Bc (P 124 [olim cod. 31]); the librarian reports that this copy cannot be located.

NOTE – The description has been taken from a catalogue entry kindly supplied by the library.

BIBLIOGRAPHY – Trovato, p. 38, no. 16; Walker, p. 398

POINTEL 11: TITLE – [Within a decorative border of instruments and foliage] LES I SIMPHONIES I à 4. I AVEC LES AIRS I *ET TRIOTS,* I DE I CADMUS. I MISE EN MUSIQUE I *Par* Monsieur de LULLY. I [rule] I *DESSUS.* I [printer's mark] I A AMSTERDAM, I Par A. POINTEL.

DATE – [*c.* 1687–1700: SchneiderC, p. 210]

CONTENTS – Contains twenty pieces arranged in strict LWV order (with the exception of LWV 49/5 and 6, which are reversed) including **LWV 49:** 1, 6, 5, 8, 10, 15, 17, 18, 22, 27, 34, 36, 37, 42, 44, 47, 51, 54, 55, 57

DESCRIPTION – Four parts: Dessus (12 pp.); [Haute-contre], [Taille], [Basse] no
copies located
COPY – A-Wn (S.A.79.C.20) [Ds only]
BIBLIOGRAPHY – *RISM* A/I, L 2983; SchneiderC, p. 210; SchneiderR, p. 333

POINTEL 12: TITLE – [Within a decorative border of instruments and foliage] LES
I SIMPHONIES I à 4. I AVEC LES AIRS I *ET TRIOTS,* I DES FESTES I DE L'AMOUR
I ET DE BACCHUS. I *Par* Monsr. de LULLY. I [rule] I *DESSUS.* I [printer's mark] I A
AMSTERDAM, I Par A. POINTEL.
DATE – [*c.* 1687–1700: SchneiderC, p. 204]
CONTENTS – Contains twenty-two pieces arranged in strict LWV order (with the
exception of LWV 47/21 and 22, which are reversed) including **LWV 47:** 1 [= 43/1],
3 (G: lacking first measure), 5, 9, 11, 12 [= 41/10], 15 [= 42/11], 16 [= 42/12], 18
[= 42/14], 20 [= 42/16], 21 [= 40/18 and 52/47], 22 [= 40/14], 23, 25 [= 33/1 and
46/17], 27 [= 33/3 and 46/19], 29, 31, 40, 41 [= 38/7 and 46/22], 45 [= 38/11 and
46/26], 46 [= 38/12 and 46/27], 48 [= 38/14 and 46/29]
DESCRIPTION – Parts: Dessus (12 pp.); [Second Dessus], [Taille], [Basse] no
copies located
COPY – A-Wn (S.A.79.C.21) [Ds only]
BIBLIOGRAPHY – *RISM* A/I, L 2987; SchneiderC, p. 204; SchneiderR, p. 333;
Walker, p. 398

POINTEL 13: TITLE – LES AIRS I DE LA GROTTE I DE VERSAILLES, I ET I DE LA
MASCARADE. I *Propres à Chanter & à Joüer sur toutes* I *sortes d'Instruments.* I Par
Monsieur DE LULLY, Sur-Intendant de la I Musique du Roy. I [rule] I THE AIRS I
OF THE GROTTI I OF VERSAILLES, I SING I OF THE MASCARADI. I *Fit for to
sing and to playd uppon all sorts* I *of Instruments.* I By Monsieur DE LULLY, Sur-
Intendant I of the Kings Musicke, I [ornament] I AMSTERDAM, I [rule] I By
ANTHONY POINTEL, *in die Kalver-straat, in de Rozeboom,* I *is alderlay gelineert
Papier en Musyc te koop. 1700.*
DATE – 1700
DESCRIPTION – Short score (voice and Bc): 59 + [1] pp.
CONTENTS – Contains seventeen pieces arranged as suites including **LWV 39:** 2
(1), 4 (2), 5 (3), 6 (4), 7 (5), 8 (6), 10 (7), 11 (8); **LWV 36:** 2 (1); **LWV 19:** 12 (2), 13
(3); **LWV 34:** 1 (4 "Air"), 2 (5 "Air"); **LWV 41:** 16 (C: 6), 2 (7 "Air"), 3 (8); **LWV 43:** 3
(9 "Air" [= 46/47 and 52/28])
NOTE – The "TABLE I Des Airs de la Grotte de Versailles, I & du Carnaval,
Mascarade" on p. (60) lists twenty-one pieces.
COPIES – D-ZW (K 17); F-BO (14004) [see Ducoin, p. 458], Pn (Rés. Vm^7 602 and
Rés. Vm Crlt 241) [copy from the collection of Sébastien de Brossard: see LesureC,
p. 406]
BIBLIOGRAPHY – *RISM* A/I, L 3043; SchneiderC, pp. 155 and 266

POINTEL 14a: TITLE EDITION 1 – LES AIRS, I DE LA I TRAGEDIE I DE PERSE'E.
I *Propres à Chanter & à Joüer sur toutes* I *sortes d'Instruments,* I Par Monsieur DE
LULLY, Sur-Intendant de la I Musique du Roy. I [rule] I THE AIRS, I OF THE I
TRAGEDY I OF PERSE'E. I *Fit for to sing and to playd uppon all sorts* I *of Instruments.*
I By Monsieur DE LULLY, Sur-Intendant I of the Kings Musicke. I [ornament] I
AMSTERDAM, I [rule] I *By* Anthony Pointel, *in de Kalver-straat, in de Roozeboom,* I
is alderley gelinneert Papier en Musyc te koop. 1688.
[bound with] SECONDES PARTIES, I DES AIRS I DE LA I TRAGEDIE I DE I
PERSÉE, I A DEUX & A TROIS. I *Pour les Curieux, qui s'en voudront servir* I *dans les*
concerts. I Par Monsieur DE LULLY, Sur-Intendant I de la Musique du Roy. I *Suivant*
la Copie Imprimée I *à Paris.* I [ornament] I AMSTERDAM, I [rule] I *By* Anthony
Pointel, *in de Kalver-straat, in de Roozeboom,* I *is alderley gelineert Papier en Musyc te*
koop. 1688.

POINTEL 14b: TITLE EDITION 2 – LES AIRS I DE LA I TRAGEDIE I DE PERSE'E I
Propres à Chanter & à JOüER sur toutes I *sortes d'Instruments.* I Par Monsieur DE
LULLY, Sur-Intendant de la I Musique du Roy. I [rule] I THE AIRS I OF THE I
TRAGEDY I OF PERSÉE, I *Fit for to sing and to playd uppon all sorts* I *of Instruments.*
I By Monsieur DE LULLY, Sur-Intendant I of the Kings Musicke. I [ornament] I
AMSTERDAM, I [rule] I *By* Anthony Pointel, *in die Kalver-straat, in de Rozeboom.* I
is alderlay gelineert Papier en Musyc te koop. 1688.
DATE – 1688
DESCRIPTION – Short score: 63 + [1] + 8 pp.
CONTENTS – Contains twenty-eight pieces including **LWV 60:** 5 (1), 11 (2), 15 (3),
17 (4), 18 (5), 19 (7), 20 (8), 21 (9), 22* (10), 23 (11), "Quel plaisir prenez-vous"
(12), 24 (13), 25 (14), 33 (15), 36 (16), 37 (17), 38 (18), 39 (19), 40 (20), 41 (21), 42
(22), 43 (23), 46 (24), 62 (25), 65 (26), 72 (27), 73 (28)
COPIES – **C**-Lu (MUSIC GM/AR.016) [see Neville, p. 280, no. 145]; **F**-G, Pn (Rés.
Vm Crlt 238) [Edition 14b: see LesureC, p. 407]; **GB**-Lbl (A.409.(4.)) [Edition 14b:
see *CPM*, XXXVI, p. 375]; **I**-Bc (AA. 214) [see Gasparini, vol. III, p. 314]; **US**-
BEfelker [Edition 14a: this exemplar was purchased from William Salloch]
BIBLIOGRAPHY – *RISM* A/I, L 3001; SchneiderC, p. 369; SchneiderR, p. 331;
Walker, p. 398

POINTEL 15*: TITLE – Airs pour les violons ou pour les flûtes. Persée. à 3.
parties.
DATE – Before 1689
DESCRIPTION – Three parts
CONTENTS – Excerpts from **LWV 60**
NOTE – Advertised in *Cattalogue, des Livres de Musique, à Chanter et à Joüer* (see
Pointel 19) as "*Les Livres de Violons de l'Opera de Persée, à 3. Parties, et les*
Diminutions des Airs dans le Dessus et la Basse."
COPY – None located

139

CARL B. SCHMIDT

BIBLIOGRAPHY – Walker, p. 398 as advertised in *CATALOGUE DES LIVRES DE MUSIQUE, A CHANTER ET A JOUER* (1689)

POINTEL 16: TITLE – [Within a decorative border of instruments and foliage] LES I SIMPHONIES I à 4. I AVEC LES AIRS I *ET TRIOTS,* I DE I PHAETON. I MISE EN MUSIQUE I *Par* Monsieur de LULLY. I [rule] I *DESSUS.* I [printer's mark] I A AMSTERDAM. I Par A. POINTEL.
DATE – [*c.* 1687–1700: SchneiderC, p. 389]
CONTENTS – Contains thirty-three pieces generally in LWV order except for three instances: LWV 61/25 follows 61/18, LWV 61/40 follows 61/45, and LWV 61/57 follows 61/50. Includes: **LWV 61:** 1–4, 7, 10, 11, 14–16, 18, 23 (rit. only), 23 (air only), 24, 25, 27, 35, 37, 40, 41, 45, 47, 48, 50, 53 (rit. only), 53 (air only), 56–58, 59, 67, 68
DESCRIPTION – Four parts: Dessus (18 pp.); [Haut-contre], [Taille], [Basse] no copies located
COPY – A-Wn (S.A.79.C.21) [Ds only]
BIBLIOGRAPHY – *RISM* A/I, L 3013; SchneiderC, p. 389; SchneiderR, p. 333

POINTEL 17a: TITLE EDITION 1 – LES AIRS I DE LA I TRAGEDIE I DE I PROSERPINE, I *Propres à Chanter & à Joüer sur toutes sortes* I *d'instruments,* I Par Monsieur DE LULLI Sur-Intendant de la I Musique du Roi. I [rule] I THE AIRS I OF THE I TRAGEDY I OF PROSERPINE, I *Fit for to sing and to playd uppon all sorts of Instruments.* I By Monsieur DE LULLI Sur-Intendant of the I Kings Musicke. I [ornament] I AMSTERDAM, I [rule] I *Chez* Antoine Pointel, *dans le Kalver-straat au Rosier,* I *se vend toutes sortes de Papier ligne & Musiques.* 1689
POINTEL 17b: TITLE EDITION 2 – LES AIRS I DE LA I TRAGEDIE I DE I PROSERPINE, I *Propres à Chanter & à Joüer sur toutes sortes d'instruments,* I Par Monsieur DE LULLI Sur-Intendant de la I Musique du Roi. I [rule] I THE AIRS I OF THE I TRAGEDY I OF PROSERPINE, I *Fit for to sing and to playd uppon all sorts of Instruments.* I By Monsieur DE LULLI Sur-Intendant of the I Kings Musicke. I [ornament] I AMSTERDAM. I [rule] I *Chez* Antoine Pointel, *dans le Kalver-straat au Rosier,* I *se vend toutes sortes de Papier ligne & Musiques.* 1689
SECONDES PARTIES I DES AIRS I DE LA I TRAGEDIE I DE I PROSERPINE, I A DEUX ET A TROIS. I *Pour les Curieux qui s'en voudront servir* I *dans les Concerts,* I Par Monsieur De LULLY, Sur-Intendant I de la Musique du Roy. I *Suivant la Copie Imprimée* I *à Paris.* I [design] I A AMSTERDAM, I [rule] I *Chez* Antoine Pointel, *dans le Kalver-strat au Rosier,* I *se vend toutes sortes de Papier ligné & Musiques.* 1689
DESCRIPTIONS: EDITION 1 – Short score: 58 + [2] + 4 pp.; EDITION 2 – Short score: 58 + [1] + [1] + 4 pp.
DATE – 1689
CONTENTS – Contains thirty-one excerpts arranged in strict LWV order including **LWV 58:** 8, 11, 12, 14, 17–19; two separate pieces now occur which continue LWV 58/19 to the end of the scene and do not have separate LWV

numbers: "Je crains enfin" (sung by Aréthuse) and "Aimez sans vous contraindre"
(sung by Cérès), 20, 21, 31, 32, 34–36, 38–43, 45, 46, 50, 51, 65–67, 72, 73, 75, 81
NOTES – The two editions contain numerous differences: Edition 1 uses lozenge-
shaped notes and Edition 2 diamond-shaped notes, and Edition 1 uses smaller type
and sometimes contains fewer bass figures in the Bc.
COPIES – F-Pn (Rés. Vm Crlt 240) [Edition 1: see LesureC, p. 407]; GB-Lbl
(A.409.(1.)) and (Hirsch III. 908.: part one only) [Edition 2 and 1 respectively: see
CPM, XXXVI, p. 376]; US-BAo'keefe
BIBLIOGRAPHY – RISM A/I, L 3019; SchneiderC, p. 333; SchneiderR, p. 331;
Walker, p. 398

POINTEL 18: TITLE – [Within a decorative border of instruments and foliage] LES
| SIMPHONIES | à 4. | AVEC LES AIRS | ET TRIOTS, | DE | PSICHE'. | MISE EN
MUSIQUE | Par Monsieur de LULLY. | [rule] | DESSUS. | [printer's mark] | A
AMSTERDAM, | Par A. POINTEL.
DATE – [c. 1687–1700: SchneiderC, p. 310]
CONTENTS – Contains twenty-seven excerpts arranged in strict LWV order (with
the exception of the addition of LWV 53/58 between LWV 10 and 13) including
LWV 56: 1 [= 45/1], 4 [= 45/4 and 46/8], 6 [= 45/6 and 46/10], 9, 10; LWV 53: 38;
LWV 56: 13 [= 45/8 and 46/13], 15 [= 45/10 and 46/15], 16, 17 [= 45/11], 18 [=
45/12] and 46/33], 22–24, 28 [= 45/15], 31, 36 [= 45/18], 40, 45 [= 45/22 and
46/65], 48 [= 45/25 and 46/68], 49 [= 45/26 and 46/69], 51 [= 45/28 and 46/71], 53
[= 45/30 and 46/73], 56 [= 45/33 and 46/76], 57 [= 45/34 and 46/77], 58 [= 45/35
and 46/78], 59 [= 45/36 and 46/79]
DESCRIPTION – Four parts: Dessus (15 pp.); [Haut-contre], [Taille], [Basse] no
copies located
COPY – A-Wn (S.A.79.C19) [Ds only]
BIBLIOGRAPHY – RISM A/I, L 3026; SchneiderC, p. 310; SchneiderR, p. 333

POINTEL 19: TITLE – RECUEIL, | [next eight lines all within a decorative border]
De tous les | plus beaux AIRS de | L'OPERA | DE | ROLAND. | Propre pour toutes
sortes | de Voix, Et d'In- | struments. | [below the border] Se vendent chez Anthoine
Pointel, dans le Jonge Roelof- | steech, in't Musicq-stuck, tot Amsterdam.
DATE – [c. 1687–1700; SchneiderC, p. 429 gives c. 1685–86, but Pointel is not
known to have been active as a printer before 1687]
DESCRIPTION – Score: [2] + 32 + [2] pp. [voice or voices with guitar tablature or
Bc]
CONTENTS – The print claims to contain thirty-one numbers, but lists thirty-two
titles with thirty-three actual pieces present including LWV 65: 3 (23), 6 (31), 13
(3), 15 (1), 20 (2), 23 (4), 25 (6), 26 (25), 28 (24), 32 (10), 33 (20), 34 (19), 35 (22),
36 (16), 37 (15), 38 (18), 41 (13), 43 (14), 45 (11), 46 (17), 48 (12), 52 (32), 54 (21),
59 (5), 64 (9), 65 (8), 68 (7 one voice of duet), 68 (9 second voice of duet), 70 (26),
71 (27), 72 (29), 74 (28), 77 (30)

CARL B. SCHMIDT

NOTES – This print does not contain LWV 65/1 as indicated in SchneiderC, p. 430. "Dans ces sombres retraittes" listed in the "Tables des Airs" as on p. 18 is in error and 34(19) and 70(27) are not in the "Tables des Airs." Page [2 initial sequence] reads "REcueil, de tous les plus beaux AIRS de L'OPERA DE ROLAND; Jusq'aux nombre de Trente un. Propre pour toutes sortes de Voix, et d'Instruments. à un, deux, et trois parties; Avec une maniere toute particuliere, que le S*r.* Derosier, à Inventé pour accompagner parfaitement avec la Guittarre, par les Lettres Capitales, augmentées sur l'*Alphabeth Italienne,* avec une bref Instruction, qui se void dans le huitiesme Feüillet, ou l'on poura voir toutes les significations des Lettres Capitales, pour la *Guittarre:* Quand il se trouve des Chiffres devant les Lettres, ce la fait Monter l'accord d'auttant de Touche que le nombre qui se void devant la Lettre. Par example, si l'Accord se prend sur la Premiere touche, comme le premier P. et qu'il y est un Chiffre 2. devant la Lettre, cela veut dire qu'il faut avanser toute la Main d'une Touche, et ainsi des autres, &c." This print also contains the following catalogue at the end: "*Cattalogue, des Livres de Musique,* | *à Chanter et à Joüer; Gravé par Anthoine Poin-* | *tel, in de Jonge-Roelof-steegh, in't Musicq-stuck,* | *tot Amsterdam.* | *LEs Livres de Violons de Roland, à 3. et 4. et 5. Parties, avec* | *quelque Diminutions pour le Dessus de Violon.* | *Les Livres de Violons d'Amadis, à 3. 4. 5. et 6 Parties.* | *Les Livres de Violons du Triomphe de l'Amour, à 3. Parties.* | *Les Livres de Violons de l'Opera de Persée, à 3. Parties, et les* | *Diminutions des Airs dans le Dessus et la Basse.* | *Simphonie del S*r.* Corelly, à 2. Violons et B. C. propre pour* | *l'Eglise, et pour la Chambre.* | *Les Livres du S*r.* Nicolas Mattheys, à 2. 3. et 4. Parties.* | *imprimé à Londre.* | *Le Livre d'Air d'Amadis, augmentez à 1. 2. 3. Voix.* | *Les Livres, de differents Autheurs, Imprimé à Paris.* | *Le Livre d'Air de Roland, à 1. 2. 3. Voix.* | *Le Triomphe de la Guittarre. Par le S*r.* Nicolas Derosier.* | *Vn petit Livre pour ceux qui commence pour la Guittarre, ou sont* | *tous les principes, et toutes les petites Piesces Gallantes, avec les Parolles. &c.*"
COPIES – F-Pn (Rés. Vmd. 106) [purchased from William Salloch]; I-Bc (AA. 212) [see Gasparini, vol. III, p. 314]; note: F-BO reports it does not own the copy attributed to it in *RISM*.
BIBLIOGRAPHY – *RISM* A/I, L 3035; SchneiderC, p. 429; SchneiderR, p. 331; Selhof, p. 179, no. 1582 (Nicolas Selhof apparently owned a copy of this edition; his collection was sold in 1759); Walker, p. 398

POINTEL 20*: TITLE – Airs pour les violons ou pour les flûtes. Roland. à 4. parties.
DATE – Before 1689
CONTENTS – Excerpts from **LWV 65**
NOTE – Advertised in *Cattalogue, des Livres de Musique, à Chanter et à Joüer* (see Pointel 19) as "*LEs Livres de Violons de Roland, à 3. et 4. et 5. Parties, avec quelque Diminutions pour le Dessus de Violon.*"
COPY – None located
BIBLIOGRAPHY – Walker, p. 398 as advertised in *CATALOGUE DES LIVRES DE MUSIQUE, A CHANTER ET A JOUER* (1689)

142

[POINTEL] 21: TITLE – [within a decorative border of Putti and instruments] *Le Temple | de | LA PAIX. | BALLET. | Dansé devant sa Majesté | à Fontaine-bleau | t. Amsterdam Au Rosier. int Musickt stuck.* | [and below in a drapery held by Putti] *Int Musick-Stuck | t'Amsterdam.*

DATE – [*c.* 1687–1700: SchneiderC, p. 453]

DESCRIPTION – Four (?) parts: [Premier Dessus] (11 pp.); [Second Dessus] (11 pp.); [Taille], [Basse] no copies located

CONTENTS – Contains eighteen pieces grouped in suites by key including **LWV 69**: 1 (1), 6 (2 "Air"), 7 (3), 13 (4), 14 (5), 15 (6), 16 (14), 24 (18), 26 (9), 27 (8), 30 (10), 31 (15), 32 (16), 34 (17), 37 (C: 11 "Gigue"), 39 (C: 12), 40 (C: 13), 45 (7)

NOTES – Though Pointel is nowhere named as the publisher, the title page contains the same decorative border used in other Pointel prints and is similar to Pointel editions.

COPY – **GB**-Lbl (K.7.c.2.(16.)) [Ds I and Ds II only: see *CPM*, XXXVI, p. 376]

BIBLIOGRAPHY – *RISM* A/I, L 3051; SchneiderC, p. 453; SchneiderR, p. 333

POINTEL 22*: TITLE – Airs à chanter des operas. Le Temple de la Paix. à 1. 2. & 3. voix.

DATE – Before 1689

CONTENTS – Excerpts from **LWV 69**

COPY – None located

BIBLIOGRAPHY – Walker, p. 398 as advertised in *CATALOGUE DES LIVRES DE MUSIQUE, A CHANTER ET A JOUER* (1689)

POINTEL 23: TITLE – LES AIRS | DE LA | TRAGEDIE | DU TRIOMPHE | DE L'AMOUR | *Propres à Chanter & à Joüer sur toutes sortes d'Instruments,* | Par Monsieur DE LULLI Sur-Intendant de la | Musique du Roi. | [rule] | THE AIRS | OF THE | TRAGEDY | OF THE TRIOMPHE | OF L'AMOUR | *Fit for to sing and to playd uppon all sorts of Instruments.* | By Monsieur DE LULLI Sur-Intendant of the | Kings Musiche. | [ornament] | AMSTERDAM. | [rule] | *By* Anthoni Pointel, *in de Kalver-straat in de Roozeboom,* | *is alderley gelineert Papier en Musyc te koop.* 1688

DATE – 1688

DESCRIPTION – Short score: 47 + [1] pp.

CONTENTS – Contains twenty-five pieces arranged in strict LWV order including **LWV 59:** 3 (air only), 4, 7, 9, 11 (air only), 15 (air only), 17–19, 21, 24, 29 (air only), 31, 33, 36 (air only), 38 (air only), 39 (follows 39 "Malgre tous mes eforts"), 47 (air only), 49, 56 (air only), 63 (first couplet), 63 (second couplet), 67, 68 (air only), 70

NOTE – p. 6 not numbered

COPY – **C**-Lu (MUSIC GM/AR.015) [see Neville, pp. 296–297, no. 153]; the copies listed in *RISM* as being at **GB**-Lbl (A.409.(2.)) [see *CPM*, XXXVI, p. 377] and **NL**-DHgm are actually copies of *RISM* A/I, L 3057 – see Pointel 24

BIBLIOGRAPHY – *RISM* A/I, L 3058; SchneiderC, p. 351; SchneiderR, p. 331; Walker, p. 398

[**POINTEL**] 24: TITLE – [within a simple decorative border] *Ouverture du Triomphe de L'Amour | avec tous Les Airs de Violon. Composez Par Monsieur | de Lully Secretaire Conseiller du Roy, a Paris* | [and continuing at the bottom of the page under the music] *Se Vandent int Musick stuck inde Jonge Roelefs Steeg t Amsterdam.*
DATE – [*c.* 1687: SchneiderC, p. 351]
DESCRIPTION – Three parts: [Premier Dessus de Violon] (16 pp.); [Second Dessus de Violon (title page wanting?)] (16 pp.); [Basse de Violon (title page wanting?)] (16 pp.)
CONTENTS – Contains thirty-five pieces arranged in strict LWV order (with the exception of LWV 59/12 and 13, which are reversed) including **LWV 59:** 1, 3, 5–8, 10, 12, 13, 14, 20*, 22, 23, 25, 26*, 27, 28, 30, 32, 34, 35, 41, 46, 47, 51–53, 58, 59, 62, 64–66, 69, 71
NOTES – Though Pointel's name is not given on the title page, he is the printer of this volume. Advertised in *Cattalogue, des Livres de Musique, à Chanter et à Joüer* (see Pointel 19) as "*Les Livres de Violons du Triomphe de l'Amour, à 3. Parties.*"
COPIES – **GB**-DRc (C55(iii)) [see Harman, p. 89, no. 533], Lbl (A. 409.(2.)), (K.7.c.2.(15.)) [see *CPM*, XXXVI, p. 377]; **NL**-DHgm [see ScheurleerM, 2, p. 370]; **USSR**-Mrg (M3 P-NH/107) [DsVn I & II only: see *GOL*, p. 75, no. 1572]
BIBLIOGRAPHY – *RISM* A/I, L 3057; SchneiderC, p. 351; SchneiderR, p. 333; Selhof, p. 139, no. 917 (Nicolas Selhof apparently owned a copy of this edition; his collection was sold in 1759)

POINTEL 25*: TITLE – DEUSIESME | RECUIEL, | DES DANCES ET | CONTRE-DANCES, | *Avec la Basse Continue. Propre à Joüer sur | toutes sortes d'Instruments. Par divers | Auteurs.* | [rule] | TWEEDE | VREUGDE-MUSICQ. | *Inhoudende alle de Danssen en* | CONTRE-DANSSEN, | *Bequaem om te speelen op alle soorten van Instru-* | *menten. Gecomponeert door verscheyde | Autheurs.* | [type-ornament] t'AMSTERDAM, | [rule] | *Gedrukt by* Anthony Pointel, *in de Kalver-straat, by de | Kapel, in de Roozeboom,* is alderley gelineert Papier | en Music te koop. 1688.
DATE – 1688
DESCRIPTION – Two parts: [Dessus, Basse continue] (both 36 pp.)
CONTENTS – **LWV 73:** 15 ("Menuet de Galatée" p. 7)
NOTES – Only one of the sixty-five pieces, none of which is attributed in the print, is known to be by Lully. The remaining music consists of titled pieces plus numerous different dances.
COPY – **F**-Pn (Vm^7 3638)
BIBLIOGRAPHY – Walker, p. 398 as advertised in *CATALOGUE DES LIVRES DE MUSIQUE, A CHANTER ET A JOUER* (1689)

BALLARD/POINTEL 26: TITLE – AIRS DE DANSES | ANGLOISES, HOLLANDOISES, | ET FRANÇOISES, | A DEUX PARTIES. | Nouvellement recueillies par ANTOINE POINTEL. | *DESSUS.* | [printer's mark] | A

AMSTERDAM, | Dans le Nest, proche le long-Pont. | Imprimez | A PARIS, | Chez
CHRISTOPHE BALLARD, Seul Imprimeur du Roy | pour la Musique, ruë S. Jean de
Beauvais, | au Mont-Parnasse. | [rule] | M.DCC. | *AVEC PRIVILEGE DU ROY.*
DATE – 1700
DESCRIPTION – Two parts: Dessus, Basse both ([4] + 44 pp.)
CONTENTS – Contains 118 numbered pieces of which only the following are by
Lully: **LWV 2:** 4 (96 "La Mariée" [= LWV 19/3]); **LWV 31:** 1 (87), 2 (88), 3 (89), 4
(90)
NOTE – This edition, published in Paris by Ballard using his normal type, contains
an "EXTRAIT DU PRIVILEGE." confirming Ballard's exclusive right granted by
Louis XIV to print, sell, and distribute music.
COPIES – F-V (MSL In 4°) [B only]; NL-DHgm (21 F 21–22) [see ScheurleerM, 1,
p. 395]; US-Wc (M1450.A2A28) [Ds only]
BIBLIOGRAPHY – *RISM* B/I, 1700⁵; SchneiderC, pp. 123–24 (LWV 2/4*; LWV 31/2
and 31/4 incorrectly listed as no. 89)

Edition by Jean Stichter containing music by Jean-Baptiste Lully
STICHTER 1: TITLE – RECUEIL. | De tous les Airs à Joüer sur le Violon & sur la
Flute | DE L'OPERA | D'ARMIDE, | *Fait par Monsieur de* Lully, *Escuyer, Conseiller
Secretaire du Roy, Maison,* | *Couronne de France, & de ses Finances, & sur Intendant* |
de la Musique de sa Majesté. | Suivant la Copie du grand Livre de Paris. | [design] | à
AMSTERDAM, | [rule] | *Imprimé chez* Jean Stichter, *dans le Kalver-straat, pour*
Nicolas de Rosier.
DATE – ? (Nicolas Derosier, for whom the edition was printed, was still alive in
1699, but cannot be documented with certainty beyond that date.)
DESCRIPTION – Three parts: [Dessus premier], [Dessus second], [Basse] all 28
pp.
CONTENTS – Contains thirty pieces grouped as suites by key including **LWV 71:**
1 (1), 7 (13 "Air pour les Flutes et Violons"), 8 (14 "Menuet pour les Flutes"), 9 (15
"Gavotte en Rondeau"), 12 (3), 13 (2), 14 (5 "Menuet pour les Hautbois"), 15
(12), 16 (16), 24 (7), 26 (6), 27 (8), 28 (19), 29 (20), 33 (29), 34 (28), 35 (21), 38
(27), 39 (22), 40 (23), 41 (24), 43 (30 "Prelude"), 46 (17 "Air"), 48 (18 "Air pour la
suitte de la Haine"), 51 (11 "Les Desmons"), 52 (10), 53 (4), 54 (9), 68 (25), 69
(26)
COPY – S-Uu (Utl. instr. mus. tr. 14)
BIBLIOGRAPHY – *RISM* A/I, L 2960; SchneiderC, p. 466; SchneiderR, p. 334

Editions by P. & J. Blaeu and Amédée Le Chevalier containing music by Jean-Baptiste Lully (listed by date of publication)
BLAEU/LE CHEVALIER 1a: TITLE VOLUME 1 – LES TRIO | DES | OPERA | DE
MONSIEUR DE LULLY, | Mis en ordre pour les concerts. | *Propres à chanter, & à
joüer sur la Flute, le Violon, &* | *autres Instruments.* | PREMIER DESUS. | [printer's

mark] | *A AMSTERDAM,* | [rule] | Dans l'Imprimerie de P. & J. BLAEU, & se
vendent sur le Pype-Markt, | proche le Schilt van Vrankryk. 1690.

DATE – 1690

DESCRIPTION – Three parts: Premier Dessus [2] + ([10] + 41 pp.); Second Dessus
[2] + ([10] + 51 pp.); Basse ([2] + [10] + 82 pp.)

CONTENTS – The following contents are presented in LWV order. The number
given in parentheses shows the order in the print. **LWV 45:** 22 (23), 34 (25); **LWV
47:** 18 (84 [= 42/14]), 23 (87), 24 (88), 29 (48), 31 (62), 46 (68 [= 38/12 and 46/22]);
LWV 49: 6 (83), 17 (22), 18 (24), 24 (15), 27 (63), 36 (14), 41 (44); **LWV 50:** 20 (73),
26 (33), 27 (26), 36 (79), 39 (28), 40 (57), 67 (19), 83 (85); **LWV 51:** 18 (50), 26 (30),
46 (86), 71 (81); **LWV 53:** 18 (54), 41 (69), 55 (56), 59 (51), 74 (1); **LWV 54:** 16 (49),
18 (31), 24 (58), 39 (32), 48 and 49 (20); **LWV 57:** 50 (72), 55 (82), 66 (9 air only);
LWV 58: 35 (67), 40 (89), 70 (91), 75 (43), 76 (45), 83 (16); **LWV 60:** 15 (4), 23 (55),
24 (64), 34 (29), 48 (90), 54 (20–21), 65 (52), 74 (40); **LWV 61:** 8 (17), 10 and 11 (3),
23 and 24 (2), 39 (59), 45 (39), 56 (93); **LWV 63:** 9 (61), 20 (75), 27 (35), 39 (21), 52
(42); **LWV 65:** 8 (38), 10 (41), 30 (18), 32 (13), 50 (41), 68 (53); **LWV 71:** 15 (11), 22
(6), 23 (7), 22 (5), 57 (12), 58 (8). In addition, pieces 10, 60, 65, 66, 71, and 76 are
drawn from *Zéphire et Flore*; 37, 70, 77, 78, 80, 92, and 94 from *Achille et Polyxène*;
plus 46 and 47 from *Thétis et Pélée*.

NOTES – A dedication on pp. [5–6] reads:

> A.S.E. | MONSEIGNEUR | PHILIBERT DE LA TOUR, | *Baron de Bourdeaux,
> Conseiller d'Etat de S.A.R. President de ses finances* | *de Savoye, Intendant de
> sa Maison & Son Envoyé Extraordinaire au-* | *pres de leurs Hautes Puissances
> Messeigneurs les Etats Generaux* | *des Provinces Unies des Pays-Bas.*
>
> MONSEIGNEUR;
>
> Depuis plusieurs années le celebre Monsieur *de Lully* a esté celuy des
> Musiciens qui a merité le plus d'estime par ses Compositions; il a eu
> l'applaudissements de tous les cognoisseurs, & la plus grande partie de
> l'Europe a fait ses divertissements des Opera qu'il a mis au jour: Je prends la
> liberté, Monseigneur, d'offrir à V. E. un receüil des plus beaux [p. 6] endroits
> & des plus divertissants de cet Autheur, que j'ay mis dans une ordre tres
> commode pour les concerts; ils ont plû aux plus grands Princes de l'Europe,
> j'oze esperer qu'ils seront receus favorablement de V.E. & qu'ils pourront la
> delasser quelques moments des grandes occupations où son ministere
> l'attache. J'avois besoing d'un patron illustre dans l'entreprise que j'ay faite
> d'imprimer ces sortes d'ouvrages d'une maniere particuliere pour la
> satisfaction des curieux; je ne puis en trouver un dont la protection me soit
> plus avantageuse que celle de V.E. qui a une cognoissance si parfaite de tous
> les beaux arts; je serai trop heureux si depuis quatorze ans que ma mauvaise
> fortune m'a fait attacher à l'estude de la Musique, j'ai le plaisir de voir que
> mes soins sont agreables à Vostre Excellence, & qu'elle reçoit les premices de

mon travail comme un témoignage sincere du profond respect avec le quel je suis,

MONSEIGNEUR De V. E. Le tres-humble & tres-obéissant Serviteur

LE CHEVALLIER B.

The "AVIS | AU | LECTEUR." on p. [7] reads:

L'Empressement que l'on avoit pour les ouvrages de Monsieur de Lully s'est augmenté despuis sa mort, il n'est point de curieux en Musique qui ne les souhaitte: mais soit que l'embaras de les faire venir des pays esloignés est trop grand, où que peu de gens veulent faire une depence aussy considerable que celle de tant de Volumes, on est privé de la satisfaction de les posseder tous. Aprés avoir consulté plusieurs de mes Amis sur les moyens de satisfaire à la curiosité des uns, & à espargner la bource des autres, j'ai pris la resolution de donner des receüils entiers de touttes les OEuvres de cet illustre Autheur qui en contiendront generalement tous les beaux endroits. J'ay commencé par touttes les pieces qui sont à trois parties, comme d'une Basse qui chante avec deux instruments, avec tous les Recits qui les precedent: de trois voix; où de deux voix & une Basse: ce sont les pieces les plus recherchées, & les moins dificiles à excuter. J'ay transposé les clefs de la haute contre, de la Taille, & du Bas desus, en une seule clef qui est la plus cognue dans ces pays pour ceux qui apprennent à joüer de la Flute ou du Violon. Je continuerai de mesme touttes les impressions des autres pieces que j'ay touttes prestes à mettre au jour, tant de Simphonies que de voix. J'ay pris soing de mettre tous les tons de suite afin d'eviter l'interruption qui se fait pour entrer d'un ton à un autre, & qui trouble ordinairement les concerts. La Table que j'ay faite est suivant l'ordre que les Opera ont esté representés avec le renvoy à la page où sont les airs, & pour plus grande facilité, ils finissent à chaque page, sans estre obligé de tourner la feuille en chantant, ou en joüant, excepté dans le reçit. J'espere que le public agréera ce premier temoignage de la passion que j'ay à contribuer à ses divertissements, & à son utilité, en promettant de luy donner bien-tost d'autres pieces dignes de sa curiosité, & imprimées en caracteres plus beaux que ceux dont je me suis servi cette premiere fois.

The "PRIVILEGIE." on pp. [8–9] reads:

DE Staaten van Hollandt en Westvrieslandt, doen te weeten: Alzoo ons vertoond is by *Amedeus le Chevallier,* woonende tot Amsterdam, dat hy zich lange jaaren herwaarts hem alhier te Lande hebbende laten gebruiken tot onderwyks van de Jeugt in de Musicq, hy Suppliant hadde, dien tydt geduurende, verzameldt ende by een gebragt verscheide uitgezochte Stukken, die hy geerne in't licht zoude uitgeven, tot een opregt merkteeken van zynen yver en toegenegentheit tot die geene, dewelke aan middelen ontbreeken om hun in die loffelyke Konst van de Musicq te doen onderwyzen, als mede ten dienste van de Liefhebbers, dewelke, te verre van

hem zynnde, van hem Suppliant niet konden geinstrueert worden. Dog alzoo
hy Suppliant ettelyke jaaren, als voorsz. was, daar aan hadde gearbeidt, ende
zulks met groote kosten, zoo tot den Druk van zoodanige Stukken, als anders,
welke impressien door baatzoekende persoonen gevoehglyk nagedrukt
zouden konnen worden, waar door den Suppliant vn zyne hoope ende
oogmerk ontzet zoude worden, ende by gevolge groote schaade lyden; zoo
keerde den Suppliant, hem tot ons, ootmoedelyk verzoekende, dat het onze
goede geliefte zy, hem Suppliant te verleenen favorabel Octroy voor den tydt
van vystien a twintig aan een-volgende jaaren, ten cynde hy Suppliant, dien
tydt geduurende, zoodanige Musicale stukken, als Simphonie, Stukken a een,
twee dry a vier Stemmen, zelfs heele Stukken, zoo van *Jan Baptiste Lully,*
Colasse, en andere vermaarde Autheuren, alleen zoude mogen drukken,
uitgeven, verkoopen, ofte doen verkoopen, en debiteren in de Operaas, die
hier bevooren in Vrankryk gedrukt waaren geweest, ofte naderhandt noch
gedruktzouden mogen werden, of wel noch andere schoone en uitgelezene
Stukken van de zelve *Lully, Colasse,* ende andere Autheuren, dewelke tot nu
toe in 't licht niet uitgegeven waaren, om de zwaare onkosten, en overgroote
moeyten, die daar toe van nooden waaren, met interdictie op zeekere groote
peene, door ons te statueren, jegens de contraventeurs van zoodanige
Musicale Werken te drukken, nadrukken, of doen drukken, uitgeven,
verkoopen, doen verkoopen, ofte debiteren, onder wat pretext het ook zoude
mogen ztn, direct, noch indirectelyk, ende hier van aan den Suppliant te
doen depesscheren behoorlyk Octroy: SOO IS'T, dat wy, de zaake ende 't
verzoek voorsz. overgemerkt hebbende, ende genegen wezende, ter bede van
den Suppliant, uit onze rechte wetenschap, souveraine magt ende authoriteit,
den Supliant geconsenteert, geaccordeert en geoctroyeert hebben,
consenteren, accorderen ende octroyeren den zelven by deezen, dat hy,
geduurende den tydt van vystien agter-een-volgende jaaren, de voorsz.
Musicale Werken binnen den voorn. onzen Lande alleen zal mogen drukken,
doen drukken, uitgeven ende verkoopen. Verbiedende daarom alle ende
eenen iegelyke, dezelve Musicale Werken in 't geheel of ten deele naar te
drukken, ofte elders naargedrukt binnen den zelven onzen Lande te brengen,
uit te geven ofte verkoopen, op verbeurte van alle de naargedrukte,
ingebragte ofte verkogte Exemplaren, ende een boete van 300 Guldens daar-
en-boven te verbeuren, te appliceeren een derde part voor den Officier die de
calange doen [p. 9] zal, een derde part voor den Armen der plaatze daar het
casus voorvallen zal, ende het resteerende derde part voor den Suppliant:
Alles in dien verstande, dat wy den Suppliant met deezen onzen Oc[t]roye
alleen willende gratificeeren, tot verhoedinge van zyn schade, door het
nadrukken van de voorsz. Werken, daar door in geenigen deele verstaan den
innehoude van dien te authoriseren ofte te advoueren, en veel min dezelve
onder onze proctectie ende bescherminge eenig meerder credit, aanzien ofte

reputatue te geven, nemaar den Suppliant, in cas daar iets onbehoorlyks zoude mogen inflileuren, alle het zelve tot zynen laste zal gehouden weezen te verantwoorden: Tot dien cinde wel expresselyk begeerende, dat, by aldien hy deeze onzen Octroye voor de voorsz. Musicale Werken zal willen stellen, daar van geene geabbrevieerde ofte gecontraheerde mentie zal mogen maaken, nemaar gehouden zal weezen't zelve Octroy in't geheel, ende zonder eenige omissie, daar voor te drukken ofte te doen drukken; Ende dat hy gehouden zal zyn een Exemplaar van de voorsz. Musicale Werken, gebonden en wel gecontioneert, te brengen in de Bibliotheek van onze Universiteit tot Leiden, en daar af behoorlyk te doen blyken; alles op peene van het effect van dien te verliezen. Ende ten einde de voornoemde Suppliant deezen onzen Consente ende Octyroye mooge genieten als naat behooren, lasten wy alle ende eenen iegelyken die het aangaan mag, dat zy den Suppliant van den innehoude van deezen doen ende laten gedoogen, rustelyk, vreedelyk ende volkomentlyk genieten en gebruiken, cesserende alle belet ter contrarie. Gedaan in den Hage, onder onzen grooten Zegel hier aan doen hangen, den eersten December in't Jaar onzes Heeren ende Zaligmaakers duizendt zes hondert negen-en-tachtigh. Was geteekent, A. HEINSIUS. V^t. In dorso stondt, *Ter Ordonnantie van de Staaten.* Was geteekent, SIMON van BEAUMONT. Hebbende onder uithangen een Zegel in tooden wassche aan een dubbelde francyne staate.

The "PRIVILEGIE." on p. [10] reads:

DE Staaten Generaal de Vereenigde Nederlanden, allen den geenen die deezen zullen zien, ofte hooren leezen, Saluit, DOEN TE WETEN, Dat wy geconsenteert, geaccordeert, ende geoctroyeert hebben, gelyk wy consenteeren, accordeeren, ende octroyeeren by deezen, aan *Amedeus le Chevallier,* omme voor den tydt van vystien naastkomende achter een-volgende jaaren, met seclusie van allen anderen, binnen deeze Geunieerde Provincien, Landtschappen, Steden ende Leden van dien, te mogen doen drukken, uitgeven, venten, verkoopen, ende debiteren, zoodanige Musicale Stukken, als Simphonien, Stukken a een, twee, drie a vier Stemmen, zelfs heele Stukken, zoo van *Jan Baptist Lully, Colasse,* ende andere vermaarde Autheuren in de Operaas: Verbiedende allen, ende eenen iegelyken, Ingezetenen van de voorsz. Vereenigde Nederlanden, Landschappen, Steden, ende Leden van dien, binnen den voorsz. tydt van vystien naastkomende jaaren, de voorsz, Musicale Stukken, ende Simphonien, Stukken a een, twee, drie a vier Stemmen, ende heele Stukken, in het geheel, ofte ten deele na te drukken, doen nadrukken, uitgeven, venten, verkoopen, ende debiteren, ofte elders zoo nagedrukt binnen de opgemelte Landen te brengen, om verkogt te werden, op de verbeurte van alle de nagedrukte Exemplaren, ende daaren boven van een somme van drie-hondert Carolus Guldens, te appliceren daar van een derde-deel ten behoeve van den Officier die de calange doen zal, het

CARL B. SCHMIDT

tweede derden-deel ten behoeve van den Armen, ende het restende derden-
deel ten behoeve van den voorsz. *Amedeus le Chevallier;* behoudelyk
nochtans, dat den zelven *Amedeus le Chevallier* gehouden zal zyn, op deezen
onzen Octroye te verzocken, ook te obtineren attache van die Provincie, of
Provincien, daar hy de voorsz. Musicale Stukken, Simphonien, Stukken a
een, twee, drie a vier Stemmen, ende heele Stukken, zal willen doen drukken
uitgeven, venten, verkoopen, ende debiteren. Gedaan ter Vergaderinge van de
hoog-gemelte Staaten Generaal, in den Hage, den eersten February, Duizendt
zes-hondert tnegentig. Was geteekent, W. DE NASSAU. Onder stondt, *Ter
Ordonnantie van de zelve.* Was geteekent, F. FAGEL.

COPIES – **D**-FUl (KWF 840/600) [B only]; Dl; **F**-Pa (M. 685a-b) [Ds II only: see La
Laurencie, p. 143]; **GB**-DRc (B35a(i)) [see Harman, p. 90, no. 533a], Lbl
(C.404(1–3)) [B only: see *CPM*, XXXVI, p. 370], Ob (Mus. Sch. E. 520a-c) [see
BUC, II, p. 635] and (Mus. Sch. E. 521a, b) [Ds. I and II only]; **NL**-Lu (542 F 16.1,
17.1, & 18.1); **S**-N (Finsp. Fol. 1127:1–3) [see Davidsson, pp. 265–266, no. 321];
USSR-Mrg (ω 90–82//17) [see *GOL*, p. 77, no. 1581]

BIBLIOGRAPHY – *RISM* A/I, L 3061; ScheurleerA, SchneiderC, *passim*

BLAEU/LE CHEVALIER 1b: TITLE VOLUME 2 – identical except "1690" is
replaced by "1691" and the words "PREMIER DESSUS." are omitted.

DATE – 1691

DESCRIPTION – Three parts: Premier Dessus ([6] + 104 pp.); Second Dessus ([6]
+ 104 pp.); Basse ([4] + 88 pp.)

CONTENTS – The following contents are presented in LWV order. The number
given in parentheses shows the order in the print: **LWV 39:** 5* (84), 7* (85), 10
(113); **LWV 45:** 27 (68), 32 (48); **LWV 47:** 16 (41 [= 41/12]), 17 (189 [= 42/13]), 21
(104 [= 42/18]), 25 (185 [= 33/1 and 46/17]), 28 (186 [= 33/4 and 46/20]), 34 (99),
37 (135 [= 42/19]); **LWV 49:** 3 (123), 14 (101), 23 (21), 38 (22); **LWV 50:** 15 (4), 30
(5), 31 (164), 52 (167), 64 (82), 76 (98), 78 (166); **LWV 51:** 3 (8), 17 (6), 29 (154), 42
(169), 45 (75), 47 (187), 51 (60), 61 (59), 62 (58), 64 (170), 65 (7), 70 (38); **LWV 53:**
22 (128), 29 (54), 31 (152), 34 (28), 51 (102), 54 (97), 69 (131), 72 (43), 75 (26), 76
(24), 78 (156); **LWV 54:** 4 (110), 27 (90), 28 (119), 34 (88), 37 (184), 41 (79 verse 2
only), 44 (14); **LWV 56:** 12 (91), 25 (53), 27 (148), 30 (149 [= 45/17]), 35 (180), 37
(122), 39 (127); **LWV 57:** 3 (33), 27 (34), 29 (87), 53 (141), 65 (35 duet only); **LWV
58:** 8 (132), 11 (136 [= 78/10]), 39 (80), 43 (27), 45 (32), 46 (157), 63 (161), 64
(162), 72 (188); **LWV 59:** 11 (55), 49 (25), 55 (23); **LWV 60:** 3 (142), 5 (144), 7 (12),
9 (15), 11 (13), 16 (16), 19 (145), 25 (114), 35 (51), before 40 (69 "Ah qu'un tendre
cœur"), 41 (111), 43 (89), 51 (74), 52 (50), 55 (64), 64 (86); **LWV 61:** 3 (9), 7 (143),
16 (10), 21 (76), 34 (105), 35 (11), 53 (179); **LWV 63:** 21 (30), 31 (103), 34 (106), 35
(138), 36 (107), 56 (178), 58 (174), 62 (46), 63 (31), after 68 ("Un tendre Amour");
LWV 65: 6 (72), 25 (66), 28 (70), 39 (163 "Aimons nous"), 41 (155), 52 (137), 54
(100), 59 (134), 68 (29); **LWV 68:** 3 (71); **LWV 69:** 5 (168), 8 (165), 21 (78), 25 (1),

29 (125), 33 (2), 36 (56); **LWV 71**: 4 (17), 5 (153), 17 (73), 37 (116), 55 (146), 60 (36); **LWV 73**: before 23 (92 "Redoublons sans cesse"), 23 (94), 25 (117), before 32 (177, II,4), 41 (151), 52 (49). In addition, pieces 20, 109, 115, 118, and 126 are drawn from *Zéphire et Flore;* 40, 63, 121, 150, 173, 176, and 183 from *Achille et Polyxène*; and 44, 45, 62, 67, 77, 81, 83, 108, 130, 139, and 140 from *Thétis et Pélée.* The following pieces (cited according to attributions given in the print) cannot be matched with LWV numbers: **LWV 50**: "Ah! quelle gloire" [V, 4] (57), "Alceste, vous pleurez" [Act II, 8] (95); **LWV 51**: "Les plus douces chaines" (171), "Que de torments!" (172); **LWV 53**: "Le moindre artifice" (112), "Quels honneurs" [Act I, 3] (129); **LWV 56**: "Pleurons en des si grands malheurs" (96), "Perdez l'effroy dont vos sens sont glacez" (124), "Cependant montrons luy ce que ces lieux terribles" (182); **LWV 58**: "Loing d'icy, loing de nous" (158), "O bien heureuse" (159), "Ah! que ces demeures" (160); **LWV 69**: "Que la gloire a jamais la couronne" (2), "Quel empire eust jamais tant de charmes" (42); **LWV 71**: "Non, je perdray plustost le jour" [V, I] (37); **LWV 73**: "Brillant soleil celebrons" (18), "Qu'aujourd'huy toutte la nature" (19), "Pardonnons aux tendres Amants" (52), "Serons nous tousjours" [I, 5, before 73/20] (61), "Son jeune cœur" (120), "L'Hymen vient" (133)

COPIES – **D**-FUl (KWF 840/600) [B only]; DI; **F**-Pa (M. 685a-b) [Ds II only: see La Laurencie, p. 143], Pn (Rés. Vmc. 178 (1–2)); **GB**-DRc (B35a(ii)) [see Harman, p. 90, no. 533b], Lbl (C 404(1–3)) [B only: see *CPM*, XXXVI, p. 370], Ob (Mus. Sch. E. 522a-c) [see *BUC*, 11, p. 635] and (Mus. Sch. E. 523a, b) [Ds. I and II only]; **NL**-LU (542 F 16.2, 17.2, & 18.2); **S**-N (Finsp. Fol. 1127:1–3) [see Davidsson, pp. 266–268, no. 322]; **USSR**-Mrg (Ω 90–81H18) [see *GOL*, pp. 77–78, no. 1582]

BIBLIOGRAPHY – *RISM* A/I, L 3062; SchneiderC, *passim*

BLAEU/LE CHEVALIER 2*: TITLE – SCELTA | Delle più belle | ARIETTE, e CANZOCINE I | ITALIANE, | De' più famosi Autori, | Che in quella lingua ne habbino composte nelle Opere, | *Accommodate al suono di Flauto, Violino, & altri Stromenti,* | Racolte | D'AMADEO LE CHEVALLIER. | [printer's mark] | *IN AMSTERDAM,* | [rule] | Stampate de P. & J. BLAEU, e si vendono nel Pype- | Markt, vicino | l'Arme di Francia. 1691.

DATE – 1691

DEDICATIONS – pp. 5–7:

> *Alla Serenissima Altezza Padrona Clementissima,* | MADAMA | LA PRINCIPESSA DI SOISSONS, | CONSACRA | *in segno dell' umilissimo suo ossequio* | AMEDEO LE CHEVALLIER | queste picciola Scelta delle piu belle | Ariette Italiane.
> SERENISSIMA ALTEZZA,
> Ancorche porti il titolo d'Aria questa picciola operetta, che vengo ad offrir à VOSTRA ALTEZZA SERENISSIMA, profondissimo è nondimeno l'ossequio, che me vi astrenge, ed in vero, chi vuol' ascendere all'au- [p. 6] ge dell'eccelsi glorie di V.A.S. ha d'uopo dell'assistenza dell'Aria per inalzaruisi quasi

CARL B. SCHMIDT

Dedalo sù le ali della Fama, che le và publicando per l'Universo; In Labirinto
maggiore di quello da lui formato si troverebbe, chi inoltrar si volesse frà le
lodi delle Virtù di V.A.S., che la rendono impareggiabile nel Sesso, e crederei
d'incontrar la Sorte d'Icaro, se valicar le volessi per l'Aria, che le porta da per
tutto, laonde nella infinità de Ponti, che compongono qaueste, che le
presento, le racchiudo col silenzio, e negli assidovi sospiri, l'accerto d'haver
io da longo tempo sospirata l'occasione di consecrarle la mia
ossequiosissima servitu. L'accetti V.A.S. colla solita sua benignissima
Clemenza, e mi conceda la stimatissima grazia di potermi dire per sempre.
Di V.A.S. *Umilissimo, divotissimo & ossequiosissimo servitore*
AMEDEO LE CHEVALLIER.
[p. 7] AGLI I AMATORI I DELLA I MUSICA. I
CRederete, che pascere vi voglia d'Aria, come un Camaleonte, presentandovi
ora dell' Aria, mà se considerarete il mio intento, vedrete che prima di dar
queste alle Stampe di quella sola cravate pasciuti, mentre dopò d'haverlo
ascoltato per quell' elemento, profittar ne potrete coll' Intelletto, goderne coll'
amabile concento della Vostra voce à piacere, e farne parte altrui. Se
aggradirete questa mia fatica, mi darete campo d'inoltrarmi nel lavore,
essendovi per esporre quello, de' piu illustri soggetti che componghino oggi
giorno le Opere Italiane, dalle quali ho scelte quelle che ora vi offro, e godrete
Veder sotto il Torchio quanto essi danno di bello in luce ogni dì. Non altro, che
desiderarvi le maggiori prosperità, e buona salute per longamente goderne.
PRIVILEGES – pp. [8–10]: see Blaeu/Chevalier 1b
DESCRIPTION – Short score (voice(s) and Bc): [10] + 53 + [1] pp.
CONTENTS – **LWV 43**: 15 (= 46/38 and 52/49), 26 (= 46/52 and 52/5), and 31 (=
46/56 and 52/10)
Textual incipits for the complete volume are given below in their order of
appearance:

No.	Incipit	Pages
1	Date all'armi, ò miei pensieri, Si brani, s'uccida	1–4
2	Non vantar libertà, O mio Core se sciolto sei tu	5–7
3	Cieca diva in esorabile [Cesti: see note below]	8–10
4	Muti pur chi vuol Amor	10–11
5	Io non credo alla Speranza, Nè vuò darle albergo in seno	11–13
6	Deh piangete al pianto mio Sassi duri, antiche selve	14–15
7	Ahi martire! Empia sorte! Che condanni à morir	15–16
8	Com'esser può fravoi, ò Numi eterni	16–18
9	Ahi ch'indarno si tarda [Deh piangete, &c. Come sopra]	18–19
10	Quanto vale quanto può Bella bocca di cinabro [Cesti: see note below]	19–21

11 Cieco Dio frà tante pene [strophe I]; Dona tregua à miei martiri   22–23
    [strophe II]
12 Che farai misero core, Io ti peggio poco à poco   23–25
13 Fiero Amor tua fatal forza   25–27
14 Spargi altrove il tuo velen gelosia   27–29
15 O che felicità nel impero d'amore   30–33
16 Ove con piè d'argento porta al'adriatico   33–41
17 De l'Amore Il lieto aspetto Rasserena   42–44
18 Se ti sabir, ti respondir [Lully]   44–45
19 Berenice ove sei dove t'ascondi luce [Cesti: see note below]   45–47
20 Si crude Stelle Ch'io sempre rubelle   48–49
21 Non prendo consiglio, se non dal furor   50–51
22 Lieto ò pensiero, ch'al fin goderò   51–52
23 Ay que lo cura con tanto rigor [Lully]   53
24 Alegresse en amurando, y tome mi parecer [Lully]   53

NOTES – The volume contains a selection of arias in Italian. Except for the pieces by Lully, I have been able to identify only three excerpts from Antonio Cesti's opera *Il Tito* (Venice, 1666) including no. 3 "Cieca diva" (III, 12), no. 10 "Quanto vale quanto può" (I, 13), and no. 19 "Berenice ove sei dove t'ascondi luce" (III, 8). With the exception of these excerpts, no music from this opera is known to have been published in the seventeenth century.
COPIES – **GB**-Lbl (C. 404 (1–3)), Ob (Mus. Sch. E. 498); **S**-Uu (Utl. vok. mus. tr. 134)
BIBLIOGRAPHY – *RISM* B/II, 1691[4]; *BUC*, 2, p. 605; SchmidtT, p. 745; Selhof, p. 169, no. 1333 (Nicolas Selhof apparently owned a copy of this edition; his collection was sold in 1759).

Edition by Amédée Le Chevalier containing music by Jean-Baptiste Lully

LE CHEVALIER 1: TITLE – BELLEROPHON | TRAGEDIE. | MISE EN MVSIQVE, | *Par Monsieur De Lully,* | *Sur-Intendant de la Musique* | *du Roy.* | *Presentée,* | A. S. A MADAME LA PRINCESSE, | ET ABESSE DE MONSTERBLCE, | ET CONTESSE DASPREMONT. | ET RAYQUEM. | [decorative design] | *Se vend a Amsterdam sur le pype Marck au Schilt* | *van Vrankryk, chez Amadée le Chevalier, 1692.*
DATE – 1692
DESCRIPTION – Score (*partition réduite,* excerpts only): [2] + 69 pp.
CONTENTS – Contains thirty-six pieces arranged in the order of the *tragédie lyrique* including **LWV** 57: 2, 3, 5, 7 (octave higher), 10, 13, 14, 15, 16 (but including the preceding section beginning "Reine, vous scavez qu'en ce jour"), 17 (but including the preceding section beginning "Et je crois qu'aucune ardeur"), 26, 27, 28, 29, "Ma presence icy te fait peine?" (no Schneider number, II, 3*), "Tu me

quittes, cruel, arreste" (no Schneider number, II, 4*), 30, 31, 32, 33, 35 (listed as II, 7), 37 (listed as II, 7), 38, 39, 46, 48, 49, 50, 51*, 53, 54 (ritournelle listed in IV, 3 and duet in IV, 4), 55 (listed as IV, 6), 61 (but including the preceding section beginning "Et toy, ma Fille, abandonne ton ame"), 63, 65, 66

NOTE – SchneiderC, p. 330 incorrectly indicates that LWV 57/64 is found in this print

COPY – US-Wc (M1500.L95B4 1692 Case)

BIBLIOGRAPHY – *RISM* A/I, L 1975; *NUC*, 345, p. 432; SchneiderC, p. 316

Editions by Estienne Roger containing music by Jean-Baptiste Lully (listed alphabetically by title of composition except for the two anthologies [nos. 18 & 19] and the collection entitled De Musyk Schouwtoneel *[no. 20], which are placed at the end)*

ROGER 1: TITLE – OUVERTURE PASSACAILLE | & Tous les autres Airs à jouer de | L'OPERA | D'ACIS & GALATÉE | par M.ᴿ BAPTISTE LULY | Conseiller, Secretaire & sur intendant de la Musique du Roy | A AMSTERDAM | Aux depens d'Estienne Roger Marchand Libraire | *Chez qui l'on trouve un assortiment general de toute sorte de* | *Musique, dont on peut avoir chez lui le Catalogue. N.º 20.*

DATE – [*c.* 1708–12: LesureB, p. 72]

DESCRIPTION – Four parts: Dessus, Second Dessus, Taille, Basse all ([2] + 12 pp.)

CONTENTS – Contains twenty-two pieces including **LWV 73:** 1 (1), 5 (14), 6 (5), 7 (6), 8 (19), 11 (20), 12 (2 "Prelude") and 12 (16 "Apollon en ce jour. Adagio" [air]), 13 (3), 14 (4), 15 (15 "Menuet en Rondeau"), 24 (18), 26 (9), 27 (11), 28 (17), 32 (13), 34 (21), 35 (22), 38 (7), 42 (12), 44 (8), 9 (10)

COPY – GB-Lbl (a. 148. (5.)) [see *CPM*, XXXVI, p. 371]

BIBLIOGRAPHY – *RISM* A/I, L 2933; SchneiderC, p. 482; SchneiderR, p. 334; Selhof, p. 156, no. 1165 (Nicolas Selhof apparently owned a copy of this edition; his collection was sold in 1759).

ROGER 2: TITLE – OUVERTURE | & Tous les autres Airs à jouer de | L'OPERA | D'ALCESTE | par M.ᴿ BAPTISTE LULY | Conseiller Secretaire & sur intendant de la Musique du Roy. | A AMSTERDAM | Aux depens d'Estienne Roger Marchand Libraire. | *Chez qui l'on trouve un assortiment general de toute sorte de* | *Musique, dont on peut avoir chez lui le Catalogue. N.º 90.*

DATE – [*c.* 1709–12: LesureB, p. 72]

DESCRIPTION – Four parts: Dessus ([2] + 12 pp.); Second Dessus ([2] + 11 pp.); Taille ([2] + 10 pp.); Basse ([2] + 9 pp.)

CONTENTS – Contains twenty-four pieces including **LWV 50:** 1 (1), 4 (5), 9 (23), 11 (24), 13 (11 "Air" [chorus only]), 14 (6 "Air"), 15 (7 "Menuet"), 29 (10), 31 (2), 32 (3), 34 (18), 41 (8), 43 (12), 56 (14), 61 (9), 68 (15), 69 (16), 72 (17), 79 (20), 81 (19), 82* (22), 84 (21), 85 (C: 4 "Rondeau"); **LWV 51:** 76 (13)

COPY – GB-Lbl (a. 148. (10.)) [see *CPM*, XXXVI, p. 371]

BIBLIOGRAPHY – *RISM* A/I, L 2942; SchneiderC, p. 226; SchneiderR, p. 334

ROGER 3: TITLE – OUVERTURE | *Avec tous les Airs à joüer de* | *l'Opera* | D'AMADIS | *Par* | M.ʳ BAPTISTE LULY | *Conseiller Secretaire et sur Intendant de la Musique* | DU ROY | *a Amsterdam* | *Chez Estienne Roger Marchand Libraire.*
DATE – [1702: LesureB, p. 72]
DESCRIPTION – Four parts: Dessus, Second Dessus, Taille, Basse all ([2] + 12 pp.)
CONTENTS – Contains twenty-six pieces including **LWV 63:** 1 (1), 4 (2), 5 (3), 10 (20 "Menuet en Rondeau"), 11 (22), 12 (21), 22 (8), 23 (9), 24 (10), 26 (15), 29 (4 "Air"), 33 (19), 34 (5 "Air"), 36 (6 "Menuet"), 41 (13), 42 (12), 46 (7), 48 (16), 49 (17), 50 (18), 55 (23), 57 (24), 58 (25), 59 (26), 60 (14), 67 (11)
COPIES – **GB**-Lbl (a. 148. (2.)) [see *CPM*, XXXVI, p. 371]; the copy listed in *RISM* as at **US**-R (M1505,L956; Hc only, lacks a title page) is actually an edition by Jean Philip Heus (Amsterdam, 1684); **USSR**-Mrg (M3 P-NH/107) [Ds I & II only: see *GOL*, p. 73, no. 1561]
BIBLIOGRAPHY – *RISM* A/I, L 2950; SchneiderC, p. 411; SchneiderR, p. 334

ROGER 4: TITLE – OUVERTURE CHACONNE | & Tous les autres Airs à jouer de | L'OPERA | D'ARMIDE | par | M.ᴿ BAPTISTE LULY | Conseiller, Secretaire & sur intendant de la Musique du Roy | A AMSTERDAM | Aux depens d'Estienne Roger Marchand Libraire | *Chez qui l'on trouve un assortiment general de toute sorte de* | *Musique, dont on peut avoir chez lui le Catalogue. N.º 19.*
DATE – [*c.* 1708–12: LesureB, p. 72]
DESCRIPTION – Four parts: Dessus ([2] + 15 pp.); Second Dessus ([2] + 15 pp.); Taille ([2] + 11 pp.); Basse ([2] + 15 pp.)
CONTENTS – Contains thirty pieces including **LWV 71:** 1 (1), 7 (13), 8 (14), 9 (15 "Gavotte en Rondeau"), 12 (3), 13 (2), 14 (5), 15 (12), 16 (16), 24 (7), 26 (6), 27 (8), 28 (19), 29 (20), 33 (29), 34 (28), 35 (21), 38 (27), 39 (22), 40 (23), 41 (24), 43 (30), 46 (17 "Air"), 48 (18), 51 (11), 52 (10), 53 (4), 54 (9), 61 (31), 68 (25), 69 (26)
COPY – **GB**-Lbl (a. 148. (6.)) [see *CPM*, XXXVI, p. 373]
BIBLIOGRAPHY – *RISM* A/I, L 2959; SchneiderC, p. 466; SchneiderR, p. 334; Selhof, p. 156, no. 1166 (Nicolas Selhof apparently owned a copy of this edition; his collection was sold in 1759). Facsimile issued in Performer's Facsimiles, No. 113 (New York: [Broude Brothers] n.d.)

ROGER 5: TITLE – OUVERTURE | *Avec tous les Airs à joüer de* | *l'Opera* | D'ATIS | *par* | M.ʳ BAPTISTE LULY | *Conceiller Secretaire et Surintendant de la Musique* | DU ROY | A AMSTERDAM, | *Chez ESTIENNE ROGER Marchand Libraire*
DATE – [1704: Hortschansky, p. 277]
DESCRIPTION – Four parts: Dessus, Second Dessus both ([2] + 8 pp.); Taille, Basse both ([2] + 6 pp.)
CONTENTS – Contains eighteen pieces including **LWV 53:** 1 (1), 4 (3), 9 (7 "Gavotte en Rondeau"), 12 (9), 15 (8), 34 (11 "Air"), 46 (6 "Air"), 47 (4), 48 (5

"Air"), 54 (18), 58 (2 "Air"), 60 (13 "Air"), 62 (14), 77 (17), 79 (15), 80 (16), 86 (12 "Air"); **LWV 50:** 43 (10 "Air")

COPIES – **GB**-Lbl (a. 148. (11.)) [see *CPM*, XXXVI, p. 373]; **USSR**-Mrg (M3 P-NH/107) [Ds I & II only: see *GOL*, p. 73, no. 1562]

BIBLIOGRAPHY – LesureB, p. 72; *RISM* A/I, L 2968; SchneiderC, p. 270; SchneiderR, p. 334

ROGER 6: TITLE – OUVERTURE | *avec tous les Airs à jouer de* | *l'Opera de* | *Bellerophon* | Par | M^r. BAPTISTE LULY | *Conseiller Secretaire & surintendant de la Musique* | DU ROY | *A Amsterdam* | *Chez Estienne Roger Marchand Libraire*
DATE – [*c.* 1700–01: LesureB, p. 72]
DESCRIPTION – Four parts: Dessus, Second Dessus, Taille, Basse all ([2] + 9 pp.)
CONTENTS – Contains twenty pieces including **LWV 57:** 1 (1), 4 (12), 7 (15), 8 (13), 9 (5), 18 (21), 19 (2), 23 (3), 24 (19), 25 (20), 34 (22 "Premier Air des sorciers"), 36 (11), 42 (17), 45* (18), 58 (14), 59 (10), 64 (8), 67 (9), 68 (4), 69 (6), 70 (7)
COPIES – **B**-Br (Cl.12.000 Mus. [7^e cl.V.K.Lull.: B only]) [see Huys, p. 268, no. 401]; **GB**-Lbl (a. 148. (7.)) [see *CPM*, XXXVI, p. 373]; **USSR**-Mrg (M3 P-NH/107) [Ds I & II only: see *GOL*, p. 73, no. 1563]
BIBLIOGRAPHY – *RISM* A/I, L 2977; SchneiderC, p. 316; SchneiderR, p. 334

ROGER 7: TITLE – OUVERTURE | *avec tous les airs à jouer de* | *l'Opera de Cadmus* | *Par* | Mr BAPTISTE LULY | *Conseiller secretaire & surintendant de la Musique* | *du Roÿ* | *A Amsterdam* | *Chez ESTIENNE ROGER Marchand libraire*
DATE – [1702: LesureB, p. 72]
DESCRIPTION – Four parts: Dessus, Second Dessus both ([2] + 10 pp.); Taille, Basse both ([2] + 9 pp.)
CONTENTS – Contains twenty-two pieces including **LWV 49:** 1 (1), 4 (17), 5 (15), 8 (12), 10 (16), 14 (2), 15 (3), 22 (19), 34 (4), 36 (5), 42 (9), 44 (10), 47 (11), 51 (7), 54 (13), 55 (14), 56 (8), 57* (6); **LWV 59:** 54 (18); plus three unidentified "Menuets" (20–22)
NOTE – The three unidentified "Menuets" also occur in an edition printed by Jean Philip Heus (Amsterdam, 1682); see Heus 1.
COPIES – **GB**-Lbl (a. 148. (8.)) [see *CPM*, XXXVI, p. 374]; **USSR**-Mrg (M3 P-NH/107) [Ds I & II only: see *GOL*, p. 73, no. 1564]
BIBLIOGRAPHY – *RISM* A/I, L 2982; SchneiderC, p. 210; SchneiderR, p. 334; Selhof, p. 156, no. 1167 (Nicolas Selhof apparently owned a copy of this edition; his collection was sold in 1759).

ROGER 8: TITLE – OUVERTURE | *Avec tous les Airs a jouer* | *de l'Opera* | D'ISIS | Par | Mr BAPTISTE LULY | *Conseiller Secretaire & surintendant de la Musique* | DU ROY | *A Amsterdam* | *chez Estienne Roger Marchand libraire*
DATE – [1701: LesureB, p. 72]

DESCRIPTION – Four parts: Dessus, Second Dessus, Taille, Basse all ([2] + 8 pp.)
CONTENTS – Contains twenty-four pieces including **LWV 54:** 1 (1), 4 (8), 5 (9), 10
(2), 11 (3), 12 (18), 21 (11), 22 (12), 24 (6), 29 (15), 31 (16 "Menuet"), 33 (4), 35 (5),
36 (7), 42 (14), 43 (17 "March des bergers"), 44 (22), 45 (21), 51 (10), 54 (23), 56 (13
"Les Furies"), 57 (24 "Second air des Furies"), 65 (19), 66 (20)
COPIES – **GB**-Lbl (a. 148. (4.)) [see *CPM*, XXXVI, p. 374]; **USSR**-Mrg (M3 P-
NH/107) [Ds I & II only: see *GOL*, p. 74, no. 1565]
BIBLIOGRAPHY – *RISM* A/I, L 2991; SchneiderC, p. 293; SchneiderR, p. 334

ROGER 9: TITLE – OUVERTURE | *avec tous les airs à joüer de* | *l'Opera de Persée* |
Par Mr BAPTISTE LULY | *Conseiller secretaire & surintendant de la Musique* | *du Roy*
| *A Amsterdam* | *Chez ESTIENNE ROGER Marchand libraire*
DATE – [1702: LesureB, p. 72]
DESCRIPTION – Four parts: Dessus, Second Dessus, Taille, Basse all ([2] +12 pp.)
CONTENTS – Contains twenty-nine pieces including **LWV 60:** 1 (1), 6 (6), 10 (10
"Rondeau"), 11 (9), 26 (20), 28 (14), 29 (15), 30 (13), 31 (19), 44 (25), 45 (12), 47
(26), 49 (27), 50 (17), 56 (18), 57* (16), 59 (24 "Prelude"), 69 (29), 70 (22 "Prelude"),
71 (21), 72 (23), 73 (28), 76 (4), 77 (3), 78 (7), 79 (8), 81 (11), 82 (5), 84 (2)
COPIES – **GB**-Lbl (a. 148. (12.)) [see *CPM*, XXXVI, p. 375]; **USSR**-Mrg (M3 P-
NH/107) [Ds I & II only: see *GOL*, p. 74, no. 1566]
BIBLIOGRAPHY – *RISM* A/I, L 3000; SchneiderC, p. 370; SchneiderR, p. 334

ROGER 10: TITLE – OUVERTURE | *Avec tous les Airs a jouér de* | *l'opera de* |
Phaeton | *par* | MR BAPTISTE LULY | *Conseiller Secretaire et Sur Inteneant de la*
Musique | DU ROY | [rule] | *a Amsterdam ches* | *Estienne Roger Marchant* | *Libraire*
DATE – [1697: LesureB, p. 72]
DESCRIPTION – Four parts: Dessus, Second Dessus, Taille, Basse all ([2] + 12 pp.)
CONTENTS – Contains twenty-eight pieces (not numbered in the print) including
LWV 61: 1 (1), 2 (4), 6 (17), 7 (18), 8 (5), 14 (2), 15* (3 "Bourée pour les Mesmes"),
23 (7 "Pour les Hautbois"), 25 (6), 27 (8), 29 (16), 37 (9), 40* (15), 41 (13), 47 (26),
48 (20), 50 (27), 52 (19), 53 (24), 55 (25), 57 (10), 58 (11), 59 (12), 61 (14), 66 (23),
67 (21), 68 (22), 72 (28)
NOTES – The engraving in this edition is cramped and of inferior quality when
compared to later Roger editions. It is also the only Roger edition of Lully to use
large double-lined letters for words like "Ouverture."
COPIES – **GB**-Lbl (A. 148. (9.)) [better quality paper than the following exemplar]
and (K.7.c.2.(14.)) [Ds II only: see *CPM*, XXXVI, p. 375]; **USSR**-Mrg (M3 P-
NH/107) [Ds I & II only: see *GOL*, p. 74, no. 1567]; a copy of the Taille part was
offered for sale by Scientific Library Service, see cat. 59, no. 357.
BIBLIOGRAPHY – *RISM* A/I, L 3012; SchneiderC, p. 389; SchneiderR, p. 334;
Selhof, p. 156, no. 1168 (Nicolas Selhof apparently owned a copy of this edition; his
collection was sold in 1759).

ROGER 11: TITLE – EXTRAIT | *DE* | L'OPERA | *DE* | PHAËTON, | Où Recüeil des plus beaux endroits à chanter, à une, deux, & | trois voix, avec les Accompagnemens, Préludes, | & Ritournelles. | [printer's mark of a bowl of flowers and foliage] | *A AMSTERDAM*, | Aux Dépens de Mr. CHAMPERREUX & se vend chez ESTIENNE ROGER, Marchand | Libraire où l'on trouve un assortiment général de toute sorte de Musique.

DATE – [1706: Hortschansky, p. 278]

DESCRIPTION – Score: [2] + 114 pp.

CONTENTS – Contains forty-six pieces (not numbered in the print) including **LWV 61**: 3–5, 7–12, 16–21, "Vous passez sans me voir" before 22 (opening of I, 3 [Théone]), "Vous paroissez chagrin" I, 4 [Clymène], 23, 24, 26, 28, 32–39, 42–46, 49, 53, 54, 56, 59, 63–66, 69, 71

NOTE – This edition has been printed rather than engraved.

COPY – **CH**-N (5R 842)

BIBLIOGRAPHY – LesureB, p. 72; *RISM* A/I, L 3010; SchneiderC, p. 389; SchneiderR, p. 332

ROGER 12: TITLE – OUVERTURE | *avec tous les airs á jouer de* | *l'Opera de Proserpine* | *par* | Mr BAPTISTE LULY | *Conseiller secretaire & surintendant de la Musique* | *du Roÿ* | *A Amsterdam* | *Chez ESTIENNE ROGER Marchand libraire*

DATE – [1706: LesureB, p. 72; [1702]: SchneiderC, p. 333]

DESCRIPTION – Four parts: Dessus ([2] + 11 pp.); Second Dessus ([2] + 10 pp.); Taille ([2] + 9 pp.); Basse ([2] + 11 pp.)

CONTENTS – Contains twenty-three pieces including **LWV 58**: 1 (1), 3 (11), 4 (9 "Air pour les Trompetes"), 5 (10), 10 (12), 11 (B♭: 23 "Menuet" [= 78/10]), 13 (3), 14 (4 "Menuet"), 23 (14), 26 (16), 27 (17), 28 (15), 44 (6 "Air Pour les Flustes & Violons"), 47 (19), 53 (5), 58 (7), 69 (21), 71 (22), 73 (13 "Air"), 78 (2), 82 (8), 84 (20), 85 (18)

COPIES – **B**-Lc (Rés. 032) [Ds II and B only]; **GB**-Lbl (a. 148. (13.)) [see *CPM*, XXXVI, p. 376]; **USSR**-Mrg (M3 P-NH/107) [Ds I & II only: see *GOL*, p. 75, no. 1569]

BIBLIOGRAPHY – *RISM* A/I, L 3021; SchneiderC, p. 333; SchneiderR, p. 334; Selhof, p. 156, no. 1169 (Nicolas Selhof apparently owned a copy of this edition; his collection was sold in 1759).

ROGER 13: TITLE – OUVERTURE | *Avec tous les Airs à jouer* | *du Ballet* | DE PSICHE | *par* | Mr BABTISTE LULY | *Conceiller Secretaire et Surintendant de la Musique* | DU ROY | A AMSTERDAM | *Chez ESTIENNE ROGER Marchand Libraire*

DATE – [1705: Hortschansky, p. 278]

DESCRIPTION – Four parts: Dessus ([2] + 8 pp.); Second Dessus, Taille, Basse all ([2] + 6 pp.)

CONTENTS – Contains fifteen pieces including **LWV 56**: 1 (1 [= 45/1]), 4 (2 [= 45/4 and 46/8]), 6 (3 [= 45/6 and 46/10]), 15 (4 "Les Femmes Eschevelées" [= 45/10 and 46/15]), 17 (6 "Air" [= 45/11]), 18 (5 "Les Forgerons" [= 45/12 and 46/33]), 28 (15 [= 45/15]), 36 (7 "Les Demons" [= 45/18]), 42 (7 [= 45/19 and 46/62]), 48 (10 [= 45/25 and 46/68]), 51 (8 "Les Bacchanelles" [= 45/28 and 46/71]), 53 (9 "Les Voltigeurs" [= 45/30 and 46/73]), 56 (11 [= 45/33 and 46/76]), 58 (12 "Echo" [= 45/35 and 46/78]), 59 (13 "Rondeau pour les Trompettes" [= 45/36 and 46/79]), 60 (14 [45/37 and 46/80])

COPIES – **GB**-LBL (a. 148. (3.)) [see *CPM*, XXXVI, p. 376]; **USSR**-Mrg (M3 P-NH/107) [Ds I & II only: see *GOL*, p. 74, no. 1568]

BIBLIOGRAPHY – LesureB, p. 73; *RISM* A/I, L 3025; SchneiderC, p. 310; SchneiderR, p. 334

ROGER 14: TITLE – OUVERTURE I *Avec tous les Airs à joüer de* I *l'Opera de* I ROLAND I *par* I M.ʳ BAPTISTE LULY I *Conceiller Secretaire et Sur Intendant de la Musique* I DU ROY I *A AMSTERDAM.* I *Chez ESTIENNE ROGER Marchand Libraire*

DATE – [1704: Hortschansky, p. 278]

DESCRIPTION – Four parts: Dessus ([2] + 9 pp.); Second Dessus ([2] + 8 pp.); Taille ([2] + 8 pp.); Basse ([2] + 9 pp.)

CONTENTS – Contains nineteen pieces including **LWV 65:** 1 (1), 4* (9), 11 (2), 12 (3), 13 (4), 21 (6), 24 (5), 26 (7), 40 (11), 42 (12), 55 (10), 56 (8), 63 (19), 65 (14), 66 (15), 67 (18), 75* (13), 82 (16), 83 (17)

COPIES – **GB**-Lbl (a. 148. (1.)) [see *CPM*, XXXVI, p. 376]; **USSR**-Mrg (M3 P-NH/107) [Ds I & II only: see *GOL*, p. 75, no. 1570]

BIBLIOGRAPHY – LesureB, p. 73; *RISM* A/I, L 3034; SchneiderC, p. 429; SchneiderR, p. 334

ROGER 15: TITLE – OUVERTURE I *avec tous les airs á joüer de* I *L'Opera du Temple de la Paix* I *Par* I Mʳ BAPTISTE LULY I *Conseiller secretaire & surintendant de la Musique* I *du Roy* I A Amsterdam I *Chez ESTIENNE ROGER Marchand libraire*

DATE – [1703: LesureB, p. 72]

DESCRIPTION – Four parts: Dessus, Second Dessus, Taille, Basse all ([2] + 8 pp.)

CONTENTS – Contains eighteen pieces arranged in strict LWV order (with the exception of LWV 69/34 and 45, which are reversed) including **LWV 69:** 1, 6 ("Air"), 7, 13–16, 24 ("Air"), 26, 27, 30, 31 ("Trio"), 32, 34, 37, 39, 40, 45

COPIES – **GB**-Lbl (a. 148. (14.)) [see *CPM*, XXXVI, p. 376]; **USSR**-Mrg (M3 P-NH/107) [Ds I & II only: see *GOL*, p. 75, no. 1571]

BIBLIOGRAPHY – *RISM* A/I, L 3050; Schneider, p. 453; SchneiderR, p. 334

ROGER 16a (Nos. 1–61): TITLE – TRIOS I *de* Differents Autheurs I *Choisis & Mis en ordre* par I M.ᴿ BABEL I *Ce Livre sera Suivi dans peu d'un Second* I *qui contiendra la Suite de ces pieces icy* I *jusques au Nombre de 130.* I *LIVRE PREMIER* I [rule] I *a Amsterdam Ches* I *Estienne Roger Marchand Libraire.*

ROGER 16b (Nos. 62–129): TITLE – TRIOS I *de Differents Autheurs* I *Choisis et Mis* *en ordre par* | MR BABEL | LIVRE SECOND | *a Amsterdam chez Estienne Roger* | *Marchand Libraire*

DATES – [Vol. I was first advertised in 1697 and vol. II in 1700. See LesureB, p. 35 and GustafsonLI, p. 506. Schmieder, p. 439 suggests 1689 as the date for vol. II.]

DESCRIPTIONS – Three parts: vol. I Dessus ([2] + 39 pp.); Second Dessus ([2] + 35 pp.); Basse [Continue] ([2] + 34 pp.); vol. II Dessus (33 pp.); Second [Dessus] (30 pp.); Basse Continue (26 pp.)

CONTENTS – Contains 129 pieces including **LWV 11:** 29 (13a); **LWV 14:** 10 (23); **LWV 15:** 3 (3 "Ritournelle de Pluton"); **LWV 18:** 11 (96 [= 35/13]), 21 (97 "R[ecit] Escalope"), 25* (51 "Les Mors" [contains a unique prelude]); **LWV 21:** 38 (60 "Les Gojats"); **LWV 27:** 32 (84 [= 35/11 and 79/37]); **LWV 31:** 23* (40); **LWV 32:** ? (54); **LWV 35:** 1 (67), 2 (71), 3 (69), 4 (73), 5* (72 "Imitation"), 6 (74), 7 (68), 9 (66), 10 (90), 11 (87), 12 (88), 42* (125); **LWV 38:** 2 (124 "A Moy camarade" [= 79/48]), 3 (B♭: 58 [= 35/49 and 79/49]); **LWV 39:** 1* (1), 5 (16), 10 (C: 80); **LWV 43:** 15 (5 [= 46/38 and 52/49]), 38 (77 [= 35/50 and 79/42]); **LWV 45:** 27 (g: 19); **LWV 49:** 5* (61 "Air de Pan"), 14 (12), 50 (117); **LWV 50:** 30 (81), 31 (101), 70 (126), 79 (14), 83 (55); **LWV 51:** 29 (43), 51* (11), 64 (95), 65 (82), 68 (22), 76 (64 "La Gloire"); **LWV 53:** 78 (41), 81 (111), 85 (89); **LWV 54:** 4 (30), 8 (2), 14 (44), 34* (100), 44 (76), 58* (B♭: 47); **LWV 56:** 22 (129), 31 (4), 40* (113); **LWV 58:** 30 (103), 60 (36 "Les Champs elisées"), 65 (10), 72 (50 "Les Ombres"), 80 (6 "Prelude"); **LWV 59:** 15 (27); **LWV 60:** 5 (39), 11 (75); **LWV 61:** 23* (70), 53 (57); **LWV 63:** 34 (18), 36 (15), 58 (79); **LWV 65:** 6 (128), 25 (108); **LWV 68:** 8 (105); **LWV 69:** 2 (d: 104); **LWV 71:** 16 (123); numbers not listed above are either anonymous or the work of other authors. For a full inventory of these pieces, see GustafsonLI, pp. 506–509.

NOTES – This work was sold on two types of paper: "Beau papier" for "f. 9.0" and "petit papier" for "f. 6.0."

COPIES – D-W (6.1–6.3 Musica div. (1.2)) [see Schmieder, pp. 439–440, no. 636]; GB-DRc (*C53(i) and (ii)) [see Harman, pp. 102–103, nos. 533a and 533b]

BIBLIOGRAPHY – LesureB, p. 73; *RISM* BI/1, pp. 575 ([1697]^4) and 587 (1698)^5; SchneiderC, *passim*; Selhof, p. 141, no. 964 (Nicolas Selhof apparently owned a copy of this edition; his collection was sold in 1759).

ROGER 17*: TITLE – Les airs pour les violons flustes &c. de l'opera le triumphe de l'amour

DATE – [1697: Hortschansky, p. 278]

DESCRIPTION – [Three parts: LesureB, p. 21]

CONTENTS – Excerpts from **LWV 59**

COPY – None located

BIBLIOGRAPHY – Hortschansky, p. 278; LesureB, p. 73; SchneiderC, p. 351

ROGER 18*: TITLE – SUITTES FACILES | *Pour 1 Flute ou 1 Violon & 1 Basse Continuë* | *de la Composition de* | *Messieurs* | DU FAU, L'ENCLOS, PINEL, LULLY |

BRUYNINGHS, LE FEVRE | & autres habiles Maistres | Avec les agrèements marquez en faveur de | Ceux qui Commencent a aprendre | A Amsterdam | Chez Estienne Roger Marchand libraire | LONDON sold by Francis Vaillant french bookseller in the [. . .] and | where you may be furnished with all sorts of musick

DATE – [1700: Hortschansky, p. 281; c. 1710: Harman, p. 100; [1703]: SchneiderC, p. 499]

DESCRIPTION – Two parts: Dessus (13 pp.); Basse Continue (11 pp.)

CONTENTS – Because an inventory of this volume has not appeared in print, the full title of each excerpt it contains is listed below. Most of the pieces lack composer attributions in the print.

1. Gavote	17. Rondeau
2. Tombeau de Mr Lenclo	18. Allemande de M.^{r} du fau
3. Courante la belle homicide	19. Courante
4. Sarabande	20. Sarabande
5. Allemande de Mr de Lully (g: LWV 75/19 [= 27/4 and 35/40]	21. Gavote
	22. Gigue
	23. Allemande la Royalle
6. Gigue	24. Courante
7. Allemande	25. Sarabande
8. Courante	26. Rondeau
9. Sarabande	27. Marche pour M.^{r} L'Electeur Palatin
10. Gigue	28. Allemande de M.^{r} le fevre
11. Gavote	29. Courante
12. La Caquet des femmes	30. Sarabande
13. Gavote	31. Gavote
14. Allemande de Mr Brunings	32. Gigue de Mr Pinel
15. Courante la toute belle	33. Passacaille de M.^{r} le fevre
16. Sarabande	34. Rondeau

NOTE – This volume was sold for "f. I. 10."

COPY – GB-DRc (*C99) [see Harman, pp. 100–101, no. 589, and BUC, vol. II, p. 988]

BIBLIOGRAPHY – LesureB, p. 87; SchneiderC, p. 499 (from his description it is clear that Schneider has seen this print); SchneiderR, p. 334 (no copy listed)

ROGER 19*: TITLE – Suittes pour un Lut avec un violon, ou une flûte & une basse continue ad libitum de la composition de Mrs. du Fau, l'Enclos, Pinel, Lully, Bruyninghs, le Frevre & autres habiles maîtres grav. 4.

DATE – [1700: Hortschansky, p. 281]

CONTENTS – Unknown

COPY – None located

BIBLIOGRAPHY – LesureB, p. 87

CARL B. SCHMIDT

ROGER 20*: TITLE –De Musyk Schouwtoneel
DATE – [*c.* 1712–15: LesureB, p. 85]
DESCRIPTION – unknown
NOTES – According to LesureB, p. 85, this set includes twenty-five volumes (each selling for "f. 0.10"), of which 1–7 and 23–25 are not by Lully. Lesure does not attribute no. 22 to Lully, but it is probably *Le Triumph de l'Amour*. The following list of Lully contents is quoted from LesureB:

> Achste boek, Armida
> Negende boek, Acis en Galatea
> Tiende boek, Alcestus
> Elfde boek, Phaëton
> Twaalfde boek, Bellérophon
> Dertiende boek, Isis
> Veertiende boek, Amadis
> Vyftiende boek, Cadmus
> Sestiende boek, Perseus
> Seventiende boek, Proserpina
> Achtiende boek, de Tempel der Vreede
> Negentiende boek, Roland
> Twentigst boek, Atys
> Een-en-twentigste boek, Psiché
> Twee-en-twentigste boek, De Triumph der Liefde

COPY – None located
BIBLIOGRAPHY – LesureB, p. 85; Selhof, p. 237, no. 2748 (Nicolas Selhof apparently owned a copy of no. 20 (*Atys*); his collection was sold in 1759).

Editions by Pierre Mortier containing music by Jean-Baptiste Lully (listed by date of publication)

MORTIER 1: TITLE – PHAËTON, I *TRAGEDIE* I MISE I EN I MUSIQUE, I PAR MONSIEUR DE LULLY, ESCUYER, I *Conseiller Secretaire du Roy, Maison, Couronne de* I *France & de ses Finances, & Sur-Intendant* I *de la Musique de Sa Majesté.* I TROISIE'ME EDITION. I [decorative design] I A AMSTERDAM, I [rule] I Chez PIERRE MORTIER, Sur le Vygendam. I *Qui vend toutes sortes de Musique, les plus belles & Correctes qu'il y ait au Monde. Et il* I *donnera tous les Operas de* Mr. LULLY, *de la même beauté que cet Ouvrage.* I MDCCXI.
DATE – 1711
DESCRIPTION – Score (*partition générale*): [2] + 341 pp.
NOTES – According to a *CATALOGUE Des Livres de Musique qui se trouvent Chez Ledit MORTIER* bound in the US-Wc copy, this score sold for "7 Livres." Contains the same six engravings found in the "Seconde edition" engraved by Henri de Baussen (Paris, 1709: see *RISM* A/I, L 3003).

162

COPIES – B-Br [see Fétis, p. 327]; F-LB (2325) [see Libourne, p. 191], Pn (Vm² 70),
(Vm² 70a), (Rés. F. 611) [see LesureC, p. 407], Pmeyer [see LesureCM, p. 48], Sim
(Rm 23); **US**-Wc (M1500.L95.P44) [see Sonneck, p. 100]; USSR-Mrg (M3 P-
NH/160): see *GOL*, p. 76, no. 1576]
BIBLIOGRAPHY – Goovaerts, p. 451, no. 990; *RISM* A/I, L 3004; SchneiderC, p. 389

MORTIER 2: TITLE – ROLAND, I *TRAGEDIE* I MISE I EN I MUSIQUE, I PAR
MONSIEUR DE LULLY, ESCUYER, I *Conseiller Secretaire du Roy, Maison,*
Couronne de I *France & de ses Finances, & Sur-Intendant* I *de la Musique de Sa*
Majesté. I [printer's mark] I A AMSTERDAM, I [rule] I Chez PIERRE MORTIER,
Sur le Vygendam. I *Qui vend toutes sourtes de Musique, les plus belles & Correctes qu'il*
y ait au Monde Et il I *donnera tous les Operas de* Mr. LULLY, *de la même beauté que cet*
Ouvrage. I MDCCXI.
DATE – 1711
DESCRIPTION – Score (*partition générale*): [4] + 400 pp.
NOTES – According to the *CATALOGUE Des Livres de Musique qui se trouvent*
Chez Ledit MORTIER (bound in the US-Wc copy of *Phaéton*, also published by
Mortier), this score sold for "7 Livres." The page layout of this edition follows
that of the Christophe Ballard first edition (Paris, 1686: see *RISM* A/I, L 3027)
except that the Paris edition numbers the prologue i–lxvj and Acts I–V 1–273,
while Mortier numbers the prologue and Acts I–V consecutively 1–341. Mortier
omits the "Au Roy" found in Paris, but adds engravings and descriptions of the
scenery at the beginning of each act. Many of the manuscript ink corrections
found in copies of the Ballard print have been incorporated into the Mortier
edition.
COPIES – D-Sl (Lul 60/5001); DK-Kk (U6); F-private coll., Po (A.17.c.); **GB**-Ltc
[see *BUC*, vol. II, p. 635]; **MO**-Ml'oiseau-lyre; NL-DHgm [see ScheurleerM, vol. II,
p. 371]; USSR-Mrg (M3 P-NH/327) [see *GOL*, p. 76, no. 1577]; Eitner, vol. VI, p. 246
also listed copies in Copenhagen, Rostock, and at D-Bds, which can no longer be
located.
BIBLIOGRAPHY – *RISM* A/I, L 3029; SchneiderC, p. 429

MORTIER 3: TITLE – PERSE'E, I *TRAGEDIE,* I MISE EN MUSIQUE, I Par
Monsieur de LULLY, Escuyer, Conseiller Secretaire du Roy, Maison, Couronne de I
France & de ses Finances, & Sur-Intendant de la Musique de Sa Majesté. I
NOUVELLE EDITION. I [printer's mark] I A AMSTERDAM, I [rule] I Chez
PIERRE MORTIER, Libraire, I *Qui vend toutes sortes de Musique, les plus belles &*
Correctes qu'il ait au Monde. Et il I *donnera tous les Operas de* Mr. LULLY, *de la même*
Grandeur & beauté que cet Ouvrage.
DATE – [1710?]
DESCRIPTION – Score (oblong 4°: *partition réduite*): [2] + 384 pp.
NOTES – According to the *CATALOGUE Des Livres de Musique qui se trouvent Chez*
Ledit MORTIER (bound in the US-Wc copy of *Phaéton*, also published by Mortier),

this score sold for "5 Livres." This edition is not a copy of the Henri de Baussen (Paris, 1710: see *RISM* A/I, L 2993) *partition réduite*.
COPIES – D-ROu (Mus. saec. XVII.18.24¹); F-Pn (Rés. 690) [see LesureC, p. 406]
BIBLIOGRAPHY –*RISM* A/I, L 2997; SchneiderC, p. 369

MORTIER 4a*: TITLE – LES | TRIOS | DES | OPERA | DE MONSIEUR DE LULLY, |
Mis en ordre pour les concerts. | *Propres à chanter, & à joüer sur la Flute, le Violon, &* | *autres Instruments*. | PREMIER DESSUS. | [printer's mark] | *A AMSTERDAM*, |
[rule] | Chez PIERRE MORTIER Libraire sur le Vygendam, qui continuera d'imprimer les Livres | nouveaux en Musique, avec la même beauté & exactitude que cet Ouvrage. S'il y a des Musiciens qui en aient quelques-uns à faire graver ou imprimer, ils n'ont qu'à | s'addresser au dit Mortier.
DATE – [by February 1711: LesureC, p. 408 suggests *c*. 1710]
DESCRIPTION – Three parts: Premier Dessus ([2] + 51 + [1] pp.); [Second Dessus], [Basse] no copies located
CONTENTS – follow Blaeu edition 1a
NOTE – This edition is a reprint of Blaeu edition 1a except that the dedication, "AVIS AU LECTEUR," and "PRIVILEGIE" have been omitted and the "Table des Airs contenus dans ce Volume" now follows the main contents.
COPY – F-Pn (Rés. 692) [Ds I only]
BIBLIOGRAPHY – *RISM* A/I, L 3064; Selhof, p. 179, no. 1586 (Nicolas Selhof apparently owned a copy of this edition; his collection was sold in 1759).
MORTIER 4b*: TITLE – follows Mortier 4a
DATE – [by February 1711: LesureC, p. 408 suggests *c*. 1710]
DESCRIPTION – Three parts: Premier Dessus ([2] + 104 + [2] pp.); [Second Dessus], [Basse] no copies located
CONTENTS – follow Blaeu edition 1b
NOTE – This edition is a reprint of Blaeu edition 1b except that it contains a "Table des Airs" at the end that is not found in the Blaeu edition.
COPY – F-Pn (Rés. 693) [Ds I only]
BIBLIOGRAPHY – *RISM* A/I, L 3064

Editions by Michel Charles Le Cène containing music by Jean-Baptiste Lully (listed alphabetically by title of composition)
LE CENE 1: TITLE – PERSE'E, | *TRAGEDIE*, | MISE EN MUSIQUE, | Par Monsieur de LULLY, Escuyer, Conseiller Secretaire du Roy, Maison, Couronne de | France & de ses Finances, & Sur-Intendant de la Musique de sa Majesté. | NOUVELLE EDITION. | [printer's mark] | A AMSTERDAM, [rule] | Chez MICHEL CHARLES LE CENE, Libraire, chez qui l'on trouve | un assortiment general de Livres de Musique Vocale & Instrumentale.
DATE – 1723 or later [LesureC, p. 407 suggests *c*. 1724]
DESCRIPTION – Score (oblong 4°, *partition réduite*): [2] + [4] + 384 pp.

NOTE – This edition is a reprint of Mortier 3 with an added engraved frontispiece signed "*Deur f.*"
COPY – F-Pn (X. 1092) [see LesureC, p. 407]; Eitner, vol. VI, p. 245 also listed copies in Rostock and at D-Bds, which can no longer be located
BIBLIOGRAPHY – *RISM* A/I, L 2996; SchneiderC, p. 369

LE CENE 2: TITLE – PHAËTON, I *TRAGEDIE* I MISE I EN I MUSIQUE, I PAR MONSIEUR DE LULLY, ESCUYER, I *Conseiller Secretaire du Roy, Maison, Couronne de* I *France & de ses Finances, & Sur-Intendant* I *de la Musique de sa Majesté.* I TROISIE'ME EDITION. I [printer's mark] I A AMSTERDAM, I [rule] I Chez MICHEL CHARLES LE CENE, Libraire, chez qui l'on trouve I un assortiment general de Livres de Musique Vocale & Instrumentale.
DATE – 1723 or later [LesureC, p. 407 suggests *c.* 1725]
DESCRIPTION – Score (*partition générale*): [2] + 341 pp.
NOTE – this edition is a reprint of Mortier 1
COPIES – B-Bc (1748) [see Eitner, vol. VI, p. 245]; F-Pn (Rés. F. 612) [see LesureC, p. 407], TLm (Conservatoire 32(1)); GB-DRu (x+782.14) [see *BUC*, vol. II, p. 635; incorrectly reported by *RISM* as in DRc].
BIBLIOGRAPHY – *RISM* A/I, L 3005; SchneiderC, p. 389

LE CENE 3: TITLE – ROLAND I *TRAGEDIE* I MISE I EN I MUSIQUE, I PAR MONSIEUR DE LULLY, ESCUYER, I *Conseiller Secretaire du Roy, Maison, Couronne de* I *France & de ses Finances, & Sur-Intendant* I *de la Musique de sa Majesté.* I TROISIE'ME EDITION. I [printer's mark] I A AMSTERDAM, I [rule] I Chez MICHEL CHARLES LE CENE, I Libraire, chez qui l'on trouve I un assortiment general de Livres de Musique Vocale & Instrumentale.
DATE – 1723 or later [LesureC, p. 407 suggests *c.* 1725]
DESCRIPTION – Score (*partition générale*): [4] + 400 pp.
COPIES – F-Pn (Vm^2 81) [see LesureC, p. 407], V (MSD In f° 49); I-PAc (Sez. mus. bibl. pal. 17736) [see Parma, pp. 118–119].
BIBLIOGRAPHY – *RISM* A/I, L 3032; SchneiderC, p. 429

7 "Pourquoi toujours des bergers?" Molière, Lully, and the pastoral *divertissement*

JOHN S. POWELL

Notwithstanding the claims that they had scoffed at the idea of pastoral opera in the French language until they witnessed the success of *Pomone*,[1] Molière and Lully introduced rustic characters, Arcadian themes, and operatic pastoral scenes in many of the court *divertissements* they created for Louis XIV. The trademark shepherds, nymphs, satyrs, and magicians of the pastoral genre had long been standard figures in *ballet de cour*. Yet, the chains of rustic lovers, lyric monologues and lovers' laments, the echo dialogues and song contests, and the mock suicides and sleep scenes found in their *comédies-ballets* reveal that pastoral commonplaces were a source of ongoing comic inspiration for *les deux grands Baptistes*.

By the 1660s, the pastoral genre in France was largely démodé as serious dramatic literature. The early pastorales of Nicolas de Montreux (*Arimène*, 1596), Montchrétien (*Bergerie*, 1600), Chrestien des Croix (*Les Amants, ou la grande pastourelle*, 1613), and Isaac du Ryer (*La Vengeance des satyres*, 1614) had been inspired by earlier Italian and Spanish models. With Honoré d'Urfé's multi-volume novel *L'Astrée* (1607–27) the pastorale took on a more Gallic character, and established a new pastoral ethic that was in harmony with the fashionable *esprit précieux* of the 1620s.[2] This imaginary

---

I wish to thank Perry Gethner and Stephen Fleck for their careful reading of and thoughtful comments on earlier drafts of this article.

1   *Mémoires de ma vie, par Charles Perrault*, ed. Paul Bonnefon (Paris, 1909), 126–127 and Antoine Bauderon de Sénecé, *Lettre de Clément Marot, a monsieur de *** touchant ce qui s'est passé à l'arrivée de Jean-Baptiste de Lulli aux champs Elisées* (Cologne: P. Marteau, 1688), 54–55.
2   Tallemant de Réaux relates that "In the company of the family of Mme de Guéméné, they entertained themselves, among other things, with writing some questions on *L'Astrée*; and he who did not answer well paid for each mistake with a pair of frangipani gloves. Two or three questions were written down on paper and

utopia of noble *bergers* and *bergères* provided contemporary French society with a poetic and moral code – to the extent that "knowing one's *Astrée* well" became a mark of the cultured gentleman. Pastoral drama reached its zenith in the 1620s and 1630s with Racan's *Les Bergeries* (1625), Mairet's *Sylvie* and *Silvanire* (c. 1625–29), and Gombauld's *Amaranthe* (1631), but quickly declined thereafter. Twenty years later, Tristan l'Hermite's play *Amarillis* (1653) initiated a nostalgic revival of the pastoral genre that coincided with the first *pastorales en musique* of Dassoucy (*Les Amours d'Apollon et de Daphné*, 1650), Charles de Beys (*Le Triomphe de l'Amour*, 1654, rev. 1657), and Pierre Perrin (*Pastorale d'Issy*, 1659).[3] However, Thomas Corneille's satire *Le Berger extravagant* (1653) pointed up the absurdities of the pastoral genre when its protagonist, after reading *L'Astrée* and seeing a performance of Tristan's *Amarillis*, dons shepherd's garb and lives out his own Arcadian fantasy.[4]

A decade later, Molière and Lully would find comic inspiration in the threadbare conventions of the pastorale. Many of the bucolic motifs in their *divertissements* derive from the pastoral poetry of antiquity. The allusions to the innocent and happy love among the birds and animals in *La Pastorale comique*, *Le Sicilien*, and *Les Amants magnifiques*, according to Jacques Morel, stem from *De rerum natura* of Lucretius, "which Tasso transmitted to the French authors of pastorales."[5] Moreover, on two occasions Molière

sent to a person – as, for example, on which side was Bonlieu upon leaving the Bouteresse bridge, and other such things, be it on history or geography; this was the means of knowing one's *Astrée* well. There had been so many pairs of gloves lost on all sides that when one came to count them (for we scored carefully), it was found that practically nothing was owed by anyone" (Tallemant des Réaux, *Historiettes*, ed. Antoine Adam, 2 vols. [Paris, 1960], "Le Cardinal de Retz," vol. II, 305).

3 For more on these early musical settings see Louis E. Auld, "'Dealing in Shepherds': The Pastoral Ploy in Nascent French Opera," in *French Musical Thought 1600–1800*, ed. Georgia Cowart (Ann Arbor, Mich.: UMI Research Press, 1989), 53–79.

4 Corneille based his "pastorale burlesque" on Paul Sorel's 1628 comic novel, *Le Berger extravagant*; but whereas Sorel's spoof, contemporaneous with the appearance of the final volume of *L'Astrée*, had little effect on the latter's success, Corneille's play appears to have contributed to the decline in popularity of pastoral drama. I am indebted to Professor Perry Gethner for pointing this connection out to me.

5 Jacques Morel, "Le Modèle pastoral dans l'œuvre de Molière," in *Le genre pastoral en Europe du XVe au XVIIe siècle: Actes du colloque international tenu à Saint-Etienne du 28 septembre au 1er octobre 1978* (Université de Saint-Etienne, 1980), 337–347 [340].

directly imitated classical models: the singing contest of the Quatrième
Intermède of *La Princesse d'Elide* imitates the Anacreontic pastoral lyric,
while the "dépit amoureux" of the Troisième Intermède of *Les Amants
magnifiques* is a French translation of an ode of Horace ("Donec gratus
eram tibi," Ode IX of Book III).[6]

Other pastoral situations, scenes, and characters look to the *seicento*
Italian pastorale for inspiration. The *comédies-ballets* designed for court
fêtes borrow heavily from these Italian sources – for, according to Athénaïs
de Montespan (Louis XIV's mistress from 1667 to *c.* 1673), Guarini's *Pastor
fido* and Tasso's *Aminta* were among the king's favorite works.[7] It is no accident that the action of *La Princesse d'Elide* (1664), like that of *Pastor fido*,
begins immediately after a boar hunt,[8] or that the Princess, like Silvia in
Aminta, prefers the excitement of the hunt over the attentions paid her by
her noble suitors. Meanwhile, her court fool Moron follows the example of
Aminta, and affects to kill himself for the love of a shepherdess. For Morel,
the disdainful shepherdesses of *Mélicerte* (1666) are "d'une allure guarini-
enne,"[9] while the two satyrs rejected by Caliste in the Troisième Intermède
of *Les Amants magnifiques* call to mind the satyr spurned by Corisca in
Pastor fido.[10]

Other Arcadian borrowings look to contemporary French pastorales. The *Ballet des Muses* (1666–67) contains no less than three of
Molière and Lully's early attempts at the genre. *Mélicerte*, Molière's only
spoken pastoral comedy, originally served as the Troisième Entrée dedicated to the comic muse Thalia. While later editions of this *comédie pastorale-héroïque* do not call for music or dance, the *entrée* following it in the
Ballet des Muses celebrated Euterpe, the pastoral muse, and featured pastoral songs, choruses, and dances – some of which may have originated as
musical *intermèdes* performed between the acts of the play. *Mélicerte* is

---

6 Eugène Despois and Paul Mesnard, eds., *Œuvres de Molière*, 14 vols. (Paris,
   1873–1900), vol. VII, 372.
7 Etienne Léon de Lamothe-Langon, trans., *Memoirs of Madame La Marquise de
   Montespan*, 2 vols. (London: H. S. Nichols, 1895), vol. I, 102.
8 Another boar hunt figures in the *dénouement* of *Les Amants magnifiques*.
9 Morel, "Le Modèle," 341.
10 It is also tempting to view Lycas of *La Pastorale comique*, the ugly but rich
   shepherd-suitor to Iris (with his "museau tondu tout frais"), as akin to the satyr
   from *Pastor fido*.

based on an episode in Mlle de Scudéry's popular pastoral romance *Artamène, ou le Grand Cyrus* (1649–53). Its plot revolves around a conventional chain of pastoral lovers: Acanthe and Tyrène are in love with Daphné and Eroxène, who both love Myrtil, who in turn loves and is loved by Mélicerte. Molière grants the minor characters so little individualizing personality that they merely parrot each other's lines. The opening scene, for example, mimics the balanced exchanges that informed much of Perrin's *Pastorale d'Issy* (and, to an even greater extent, Beys's *Le Triomphe de l'Amour*):

Molière, *Mélicerte*, I, 1

ACANTE	ACANTE
Ah! charmante Daphné!	Ah! charming Daphne!
TYRÈNE	TYRÈNE
Trop aimable Éroxène.	Too lovely Eroxène.
DAPHNÉ	DAPHNÉ
Acante, laisse-moi.	Leave me, Acanthe.
ÉROXÈNE	ÉROXÈNE
Ne me suis point, Tyrène.	Do not follow me, Tyrène.
ACANTE	ACANTE
Pourquoi me chasses-tu?	Why do you drive me away?
TYRÈNE	TYRÈNE
Pourquoi fuis-tu mes pas?	Why do you fly from me?
DAPHNÉ	DAPHNÉ
Tu me plais loin de moi.	You please me most when far away.
ÉROXÈNE	ÉROXÈNE
Je m'aime où tu n'es pas.	I love to be where you are not
ACANTE	ACANTE
Ne cesseras-tu point cette rigueur mortelle?	Why not cease this killing severity?
TYRÈNE	TYRÈNE
Ne cesseras-tu point de m'être si cruelle?	Why not cease to be so cruel to me?
DAPHNÉ	DAPHNÉ
Ne cesseras-tu point tes inutiles vœux?	Why not cease your useless protestations?
ÉROXÈNE	ÉROXÈNE
Ne cesseras-tu point de m'être si fâcheux?	Why not cease to be so annoying to me?

ACANTE	ACANTE
Si tu n'en prends pitié, je succombe à ma peine.	If you will not pity me, I succumb to my grief.

TYRÈNE	TYRÈNE
Si tu ne me secours, ma mort est trop certaine.	If you will not succour me, my death is but too sure.

DAPHNÉ	DAPHNÉ
Si tu ne veux partir, je vais quitter ce lieu.	If you insist on not going, I shall leave this place.

ÉROXÈNE	ÉROXÈNE
Si tu veux demeurer, je te vais dire adieu.	If you insist on remaining, I shall say goodbye.

However, we soon discover that the playwright has reserved such symmetrical, repetitive passages for these thoroughly conventional pastoral lovers – while he reserves more poignant lyricism for his main characters, Myrtil and Mélicerte (for instance, compare the above scene (I, 1) with Myrtil's opening speech in I,5 – a lyric monologue in *vers mêlés*).

Molière and Lully's next *comédie-ballet*, also written for *Le Ballet des Muses*, was a full-fledged *pastorale en musique*. Entitled *La Pastorale comique*, it follows the example of d'Urfé's *L'Astrée* to take on a measure of contemporary social relevance.[11] Lycas and Filène, two "riches pasteurs," court the young shepherdess Iris, who instead loves the poor but noble-hearted Coridon. However, Molière quickly turns pastoral convention on its head when the rich but ugly Lycas consults some magicians – who invoke the goddess of love in a hymn ("Déesse des appas"), dress the shepherd up in ludicrous fashion, and then deride him in song and dance ("Qu'il est joli!"). In scene 3 Filène tries his hand at the lyric monologue, a long-standing commonplace of the dramatic pastorale. But while Filène waxes poetic, his soliloquy is considerably more flat-footed than that of the idealized shepherd-lover; rather than delivering the traditional apostrophe to the flora and fauna of the bucolic landscape, Filène instead seeks consolation in his beloved flock of sheep ("Paissez, chères brebis"). Soon thereafter, a singing contest brings Filène and Lycas to the point of blows; when some peasants later arrive to separate them, the group only ends up fighting amongst itself.

11 None of the spoken texts of *La Pastorale comique* survives – only the *livret* of the *Ballet des Muses* (which includes a list of the characters in each scene, a summary of the action, and the sung lyrics) and Lully's musical score.

In typical *comédie-ballet* fashion, Molière and Lully mimetically defuse the impending violence by transforming this altercation into dances of battle (*Les Paysans combattant avec des bâtons*) and of reconciliation (*Les Paysans réconciliés*). In the end, Lycas and Filène, having both been rejected by Iris, resolve to commit suicide (the only recourse of the spurned pastoral lover). Yet Molière gives this scene comic spin, by having the rival lovers argue over who is to do himself in first. Thereupon a joyful shepherd – the *raisonneur* of Molière's urban comedies – arrives to chide these despondent lovers for thinking of killing themselves for something as silly as unrequited love ("Ha! quelle folie!"). Here and elsewhere, Molière recasts the commonplaces of the pastorale in dramatically apposite, pointedly comic fashion.

As the 1667 Carnival performances of *Le Ballet des Muses* came to a close at court, Molière and Lully added *Le Sicilien, ou l'Amour peintre* as the final Quatorzième Entrée. This *comédie-ballet* features a pastoral "scène de comédie chantée" performed by some Turkish singers, in which two archetypal shepherds decry the harshness of their respective mistresses. Even the rocks will be moved upon hearing of Philène's anguish ("Si du triste récit"), while Tircis's sighs commence anew each dawn when the birds begin to sing ("Les oiseaux réjouis, dès que le jour s'avance"). After the disheartened shepherd-lovers commiserate in anguished exclamations, they join in weepy duet on a saccharine conceit:

Molière, *Le Sicilien, ou l'Amour peintre*, scene 2

SECOND MUSICIEN	SECOND MUSICIEN
Ah! mon cher Filène.	Ah! dear Filène.
PREMIER MUSICIEN	PREMIER MUSICIEN
Ah! mon cher Tìrcis.	Ah! dear Tircis.
SECOND MUSICIEN	SECOND MUSICIEN
Que je sens de peine!	What grief I feel!
PREMIER MUSICIEN	PREMIER MUSICIEN
Que j'ai de soucis!	What cares I have!
SECOND MUSICIEN	SECOND MUSICIEN
Toujours sourde à mes vœux est l'ingrate Climène.	Ever deaf to my sighs is the ungrateful Climène.
PREMIER MUSICIEN	PREMIER MUSICIEN
Cloris n'a point pour moi de regards adoucis.	Cloris has for me no sweet looks.

JOHN S. POWELL

TOUS DEUX	TOUS DEUX
Ô loi trop inhumaine!	O too inhuman law!
Amour, si tu ne peux les contraindre d'aimer,	Cupid, if you cannot compel them to love,
Pourquoi leur laisses-tu le pouvoir de charmer?	Why do you leave them the power to charm?

Once again, a worldly-wise shepherd intervenes, and sings an air to show these misguided lovers the error of loving "des inhumaines" ("Pauvres amants, quelle erreur"); in his embellished *double*, he illustrates how he matches his lovers' affections in kind – whether tender or fierce.[12]

Molière and Lully also experimented with juxtaposing a self-contained, musical comedy presented in *intermèdes* with the main action of a heroic spoken play – thereby making the former a pastoral reflection or reinterpretation of the latter. In *La Princesse d'Elide*, the Princess's maid in the play doubles as the "shepherdess" Philis in the pastoral *intermèdes*, wherein the court fool Moron aspires to be her shepherd-lover. (We cannot help but wonder if some of the other rustic characters of the pastorale – Tircis, Clymène, the satyr – might not also hold "day-jobs" at court.) Before the play begins the court has been hunting, and the Prince of Messina has saved the Princess from a wild boar. But rather than showing gratitude, the Princess expresses outrage at his interference and reproaches him for lacking confidence in her hunting abilities. Likewise, Moron undergoes a similar test of his mettle in the Deuxième Intermède, when he faces a charging bear unarmed. According to Molière's synopsis, some huntsmen arrive to rescue the fool, who "having grown bold by the removal of danger, wishes to go give a thousand blows to the animal, no longer able to defend himself, and does all that a braggart, not overly brave, would have done on such an occasion." Moron's cowardice thus serves as a comic foil to the Princess's bravery, while the huntsmen's joy provides a choreographic counterpoint to the Prince's chagrin.

The amorous misadventures of Moron in the pastoral *intermèdes* also mirror the heroic play's etiquette of love and courtship. Moron, the wily if cowardly servant of the court, is out of his element in a world ruled by a pastoral code of conduct, and his ineptitude at mastering the conventions of the lyric arts plays off of the verbal gallantry of the Princess's noble

12 Manuel Couvreur views this "scène de comédie chantée" as the prototype for the *George Dandin* pastorale; see CouvreurL, 171.

172

suitors.[13] As Ada Coe observes, "this is not the stylized, mythical Arcadia, but a comic world in which values are turned topsy-turvy."[14] For example, in the Deuxième Intermède Moron goes off to a solitary place to confess his love for Philis, and tries his hand at fashioning a lyric monologue. But Moron, no gallant shepherd, soon violates the *bienséances* forbidding the mention of things in life held to be beneath notice of the noble mind, and his injudicious choice of poetic images soon turns this lyric composition into a parody of the pastoral lament.[15] He begins well enough,

> Bois, prés, fontaines, fleurs, qui voyez mon teint blême
> Si vous ne le savez, je vous apprends que j'aime.
>> Philis est l'objet charmant
>> Qui tient mon cœur à l'attache;

> Woods, meadows, fountains, flowers, that behold my pale countenance,
> if you do not know it, I tell you I am in love.
>> Philis is the charming object
>> who has fixed my heart;

until the fool goes on to describe his carnal feelings while watching his beloved milk a cow. As his imagery becomes increasingly earthy and tactile, the accretion of proscribed words soon reaches critical mass, resulting in Moron's exclamation:

> Et je devins son amant
> La voyant traire une vache.
> Ses doigts tout pleins de lait, et plus blancs mille fois,
> Pressaient les bouts du pis d'une grâce admirable.
>> Ouf! Cette idée est capable
>> De me réduire aux abois.

> And I became her lover
> by seeing her milk a cow.

13 Further connections exist between the Princess and her fool: the former is a skilled singer who refuses to sing for anyone *except* Prince Euryale; Moron, on the other hand, is a non-singer, who attempts to learn to sing in order to compete for the affections of his beloved shepherdess.
14 Ada Coe, "'Ballet en comédie' or 'comédie en ballet'? *La Princesse d'Elide* and *Les Amants magnifiques*," *Cahiers du Dix-Septième* 2/1 (Spring 1988), 109–122 [112].
15 The following discussion of the Deuxième Intermède is inspired by Louis Auld's analysis of this scene in "Molière as Dramatic Lyricist" (p. 6), an unpublished paper delivered at the 110th Convention of the Modern Languages Association in 1995.

> Her fingers, quite full of milk, and a thousand times whiter,
> squeezed the udder with an admirable grace.
> > Whew! The very thought of it
> > drives me crazy.

Moron's qualifications as a pastoral lover then are further thrown into question by another Arcadian commonplace: the echo. This echo stubbornly refuses to repeat the name of his beloved – but instead responds with facetious repartee.

Later juxtapositions of speech and song point up the fool's basic incongruity with his pastoral surroundings. In the Troisième Intermède Moron meets up with a singing satyr, who had once promised to teach him to sing. The satyr is one of these mythic woodland beings for whom music comes naturally – to the extent that, as Moron observes, "he is so used to singing that he doesn't know how to speak in any other way." Moron asks the satyr to sing a *chanson* that he heard him sing some days before ("Dans vos chants si doux"), and then begs to learn it. But when the satyr uses solmization syllables to teach him the melody (see Example 7.1), the fool construes an insult in "fa" ("fat," pronounced like "fa" in the seventeenth century, means "idiot" or "imbecile"). Just as the two are about to come to blows, the violins strike up an air – which, in *comédie-ballet* fashion, transforms their altercation into ballet-pantomime.

In the following *intermède* Moron encounters the shepherd Tircis, whom his beloved Philis seems to favor. This scene introduces another pastoral commonplace: the singing contest. Tircis extemporizes two thoroughly conventional airs – one a lover's protestation ("Tu m'écoutes hélas! dans ma triste langueur"), the other a plainte ("Arbres épais, et vous, prés émaillés"). While capably composed, the shepherd's tunes, dominated by triadic outlines and anapestic rhythms, show little melodic inspiration (Examples 7.2a and 2b). Moron responds with his own lyric composition, based on another well-worn poetic *topos*: he has been fatally wounded by love, and the lady alone possesses the power to heal him ("Ton extrême rigueur"; Example 7.2c). To our surprise, Moron not only successfully imitates the fashionable style of the *air tendre*, but his musical invention surpasses that of Tircis in elegance and suppleness. His opening gesture consists of two beautifully crafted phrases of unequal length. The first phrase (mm. 1–5) begins on the upper tonic, fills in a descending seventh,

Example 7.1
La Princesse d'Elide (1664)
Troisième Intermède, scene 2 (after F-Pn, Rés. F 531)

and then doubles back to the dominant before completing its descent to the lower tonic (the deceptive cadence in m. 5 on "cœur" is an unexpected poetic touch). Moreover, Moron evidently stole a melodic motive (on the words "sur mon cœur," marked with asterisks in Example 7.2c) from his rival's second air (marked with asterisks in Example 7.2b). His second phrase (mm. 5–8) consists of a pair of langorous 7–6 suspensions which conclude with a hauntingly beautiful Phrygian cadence on "trépasse." Moron has proven himself to be a surprisingly quick study – considering that he could scarcely match pitch in the preceding *intermède*.

But once again, the fool tips his hand by allowing vulgarity of expression to creep into his final argument ("Will you be the fatter for it, having allowed me to die?"; Example 7.2d). He performs trills on both half-notes of "grasse" and gives the final, mute syllable a clumsy agogic accent. To make matters worse, his melodic line underscores the gaffe – ascending to a high note on the proscribed word, and then dramatically falling the *chute* of a ninth to the final cadence. Even though Moron professes willingness to die for the love of Philis, the crudeness of his poetic and musical rhetoric breaks the spell. In an ideal Arcadia, no self-respecting shepherdess would have the bad manners to accept a lover's offer of suicide. However, to the fool's chagrin, Philis expresses delight at the thought. While Moron meekly protests, Tircis enthusiastically supports his suicide plan ("Ah! how pleasant it is to die for the object one loves"; Example 7.2e) and urges him on ("Take courage, Moron! Die quickly, like a generous lover") – using the borrowed 2–3–1 motive (marked with asterisks) and ascending chromaticism (on "de mourir," an inversion of "Ah! Philis, je trépasse" in Example 7.2c) to underscore his mocking sarcasm. At the moment of truth with dagger poised, the not-so-foolish Moron abruptly changes his tune and abruptly bids farewell to these bloodthirsty pastoral lovers with "Je suis

Example 7.2

La Princesse d'Elide (1664)

Quatrième Intermède, scenes 1–2 (after F-Pn, Rés. F 531)

176

votre serviteur: quelque niais" ("I am your servant; I am not such a fool as I look.").[16]

Molière and Lully once again experimented with intercalating a spoken comedy with a self-contained *pastorale en musique* (presented as *intermèdes*, with its own cast of characters) in the *Grand Divertissement Royal de Versailles* (1668). According to the published *livret,* "even though it appears that this might be two comedies performed at the same time, of which one is in prose and the other in verse, they are however so well joined to a common subject that they are the self-same piece and depict but a single action."[17] This "common subject" that links the pastorale and the play *George Dandin* is the ongoing battle between the sexes. Here, the protagonist of the play furnishes *liaison de scène* with the operatic *intermèdes*; but unlike the fool Moron, who actively participated in both worlds, Dandin only witnesses the events that unfold in this parallel, pastoral realm. For example, at the end of Act I Dandin "is interrupted by a shepherdess, who comes to give him an account of the two shepherds' despair; he leaves her in anger, and makes way for Cloris who, on the death of her lover, comes to perform a musical lament." Unlike the lighthearted satire of the surrounding pastoral scenes, this *intermède* is of a serious character. To depict the shepherdess's anguish Lully drew upon the usual expressive musical gestures of the Italian *lamento*: a descending ostinato

16 Purkis ("Le Chant pastoral chez Molière," 137) points out that: "Singing is an attractive manner of declaring one's love, and every woman loves to hear her praises from the mouth of the one who pleases her, all the while refusing to take literally the words uttered . . . to declare oneself ready to die is to indicate at which point life would be empty without the beloved. This manner of expression is thus both convention and symbol. This is what Moron does not understand. He takes the notion of suicide literally, and refuses to go through with it. Now, this refusal is also symbolic: it indicates that Moron, too selfish to kill himself, is incapable of loving." I disagree with Purkis's analysis, insofar as I would suggest that Moron is too clever to fall into an obvious trap laid by the shepherdess – who clearly prefers his rival and would no doubt just as soon be rid of the fool.

17 André Félibien, *Relation de la Feste de Versailles du 18 juillet mil six cens soixante-huit* (Paris: Imprimerie Royale, 1679), 13. Morel refers to this as "le dialogue d'un genre littéraire et d'un autre, et plus précisément, si on veut, le dialogue de *La Jalousie du Barbouillé* et de la *Pastorale comique*"; see Morel, "Le Modèle," 342. For detailed analysis of how the pastorale relates to the comedy, see Helen Purkis, "Les Intermèdes musicaux de *George Dandin*," *Baroque* 5 (1972), 63–69.

Example 7.3
George Dandin (1668)
Second Intermède (after F-Pn, Rés. F 526)

bass, passionate exclamations followed by expressive silences, chains of suspensions, drooping melodic lines, and phrases that cadence with a fatalistic regularity (Example 7.3).[18]

Elsewhere, Molière endows the shepherd-lovers with little individualizing personality, and the musical symmetry of their paired exchanges resembles a four-way *dialogue en musique*. In the *intermède* preceding the shepherdess's lament, two shepherds respond in duo-recitative to the harshness of their respective shepherdesses and resolve to commit suicide. Lully's music, with its parallel thirds and short bits of imitation, confirms that these spurned lovers are merely clones of one another. As Molière wryly notes in a rubric found at the end of this scene, "these two shepherds go away in despair, following the custom of lovers of old who would despair over trifles." Their music, with its mindless repetitions,

---

18 Lully's prototype for the "Plainte de Cloris" can be found in the "Récit
d'Armide" ("Ah Rinaldo, e dove sei?"), the Italian *lamento* he composed for the
Huitième Entrée of the *Ballet des Amours déguisez* (1664). For comparison of
these two laments, see Denise Launay, "Les Airs italiens et français dans les
ballets et les comédies-ballets," in Heidelberg87, 31–49 [specifically 38–42 and
45–47].

178

Example 7.4

George Dandin (1668)

Premier Intermède (after F-Pn, Rés. F 526)

jaunty dance-rhythms, and obligatory chains of mock-pathetic suspensions, further deflates the gravity of the situation (Example 7.4).

After *George Dandin*, Molière and Lully abandoned the parallel, ongoing *pastorale en musique* and reverted to their earlier format of introducing pastoral episodes as performances within the context of the spoken

Example 7.4 (*cont.*)

play. In *Les Amants magnifiques* (1670), the *intermèdes* constitute various musical and balletic *divertissements* given for the court of Thessaly. Like Iris in *La Pastorale comique*, who prefers Coridon over the two "riches pasteurs," Princess Eriphile favors the noble-hearted Sostrate – a general in the army who, because of his low station, feels that he cannot compete with her princely suitors. Sostrate goes through much of the play trying to conceal his love for Eriphile, and, like the archetypal shepherd lover, he is prepared to die either from grief (in I, 1) or from happiness (in IV, 4).

Molière takes these associations between the play's characters and their pastoral counterparts to a higher, meta-theatrical level in the Troisième Intermède, when Prince Timoclès (one of the noble suitors) arranges for the performance of a *pastorale en musique*. Its prologue, like that of *Pastor fido*, serves a double function: it pays tribute to the guest of honor (Princess Eriphile), and introduces the subject of the entertainment. Furthermore, the action and characters of this *pastorale en musique* can be viewed as a symbolic reflection of the spoken play.[19]

In the first scene, the shepherd Tircis sings a stock lyric monologue ("Vous chantez sous ces feuillages"); but his triple-meter dance rhythms and active bass line tells us that his grief is trivial rather than tragic. Then two other shepherds, Lycaste and Ménandre, arrive and try to console Tircis. These minor characters behave like identical twins: they respond in tandem, and their extravagant outbursts of empathy, formulated in *répétition de paroles*, verbal symmetries and stichomythia, are once again designed for parodic effect:

19 Such strata of theatrical illusion would compound in *Le Malade imaginaire* (1673), where the spoken comedy becomes a play-within-the-eclogue and featuring its own pastoral operetta. Although *Le Malade imaginaire* lies beyond the scope of this study, a close examination of the pastoral elements reveal new levels of comic meaning. For example, in the *petit opéra impromptu* of II, 5, Molière playfully underscores the "impromptu" aspect of this performance: after Cléante relates to the girl's father and her fiancé the events which preceded this pastoral scene, he thrusts into Angélique's hand some untexted (and passionate) music – for which she has to extemporize the appropriate words and emotions. The plot, as explained to the girl's father and her intended fiancé, is the story of Cléante and Angélique in pastoral guise: the young shepherd saves a shepherdess from the advances of a boorish lout (recalling the satyr of *Aminta*), falls in love with her at first sight, obtains her promise to marry him by means of a letter, and attempts to see her again – only to learn that her father has arranged for her to marry another (a theme of *Pastor fido*). Casting aside all restraint, the shepherd breaks his silence and, in a "transport of love," expresses his feelings in song. Here, the pastoral convention of the *dialogue en musique* allows Cléante and Angélique, through their pastoral alter-egos Tircis and Philis, to develop their courtship before Argan and Thomas Diafoirus – the urban counterparts of the shepherdess's father and the "unworthy rival." This *petit opéra impromptu* thereby epitomizes the overall dramatic action of the spoken comedy – and its happy outcome anticipates the play's musical *dénouement*. For further discussion see my article, "Music, Fantasy and Illusion in Molière's *Le Malade imaginaire*," *Music & Letters* 73/2 (1992), 222–243 [230–233].

Molière, *Les Amants magnifiques*, Troisième Intermède, scene 2

LYCASTE ET MÉNANDRE	LYCASTE ET MÉNANDRE
Ah! Tircis!	Ah! Tircis!
TIRCIS	TIRCIS
Ah! Bergers!	Ah! shepherds!
LYCASTE ET MÉNANDRE	LYCASTE ET MÉNANDRE
Prends sur toi plus d'empire.	Take control of yourself.
TIRCIS	TIRCIS
Rien ne me peut plus secourir.	Nothing can come to my aid.
LYCASTE ET MÉNANDRE	LYCASTE ET MÉNANDRE
C'est trop, c'est trop céder.	It is giving way too much, too much.
TIRCIS	TIRCIS
C'est trop, c'est trop souffrir.	It is suffering too much, too much.
LYCASTE ET MÉNANDRE	LYCASTE ET MÉNANDRE
Quelle faiblesse!	What weakness!
TIRCIS	TIRCIS
Quel martyre!	What martyrdom!
LYCASTE ET MÉNANDRE	LYCASTE ET MÉNANDRE
Il faut prendre courage.	You must take courage.
TIRCIS	TIRCIS
Il faut plutôt mourir.	Rather let me die.

This scene, however, lacks the shepherd-*raisonneur* of *La Pastorale comique* and *Le Sicilien*, who represented a sane voice in the midst of pastoral delirium.

In the next scene, the shepherdess Caliste confesses in an expressive *plainte* ("Ah! que sur notre cœur") that despite her will she has fallen in love with Tircis. After she has become overtaken by sleep, Tircis and his companions arrive to sing her a kind of lullaby similar to the traditional *sommeil* music (see Example 7.5).[20] Caliste awakens, is surprised to find that Tircis has followed her and admits that pity has aroused her true affections. The key shifts from G minor to B♭ major when Caliste surrenders her heart to her shepherd-lover. Tircis, stunned ("Ah! I am beside myself!"), momentarily

---

20 The *sommeil* was a commonplace of Italian operas of the time – for example in II, 9 of Rossi's *Orfeo* (1647), the chorus sings a lullaby ("Dormite begli'occhi") to the unconscious Euridice. Dassoucy imitated this scene in III, 4 of *Les Amours d'Apollon et de Daphné* (1650), where Apollo sings the same words to the sleeping Daphne ("Dormite belli ochi").

Example 7.5

Les Amants magnifiques (1670)

Troisième Intermède, scene 4 (after F-Pn, Rés. F 531)

Example 7.6

Les Amants magnifiques (1670)

Troisième Intermède, scene 4 (after F-Pn, Rés. F 601)

loses track of his key as he wanders through B♭, G major, C minor, and finally settles on D major; his friends, in response to his good fortune, bring the music back to G (Example 7.6). Here Lully's setting has an arioso-like expressiveness that features the prominent anapests, triadic outlines, and downbeat end-rhymes typical of his later operatic recitative.

184

Example 7.7

Les Amants magnifiques (1670)

Troisième Intermède, scene 5 (after F-Pn, Rés. F 601)

By way of contrast, scene 5 introduces two new characters – the satiric counterparts of Lycaste and Ménandre. These woodland creatures had been former rivals for Caliste's affections, and they are now taken aback by the sudden revelation of her new-found love for Tircis. Often presented as a comic villain in pastoral comedy, the satyr was traditionally lewd in his behavior and bestial in his desires. These, however, are gallant satyrs, who express their just indignation at Caliste's rejection in *précieux* language. Returning to the key of B♭, the first satyr, in rapid, conversational speech-rhythms over a static bass, reproaches Caliste for granting her love to a mere shepherd; the second satyr echoes these sentiments in the key of F, and complains of Caliste's callous disregard for his feelings (Example 7.7). The shepherdess's nonchalant response, set to a dance-like, triple-meter melody,

185

suggests a new side of her personality – that of a consummate coquette. Since destiny wills her to fall in love with Tircis (so she tells the satyrs), both must bear their fates patiently. As unlucky in love as their forebears, the two disheartened satyrs resolve to drown their sorrows in wine ("Aux amants qu'on pousse à bout").

In the denouement to the Troisième Intermède, the shepherds, shepherdesses, and satyrs join in chorus to summon the woodland divinities ("Champêtres divinités"), whereupon some dryads and fauns emerge from their grottos to perform an *entrée de ballet*. Next, they present a musical performance featuring two pastoral lovers, Philinte and Climène, whose story (taken from an ode of Horace) raises the *divertissement* to yet a higher level of meta-theatrical abstraction. Having formerly sought consolation in the arms of others, the inconstant lovers enact a *dépit amoureux* that concludes in a duet of reconciliation. As they now declare eternal fidelity, their melodic lines intertwine in imitation and combine in thirds and sixths – symbolic of their new-found harmony. After the performance-within-the-play ends, "tous les acteurs de la Comédie" momentarily step out of character and join in chorus to exhort lovers everywhere to quarrel, so that they may enjoy the pleasures of making up ("Amants, que vos querelles"). In this final number, "the fauns and the dryads recommence their dance, which the singing shepherdess and shepherds intermingle with their songs, while three little dryads and three little fauns reproduce upstage everything that happens downstage."

This mirror reflection projected by the little dryads and fauns represents the symbolic relationship that exists between the pastoral Troisième Intermède and the spoken play. Tircis, the suffering shepherd of the opera, can be viewed as the pastoral counterpart to General Sostrate, the suffering lover of the play, and Caliste's preference for a mere shepherd over the two rival satyrs is analogous to Eriphile's choice of Sostrate over the two rival princes. Moreover, Caliste's pronouncement to her satyr-suitors "le destin le veut ainsi" (scene 5) predicts the denouement of the play, when an unforeseen twist of fate decides the princess's future husband.[21] The

21 Venus appears in IV, 2 of the play to tell Queen Aristione that the gods wish to reward her with the best possible match for her daughter, and they will give her a sign: her life will be saved by the man who should marry Eriphile. While the miraculous appearance of Venus is merely a ruse concocted by the astrologer

association of the rival princes with the courtly satyrs is a clever, parodic touch – particularly later on, when their outrage at Eriphile's choice matches the satyrs' indignation. Moreover, Caliste's nonchalant reaction to the satyrs' distress recalls the behavior of Princess Eriphile, who also trifles with the affections of her royal suitors and plays games with Sostrate.[22] Declaration of her love must wait until IV, 4 – when Sostrate's ecstatic reaction ("Ah! Madame, c'en est trop pour un malheureux: je ne m'étais pas préparé à mourir avec tant de gloire . . .") recalls that of the shepherd Tircis in scene 4 of the Troisième Intermède ("Ô Ciel! Bergers! Caliste! Ah! je suis hors de moi. / Si l'on meurt de plaisir je dois perdre la vie").

Whatever reservations Molière may have had about pastoral opera, he seems to have taken considerable pride in this *pastorale en musique* – that is, assuming that Aristione (Eriphile's mother) voiced the playwright's sentiments when she exclaimed "That is admirable! Nothing could be more beautiful! It surpasses all that has ever been seen." But this pronouncement might carry a hidden meaning – given that, beginning with *Les Amants magnifiques*, Molière took over Benserade's position of poet for court ballets. Moreover, Molière and Lully's accomplishment surpassed that of Perrin's Académie Royale des Opéra, which had been in existence since 1669 but had yet to stage an opera. Indeed, Manuel Couvreur judges that "by the quality of the versification, by the varied beauties of the score, this pastorale is much superior to the famous *Pomone* – which would be created the following year."[23]

Molière and Lully renewed their satire of pastoral opera in *Le Bourgeois Gentilhomme* (1670), where their barbs became increasingly directed at Perrin and his forthcoming ventures in pastoral opera. In Act I, scene 2, three professional singers appear before M. Jourdain to perform a musical dialogue "upon the different passions that music can express." Moreover, the Maître de Musique directs M. Jourdain to imagine them

Anaxarque (on behalf of the rival princes), fate steps in when the queen is attacked by a wild boar, and it is Sostrate who saves her life and thereby wins the princess.

22 In Act II, the court fool Clitidas awakens Eriphile's jealousy when he pretends that Sostrate is in love with one of her maids, and asks for her aid with his suit. Eriphile in turn torments Sostrate by asking advice on her choice between the rival princes.

23 CouvreurL, 181.

dressed as shepherds. "Why always shepherds?" the bourgeois asks, "We see nothing else everywhere." But his Maître à Danser patiently explains that "When we have characters that are to speak in music, it is necessary for the sake of verisimilitude to give it as a pastorale; song has always been assigned to shepherds, and it is hardly natural in dialogue for princes or shopkeepers to sing their passions."[24] These singers, however, portray neither real shepherds nor their Arcadian ideals, but rather nameless, abstract pastoral personas. Like the shepherdess Caliste, "la musicienne" (*dessus*) prizes her freedom over love. The "premier musicien" (*haute-contre*) embraces the philosophy of the *berger fidèle*, while the "second musicien" (a more worldly-wise *basse-taille*) wants nothing more to do with "ce sexe inconstant."

At any rate, Molière and Lully depict all three pastoral archetypes with tongue in cheek. The shepherdess mocks the sentiments of the infatuated lover ("On dit qu'avec plaisir on languit, on soupire") by a long, drawn-out suspension and cadence, and yet she quickly gives up her prized *liberté* later on to win the heart of the discouraged shepherd. While the air of the faithful shepherd ("Il n'est rien de si doux que les tendres ardeurs") begins with a parody of her last line ("Il n'est rien de si doux que notre liberté"), the chromatic *lamento* bass underlying this phrase foretells that grief awaits him. By way of contrast, the discouraged shepherd's melodramatic outbursts ("Mais, hélas! ô rigueur cruelle!") are delivered in recitative that apes the passionate extremes of a larger-than-life, "operatic" figure.

After each pastoral persona establishes his philosophy of love in an opening number, the three juxtapose their contradictory views in an exchange of balanced phrases ("Aimable ardeur, / Franchise heureuse, / Sexe trompeur, / Que tu m'es précieuse! / Que tu plais à mon cœur! / Que tu me fais d'horreur!") which soon reaches a reconciliation. Siding with the faithful shepherd, the shepherdess joins her melody to his in thirds and sixths; accepting her offer (or rather challenge) of love, the discouraged shepherd abandons his angry recitative for lyrical melody. Amusingly, the reformed misogynist now intones the mantra "Ah! qu'il est doux d'aimer /

---

24 Here, Molière and Lully parody the aesthetic of Perrin's operas, which sought to avoid the pitfalls of narrative singing by replacing all "serious discourse" with the lyric sentiments most suitable for musical expression – love, joy, despair, etc. Indeed, all three pastoral personalities introduced in this *dialogue en musique* seem to be inspired by the inconstant Sylvie, the faithful Tyrsis, and the rejected satyr of Perrin's *Pastorale d'Issy*.

Quand deux cœurs sont fidèles" to a descending, *lamento* bass (this time in diatonic form) – as if to suggest that his fate is now bound to that of the faithful but doomed shepherd. In the final trio, the three singers resolve their differences, while imitative and chordal passages homogenize their previously distinct musical personalities into one.[25]

With *Psyché* (1671), Molière and Lully (in collaboration with Corneille and Quinault) transformed the genre of *comédie-ballet* by grafting *ballet de cour* onto a mythological *pièce à grand spectacle*. Manuel Couvreur has shown that several passages stem from the unfinished *comédie pastorale-héroïque Mélicerte*.[26] But another point of contact between the pastoral genre and this mythological *tragédie-ballet* can be found in the Premier Intermède, the Italian lyrics of which may well have been written by Lully himself.[27] The model for this vocal trio is the pastoral commonplace of the *plainte* or *stances*, a lyric address to the gods and to nature that traditionally takes place in a solitary and deserted place.[28] Here Lully paints a vivid portrayal of desolation. Example 7.8 illustrates the opening bars of an expressive monody, in which a "femme désolée" (an incarnation of Psyche's despair) exhorts the rocks, rivers, and savage tigers to join their tears with hers. In a highly ornamented and melismatic *double* composed by Michel Lambert (Lully's father-in-law), she later graphically

25 The musical examples required to illustrate these points are too numerous and lengthy to include here; the entire *dialogue en musique* can be consulted in LullyOC, "Les Comédies-Ballets," vol. III (1938), 55–71. For a provocative analysis of Lully's music, see Stephen H. Fleck, *Music, Dance, and Laughter: Comic Creation in Molière's Comedy-Ballets*, Biblio 17 (Paris–Seattle–Tübingen: Papers on French Seventeenth-Century Literature, 1995), 105–111.

26 CouvreurL, 242–245. Other passages from *Mélicerte* seem to have influenced later *comédies-ballets*. For instance, the scene in which Lycarsis reveals his secret to Mopse and Nicandre after declaring that they should know nothing (I, 3) recurs in *George Dandin* (II, 5), while Myrtil's speech to assuage Lycarsis in II, 5 is reproduced almost verbatim in IV, 3 of *Tartuffe*, when Marianne attempts to soften the heart of Orgon.

27 ParfaictH, vol. XI, 127, attributes these lyrics to Lully.

28 For more on the *stance* in French plays of the early seventeenth century, see H. Carrington Lancaster, "The Origin of the Lyric Monologue in French Classical Tragedy," *Publications of the Modern Language Association* 42 (September 1927), 782–787; Gustave W. Andrian, "Early Use of the Lyric Monologue in French Drama of the Seventeenth Century," *Modern Language Notes* 68 (1953), 101–105; Jacques Morel, "Les Stances dans la tragédie française au XVIIe siècle," *XVIIe Siècle* 66 (1965), 43–56; and Marie-France Hilgar, *La Mode des stances dans le théâtre tragique français* (Paris, 1974).

Example 7.8

Psyché (1671), Premier Intermède

Plainte italienne (x) (after *Airs du Ballet Royal de Psiché* (Paris, 1670; 2nd edn. 1673); *double* (y) by Michel Lambert after *Le Ballet des ballets* (1671; F-B, 13.741)

190

Example 7.8 (*cont.*)

Example 7.8 (*cont.*)

NB: The incomplete notation of the diminutions in measures 21 and 32 is given as in the original.

commands the grottos and caverns to resound her lament.[29] Vigarani's scenery portrayed a bleak desert landscape ("la scène est changée en des rochers affreux, et fait voir en éloignement une grotte effroyable"), while a "troupe désolée" mimetically projects the prevailing mood "by a dance full of every mark of the most violent despair" (*Entrée d'Hommes affligez et de Femmes desolées*). Here, all of the arts – music, poetry, pantomime, costumes, and painting – join in a tragic expression devoid of any hint of the parody that figured prominently in Molière and Lully's earlier pastoral collaborations.

After *Psyché*, Lully composed no more pastoral *divertissements* for Molière's plays. *La Comtesse d'Escarbagnas* (1671) contained musical episodes pieced together from earlier *comédies-ballets*: a prologue (taken from the Premier Intermède of *Les Amants magnifiques*, followed by portions of the prologue to *Psyché*), an epilogue (the final *intermède* of *Psyché*), and a lost pastorale that was performed in scene 7 of the play by some actors, for which musical *intermèdes* framed the five scenes. All we know about this pastorale is that there were seven characters – a nymph (played by Mlle de Brie), a shepherdess dressed as a man (Mlle Molière), a shepherdess dressed as a woman (also Mlle Molière), a shepherd-lover (Baron), a herdsman (Molière), a Turk (also Molière), and another herdsman (La Thorillière) – and that the play's *intermèdes* included the *plainte italienne* from *Psyché*, the magic ceremony of *La Pastorale comique* (scene 2), the pastoral ballet that concluded *George Dandin*, the gypsy entertainment of *La Pastorale comique* (scene 5), the Turkish Ceremony of *Le*

---

29 Despite the Italian text and emotional excesses, Anthony views this lament as "a synthesis in which French elements dominate." He points to its narrowness of range, its discreet use of melismas and restrained use of dissonance, its ABA form (found in many Lully operatic airs), and the fact that "in the best tradition of the *air sérieux*, it is followed by a *double*" (James R. Anthony, "Air and Aria added to French Opera," *Revue de musicologie* 77/2 [1991], 201–219 [202]). On the other hand, Denise Launay believes that the Italian features are most pronounced: "To the remarks made previously with regard to the *Ballet des Amours déguisez* and the *Plainte d'Armide*, which apply just as well to the *Plainte de la Femme désolée*, [from *Psyché*], it could be added that: the accentuation of the Italian words encouraged Lully to multiply the anacruses, preceded by silences beneficial to the emotive effect. The last measures of the air include, in addition, notes prolonged by Italianate vocalises" ("Les Airs italiens et français dans les ballets et les comédies-ballets," 41–43).

Bourgeois Gentilhomme, and the Italian and Spanish *entrée* of *Le Ballet des nations*.[30]

After his break with Molière in the spring of 1672, Lully's next project was a pastoral opera, *Les Festes de l'Amour et de Bacchus* (1672) – for which Philippe Quinault[31] was charged with the task of constructing a libretto incorporating pastoral *intermèdes* borrowed from three of the *comédies-ballets* least familiar to the Parisian public: *Les Amants magnifiques*, *La Pastorale comique*, and *George Dandin*.[32] Quinault added some connecting scenes to tie together these disparate fragments and to prepare for the concluding festival – the Troisième Intermède of *George Dandin*.[33] Not surprisingly, *Les Festes de l'Amour et de Bacchus* owes much

30 *Ballet des ballets, dansé devant Sa Majesté en son Chasteau de S. Germain en Laye au mois de Decembre 1671* (Paris: Robert Ballard, 1671). The *livret* indicates where scenes of "la comédie" intervene, but it is by no means always clear which scenes are from *La Comtesse d'Escarbagnas* and which are from the lost pastorale.

31 There remains some confusion regarding the author(s) of the libretto. According to many modern sources, Isaac Benserade and the Président de Périgny helped Quinault piece together the *livret* from fragments by Molière, to which they added some new scenes of their own. However, since Perigny died in 1670, it is unlikely that he provided much assistance with the project. The notion that Benserade contributed verses to *Les Festes de l'Amour et de Bacchus* may stem from the fact that excerpts were borrowed from *Les Amants magnifiques* (1670). Robinet incorrectly attributed the verses of *Les Amants magnifiques* to Benserade in his premature review of the court premiere (letter of February 8, 1670), and later corrected his error (letter of February 22, 1670; see William Brooks, ed., *Le théâtre et l'opéra vus par les gazetiers Robinet et Laurent, 1670–1678* [Paris, Seattle, Tübingen, 1993], 27–31). As far as we know, nothing contradicts Tralage's assertion that "les vers sont de M. Quinault et de M. de Molière, la musique de M. Lully" (Jean Nicolas de Tralage, *Notes et documents sur l'histoire des théâtres de Paris au XVIIe siècle* [c. 1697], ed. Paul Lacroix [Geneva, 1867; reprint Geneva, 1969], 110).

32 *La Pastorale comique* and *Les Amants magnifiques* were never performed publicly at the Palais Royal, and *George Dandin* was given there as a non-musical play shorn of its pastoral *intermèdes*.

33 The borrowings for *Les Festes de l'Amour et de Bacchus* are as follows: Ouverture (from *Le Bourgeois Gentilhomme*); Prologue, Part I, scene 1 (Première Entrée of *Le Ballet des Nations*), Première Entrée, *Le Donneur de livres, Quatre Importuns* (Seconde Entrée of *Le Ballet des Nations*), Part II, scenes 2–5 (new material by Quinault), Seconde Entrée, *Quatre Héros, quatre Pâtres & quatre Ouvriers*; Act I, scenes 1–2 (from Molière's *Les Amants magnifiques*, Troisième Intermède, scenes 1–2), scene 3 (new material by Quinault), scenes 4–6 (from Molière's *Les Amants magnifiques*, Troisième Intermède, scenes 3–5), Troisième Entrée, *Quatre Faunes, quatre Dryades*; Act II, scenes 1–2 (new material by Quinault), Quatrième Entrée (from Molière's *La Pastorale comique*, sc. 1), scenes 3–5 (new material by Quinault), scenes 6–7 (from Molière's *Les Amants magnifiques*,

to both the large-scale, heroic *comédies-ballets* (*Les Amants magnifiques*, *Psyché*) and the mythological, semi-operatic machine-plays of the past decade (especially Boyer's *Les Amours de Jupiter et de Sémélé* and De Visé's *Le Mariage de Bacchus et d'Ariane*). Owing to the wholesale borrowings from Molière, this opera *pastiche* features an unusually large cast of characters: fifteen singing roles (five shepherds, five shepherdesses, two satyrs, and three sorceresses), two independent choruses and two instrumental ensembles representing the followers of Cupid and Bacchus respectively, thirty-two dancing characters (fauns, dryads, magicians, demons, shepherds, shepherdesses, satyrs, bacchantes), and eleven supernatural characters (seven flying demons, two sirens, a flying sorceress, a flying goblin). Moreover, Quinault's classification of the dramatic characters by function (i.e., those who sing, those who dance, and those who are transported by machines) follows that of *Pomone*, and thereby underscores the three main elements that comprised French opera: music, ballet, and scenic spectacle. Although the frères Parfaict felt that this mélange "produced but a mediocre spectacle,"[34] the appeal of a pastoral celebration of idyllic love – adorned with Vigarani's magnificent scenery and spectacular machine effects, Des Brosses's dance *entrées*, and Lully's music – made *Les Festes de l'Amour et de Bacchus* popular enough with the Parisian public to warrant revivals in 1689, 1696, 1706, 1716, and 1738.[35]

Of immediate interest is the prologue, which begins with the opening scene from the "Ballet des Nations" (originally performed as the balletic conclusion to *Le Bourgeois Gentilhomme*). Here a crowd of spectators is shown awaiting the start of a *ballet de cour*. A dancer arrives and begins handing out *livrets* (Première entrée: *Le Donneur de livres*), "but he is hindered by the demands of people of different ranks, provinces, and nationalities, and by three troublemakers who follow hard on his heels" (Seconde Entrée: *Les Trois Importuns*). What follows stands as the first operatic collaboration of Lully and Quinault, and a statement of the philosophy of

---

Troisième Intermède, scene 5), scene 8 (new material by Quinault); Act III, scene 1, Cinquième Entrée, scene 2, Sixième Entrée, scene 3, Dernière Entrée: *Quatre Bergers, quatre Bergères, quatre Satyres & quatre Bacchantes* (all from *George Dandin*, Troisième Intermède).

34 ParfaictH, 15.
35 ParfaictH, vol. I, 550 (s.v. "*Les Fêtes de l'Amour et de Bacchus*").

the new Académie Royale de Musique. The boisterous gaiety of the *comédie-ballet* is quelled when Polymnie, the Muse of Pantomime, exhorts the performing arts henceforth to show the dignity befitting their royal patron. Melpomene and Euterpe then arrive to advocate for the tragic and pastoral genres, and afterwards the three sister-muses agree to join forces "pour plaire au plus grand des rois."

In fact, the latter half of the prologue seems to have been modeled after the prologue to *Les Amours de Jupiter et de Sémélé* (1666) of Claude Boyer, which also debated the efficacy of the different dramatic genres in celebrating the *gloire* of Louis XIV. Boyer began his tribute in much the same manner: his muses also arrive to their characteristic music – Melpomene to the clarions and trumpets of tragedy, Thalia to the fiddles of comedy, and Euterpe to musettes and oboes of the pastorale – and advocate for their respective genres. But unlike Boyer, who wrote his prologue entirely in alexandrines, Quinault assigns his muses verse-forms befitting their literary genres: alexandrines and octo-syllables for the high style of tragedy, shorter *chanson* verses for the pastorale. Moreover, in contrast to the isometric music of Euterpe's dance song, Lully set Melpomene's "nobles récits" with their characteristic anapestic rhythms in the declamatory style of French recitative (Example 7.9).

That Molière's comic muse Thalia did not appear with the triumvirate of muses on the stage of the Académie Royale de Musique was symbolic: the age of *comédie-ballet* had given way to the dawn of a new, more lofty and less humorous epoch – one marked by Louis XIV's deepening attachment to projection of an image of *gloire*, to the exclusion of ribald gaiety and self-laughter. While Polymnie agrees to support both, she confides to the tragic muse: "I reserve for you my greatest works." Indeed, this comment proved to be prophetic, for, with the exception of one *pastorale héroïque, Acis et Galathée* (1686), Lully's subsequent French operas would all be heroic *tragédies lyriques* on mythological or legendary subjects.

Example 7.9

Quinault, *Les Festes de l'Amour et de Bacchus* (1672)

Prologue (after *Les Festes de l'Amour et de Bacchus* (Paris, 1717))

Example 7.9 (*cont.*)

198

8 The presentation of Lully's *Alceste* at the Strasbourg Académie de Musique

CATHERINE CESSAC

Like most of his contemporaries, Sébastien de Brossard (1655–1730) professed a profound admiration for Jean-Baptiste Lully. The commentary he left in his *Catalogue des livres de Musique*[1] presents no ambiguity: "He [Lully] was by nationality Italian, but almost from his childhood was raised in France. He had an admirable genius for music, and had worked a long while for the ballets and other diversions of his Majesty, for which he was very well known and very much esteemed."[2] Furthermore, reflecting on the death of the *Surintendant de la musique du Roi*, Brossard wrote: "All music suffered this tragic death on March 22, 1687. I left for Strasbourg the following May 1 and I did not fail to take along everything I could then find of this illustrious author's works, both

1 *Catalogue des livres de Musique Theorique et Prattique, vocalle et instrumentalle, tant imprimée que manuscripte, qui sont dans Le cabinet du Sr. Sebastien de Brossard chanoine de Meaux, et dont il supplie tres humblement Sa Majeste d'accepter le Don, pour être mis et conservez dans sa Bibliotheque. Fait et escrit en L'année 1724*, ms., 546 p., (F-Pn) Rés Vm[8] 20. There is also a copy next to it (F-Pn) Rés Vm[8] 21. The *Catalogue* has been published in a critical edition by Yolande de Brossard: BrossardC. The notes here refer to that work.

2 BrossardC, 274. There are other examples offering evidence of the esteem that Brossard held for Lully as a composer. Staunch champion of Marc-Antoine Charpentier, Brossard produced a lengthy homage to Charpentier's *tragédie en musique Médée*, without neglecting the quality of Lully's work in that genre: "Moreover, to return to his opera *Medée*, it is without doubt the most learned and the most carefully constructed of all those that have been published, at least since the death of Lully (*ibid.*, 276). And with regard to Johann Sigismund Kusser, whose *Composition de musique suivant la methode françoise contenant six ouvertures de theatre accompagnées de plusieurs airs* (Stuttgart: P. Treu, 1682. [F Pn] Vm[7] 1484) Brossard owned, he noted "that of all the Germans, he (Kusser) best penetrated the manner of the French taste and best imitated the famous J. B. Lully" (*ibid.*, 362).

in print and in manuscript form."[3] There is no doubt that Brossard appreciated Lully's work enormously, to the extent that he copied and preserved a large portion of the Florentine composer's secular and religious pieces.

Sébastien de Brossard, composer and theoretician, is known today mainly for his famous *Catalogue*, a testament to his efforts as a bibliophile. Thanks to the huge number of volumes he collected we have many musical works and theoretical writings drawn from a large part of Europe from the end of the sixteenth to the beginning of the eighteenth century, works that otherwise may have been lost. But Brossard was not content just to collect musical scores, both in manuscript and in print. Upon occasion, he "arranged" certain pieces to conform to the taste of the day, adding a *basse continue* and sometimes even an orchestra, as he did, for instance, with the masses of François Cosset (*c.* 1610–after 1664) and Charles d'Helfer (d. after 1664). These he had performed in Strasbourg and Meaux, cities in eastern France where from 1687 on he spent most of his career. He also made an arrangement of Lully's *Alceste* for the Académie de Musique in Strasbourg.

Alceste, a tragedy set to music by Lully

Alceste, the second *tragédie en musique* by Philippe Quinault and Jean-Baptiste Lully, was first performed on January 18, 1674, at the Académie Royale de Musique, and presented again at Versailles on July 4 of the same year. The first rehearsals, attended by the king, took place at Versailles in November 1673, and promised a great success: "They often rehearse the overture; it goes beyond anything ever heard before. The king said the other day that if he were in Paris when the opera was playing, he would go every day. This work alone will be worth 100,000 francs to Baptiste."[4] The public reception, however, was not unanimous: "We go often to the opera: we find the other one [*Cadmus and Hermione*] more pleasing. Baptiste thought that he had improved on it; but even the most just of men can be mistaken."[5] In fact, the quality of the opera was not in doubt; the principal agents of this cabal were those whom Lully had eclipsed from the stage of the Académie Royale (Molière's former troupe, actors

3 *Ibid.*, 274.
4 Sévigné, Madame de, *Correspondance* (Paris, Gallimard, Bibliothèque de La Pléiade, 1972), vol. I, 630–631.
5 *Ibid.*, 686.

from the Hôtel de Bourgogne and the Italian Comedians, the theatre poets, etc.).[6] Nevertheless, the opera succeeded: indeed, by 1715, the year of Louis XIV's death, *Alceste* had enjoyed no less than five revivals.[7]

Although the libretto was published the very year of the opera's creation, the first edition of the music (in a reduced version of the score, as was common at the time) was not published until 1708, twenty-one years after Lully's death.[8] Then there followed several other editions in 1708, 1716, 1720, and 1727. Along with these we possess a large number of manuscript copies, mostly without dates.[9]

Sébastien de Brossard and the Strasbourg Académie de Musique

In May 1687 Brossard left Paris, where at Notre Dame he had the function of "buretier" (one who oversees the supply and use of communion wine), to become an honorary canon at Strasbourg cathedral,[10] a position which was naturally much better paid. Two years earlier, on March 31, 1685, the cathedral officials had decided to appoint Mathieu Fourdaux, the *maître de chapelle* of Metz, to this position at Strasbourg. Because Fourdaux failed to appear, Brossard was chosen in his place.[11] But in 1688 Alsace had fallen victim to new military conflicts (i.e. the war of the Augsburg League) as well as to a bad harvest following a particularly severe winter. Faced with a decrease in revenue, cathedral officials decided the next year to abandon the cathedral's musical activities and at the same time to reduce the emoluments of the *maître de chapelle*, leaving Brossard a diminished allocation for the support of his children. It is at that point that Brossard established an Académie de Musique.[12] We have few direct accounts of the activities of this

---

6 La GorceO, 50–51.
7 September 1677, January 1678, September 1682, November 1706, and February 1707. See *ibid.*, 198–201.
8 *Alceste./ Tragedie. / Mise en Musique / Par feu Monsieur De Lully, Ecuyer, / Conseiller-Secretaire du Roy, Maison, Couronne / de France Et de ses Finances, et Sur-Intendant / de la Musique de Sa Majesté / Première Edition / Gravée par H. de Baussen. / A Paris, / On la vend/ A l'Entrée de la Porte de l'Academie Royale de Musique, au Palais / Royal, rüe Saint honoré. / M.DCC.VIII. / Avec Privilege de sa Majesté.*
9 See SchneiderC, 225.
10 Strasbourg had become a French city on September 30, 1681.
11 See BrossardY, 20.
12 *Ibid.*, 22–23.

Académie. Brossard specifies these clearly only twice, mentioning Lully's *Alceste* and Elisabeth Jacquet de La Guerre's *Céphale et Procris*.[13] Certain references, however, such as singers' names in other manuscripts preserved by Brossard (including Lully's *Atys*, *Persée*, the *grands motets Miserere*, *Dies irae*, and the *Te Deum*), show that these works were performed in Strasbourg at either the Académie or the cathedral. Indeed, the names of these musicians appear in the chapter's records,[14] and indications in Brossard's scores confirm that these musicians also participated in the concerts of the Académie de Musique. For example, at the funeral of one of the most celebrated members of the Académie, held in the church of Saint Pierre le Jeune, the *Requiem* by Giovanni Paolo Colonna[15] was sung "in Strasbourg by the musicians of an Academy which [Brossard] had assembled and established there."[16]

Brossard as arranger of *Alceste*

Brossard describes and comments upon the copy he made of Lully's *Alceste* in these terms:

> I: Manuscript score, oblong octavo, of the opera titled *Alceste ou le Triomphe d'Alcide* set to music by the late M. de Lully. In its entirety, this score contains only the prologue in praise of King Louis XIV as well as several pieces removed from the body of the opera and suitable for a concert of about one hour's duration to be used by the Académie established in Strasbourg by Seb. de Brossard.[17]

What were Brossard's sources for his arrangement? During the years 1691 to 1695 (see below for the relevant dates) no edition had yet been issued in

---

13 See Catherine Cessac, "Les Relations musicales de Sébastien de Brossard et d'Elisabeth Jacquet de La Guerre," *Sébastien de Brossard musicien* (Versailles, Editions du Centre de Musique Baroque de Versailles; Paris, Editions Klincksieck, 1998), 43–57.

14 See Sébastien de Brossard, *Les Grands motets*, ed. Jérome Krucker (Versailles, Editions du Centre de Musique Baroque de Versailles, 1995), viii.

15 *Messa, salmi e responsori per li defonti a otto voci pieni*... (Bologna: Giacomo Monti, 1685; separate parts, F-Pn Vm1 906). From this source Brossard prepared the score *Missa pro defunctis. a 2. chor. de Gio' Paolo Colonna opera VIa.*, (F-Pn) Vm¹ 907. The name "mr Robert" appears on p. 50.

16 BrossardY, 126. Colonna was a composer whom Brossard considered "a musician's musician."

17 *Ibid.*, 498.

print. Thus Brossard's source could only have been manuscript copy. Brossard, however, mentions no such score in his *Catalogue*, whereas elsewhere he lists several manuscripts of *tragédies en musique* by Lully.[18] Comparing sources is thus a very difficult task, given that we are unsure of the source Brossard consulted. Several indications, however, have led me to consider one particular handwritten score as the possible candidate. This is a copy by Philidor l'aîné[19] preserved in the Bibliothèque municipale de Versailles. Research[20] has shown that Brossard had knowledge of manuscripts that Philidor copied (and had others copy) for the Bibliothèque royale.[21] It is hardly likely that Brossard would have copied Philidor's score himself, but without doubt he owned a copy either acquired before his departure for Alsace, during his stay in Paris in 1695,[22] or sent to him in Strasbourg. Whatever the case, this copy seems now to be lost. But we do have the Philidor source which, with respect to different manuscript sources consulted, appears to be the nearest to what Brossard could have known.

Description of the sources

1 Alceste a Philidor L'ainé / ord.^re de la musique du Roy/16 [?] [LWV 50]. Original manuscript in the hand of Philidor l'aîné, full score, 44 × 28.5 cm, 210 pp. (F-V) Ms mus 94. The copy probably dates from *c.* 1690–1702.[23]

18 A complete listing of Lully's works that appear in the Brossard Collection is given in Catherine Cessac, "Les Sources lullystes dans la Collection Brossard," in Sèvres98, 88–102.

19 Violinist of the Chapelle Royale and of the Chambre, composer André-Danican Philidor (1647–1730) was commissioned around 1684 to be the custodian of the Royal Library, along with François Fossard, with whom he shared this official responsibility. But it is primarily from Philidor that numerous manuscript copies of music have come to us.

20 Jean Duron, *L'Œuvre de Sébastien de Brossard (1655–1730), Catalogue thématique* (Versailles, Editions du Centre de Musique Baroque de Versailles; Paris, Editions Klincksieck, 1995), xliv–xlv, 330–331; and Catherine Cessac, *L'Œuvre de Daniel Danielis (1635–1696), Catalogue thématique* (Versailles, Editions du Centre de Musique baroque de Versailles, forthcoming).

21 For example the *Petits Motets et Elévations de Messieurs Carissimi, Lully, Robert, Danielis et Foggia . . . Recueillis par Philidor l'aisné, Ordinaire de la Musique du Roy, en 1688*, (F-Pn) Rés Vmb ms 6.

22 BrossardC, 309.

23 See Denis Herlin, *Catalogue du fonds musical de la Bibliothèque de Versailles* (Paris: Société française de musicologie, Klincksieck, 1995), 384.

Plate 8.1   Brossard's score of *Alceste. ou le Triomphe d'alcide. mis en musique par m*[r] *de Lully* in Brossard's own hand. F-Pn Vm² 12bis

2   Alceste. ou le Triomphe d'alcide. mis en musique par m[r] de Lully [Sdb.264]. Original manuscript in the hand of Brossard, full score, 13.3 × 21 cm, 39 pp., (F-Pn) Vm² 12bis. The copy probably dates from about 1691–1695.[24]

The Brossard manuscript preserved in the Bibliothèque Nationale is incomplete. The first page of music is shown in Plate 8.1. The score includes two bound gatherings, the first of six sheets, the second of four, all folded in two. Missing is a third gathering which contained the end of the *Pompe funèbre* of Act III and perhaps other passages like the *fête de réjouissance* at the end of the last act. Brossard's remark ("for a concert of about one hour's time") can help to reconstitute what is missing from the current manuscript. A complete summary of the source is shown in Table 8.1.

Comparison of the Brossard and Lully versions

The occasion that prompted the first performance of Brossard's arrangement of *Alceste* at the Académie de Musique in Strasbourg remains unknown.[25] Brossard's editorial selection is reflected in the prologue to the

24   See Duron, *L'Œuvre de Sébastien de Brossard*, 348.
25   It should be remembered that Brossard remained in Strasbourg until 1698.

204

Table 8.1. *Organization of Brossard's arrangement of Lully's Alceste*

Folio	Title, and incipit	Parts affected[a]	Measure	Number of measures (without reprises)	Number of measures (with reprises)
[Prologue]					
[1–1v]	*Ouverture* Grave–Presto	2 G1,C1,F4	2–6/4	42	84
[2]	*La nymphe de La Seine. ou C.P°.* "Le heros que j'attens"	C1/F4	3	50	64
[2v]	Allegro	2 G1,C1,F4	3	6	
[2v]	"Quel bruit de guerre"	C1/F4	3	4	
[2v–3]	*Allegro Rondeau*[b]	2 G1,C1,F4	¢	43	
[3–3v]	*La Seine* "Helas superbe gloire"	C1/F4	3	28	
[3v–4]	*La Gloire* "Pourquoy tant murmurer"	C1/F4	c	13	
[4]	*La Seine. C. P°.* "On ne voit plus icy paroistre"	C1/F4	3	16	32
[4]	*La Gloire* "Il revient et tu dois m'en croire"	C1/F4	c	11	
[4–4v]	[Duo] "Qu'il est doux d'accorder"	2 C1/F4	3	26	

Table 8.1 (cont.)

Folio	Title, and incipit	Parts affected[a]	Measure	Number of measures (without reprises)	Number of measures (with reprises)
[4v–6]	*Allegro Tutti* "Qu'il est doux d'accorder"	*C1,C3,2 C4,F4/* 2 G1,C1,F4	3	53	
[6]	*Adagio*	2 G1,C1,F4	3	8	
[6–6v]	*Ten. I°* "L'art d'accord avec la nature"	*C4/F4*	3	40	48
[6v–7]	*Air pour les nimphes*	2 G1,C1,F4	3	20	40
[7]	*Tenore. 2°.* "L'onde se presse"	*C4/F4*	3	18	36
[7–7v]	*Air pour les fleuves*	2 G1,C1,F4	6/4	16	32
[7v–8]	*Allegro. Duo Alto Ten. I°* "Que tout retentisse"	*C3,C4/2 G1^c, F4*	3	28	
[8–9v]	*Chœur* "Que tout retentisse"	*C1,C3,2 C4,F4/* 2 G1,C1,F4	3	66	
[9v–10]	*Air*	2 G1,C1,F4	3	41	49
[10]	*Duo* "Quel cœur sauvage"	*C1,F4/F4*	3	8	
[10v]	*Tutti* "Quel cœur sauvage"	*C1,C3,2 C4,F4/* 2 G1,C1,F4	3	8	
[10v]	*Duo T. I°* "Nous allons voir les plaisirs"	*C4,F4/F4*	3	12	

Folio	Description	Clefs	Meter		
[11]	Tutti "Nous allons voir les plaisirs"	C1,C3,2,C4,F4/ 2 G1,C1,F4	3	16	32
[11v–12]	Adagio–Allegro "Revenez plaisirs exilés"	C1,C3,2 C4,F4/ 2 G1,C1,F4	3	16	32
[Acte I]					
[12v]	Les vents. ou scene derniere du Ier acte.	2 G1,C1,F4	3/8	30	
[13]	Scene 9e. du Ier acte. Ritourn.	2 G1,C1,F4	3	10	
[13–13v]	Ten. 2o "Le ciel protege les héros"	F3/ 2 G1,F4	3	39	
[Acte II]					
[14]	Le combat. ou scene du 2d acte. Marche. Allegro	2 G1,¢ C1,F4	¢	32	51
[14v–15v]	Allegro. Tutti "A l'assaut, aux armes"	C1,C3,2 C4,F4/ 2 G1,C1,F4	¢	51	
[15v–16]	Prestissimo. "Donnons de toutes parts"	C1,C3,2 C4,F4/ 2 G1,C1,F4	¢	20	
[16–17]	Tutti Presto. "Courage, ils sont a nous"	C1,C3,2 C4,F4/ 2 G1,C1,F4	3/8	42	
[17–17v]	Les combattans.	2 G1,C1,F4	3/8	25	
[17v]	"Courage enfans"	C4/F4	c	9	
[17v–18]	Air. adagio "Que la vieillesse est lente"	C4/F4	3	25	

Table 8.1 (*cont.*)

Folio	Title, and incipit	Parts affected[a]	Measure	Number of measures (without reprises)	Number of measures (with reprises)
[Acte III]					
[18]	*Pompe funebre ou Scene. V^e du 3^e acte. Prelude Grave*	2 G1,C1,F4	¢	18	
[18v–19]	*Ten. 2°.* "La mort barbare"	C4/2 G1,F4	¢	36	
[19]	*Tutti. Molto adagio* "Rendons hommage"	C1,C3,2 C4,F4/ 2 G1,C1,F4	¢	8	
[19–20]	"Versons des pleurs"	C1,C3,2 C4,F4/ 2 G1,C1,F4	2	26	
[20–20v]	"Alceste, la charmante Alceste" [INCOMPLETE]	C1,C3,2 C4,F4/ 2 G1,C1,F4	c	10	

[a] Vocal clefs are italicized, instrumental clefs are in roman.

[b] The first part of the Rondeau indicates in alternation "Trompettes" and "Violons." In the refrain (mm. 19–25, 36–43) only the dessus part has been recopied, as well as that of the bass continuo.

[c] "hautbois."

[d] Brossard's error. It is actually the eighth and second-last scene of Act I.

[e] The first part indicates in alternation "Trompettes" and "Violons."

glory of Louis XIV, a section at the end of act I (the *symphonie* "Les vents" and the last scene), the *Combat* from Act II and the (incomplete) *Pompe funèbre* from Act III. In making his choices (excluding the prologue, which is presented in its entirety), Brossard gives a privileged place to the choruses and the instrumental sections. He also included some reworkings that involved the organization of certain sections, the tessitura of the soloists' roles, and the internal disposition of the orchestra and choruses. Brossard added Italian tempo indications – Grave, Presto, Prestissimo, Allegro, Adagio, Molto adagio – to the movements. Other elements such as figured bass, ornamentation, rhythmic and melodic variations must be considered with caution given the absence of the source Brossard consulted directly.

Treatment of form

In the prologue, Brossard generally follows Lully's score. However, he makes certain additions: the texts "Quel cœur sauvage" and "Nous allons voir les plaisirs," given only to the chorus in the Lully version, are now given first to a duo (C3 and F4). Brossard again varies slightly from the model in the different sections of the prologue: he includes brief transitional passages where they did not exist in the original (for example a measure marked Adagio in the *basse continue* before the chorus "Que tout retentisse," fol. 7v), and conversely at the end of the chorus "Qu'il est doux d'accorder," fol. 6,[26] provides a full pause instead of a short transitional passage. His emphasis on the caesura between the two parts of the chorus "Revenez plaisirs exilés" et "Volez de toutes parts" (fol.11v) is noteworthy: a pedal point is added under the quarter-note rest of Lully's version and the contrast between the two sections is emphasized by two different tempi: adagio then allegro. Finally the C♯ in place of the B and the addition of the B♭ offers a richer harmonic color. Moreover, the chorus is repeated in its entirety in Brossard's version but not Lully's (Ex. 8.1a and b).

Subsequent to making this arrangement, Brossard takes greater liberty with Lully's *tragédie*, choosing only excerpts from Acts I, II, and III. Moreover, even within sections he makes modifications. Brossard retains

26 Originally Philidor's score was identical to Brossard's in this passage. The transitional music was subsequently added (as can be seen from the scratching out of a double bar and the use of a lighter colored ink for three extra notes in the bass).

CATHERINE CESSAC

Example 8.1

(a) Chorus "Revenez plaisirs exilés," Lully's version, p. 15[27]

scene 2 in *Le Combat* of Act II, and then the end of scene 4, but truncates the trio "A moi compagnons" by eight measures, the final instrumental section of the chorus "Donnons de toutes parts" by fifty-three measures, and the chorus "Courage, ils sont à nous" by fifteen measures.[28] He completely eliminates the last chorus "Achevons d'emporter la place." Scene 5 is included in its entirety, but scenes 6, 7, 8, and 9 are absent. *La Pompe funèbre* of Act II also undergoes a profound reorganization with notable variants such as those found in the final *ritournelle* of the recitative "La mort barbare" (Ex. 8.2a and b).

The orchestra

Lully's version of *Alceste* includes, of course, an orchestra scored in the French style for five parts (*dessus, hautes-contre, tailles, quintes,* and *basses*

27 The orchestra parts are not entered in Philidor's manuscript. A marginal note, however, indicates that the strings and the oboes should double the choral parts ("Il faut le [sic] violons et hautbois dan le chœur [sic]").

28 A slip of paper in Philidor's copy hides three measures at the end of this chorus. Those measures also are absent in Brossard's copy.

210

Example 8.1 (*cont.*)

(b) Chorus "Revenez plaisirs exilés," Brossard's version, fol. 11v

de violon). Brossard's instrumental ensemble in the arrangement includes four parts in the Italian style (two *dessus de violon*, one part for the *haute-contre de violon*, and continuo). The replacement of one style of orchestration by another, mainly affecting the inner parts, was accomplished in various ways, one of which consisted of giving the part of the *haute-contre de violon* to the second *dessus de violon* and forming the *haute-contre* from elements taken from the *taille* and the *quinte* (Ex. 8.3a and b).

Sometimes Brossard rewrote the two inner parts (Ex. 8.4a and b). Brossard's score includes instrumental indications that are important

211

Example 8.2

(a) *Pompe funèbre*, ritournelle, Lully's version, p. 125

(b) *Pompe funèbre*, ritournelle, Brossard's version, fol. 18v

because they tell us something about the musicians at the Académie de Strasbourg. Besides the string parts designated by the clefs, oboes (fol. 8) and trumpets (fols. 2v and 14 are specified).

The soloists

The solo parts of the prologue for *La Nymphe de la Seine*, *La Gloire*, *La Nymphe des Tuileries*, and *La Nymphe de la Marne* are assigned entirely to the *dessus* and notated in the C1 clef. Perhaps because he lacked four voices of solo capability and wished to include all of his singers (two sopranos, an alto in C3 clef, two tenors,[29] and a bass), Brossard distributed the roles differently.[30] In his arrangement only two characters are named: "La Nymphe de la Seine ou C.Iº." (C1) and "La Gloire" (C1). The two others sung by male voices have no names. Moreover, the duo "Que tout retentisse" sung by La Gloire and La Nymphe de la Seine is assigned to an alto (C3) and to the first tenor (C4). In Lully's version the characters change after this short duo ("La Nymphe des Tuileries" in "Que tout fleurisse" and

---

29 The second tenor part is notated in F3.
30 Brossard's concert version probably did not involve staging.

Example 8.3

(a) Chorus "Qu'il est doux d'accorder," Lully's version, p. 10

(b) Chorus "Qu'il est doux d'accorder," Brossard's version, fols. 4v–5

"La Nymphe de la Marne" in "Que le chant des oiseaux"); Brossard, however, preserves the voices of the preceding duo.

In the sections that follow, the characters are not specifically identified. Although the characters Eole (F3), Alcide (C4), and Pheres (C4) have the same voice ranges as in Lully's version, the role of "Une femme affligée" (C1) in Brossard's version is sung by a second tenor.

213

Example 8.4

(a) *Entrée des Aquilons*, Lully's version, p. 61

(b) *Les vents*, Brossard's version, fol. 12v

The chorus

In Strasbourg Brossard had a sufficient number of singers but not the orchestral resources to compete with Lully. Therefore for practical reasons Brossard reduced the number of instrumental parts, a measure he compensated for, in a sense, by the increased size of the choir.[31] In Lully's version the

31 It is possible that the choir consisted of the combined soloists, for the tessituras of the two groups (soloists and choir) are the same.

Example 8.5

Chorus "Que tout retentisse," Lully's version, p. 24 and Brossard's version, fol. 9

latter has four parts (*dessus, haute-contre, taille, basse*) and in Brossard's five, the additional part being a second *taille*, notated in C4 on the same staff as the first.[32] Compared to the original *taille* the second is sometimes higher, sometimes lower (Ex. 8.5a and b).

Conclusion

The works of Lully that Brossard copied and preserved constitute a corpus of great interest that enables us to understand the diffusion of Lully's work after his death, beyond the Court, and outside Paris. In this regard *Alceste* is certainly one of the most precious examples of how Brossard the arranger brought his artistic skills to a work of the first order of importance, showing how Brossard appropriated the work of a musician whom he admired and who, by the end of the seventeenth century, enjoyed a reputation throughout all of Europe. For Brossard, music of the past (since *Alceste* by 1690 was already a work of the past) must continue to be performed, even if the means he has at his disposal are not those originally conceived for the work. This is undoubtedly the greatest mark of respect that one composer can have for another: that of ensuring the continued life of his work.

32 In an anonymous motet ([F-Pn] Vm¹ 1179) Brossard added a "Tenore 2" part with the note "additum per SB 1696." This motet was filed in the same carton as Lully's *O Lachrymae*. See BrossardC, 441–442.

9 Walking through Lully's opera theatre in the Palais Royal

BARBARA COEYMAN

Introduction

In the March 1678 issue of the *Mercure Galant* an unidentified visitor to the Paris Opera recorded observations about the layout of the theatre.[1] Seeking diversion for a few hours, this anonymous patron, certainly a dilettante of the arts, and, in the absence of national identification, probably a Frenchman, decided to attend the opera, located in the Palais Royal. He found his place in the third and highest balcony, the *paradis*, on the king's side of the auditorium. The *paradis* did not have separate boxes, as did the first two balconies. Instead, it functioned in part as a gallery, around which he and his friends could walk and where they could do more or less as they pleased. The visitor also described easy access from the *paradis* to the lower two balconies and the amphitheatre. Watching the opera was, evidently, only one of several agreeable activities available.[2] This account in the *Mercure* illustrates how attendance at the opera in seventeenth-century Paris had multiple levels of meaning. Music combined with visual effects to create multi-media artistic experiences. These experiences were overlaid with social and even political dynamics that may have been as important to the attendee as the opera itself, or even more so.[3]

Our visitor's observations are very welcome. Most other eyewitness accounts of the opera during Lully's lifetime comment on the skill of the

A version of this essay was originally presented at the annual meeting of the Society for Seventeenth-Century Studies at Wellesley College in April 1996.

1 *Mercure Galant*, March 1678, 17–27.
2 The report says "elles n'estoient pas là pour le seul plaisir de la musique ..." *Mercure*, p. 24.
3 The report does not specify which production they attended, but it was probably *Atys*, which played in revival in February 1678 (see Table 9.1).

performers, the costumes and stage effects, or the genius of Lully's music, but rarely on the theatre itself, particularly in relation to how it accommodated people. After acquiring rights to the Académie Royale de Musique in 1672, Lully transformed this former court theatre into the first public opera house in Paris. He opened the theatre with the tragedy *Alceste* on January 19, 1674, and the hall served as the home of the Opera for ninety years, until razed by a devastating fire in 1763. The theatre was the site of public performances of Lully's secular repertoire in Paris during his lifetime. Our investigation of the Palais Royal as it accommodated artistic creators, audiences, and performers informs our understanding of the presentation of Lully's repertoire, as well as his career in his roles as public administrator and designer.[4]

By researching a variety of sources, we can reconstruct Lully's theatre and its performances in our mind's eye. We can walk through the Palais Royal as Lully knew it and observe how the site accommodated people, which suggests much about the experience of attending public opera in seventeenth-century Paris. Additionally, since Lully and designer Carlo Vigarani directly oversaw the remodeling of the theatre for use by their new Académie Royale de Musique, we may assume that reconstruction of the site informs our understanding of Lully's original intentions and concepts for productions, because he could create repertoire with a particular performance venue in mind.[5]

In our tour of the Palais Royal theatre I hope to combine effectively different aspects of opera, which are seldom considered together in historical studies, as we examine the physical structure in terms of its influence on repertoire and audiences. This visit expands our acquaintance with Baroque halls and suggests new dimensions for considering opera repertoire and operatic life in the seventeenth century. Our attention to the

---

4 One account of the theatre, although after Lully's lifetime, appears in La GraveT, 81–86.
5 See Table 9.1 for a list of Lully's repertoire at the Palais Royal during his lifetime, as well as dates of his ten works which premiered at court. Court premieres were in part ceremonial gestures, to give the king an advance showing of repertoire. All works which opened at court played in the Palais Royal within several months. I have constructed Table 9.1 from a combination of sources: DucrotR, 19–55, La GorceO, 197–199, SchneiderR, LaJarteB, SchmidtC, the *Mercure Galant*, 1672–73, 1677–87 and the *Gazette de France*, 1672–80.

building and consequently the institution of opera leads to consideration of the integration of Baroque performing arts with other aspects of cultural life. In particular, the theatre, as the 1678 visitor implies, held meaning for audiences that transcended the content of the repertoire. We might even question how much Lully's audiences paid attention to his repertoire, if we apply the recent research by James Johnson on the eighteenth-century Paris Opera to Lully's theatre.[6]

Analysis of the Palais Royal expands our general understanding of French seventeenth-century theatres, whose history T. E. Lawrenson views as a search for identity in his explanation for why French structures and repertoire lagged significantly behind Italian practice.[7] This identity crisis was exacerbated by at least two factors: many theatres, public and at court, were installed in pre-existing spaces and consequently were affected to a large degree by the conditions of that space; and many theatres, especially at court, were temporary, erected quickly, used for a few performances or at most a few years, and then abandoned for other sites. Thus, Lully's opening of the Palais Royal as a public theatre significantly expanded the possibilities for performance of opera and ballet.

Given his experiences in court, Lully may have initially considered the Palais Royal as yet one more temporary theatre, which he intended to use for a few years until a better site presented itself. The despotic music director may not have anticipated his ill-starred turns of fortune in the 1680s, including his falling from the king's favor and Louis XIV's flagging interest in opera.[8]

6 James Johnson, *Listening in Paris: A Cultural History* (Berkeley and Los Angeles: University of California Press, 1995). Johnson indicates that opera audiences engaged in many activities during performances. Audiences did not become silent – that is, focused on repertoire – until the end of the eighteenth century. Johnson points out that in the seventeenth century, opera was primarily royal spectacle, and that the court of Louis XIV represented controlled order. The upper nobility more or less determined modes of behavior for everyone. While court audiences may have been more controlled than those in the public theatre were, there are many images of audiences at court during Lully's lifetime talking, walking around, and otherwise not paying much attention to the stage.

7 T. E. Lawrenson, *The French Stage in the XVIIth Century* (Manchester University Press, 1957). Concern about Paris's inadequate theatres persisted through the eighteenth century. For example, in the 1740s Voltaire called for reform in Paris's theatre, on the model of Berlin's opera house. See Carlson, 72–77. The question of the relationship between physical settings and repertoire is fascinating and hardly examined to date.

8 His split with Vigarani in 1680 may suggest that Lully was planning new directions for opera.

Not only did Lully never acquire another site, but the Palais Royal was destined to serve audiences for seventy-six years after his death.

Manifestations of an identity crisis at the Opera continued throughout most of the *ancien régime* because the Palais Royal remained under the thumb of the royal family. Overseen by Louis XIV during Lully's lifetime, the palace was transferred by the king to the Orléans family in 1692, a move which kept the theatre locked in a conservative court administration. This did little to encourage artistic creativity, and even less to discourage profligate audience culture, particularly during the Regency.[9] While our focus is on the Palais Royal during Lully's lifetime, understanding its original state as a court theatre explains much about the opera house over its entire ninety-year history. Other than minor structural and cosmetic repairs, the hall remained essentially unchanged through 1763, despite significant new repertoire (e.g., Rameau's operas) and an expanding population in Paris.[10] The roots of many of the theatre's nagging problems in the mid-eighteenth century were already present as inconvenient conditions during Lully's tenure.

Historical summary and sources

As we begin our tour, a brief history of the hall as a court setting prior to Lully's directorship explains some of the conditions that continued into the time of the Paris Opera. I have defined four stages of development of the theatre, the last as the opera house. Conditions across these four periods illustrate many features generally common to French seventeenth-century theatres.[11]

---

9   The duke of Orléans was Regent of France 1715–23. Spire Pitou, *The Paris Opera: Genesis and Glory 1671–1715* (Westport, Connecticut: Greenwood Press, 1983), 14–17, reports declining culture at the Paris Opera after Lully's death.

10   The population of Paris was not systematically documented. In a census of 1715 the population was recorded as 505,000. At the outbreak of the Revolution it was reported at 600,000.

11   For more details of the first three phases, particularly in the context of repertoire, see CoeymanO, 39–74. The history of the Palais Royal theatre is discussed in many other modern historical studies, although usually without reference to repertoire. See also LagraveT, 81–96; ChampierP, 26, 29, 50–58, 160ff; Musée Carnavalet, *Le Palais Royal* (Paris: Musée Carnavalet, 1988), 13–23, 308; La GorceO, 29–79; Jean Gourret, *Histoire des salles de l'opéra de Paris* (Paris: Guy Trédaniel, 1985), 24–47; Germain Bapst, *Essai sur l'Histoire du Théâtre* (Paris: Librairie Hachette, 1893), 388–390.

BARBARA COEYMAN

The Palais Cardinal, home to Cardinal Richelieu and designed by Jacques le Mercier, opened in 1629. The building initially contained one small theatre that began operation on April 16, 1635 and accommodated several hundred spectators.[12] Richelieu, however, desired a larger setting and commissioned le Mercier to install a second hall, which opened in January 1641, with a performance of Desmaret's play *Mirame* (machines and decor by Denis Buffequin), followed one month later by the court ballet *La Prosperité des armes de la France*.[13] Two similar engravings of a performance referred to as *Le Soir* include much information about the hall's structure and accommodation of people on stage and in the auditorium.[14] Henri Sauval provides the most detailed description of the first theatre, suggesting a seating capacity of no less than 1,200.[15]

The theatre's second period occurred following Richelieu's death in 1642, when under Cardinal Mazarin theatrical activity rose to even greater prominence in court. In 1645 Mazarin invited the renowned stage designer Giacomo Torelli to Paris to prepare stage machinery for the Italian operas that the Cardinal planned to import. Luigi Rossi's *Orfeo* played in Torelli's remodeled Palais Royal in March 1647, followed by the machine play *Andromède* in 1650 using much of the same machinery.[16] Several court ballets also appeared in Torelli's site.

Surviving the civil unrest of the Fronde and other court intrigue, the palace served as the home of Louis XIV's brother, Monsieur. In 1660 the theatre entered its third period of use when Molière's acting company,

12 ChampierP, 26–27.
13 Five engravings by Stefano della Bella illustrate the stage settings and proscenium of *Mirame*. For an example, see ChampierP, 50 and Musée Carnavalet, *Le Palais Royal* (Paris: Musée Carnavalet, 1988), cat. no. 505.
14 One of the engravings is located in the Bibliothèque Nationale, Collection Hennin, and reproduced in ChampierP, 54 and in Margaret McGowan, *L'art du ballet de cour en France: 1581–1643* (Paris: Editions du Centre National de la Recherche Scientifique, 1978), pl. XXII. The other is located in the Musée des Arts Decoratif and appears in the Musée Carnavalet, *Le Palais Royal*, no. 504, and in the article on "Paris" in the *New Grove Dictionary of Opera*, 857, among many other sources. These images indicate the setting's similarity to a Renaissance great hall, with galleries along the sides and the royal family seated in the center of the floor, the center of courtiers' focus.
15 SauvalH, vol. II, pp. 158–160. Sauval probably wrote this passage *c.* 1668. His text is reproduced in ChampierP, 51–54.
16 For more on Italian opera in Paris, see AnthonyF, chapter 4 and PrunièresO.

together with the Italian *comédiens*, took it over. Several court entertainments also played there in the 1660s. Molière oversaw repairs to tailor the hall to his repertoire, including raising the stage to accommodate his machinery, installing boxes saved from the demolition of the Petit Bourbon theatre in 1660, building an orchestra area for twelve musicians, painting the hall, and decorating the ceiling. More changes, including the installation of a deeper stage for new machinery, occurred in 1671 for the production of *Psyché*. The audience capacity of Molière's hall has been estimated at just over 1,000.[17] Molière died in this theatre on February 17, 1673 after playing the lead role in *Le Malade imaginaire*.

Following Molière's death Lully moved quickly, acquiring the patent for the theatre in the name of the Académie Royale de Musique on March 13, 1673 and Carlo Vigarani as a partner in an eight-year contract on August 23.[18] After directing his first two productions, *Les Festes de l'Amour et de Bacchus* and *Cadmus et Hermione* (see Table 9.1), in the inadequate Jeu de Paume de Bel Air, Lully succeeded in acquiring the Palais Royal through Colbert's intervention, and in mid-1673 initiated repairs to the theatre. Most construction was completed by November 1673 and re-painting by December 15, 1673 (although Rouches indicates that Vigarani continued to work on the hall through February). The repair costs of 3,000 *livres* were covered by the king.[19] Vigarani's vision for the theatre may have been

17   Much documentation about Molière's theatre and audiences survives. See Madeleine Jurgens, *Cent Ans de Recherches sur Molière* (Paris: Imprimerie Nationale, 1963), 351–355; ChampierP, 160–162; Bapst, *Essai sur l'histoire du théâtre*, 342–344, 364–365; La GorceO, 32; Pierre Mélèse, *Le Théâtre et le public*, 29–36; Bert Edward Young and Grace Philputt Young, *Le Registre de La Grange 1659–1685* (Paris: Librairie E. Droz, 1947), 25–131; William Leonard Schwartz, "Molière's Theatre in 1672–73: Light from Le Registre d'Hubert," *Proceedings of the Modern Language Association* 56 (1941), 395–427, particularly 398, the source of my estimate about the audience capacity. Schwartz suggests that Molière's audiences could be relatively small, averaging less than 400.

18   See Melese, *Le Théâtre*, 36; Gabriel Rouches, *Inventaire des lettres et papiers manuscrits de Gaspare, Carlo et Lodovico Vigarani* (Paris: H. Champion, 1913), 189 fn; La GorceO, 36. Lully and Vigarani each invested 10,000 *livres* in the enterprise. Lully acquired the patent for the opera after the first public opera venture failed. It was launched by Perrin, Cambert, and Sourdéac with a performance of *Pomone* on April 18, 1671 at the Jeu de Paume de Bouteille.

19   Rouches, *Inventaire*, 194. The most complete explanation I have found to date of Lully's repairs to the hall appears in Jean Cordey, "Lully installe l'Opéra dans le théâtre de Molière," *Bulletin de la société historique de l'architecture française* (1950), 137–142.

Table 9.1. Lully's repertoire at the Palais Royal during his lifetime, 1674–87[a]

Year	Month	Premiere	Revival	Court Premier if premier not in Paris
1674	January	Alceste		
	October–November		Cadmus et Hermione	
1675	April	Thésée		April 1675
	August		Cadmus et Hermione	
	October	Le Carnaval Mascarade		
1676	April	Atys		January 1676
1677	April		Thésée	January 1677
	August	Isis		
1678	January		Thésée	
	February		Atys	
	August		Atys	
	April	Psyché		
	???		Alceste, Cadmus	
1679	January	Bellérophon		
	October		Thésée	
	November		Cadmus	
1680	July		Bellérophon	
	November	Proserpine		February 1680

1681	May	Le Triomphe de l'Amour		January 1681
	March		Proserpine	
	November		Proserpine	
1682	January		Le Triomphe de l'Amour	
	April	Persée		
	August		Persée	
	September		Alceste	
1683	April	Phaéton		January 1683
1684	January	Amadis		
1685	March	Roland		January 1685
	November	Le Temple de la Paix & Idylle sur la Paix		October 1685
1686	January		Roland	
	February	Armide		
	September	Acis et Galatée		September 1686
1687	January		Acis et Galatée	

a Works at Jeu de Paume de Bel Air prior to the opening of the Palais Royal:

1672	November	Les Festes de l'Amour et de Bacchus
1673	April	Cadmus et Hermione

inspired by his experiences, sometimes inadequate, in other court theatres. His repairs to the Palais Royal included reinforcing the space above the stage for machinery, enlarging the opening of the stage and removing on-stage pillars that interfered with scenery, rounding out the balconies at the rear into a horseshoe shape to increase visibility to the stage, enlarging the orchestra, and re-painting the room to remove memory of Molière. *Alceste*, Lully's second *tragédie lyrique*, premiered there on January 19, 1674, and the hall witnessed a total of eighteen productions by Lully, twelve of them *tragédies lyriques*, during his lifetime (see Table 9.1).[20] La Gorce reports tensions between Lully and Vigarani as early as 1675, but the designer continued as Lully's partner until August 24, 1680, designing productions at the Palais Royal from *Cadmus* (in revival) to *Bellérophon*. Jean Berain took over as designer in 1680 and remained in that post for the rest of his life, working with Lully on repertoire from *Proserpine* through *Acis et Galatée*.[21] On Lully's death in 1687 his son-in-law Jean-Nicolas de Francine became director until 1704. Louis XIV's flagging interest in the Opera may have contributed to his decision to turn over the palace, and therefore the theatre, to the duke of Orléans in 1692.[22] Under Orléans, there was little upkeep of the theatre, but public balls were initiated there in 1716. The administration of the hall remained under the Orléans family until 1749, when the city of Paris finally acquired some jurisdiction to carry out much-needed repairs.[23]

20 One work played at a time during Lully's lifetime, in part because complex stage machinery prevented much alternating of productions. See DucrotR, 40. Ducrot (p. 36) also reports that some people attended any given production up to ten times. Ducrot provides a summary of productions, discussing court versus public performances, premieres and revivals, etc.
21 The *Mercure Galant*, November 1680, 192 reports that with the association between Lully and Vigarani having ended, Berain designed his first opera, *Proserpine*, with Lully, which premiered that month. Before 1680, Berain served as a costume designer for the opera for several years, but had less experience with machinery and sets. La GorceO, 69 reports that Berain was assisted for a few years by the machinist Ercole Rivani.
22 DucrotR, 31; ChampierP, 104ff. See 112 for a map of the palace in 1692, where the theatre is indentified as "salle de l'opera."
23 Musée Carnavalet, *Le Palais Royal*, 22, 53ff. Financial problems were acerbated by the royal family giving away many tickets. La GorceO, 197 publishes the financial records of 1713–15.

As with original source materials about other elements of production, such as dance and musical scores, limited documentation survives from Lully's lifetime regarding the structure and appearance of the Palais Royal theatre. That the opening of Paris's first public opera house did not generate more public attention from eyewitnesses and artists may speak to the relatively unimportant role of public opera in Paris's public cultural life or to the unremarkable features of the new theatre.[24] Curiously, the Salle des Machines in the nearby Tuileries theatre, while used for only three productions during the reign of Louis XIV, generated much more documentation.

Architectural drawings offer some of the most substantial information about theatres of the past. Two surviving drawings of the Palais Royal of c. 1674 (see Plates 9.2 and 9.3, pp. 230–231 below) include details about the floor plan and side elevation, making it possible to visualize a three-dimensional reconstruction of the hall.[25] These drawings, in the hand of Vigarani, are our principal source of information about the theatre as Lully knew it. However, as with musical scores, these architectural drawings alone do not tell the whole story: we must call on other sources and also exercise some imagination to understand better how the theatre may have supported real-time performances. Other architectural sources help as well: some of the information missing from the Vigarani drawings appears in a set of six other drawings located in the Archives Nationales. These drawings depict the floor plans of all three balconies mentioned by our 1678 visitor, but no details of the stage.[26] Probably the most commonly reproduced

---

24 Lagrave argues that in the mid-eighteenth century unsatisfactory conditions in the theatre kept it from being included in theoretical writings about theatre at a time when analyses of other French and Italian theatres were growing. LagraveT, 82. Curiously, even the 1674 opening of the theatre attracted no special notice. For example, the *Gazette de France* dedicated only a short paragraph to the opening of *Alceste*.

25 These drawings are located today in the National Museum of Stockholm, CC175 and CC176.

26 These images are reproduced in full in LagraveT, Plates 7–12; the side elevation in Musée Carnavalet, *Le Palais Royal*, 59 (dated before 1730); four drawings in Gourret, *Histoire*, 43–46. They are located in the Archives Nationales, N III Seine 545/7–12. Most likely they originated after Lully's lifetime, perhaps as late as 1700.

images of the Palais Royal theatre were generated at least sixty years after
Lully's lifetime: two drawings in Jacques François Blondel's *L'Architecture
Française* of 1752–56, accompanied by written commentary, include exterior remodeling of the late 1740s.[27] One of the few representations of the
theatre as it accommodated people is a pen-and-wash drawing by Saint-
Aubin of the stage and front boxes during a performance of Lully's *Armide*
in 1747. Saint-Aubin's interior was probably not much different from the
theatre during Lully's lifetime.[28]

Exterior

We start our tour from the outside of the opera house (see Plate 9.1).[29]
In the 1670s the northwestern border of the city lay not far from the Palais
Royal, which was also near the Louvre, the official residence of Louis XIV
until he moved the court to Versailles in 1682.[30] As shown in Plate 9.1, rue
Saint Honoré, the street fronting the palace, was occupied with carriages
and people; it was situated near a city gate that led to the suburbs. Virtually
all structural features of the theatre were determined to some extent by the
pre-existing space in which it was installed. The great hall which later
became the theatre lay at the front of the building, to the right of the central
courtyard. (In Plate 9.1 the theatre lies behind the fourth pair of windows
from the doorway, over to the right corner of the building.)

The theatre's origins as a court site are manifest in its exterior. The
building in no way presents a physical manifestation of the performing arts'
presence in civic and social well-being, as was seen in French opera houses
in the provinces in the mid-eighteenth century. Even after becoming a

27 Jacques François Blondel, *L'architecture Française: Ou recueil de plans,
    d'élévations, coupes, et profils des églises, maisons royales, palais, hôtels, & édifices
    les plus considéréables* (Paris: C. A. Jomberteur, 1752–56; reprint Paris: Librairie
    centrale des beaux-arts, 1904–05), vol. III (1754), book 5, illus. 9, plates 2 and 3.
    Plate 2 is reproduced in Johnson, *Listening in Paris*, Plate 1, 12; Musée
    Carnavalet, *Le Palais Royal*, 132, among other places.
28 Saint-Aubin's image appears frequently in modern sources on Paris and opera.
    For example, see Neal Zaslaw, "At the Paris Opera in 1747," *EM* 12 (1983), 515.
    The drawing is located in the Museum of Fine Arts in Boston.
29 This engraving of the palace is by Israel Silvestre, *c.* 1675. For another copy, see
    ChampierP, 58.
30 In Plate 9.1, which looks north from the palace across the gardens which still
    exist today, Montmartre can be seen in the distance.

Plate 9.1   Israel Silvestre, Palais Royal, exterior, *c.* 1675

public venue, the theatre had no distinctive features signaling its identity as a civic setting for the arts, nothing to invite the passerby into the world of gods and shepherds and monsters within. Instead, the Palais Royal reminded the would-be opera-goer on the street of opera's association with the royal family. Could this anonymous exterior suggest that Paris's public was not actively invited to participate in musical theatre?

Most symptomatic of its uninviting character is the fact that during Lully's lifetime the theatre contained no public access directly from rue Saint Honoré. Instead, the public entrance and ticket office were located in the infamous "cul de sac de l'opéra" which ran along the east side of the building. This passageway, lined by neighboring buildings and visually indistinct, as seen in Plate 9.1, was no more than ten feet wide.[31] If carriages could enter at all to drop off visitors, negotiating turns and avoiding pedestrians would

---

31 A detail of the entrance is found in Coeyman, "Theatres for Opera and Ballet During the Reigns of Louis XIV and Louis XV," *EM* 18 (February 1990), Figure 14, 34.

227

have been difficult.[32] Pierre Mélèse cites the comments of a foreign visitor to the theatre in 1699, who wrote that it took four hours to perform the opera and one hour to get through the crowd at the doorway.[33]

Interior

Despite its role as the principal site for lyric theatre in France's capital city, the Palais Royal was surprisingly restricted, smaller in area than many other court and public settings.[34] Overall the theatre measured 35 meters in length and nearly 18 meters in width.[35] Public circulation space was especially limited. After passing through the cul de sac entrance and the ticket window, we visitors are greeted not by an inviting lobby but instead by five steps before a left turn, and then one flight of stairs to the first (American second) floor. Most stairways are relatively narrow: the one we've just ascended is among the wider ones in the building, measuring a little over 2 meters; other stairways are as narrow as 1 meter.

Standing on the first floor, we see limited space for socializing. Circulation around the back of the auditorium is impeded further by the back wall of the auditorium, which almost touches the south end of the building on rue Saint Honoré, a design feature intended to provide maximum space in the auditorium. Furthermore, in the entire building no areas serve specifically for socializing except a café one level below the auditorium.[36] These physical limitations support the reports of socializing

---

32 It was only in the 1749 remodeling that the ticket window was moved to the front side, on rue Saint Honoré, and a small doorway installed, granting access from the street rather than the cul de sac. The engravings in Blondel indicate this remodeling.

33 Mélèse, *Le Théâtre*, 57.

34 See my comparison plan in Coeyman, "Theatres for Opera," Figure 1, 22. Unrealized projects for expansion of the Palais Royal in the mid-eighteenth century as much as doubled the theatre's size. See Figure 12 in that same article. In 1738 Luigi Riccoboni also reported that the opera was cramped. See *Réflexions historiques*, 140 (cited in Mittman, *Spectators on the Paris Stage in the Seventeenth and Eighteenth Centuries* (Ann Arbor: UMI Research Press, 1984), 135, n. 4).

35 These and other dimensions I am quoting from LagraveT, 83. I have verified most of Lagrave's data through my own measurements.

36 This café area can be seen on Blondel's plan, *L'Architecture française*, plate 2. I am not sure when it was installed. The addition of public areas constitutes the greatest difference between Lully's theatre and the second Palais Royal theatre,

inside the theatre. As we will see, even though private boxes are not very comfortable, they offer space for socializing available nowhere else in the theatre.

Once inside the theatre, we notice the long and narrow shape of the hall typical of French theatres, in contrast with Italian ones. As shown in Plates 9.2 and 9.3, the length of the Palais Royal is divided nearly evenly between the stage and auditorium, impacting audience seating as well as use of the stage. Also, retaining the pre-existing structure of the palace, the theatre is not very high, only about 13 meters, the height of two floors of the palace. This height obviously determined the number of balconies possible, and, of course, the acoustics of the room. To date no eyewitness commentary on those acoustics has surfaced, but a hall of these relatively small proportions should have distributed the delicate nuances of French Baroque musical style well. In 1754, Luigi Riccoboni noted the small size of French theatres in comparison with Italian ones, which usually had four or five balconies.[37]

Henri Lagrave and others have estimated the audience capacity in the Palais Royal at c. 1,300–1,400, larger than Molière's hall by several hundred.[38] Lagrave reports the distribution of these places as follows:

Parterre (standing)	600
Amphitheatre (seats)	120
first balcony	190
second balcony	184
third balcony	178
boxes over stage	30+
TOTAL:	1,302+

The percentage of occupied seats during Lully's directorship has not yet been studied.[39]

opened in 1770. Designed by Moreau-Despreux, that theatre contained a spacious lobby on the ground floor, a walking gallery along two sides, and wider hallways in addition to a grand main entrance and ticket window on rue Saint Honoré.

37 See Luigi Riccoboni, *A General History of the Stage* (London, 1754).

38 LagraveT, 86. Seating estimates vary greatly. Sauval reported 3,000. See Musée Carnavalet, *Le Palais Royal*, 310.

39 For Molière's theatre in the Palais Royal, ticket receipts offer data about audience size, as reported in Schwartz, "Molière's Theatre."

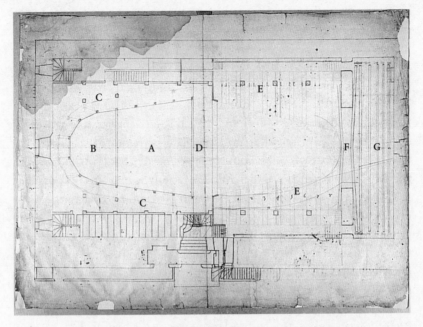

Plate 9.2   Carlo Vigarani, Palais Royal, floor plan, *c.* 1674. Stockholm, Nationalmuseum, CC175

In order to locate our places, let us now examine each of the theatre's seating areas. Even though public theatres lack the royal boxes at the center rear found in court theatres, the distribution of seating in public buildings nevertheless reflects the hierarchy of French society, especially because many members of the nobility attended opera in Paris as well as at court. Generally, the further from the center and the higher up, the less prestigious the seat. Also, the boxes over the stage afforded the best opportunities to be seen, if not to see the stage.

The Paris Opera contains a standing parterre (marked "A" on Plate 9.2), physically and socially the lowest section of the theatre. Access to the parterre is through two doors at the front of the auditorium next to the orchestra area. Built on a raked floor to enhance visibility, the parterre measures *c.* 7.5 × 13 meters. Lagrave's estimate of six hundred standing spectators in the parterre allows a little over one square foot per person when at capacity. Saint-Aubin depicts men only in the parterre, closely head-to-head, in this area which is "always on the verge of pandemonium" and filled

230

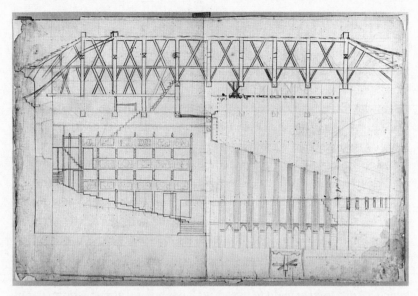

Plate 9.3   Carlo Vigarani, Palais Royal, elevation, *c.* 1674. Stockholm, Nationalmuseum, CC176

with spectators for whom entry is limited only by the cost of a ticket. Armed guards help keep order and protect the orchestra from the parterre's riffraff.[40]

Behind the parterre and separated by a barrier is the amphitheatre ("B" on Plate 9.2), which is occupied by "persons of distinction."[41] They enter from two doorways at the rear (not shown on Vigarani's drawing), and take their seats, as do those in most other parts of the theatre, on backless benches. Obviously the placement of benches may vary, but the drawing indicates nine rows, the longest nearly 5 meters and the shortest just over 2 meters. Furthermore, bench seating capacity will vary, but Lagrave estimates that we will be among 120 spectators if we sit in the amphitheatre.

40 Johnson, *Listening in Paris*, 17–18 says there were even reports of dogs being let loose in the parterre. In 1744 spectators crashed through the wall into the orchestra pit and then on to the stage. Bapst, *Essai*, 371, said there were often brawls in the parterre, citing a report from Chappazeau.
41 La GorceO, 48.

We also find bench seating in the balconies ("C" on Plate 9.2). During the first three periods of the hall's use, these balconies ran parallel and perpendicular to the walls of the theatre, but Vigarani's remodeling into a horseshoe provides enhanced visibility of the stage from the rear of the hall.[42] We also see the boxes installed by Molière, seventeen in each balcony.[43] In Lully's time the 1678 visitor reports that the third balcony, reached by a narrow stairway, has no partitions and no back walls.[44] Johnson recounts that the toilets for the theatre circled the *paradis*, and that they sometimes smelled.[45] Architectural drawings indicate that each box on the first two levels has it own doorway, and there is direct access from the palace to the Duc d'Orléans's private box over the orchestra.

As suggested earlier, the boxes provide only moderate comfort during the four-to-five-hour productions. For one, ceilings are low, no more than one foot above the heads of many of the spectators standing in the boxes, according to several images. Each box contains two or three benches, for a total of eight to twelve seats per box, estimating four persons per bench. Reminding us of the hall's earlier use for court ballet, seats in the balconies are angled toward the center of the floor, not toward the stage as in Italian theatres. Consequently, spectators need to turn on the bench to see the stage, but we may still find only a partial view because the walls of the boxes impede sightlines. Originally these walls were solid, but Lully and Vigarani installed latticework partitions to improve visibility. Surviving images suggest that our box could be the setting for conversation, gaming, and rendezvous with *filles d'opéra*.[46] After *c.* 1680 we might find our seat on

---

42 Sauval also reported that there were twenty-seven stone steps at the rear of the original hall for seating. It is not clear when these steps were removed. See SauvalH, vol. II, 161–163. The image of *Le Soir* referred to in footnote 14 offers a good impression of the continuous gallery on the sides, which was only one spectator deep, spectators facing the center of the room.

43 Two columns of boxes over the orchestra pit are not shown on the elevation in Figure 9.3 and the three columns of boxes across the back are not evident in this cut-away. Drawings by Pierre Sevin in La GorceO, 49 and 67, suggest what boxes at the Palais Royal looked like.

44 The *Mercure Galant* in June 1732, 1193, reported that fifteen loges were added to the *paradis* as well. See LagraveT, 85.

45 Johnson, *Listening in Paris*, 18.

46 See the Saint-Aubin drawing and an image by Moreau le Jeune in Johnson, *Listening in Paris*, Figure 3, 25. Images of seventeenth-century French court audiences suggest that there was also talking during performances at court.

the stage. The practice of stage seating, common in French theatres, accommodates the French nobleperson's wish to be seen at the opera, but it also cramps the space for both performers and machinery, as discussed below.[47]

Other than Sevin's images (listed in footnote 43), there are no known representations of the decor of the Palais Royal theatre as Lully knew it. However, if indeed there was no significant remodeling during the life of the theatre, then a written document of 1751 applies to Lully's era. This document describes the interior as being in greens and golds (also the colors seen in Saint-Aubin's drawing), the corridors in white with green trim, and the boxes in green satin with gold flowers, among other decorations.[48] Lully and Vigarani worked with the painters Jacob Rambour and Jean Simon for the 1673 remodeling.[49] Vigarani himself designed a ceiling image with Apollo on a horse-drawn chariot at the center, and the ceiling also included several allegorical paintings.

Let us end our tour of the auditorium by examining the orchestra area ("D" on Plate 9.2). As is typical of most Baroque theatres, the orchestra is in front of and below the stage, but not sunken as in modern halls, and is separated from the parterre audience by a partition wall and armed guards.[50] Lully greatly enlarged the orchestra area to accommodate his ensemble. According to Charles Perrault, Molière's orchestra included twelve instrumentalists, but Lully's remodeling provided for forty musicians.[51] The new

Johnson, 27, reports that in 1699 Louis XIV issued a ban preventing audiences from disrupting performers on the opera stage.

47 The best coverage of seating on French stages appears in Barbara Mittman, *Spectators on the Paris Stage in the Seventeenth and Eighteenth Centuries* (Ann Arbor: UMI Research Press, 1984). Over Lully's objections, by the 1680s spectators had bought their way on to the Paris Opéra stage. See Mittman, 19, for a quote from Du Tralage about this practice.

48 Johnson, *Listening in Paris*, 11. The document is Archives Nationales AJ 13 6.

49 Cordey, "Lully installe l'Opéra," 140–141. Cordey notes that these artists designed a view of *Amour et de Bacchus* for the Marais theatre in 1672, and also worked on operas at court. They also spruced up the loges with a new coat of paint. The painting contract was signed on November 14, 1673.

50 A good image of the frame around an orchestra appears in a view of the Dresden opera orchestra, reproduced in Roger Parker, ed., *The Oxford Illustrated History of Opera* (Oxford and New York: Oxford University Press, 1994), 60.

51 See Cordey, "Lully installe l'Opéra," 140. DucrotR, 37, cites data about the size of the orchestra on different occasions: in 1699, there were thirty-seven members; in 1704 there were first twenty-two and then forty-three players.

space measured *c.* 3 × 8 meters, allowing just over half a square meter per player in an ensemble forty strong.

Lighting in the auditorium, provided by oil lamps and wax candles, leaves many dark corners remaining, encouraging personal liaisons and illicit activities.[52] Enhanced by a row of tallow candles before the stage, lighting on stage is more brilliant than in the auditorium. In the wings, rotating light columns include reflectors behind each candle to amplify the flame. These reflectors can be turned towards or away from the scenery, as special effects require. The candle columns, connected together by ropes, provide for all lights to be adjusted simultaneously (see Plate 9.4).

The stage[53]

As in most theatres, the proscenium separates the reality of the audience's world from the fantasy of the stage. Standing on stage in the Palais Royal, we gain a sense of the scope and nature of visual components that created the mythological, historical or pastoral worlds of the repertoire. Raising the theatre's curtain, we see Vigarani's organization of the stage (see Plate 9.5) in the setting for Act V of *Thésée*, the second opera he and Lully produced in the theatre (1675). The coat of arms at the center of the arch reminds us that this is France's Academy of Music. The width of the proscenium opening, enlarged by Lully and Vigarani, is 9.5 meters, and the height approximates 8 meters. This greater height improved sight lines from the balconies.

Conditions on stage suggest the amount and complexity of machinery installed by Vigarani, as well as the somewhat cramped conditions for performers. Typifying Baroque stages, the Palais Royal contains pairs of lightweight, wooden, movable flats, which go through the stage floor for several meters and are connected by ropes to a wheel underneath, which can be seen in Plate 9.3. Vigarani's drawings (Plates 9.2 and 9.3) indicate nine pairs of flats (marked "E" on Plate 9.2) between the proscenium and the rear

52 Not much is documented about lighting in the Palais Royal. See Bapst, *Essai*, 376–378. For general commentary about light in Baroque theatres, see Ove Hidemark, Per Edström, and Birgitta Schyberg, *Drottningholm Court Theatre* (Stockholm: Byggförlaget, 1993), 82–83.
53 For general information on the Baroque stage, see Pierre Sonrel, *Traité de Scénographie* (Paris: Librarie Théatrale, 1956), chapter 8, 68–78.

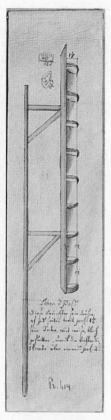

Plate 9.4   Anonymous, stage candles. Stockholm, Nationalmuseum, THC 614

structural wall (marked "F"), and six more (marked "G") beyond that wall for additional perspective.[54] As we move toward the rear of the stage, the flats themselves as well as the images on them diminish in height, which, in combination with the raked floor, exaggerates impressions of depth, as Plate 9.5 indicates. The movable flats change simultaneously in a few seconds when the wheel underneath the stage rotates. Vigarani's elevation indicates three flats on each chassis, allowing the possibility of up to three different settings within one uninterrupted segment of performance. Flies

54 Later drawings of the stage will indicate only seven pairs of flats before the wall, the front two removed to make room for spectators sitting on stage. See Figure 9.8 and La GorceE, 410.

235

Plate 9.5   Carlo Vigarani, stage decor, *Thésée*, Act V. Stockholm, Nationalmuseum, THC 662

above the stage could also be used for an upper border of scenery when needed (not used in Plate 9.5).

Apportionment of the space on the Baroque stage varied from designer to designer. Vigarani and Berain offer striking contrasts not only in their style of scenery but also their use of stage space.[55] Lully's repertoire from *Alceste* to *Bellérophon* appeared in Vigarani's settings. As Plate 9.5 indicates, Vigarani generally presents long and deep settings, creating illusions which extended far from the eye of the spectator. Following common

---

55   Agne Beijer has published a study on this subject, "Vigarani et Berain au Palais-Royal," *Revue d'histoire du théâtre* (1956), 184–196. See also Jérôme de La Gorce, "Torelli et Vigarani, initiateurs de la scénographie italienne en France," *Seicento* (1990), 13–25; La GorceE; and La GorceO, 68–69. A complete study of scenic settings in Lully's operas has yet to be done.

Italian practice, Vigarani extended the vista in *Thésée* and other settings yet further by utilizing the six rear flats beyond the structural wall, defining a second physical and dramatic space on stage. Vigarani's experience as an architect shows in his stage settings. He emphasizes buildings and other solid structures, almost always symmetrically aligned, and focused to the rear as far as possible. Majestic in their control of solid forms, straight lines dominate his drawings. Reinforcing his interest in architecture, Vigarani's stage sets usually do not include performers.[56] Whether this suggests that Vigarani personally was not the director of stage movement, or that he simply did not include figures in his drawings, remains unclear. However, his deep settings and unspecified performer locations leave open the possibility that singers and dancers could have used the entire stage depth.

Lully's stages under Berain from *Proserpine* to *Acis et Galatée* look very different.[57] Berain uses either the front portion of the stage alone, or he divides the main stage of nine flats into two sections somewhere around the fourth or fifth flats. In either case, most of his drawings focus the scenery and performers toward the front of the stage. Performing at the front is more practical, acoustically and visually, avoiding an imbalance in depth perspective between performers and scenery toward the rear. Contrasted with Vigarani's architectural quality, Berain's settings are design-oriented, focused not on structures but on their decorations. Curving lines and ornamentation enhance this attention to decor, and some images have more than one point of perspective. Of great significance for modern directors of Baroque opera, Berain includes performers in many of his drawings, suggesting that he played an active role in directing stage movement, perhaps based on his experiences as a costume designer.

The somewhat cramped conditions for audiences applied to performers as well. Floor space on stage totals about 150 square meters. As noted, Vigarani's drawings do not help us visualize how the stage may have been used before 1680. However, a drawing of unidentified repertoire (Plate 9.6) offers one good example of how Berain's stage accommodates performers.

56 The National Museum of Stockholm contains fifteen drawings of stage settings by Vigarani, eleven of these identified for Lully operas.
57 The most recent work on the designer is Jérôme de La Gorce, *Jean Berain* (Paris, 1986). See also Roger-Armand Weigert, *Jean I Berain* (Paris: Université de Paris, 1936).

Plate 9.6   Jean Berain, stage decor, unidentified. Stockholm, Nationalmuseum, THC 606

Six pairs of dancers line the two sides of the stage between the first and fifth flats, and a solo dancer appears at the center front. Twenty-one other figures, presumably singers, appear at various stations in the clouds closest to the stage floor. An ensemble of fourteen musicians and eight dancers appears above the main stage in front of a heavenly palace. These may not be actual performers on the upper stage, but images on a painted backdrop.

238

How this number of performers circulated on and off stage and around the backstage is not easy to understand. During Lully's tenure in the theatre, the backstage area offered very limited space. Performers had many access points to the stage between the flats. However, before entrances and after exits, off stage they must have been cramped owing to the very little space between the structural walls of the theatre and the edge of the flats, and there is no suggestion in Vigarani's drawings that the backstage connected to dressing rooms on the stage level. There may have been dressing rooms on the ground level, reached by stairs at the rear. The remodeling of the theatre of the mid-eighteenth century, when several backstage rooms were installed near the stage and in the building adjacent to the theatre (which was reached by two bridges built across the cul de sac) supports our thesis that the conditions in Lully's theatre were cramped.[58]

In addition to entries between the flats, performers could enter by mechanical means, up through traps in the floor, or down from the heavens on flying machines, as shown in Plate 9.7, Berain's drawing of *Hésione* in 1701. Apparently stage machinery contributed much to the spectacle and thus the popularity of performances. Audiences in Paris may have attended opera first for the machinery and the dancing (and dancers), and only after that for the music.[59] Not surprisingly, Vigarani equipped the Palais Royal with a range of machinery on par with other Parisian theatres. Unfortunately, his drawings (Plates 9.2 and 9.3) do not indicate mechanical apparatus in any detail, leaving the scope and effect of the machinery to our imaginations.

Fortunately, other visual sources, albeit after Lully's lifetime, do indicate some of the stage's mechanical capabilities. For example, an undated drawing of the stage (Plate 9.8) details the machinery on the Palais Royal stage for at least one dramatic setting. The drawing indicates two trap doors that measure *c.* 4 meters across and less than a meter wide. Traps were strong enough to support many props and many performers from subterranean worlds. Additionally there are several locations for scenery on slats that

58 These rooms are indicated in Blondel, *L'Architecture française*, plate 3.
59 Bapst, *Essai*, 339 points out the popularity of the machines in the Marais theatre in the 1650s and 1660s. Also, the Tuileries Salle des Machines was acknowledged for its machinery, although it did not succeed as a site for French opera. Riccoboni, *General History of the Stage*, 152, pointed out that what the French lacked in stage decor, they made up for in dancing.

Plate 9.7   Jean Berain, stage decor, *Hésione*, 1701. Stockholm, Nationalmuseum, THC 688

emerge from below the stage, or drop down from above. Scenery at the third, fourth, and sixth flats extends completely across the stage, the sixth flat possibly corresponding to the placement of the cloud scenery in Plate 9.6, or the balustrade across the middle of the stage in Plate 9.7.[60]

In the 1673 remodeling, Lully ordered reinforcement of the structural beams above the stage to support his machinery. Surviving drawings included few details. There seems to have been plenty of space for flying machines between the top of the sight line to the stage and the roof of the building. Vigarani's elevation (Plate 9.3) includes one suggestion of unidentified machinery, a fixture above the second pair of flats which may represent a chariot, or a drum to support ropes used to raise and lower machinery. Upper stage machinery in Lully's theatre probably included

60 Good illustrations of floor construction can be seen in Hidemark, Edström, and Schyberg, *Drottningholm Court Theatre*, 89, 91, 93, and 95.

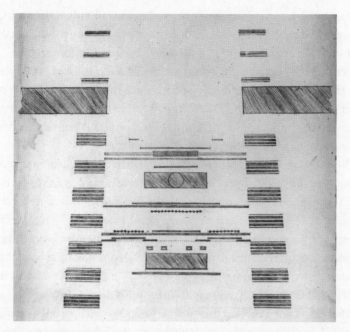

Plate 9.8   Anon. Palais Royal, stage machinery. Stockholm, Nationalmuseum, CC186

clouds, lowered from above, which could be used in part to hide the entrance of characters; flying chariots, which could hold up to several dozen performers; and other flying machines, perhaps decorated by clouds, permitting performers to move quickly across the heavens. Performers might have gained access to this flying machinery via the two flights of stairs shown ascending above the auditorium in Plate 9.3, or perhaps on ladders near the proscenium not shown in the drawings. Whatever the access Lully's singers would have found it no easy undertaking to ride on (let alone sing from) Baroque flying machines – the art of flying was then at least as important to productions as the arts of drama and music.

Conclusion

While aspects of Lully's theatre in the Palais Royal offered opportunities for spectacular productions, there were also many shortcomings for audiences and performers in the first permanent home of the Paris Opera.

How spectacular was it to experience productions in Lully's theatre? Our tour suggests a possible gap between our vision of productions based on information in *livrets*, scores, and stage designs – that is, from the consideration of opera as text – and the actual realization of repertoire – that is, from visualizing opera as performance in the context of its performance space. How much did audiences pay attention, and what does this suggest about the reception of Lully's repertoire and consequently the meanings it conveyed, to observers and artists alike?

If conditions at the Opera were as problematic as my reading suggests, why and how did Lully's opera succeed as repertoire and as an institution? Why did audiences keep coming back to the Palais Royal, not only through 1687 but as late as 1763? Even more to the point, would Lully have tolerated ongoing inferior conditions for his repertoire? Did he plan a quick turnover, moving from the Palais Royal to a more accommodating venue? Did tensions with the royal family and fellow artists weaken his monopoly over French music in the 1680s, enough to disrupt his plans? How would Lully have reacted, knowing that his opera house would stand essentially unchanged for ninety years, the subject of criticism from the likes of Voltaire? Was the 1763 fire actually a blessing? Clearly more research into the reception of Lully's repertoire and the consequent meanings conveyed through real-time performance in this seventeenth-century setting awaits an inquiring visitor to the Palais Royal theatre.

10 Gluck and Lully

HERBERT SCHNEIDER

May Virtue, from her throne, at one with the Graces, pour out her blessings upon this creative genius [Gluck]; I see nothing here but the deserved success of a great man; I rejoice in his glory almost as much as in my own.

"FROM THE ELYSIAN FIELDS. LULLY TO THE WRITERS
OF THE JOURNAL [DE PARIS, AUGUST 1779]"[1]

In fact, the qualities, even the weaknesses, of French music were sympathetic to Gluck. He found in French opera, as cultivated by Lully and Rameau, the form best suited to contain what his genius inspired in him.

(JULIEN TIERSOT, 1919)[2]

And now the Dauphine's piano teacher arrived from Vienna, in order to put music in the chains of declamation once again!

(SILKE LEOPOLD, 1985)[3]

In August 1779 the *Journal de Paris* published what purported to be a letter from Lully in the hereafter, expressing his admiration for the genius of Gluck, whose renown at that date also reflected well on Lully. In the view of

---

1 "Que sur le trône, la Vertu, unie aux Grâces, répande ses bienfaits sur ce génie créateur [Gluck]; je ne vois là que les succès mérités d'un grand Homme; je jouis de sa gloire presqu'autant que de la mienne propre." ("Des Champs-Élisées. Lulli aux auteurs du Journal [de Paris, août 1779])", re-published in G. M. Leblond, *Mémoires pour servir à l'histoire de la révolution opérée dans la musique par M. le chevalier Gluck* (Naples/Paris, 1781, reprint, Amsterdam: Antiqua, 1967), 476.
2 "De fait, les qualités, même les défauts de la musique française étaient sympathiques à Gluck. Il trouvait dans l'opéra français, tel qu'il avait été cultivé par Lulli et Rameau, la forme qui convenait le mieux pour contenir ce que son génie lui inspirait." Julien Tiersot, *Gluck* (Paris: F. Alcan, 1919), 101.
3 "Und jetzt kam der Klavierlehrer der Dauphine aus Wien, um die Musik wieder an die Fesseln der Deklamation zu legen!" S. Leopold, "Opernreformen," in *Die Musik des 18. Jahrhunderts* (Laaber: Laaber-Verlag, 1985), 251 (*Neues Handbuch der Musikwissenschaft 5*).

the anonymous authentic writer of this letter, Gluck was continuing the tradition of Lully's *tragédie en musique* at the same time as he renewed it. And if Berlioz shared Wagner's opinion that Gluck was the sole creator of a new style of musical drama, and found Lully's music poor stuff – vapid, dull, antiquated, and childish[4] – the opinion of the anonymous ghost-writer of 1779 was echoed more than a century later by Julien Tiersot, when he described Gluck as the heir of Lully and Rameau. Unfortunately there is no documentation to support Tiersot's claim that Gluck spent almost the entire year of 1745 in Paris, on his way to London.[5] Nothing came of his plan to visit Paris in 1763, but in March 1764, while Rameau was still alive, he spent about two weeks there in the company of Durazzo and Coltellini. Even if there is no evidence that he attended any performances of *tragédies lyriques* in Paris, printed scores and libretti were available. Silke Leopold maintains the questionable view that Gossec, Philidor, and Grétry had undertaken "their first essays in the field of serious opera" for Versailles in 1773, "in which they included faster recitative in the Italian manner (in 4/4 tempo) and true, symmetrically constructed arias, as well as highly dramatic accompagnato recitatives and thrilling choruses," and that Gluck put a stop to these composers' moves in the direction of "autonomous music in the aria."[6] Mueller von Asow seems to have adopted the curious premise

4 In his essay "L'Alceste d'Euripide, celles de Quinault et de Calzabigi, les partitions de Lulli, de Gluck, de Schweizer, de Guglielmi et de Handel sur ce sujet," Berlioz makes fun of Quinault's libretto, and the opera's comic characters in particular (*A travers chant* [Paris, 1880], 145–146). Berlioz has some reservations in defending Gluck's *Alceste* against the charge of "tiresome monotony" (p. 152), although a little later he describes the French *Alceste* as "one of the most magnificent realizations he ever made [of his dramatic theories]" (p. 158). Berlioz's view of *Armide* was "Gluck, in redoing *Armide*, killed Lully stone-dead" (p. 196). For Berlioz, Gluck, like Beethoven, was an "untiring Titan" (p. 198).

5 "He went to England, summoned by an engagement, and first passed through France, where he stayed for the greater part of the year 1745." *Gluck*, 25. J. G. Prod'homme denied this: "All the biographers have said, and repeated, that Gluck, after leaving Italy in the spring of 1745, stopped in France, travelling directly from Turin to Lyon, and heard operas by Rameau in Paris, notably *Castor et Pollux*... This stay of Gluck's in Paris is far from proven." *Gluck* (Paris: Société d'Editions Françaises et Internationales, 1948), 41–42. Patricia Howard, in 1963, still assumed that Gluck might have heard operas by Rameau in Paris on his way to London (HowardG, 8).

6 "ihre ersten Versuche auf den Gebiet der ernsten Oper unternommen, worin sie das schnellere Rezitativ nach italienischer Art (im 4/4-Takt notiert) und richtige,

that Gluck had fallen in line with French classical tragedy and *tragédie en musique* by accident: "Gluck's interest became involuntarily focused on France, where artists like Corneille and Racine, Lully and Rameau had flourished, artists whose talents, like his own, naturally inclined to the drama."[7] N. Miller paints a much more differentiated picture of the situation in French musical theatre and Gluck's intentions: following the Querelle des Bouffons and against the background of rejection of Rameau's artificiality, the attempt was made to supplant *tragédie lyrique* with *opéra comique*, and by this means to replace the French declamatory style with Italian melodiousness. Gluck had later opposed the vogue for the Italian style in Paris and, in order to be able to play a leading role as an opera composer who belonged to no national school, decided against presenting himself to Paris as a champion of reformed Italian opera. He tried instead to effect a rapprochement between Italian opera and French *tragédie en musique*. Miller rightly regards Gluck's *Iphigénie en Aulide* as a reworking of Racine's tragedy in a spirit close to that of Quinault's *tragédie*.[8]

In recent studies, the question of Gluck's continuation of the tradition of Lully's and Rameau's tragedies has been reduced to comparisons between the two versions of *Armide*, and in particular of the monologue "Enfin il est en ma puissance."[9] Many other issues have been ignored. Scarcely any attention has been paid to Gluck's relationship to Rameau, but

symmetrisch gebaute Arien hören ließen, außerdem aber hochdramatische Accompagnato-Rezitative und mitreißende Chöre." "Opernreformen," 249–250. Leopold does not even give titles of the operas allegedly so steeped in the Italian manner. Gossec's *Sabinus*, one of the works performed at Versailles that might qualify, belongs wholly within the tradition of Rameau, in the view of Michael Fend: "he [Gossec] clearly emulated Rameau's *tragédies lyriques*"; see "Gossec," in *The New Grove Dictionary of Opera* (London: Macmillan, 1992), vol. II, 490.

7   *The Collected Correspondence and Papers of Christoph Willibald Gluck*, ed. H. and E. H. Mueller von Asow, trans. S. Thomson (London: Barrie and Rockliff, 1962), 12.

8   N. Miller, "Christoph Willibald Gluck und die musikalische Tragödie. Zum Streit um die Reformoper und den Opernreformator," in *Gattungen der Musik und ihre Klassiker*, ed. H. Danuser (Laaber: Laaber-Verlag, 1988), 109–153.

9   Most recently G. Buschmeier, "Glucks Armide-Monolog, Lully und die 'philosophes,'" in *Festschrift Klaus Hortschansky zum 60. Geburtstag* (Tutzing: H. Schneider, 1995), 167–180, and Dörte Schmidt in her dissertation "Armide als exemplarischer Fall. Lully, Gluck und die Möglichkeiten der künstlerischen Rezeption" (Ruhr-Universität Bochum, 1997).

245

this subject cannot be discussed here for reasons of space.[10] For the same reason, little will be said here about Armide's much-discussed monologue. Instead, attention will be focused on the conception of *tragédie* represented in the works of Lully and Gluck and in particular on the relative importance of textual declamation.

The new conception of *tragédie lyrique*

What exactly does the commonplace that Gluck put drama before music, and in so doing adopted Lully's conception of opera, say about Gluck's relationship to Lully? The two composers wrote their operas in very different circumstances as regards history, musical history, and ideology. Lully and Quinault had to invent *tragédie en musique* as a wholly new genre against the background of the "tragedy with machines," Lully's own ballets de cour and *comédies-ballets*, and the pastorales of Perrin and Cambert. Gluck, for his part, having been a whole-hearted adherent of the Italian tradition to begin with, found himself faced, in the wake of the contemporary preoccupation with *opéra comique* and *tragédie lyrique* and all the talk of renewing Italian opera, with the necessity of reforming first the Italian *dramma per musica* and then opera as a whole. One of the most important reasons for his resolve to attempt a more extreme reform in Paris, going beyond French *tragédie lyrique*, was the fear that the reform he had started would not be enough to ensure the decisive and lasting success that he had in mind.[11]

10 Patricia Howard and other writers have pointed out the similarity of choruses by Gluck to those by Rameau: "The French influence in the construction of the first act [of *Orfeo*] is undeniable, and was the result of Calzabigi's fairly extensive knowledge of the French stage. More surprising is the style which Gluck brings to complete it: quite unlike anything he had written before and, at least in the opening chorus number, distinctly related to Rameau" (HowardG, 8). Elsewhere she emphasizes: "The choruses are the greatest single features of Rameau's operas, and it is these which make their most apparent mark on Gluck. The extended choral scene – 'Que tout gémisse' in *Castor et Pollux*, for example – was the exact mood that Gluck hit upon for the opening of *Orfeo*, and approaches also the monumental dignity of the prayer scenes in *Alceste* and the *Iphigénies*" (p. 27).

11 Even if the history of music credits the Italian version of *Alceste* with no influence on *dramma per musica*, contrary to Gluck's hopes, at least it was received positively by Italians writing on opera; in particular, Antonio Planelli

Operatic reform had begun independently in the two countries after the middle of the eighteenth century, and the accompanying debate, stemming from some very different impetuses, was extremely complex, contradictory, and sometimes paradoxical. Reduced to a simple formula, it produces the following discrepancy, which can be explained by the differences between the idea of *dramma per musica* and that of *tragédie lyrique*: the reform of *tragédie lyrique* postulated during the Querelle des Bouffons was inspired by the example of *opera buffa*, while the reforms proposed for *dramma per musica* were inspired by the example of *tragédie lyrique*. With his Paris reform operas, Gluck aspired to a further, universally accepted renewal, which would overcome the deficiencies of both genres and produce a supranational type of opera.

The proposals for reforming *tragédie lyrique* began in France immediately after the Querelle des Bouffons. The Abbé François Arnaud revealed an unusual breadth of vision in this heated situation, especially before the publication of Algarotti's treatise: "I compare our operas to the ancient tragedies, and I draw from the parallel many measures for rectifying the form of our lyric dramas, which are beyond question the most imperfect of all dramas, since the majority of them are nothing but a tissue of episodes not linked one to the other by either necessity or verisimilitude; I exhort our poets to abandon the prejudice that they hold only because of the weakness of the great number of musicians: since music was able to treat the tragedies of Aeschylus and Sophocles, it can without doubt treat great, tragic, and regular subjects."[12] To ameliorate this

wrote in *PlanelliO*, 148: "Questa Musica è sì conforme all'idea quì espressa della Musica Teatrale, ch'io, osservata così ben intesa composizione, mi senti inondar l'animo da un maraviglioso piacere in considerando, che mentre in questa estrema parte d'Europa io stendea un teorico saggio, ma debolissimo, e breve, di quella Musica" (This Music so fits the idea of Theatrical Music expressed here that I, having observed how well understood his composing is, felt a marvelous pleasure wash over my spirit as I considered that I, in this far off part of Europe, was meanwhile drawing up a theoretical essay, very weak, however, and brief, on that Music).

12 "Je compare nos opéra avec les tragédies anciennes, & je puise dans ce parallèle bien des ressources pour rectifier la forme de nos drames lyriques, qui de tous les drames sont sans contredit les plus imparfaits, puisqu'ils ne sont la plûpart qu'un tissu d'épisodes qui ne sont liés les uns aux autres, ni nécessairement ni vraisemblablement, j'exhorte nos poëtes à sortir du préjugé qu'ils ne tiennent que de la foiblesse du grand nombre des Musiciens; puisque la Musique a pû

unfortunate situation, Arnaud urged poets and musicians to concentrate "on the principal character of the poems . . . without ever losing sight of the whole, hastening the declamation of scenes, dwelling less upon the *airs de mouvement*, running, in a word, toward the dénouement more rapidly, and above all leaving the orchestra to its proper purpose, which is to accompany and sustain, not to swamp and dominate."[13] Already Arnaud had formulated the key terms encountered repeatedly from then until the dispute between the Gluckists and the Piccinnists: "the principal character of the poem," "hastening the declamation," and "running toward the dénouement more rapidly."

Baron Grimm, in the article "Poème lyrique" which appeared in the *Encyclopédie* in 1765, was equally critical of *tragédie lyrique* and of Metastasian *opera seria*, and created a forum for ideas of reform drawing on Algarotti's treatise[14] and Diderot's proposals, among others. For Grimm opera was incontestably "the most noble and the most brilliant of modern spectacles" and, several years before Gluck, he described music and gesture (stage movement) as universal languages.[15] Although it appears at the beginning of the article that Grimm commends the style of representation in Metastasian *opera seria* as exemplary, in the end he is relatively even-handed in his criticism of the French and Italian schools, although he excuses faults in Italian opera as due to the influence of impresarios and audiences. Many of the items in Grimm's list of demands were met by Gluck's operas for Paris.

Footnote 12 (*cont.*)
traiter les Tragédies d'Aeschyle & de Sophocle, elle peut sans doute traiter les choses grandes, tragiques & régulieres." Abbé François Arnaud, *Lettre sur la musique à Monsieur le comte de Caylus, Académicien Honoraire de L'Académie Royale des Inscriptions & belles-Lettres, & de celle de Peinture*, s.l., no imprimatur, 1754, 33–4.

13 "caractére principal des poëmes sans jamais perdre de vue l'ensemble, en hâtant la déclamation des scènes, en s'appesantissant moins sur les airs de mouvement, en courant en un mot au dénouement avec plus de rapidité, & sur-tout en rendant la symphonie à son véritable objet, qui est d'accompagner & de soutenir, & non d'engloutir & de dominer." *Ibid.*, 34.

14 The full text of Algarotti's *Saggio sopra l'opera in musica* (1755) was published in French translation only in 1773, in Paris. Excerpts from it were published in the *Mercure de France* in May 1757 (40–63).

15 "Poème lyrique," in *Encyclopédie*, 824. Grimm did not confine himself to matters of libretto-writing, but also went into décor, ballet, and performance (*exécution*) in some detail.

- Recitative should not be *chantant*, that is, written to be metrically exact or ornamented, and it should be declaimed rapidly; the declamation should reflect the age, sex, rank, and intentions of the character speaking; the alexandrine is suitable for musical setting, even in recitative.
- Unlike *chansons* and *couplets*, as Grimm terms Lully's airs, the aria should not be composed as *chant symmétrique*.
- Special attention should be paid to the alternation of recitative and aria, as it has the greatest effect.
- The course of the action should be characterized by its rapidity and simplicity, the style should be energetic, natural, and easy.
- The décor should consist of a large and beautiful building, a beautiful landscape, a beautiful ruin or a beautiful piece of architecture, but it should not be called upon to depict natural phenomena such as thunderstorms, earthquakes or "nature in motion." The phenomenon of "the marvelous" should be given expression in the "speechless and terrible eloquence of gesture" and in the music but not by the means of stage technology.[16]
- The integration of dance into the action must be reinforced by the introduction of "imitative dance" or pantomime instead of dances in regular forms, which are "academic exercises."[17]
- Grimm deplores the use of stock spectacles such as the "tempest," the "earthquake," or "the Nile bursting its banks" as symbols of emotional states or catastrophes.
- He regards the execution of pantomimic gestures in arias, especially the ritornellos, as so important that he proposes separate performers to sing and act;[18] this was first realized by Diaghilev's *Ballets russes* and Gluck did not attempt it.

Grimm found no models to serve the idea of reform in the operas of Lully and Quinault, and refers to them only when he wants negative illustrations. Thus he mentions the *air en dialogue* "Poursuivons jusqu'au trépas" and the

16 Grimm's recommendations were obviously influenced by the idea of the English landscape garden, which was very fashionable at the time.
17 Grimm castigates dances in regular forms (that is, dances with generic designations such as menuet, gigue, sarabande) in no less than three places in his article, calling them "more worthy of the dance-hall than the theatre" ("plus dignes de la guinguette que du théâtre").
18 Du Roullet spoke up strongly in favor of pantomime, and of singers receiving better training in it (see *Lettre sur les Drames-opera* [Amsterdam: chez Esprit, 1776; reprint in *Querelle des Gluckistes et des Piccinistes*, ed. F. Lesure, Geneva, 1984], vol. II). Since the publication of Grimm's article and of theoretical writings by Diderot and Noverre, growing support for such ideas had led to their being put into practice in the spoken theatre and in *opéra comique*. Performance practice has adhered to them to the present day.

chorus "Plus on connaît l'Amour" from *Armide,* and two choruses from
Atys, "Que devant vous tout s'abaisse" and "Que l'on chante," as examples
not to be followed; he also takes exception to Lully's *plein chant* for the
reasons usual at that date. On the other hand he looks on the *divertissement*
in Act IV of *Roland,* with the two menuets, the *Marche la Mariée* and the
Entrée des pastres, as the most successful thing of its kind anywhere in
French opera.

It is interesting that J. F. Reichardt, before he had seen any of Gluck's
operas at the Académie Royale de Musique in Paris,[19] compared the lament
of Admète in Lully's *Alceste* ("Sans Alceste, sans ses appas") with the equiva-
lent ("No, crudel non posso vivere") in Gluck's Italian *Alceste* of 1767.[20] He
found positive things to say about Lully's declamation and the almost
imperceptible mixture of simple and compound meters, which Gluck
employed in his opera "often with great success," but Gluck's setting struck
him as "infinitely truer and more beautiful" than Lully's. "The very choice
of key, the more plentiful significant modulations and the passionate variation of meter make it greatly superior."[21] Reichardt does not describe a
wholly characteristic formal element common to both works, which
demonstrates that Gluck's aria originated in the monologue in the French
opera with its typical reprise (the repetition of a short section from the
beginning of a number toward, or at, the end).[22] Lully brings back the first
four bars at the end, like a kind of motto. Gluck repeats the first eight bars,
which he ends on an imperfect cadence originally but on the tonic at the
reprise; unlike Lully, however, Gluck adds the twofold repeat of the two lines
in a shortened form in a kind of coda. This moved Reichardt to the enthusiastic comment: "The repetition of the first stanza pierces the soul here; and
then the enhanced expression at the end on the word 'crudel! crudel!' – that

19 When he did, Reichardt was moved to greater enthusiasm than Mozart was: "I
    had no prior conception of Gluck's opera in French throats, or of its immense
    effect." *Johann Friedrich Reichardt an das musikalische Publikum seine
    französischen Opern Tamerlan und Panthée betreffend* (Hamburg, 1787), 7.
20 See *Musikalisches Kunstmagazin* (1782; reprint Hildesheim: G. Olms Verlag,
    1969), vol. I, 88–91. The music examples from the two versions diverge at
    numerous points from the original scores.
21 *Ibid.,* 91.
22 Silke Leopold holds a different view: "The form of Gluck's arias is essentially the
    Italian form, only they lack the freedom, unity and charm of the Italian models."
    "Opernreformen," 251.

is a true stroke of genius. The short, rising ritornello [at the end] is also very eloquent."[23]

Like Arnaud, Grimm, and other writers, Marie-François-Louis Lebland Du Roullet made "rapidity" a key concept.[24] It was not only one of the three principles that should define the action of tragedy (along with simplicity and unity) but also a characteristic of recitative. In saying such things, writers on operatic theory were not primarily (as hitherto supposed) comparing Italian recitative with the slowness of French recitative; rather, they expressed a new sense of time, which was supposed to characterize the hitherto unaccustomed speed at which the action should proceed and the text be delivered. It is significant that this key term is never used for the progress of the action in the intensive discussion of the Metastasian libretto which took place in France.

With respect to the *airs de danse*, Gluck was forced to do something different from Lully, whose dances had long been replaced by newer dances when his operas were revived in Paris. Rameau had adopted Cahusac's and Noverre's ideas for reform, as many of his dances in regular forms demonstrate by the individuality of their motivic-thematic structures and their rich gestural qualities.[25] Dorat, in his "didactic poem" of 1766, gave the contemporary view of the necessity for imitative dances tailored to the individual characters:

> You wish to show us rustic dances / so let your agile leaps be not at all symmetrical; / borrow your fire from Nature alone: / a shepherd's dance is not a god's. / Do not offend our eyes with too lascivious steps: / Venus herself cannot please if she appears too much unclothed. / You wish to twine your arms about your beloved? / Go not too far, immodestly swooning in our sight, / outraging decency and, mute Siren, / suggesting to the public a pleasure it deplores.[26]

23 *Musikalisches Kunstmagazin*, vol. I, 91.
24 Du Roullet, *Lettre sur les Drames-opera*, 11 (117 in reprint) and 31 (137 in reprint).
25 The critics of Gluck's time, with few exceptions, still regarded Rameau's dances as unsurpassed. Le Suire, for example, wrote that Gluck "has claimed to compose a dramatic music with all this. We may grant that he has succeeded in the recitative. As for dance, would that we might revive Rameau." *Lettre de M. Camille Trillo [Robert-Martin Le Suire], fausset de la cathédrale d'Ausch, sur la musique dramatique* (Paris, 1777), 22.
26 "Nous représentez-vous quelques danses rustiques; / Que vos agiles bonds ne soient point symétriques; / De la Nature seule empruntez votre feu: / La danse

After the ballet reforms introduced by Angiolini and Noverre, and the polemics of various theorists against dances in regular forms, for Gluck it was out of the question that such dances – with the exception of chaconne and passacaille[27] – should have only a subordinate role, and that free pantomimic *airs* should be the true choreographic channels of expression, with the sole exception of the concluding festivities, if the opera ended happily. I cannot accept Patricia Howard's opinion that "Scene 5 of the first act of *Iphigénie* introduces Clytemnestra and Iphigenia amid a chain of dances, with short dance airs in the Lullian manner (*air gai, air gracieux*)."[28] On the contrary, the dances in regular forms in the concluding ballet of *Orphée et Eurydice*, and the menuets which Flothuis banishes to the appendix of his edition of *Iphigénie en Aulide*,[29] must be counted as "abstract" dances in regular forms without pronounced pantomimic qualities.

Numerous theorists in the age of Gluck supported the principle that operas with a *lieto fine* should end amid scenes of rejoicing, including ballet. Le Suire argued in favor of the *divertissement* finale and even of the Italian practice of a ballet or pantomime as entr'acte: "As to dance, we ought to establish, in this country of etiquette, that it should be introduced in *tragédies en musique* only when there are festivities which require it. Put pantomime in entr'actes, if you wish, as certain dramatists have done, to represent the intervening events (but then, when you have no words, the

---

Footnote 26 (*cont.*)

d'un Berger n'est pas celle d'un Dieu. / Par des pas trop lascifs n'offensez point la vue; / Vénus même déplaît, alors qu'elle est trop nue. / Enlacez-vous vos bras autour de votre Amant? / N'allez point, sans pudeur, à nos yeux vous pâmant, / Outrager la décence &, Sirène muette / Proposer au Public un bonheur qu'il rejette." Claude-Joseph Dorat, *La déclamation théatrale, poème didactique en trois chants* (Paris, 1766), "chant III, l'opéra," 125.

27   According to Arnaud, the *passacaille* in *Iphigénie en Aulide* surpassed every piece of instrumental music ever heard before in opera. He also praised "the noble style, thrown into relief by two gavottes that Rameau would have acknowledged his." See "Lettre à Madame D'Augny sur l'Iphigénie en Aulide De M. le chevalier Gluck," in *Arnaud*, vol. II, 369.

28   HowardG, 51.

29   Gluck, *Iphigénie en Aulide*, ed. M. Flothuis, *Sämtliche Werke, Abteilung I: Musikdramen*, vol. Vb (Kassel: Bärenreiter, 1989), 456–460. In another menuet (*ibid.*, 469–470) Gluck provides material for pantomimic interpretation, as Rameau did, by such means as the gestural shaping of motives, the positioning of rests, the complementarity of rhythms between different instruments and their groupings, etc.

music must be all the more expressive). Reserve your dancers' talents for a ballet at the end which will send the audience away in a merry mood. If the dénouement of the piece is happy, as in Metastasio, there is nothing to prevent this ballet being linked to the action."[30]

Du Roullet distinguished between *fêtes spectacles*, *fêtes pantomimes*, and those fêtes "which have solely dance as their object."[31] He categorically denounced dances by allegorical figures (devils, magicians, Hatred, Revenge, etc.) as offensive to reason and good sense. Except for festivities at the end of a work, he disapproved of ballet scenes in act-finales and argued in favor of the practice, often observed since Lully's time, of dramatizing a *divertissement* by interrupting it with some unexpected, important turn of events setting the music on a new course.

By desisting from dance parody, which was widespread in French opera from the first and still much used even by Rameau, Gluck distanced himself from this long-established tradition.[32]

In his efforts to have the chorus integrated into the stage action, representing emotions by means of gesture and movement, and not just singing, Gluck could refer to criticisms of choral scenes inserted into the drama that

30 "Pour la Danse, on devroit bien établir dans ce pays d'étiquettes, qu'elle ne fût introduite dans les Tragédies Musicales, que quand il y auroit des fêtes qui l'exigeroient. Mettez si vous voulez de la pantomime dans les entr'actes, comme certains Auteurs de Drames l'ont fait, pour representer les événements intermédiaires; (mais alors comme vous n'avez plus de paroles, la Musique doit être plus expressive). Réservez les talens de vos Danseurs pour un balet à la fin qui renverra gaiment les spectateurs. Si le dénouement de la Piece est heureux, comme dans Metastasio, rien n'empêche que ce ballet ne soit lié à l'action." Le Suire, *Lettre de M. Camille Trillo*, 37–38.
31 Du Roullet, *Lettre sur les Drames-opera*, 38.
32 See my recent extensive article on this question, "Parodie als Verfahren der Opernkomposition," in *Beiträge zur Musik des Barock. Tanz–Oper–Oratorium*, ed. H.-J. Marx (Laaber; Veröffentlichungen der Internationalen Händel-Akademie 6, 1998), 117–142. His *chœurs dansés* do not belong in this category, and were not performed purely instrumentally. The *Air gracieux, Animé*, "Que j'aime à voir ces hommages flatteurs," in *Iphigénie en Aulide* (Gluck, *Iphigénie en Aulide*, 447) might constitute a sole exception; however, its opening, with a unison chord for strings, is an argument against this hypothesis. Such openings are frequently encountered, following widespread criticism of the long opening ritornellos in the Italian da capo aria and in the French *ariettes* of *opéra comique*. On the other hand the second section, with its instrumental opening and the singing voice's free adaptation of the violin part, may support the hypothesis, as may also the heterometrical structure of the text (10a 8b 6b 8a).

went back to the 1760s. Dorat was not the only one to call for reform of the chorus.

> But you who, in our supposedly harmonic choruses, / come and deploy your organic mass before us / and, ranged in semicircles, / sound off in concert to try our patience; / am I to see you ever, empty of heart and spirit, / bellowing, arms folded, your insipid refrains? / . . . Let us at last discern on your expressive faces/ the meaning of the words uttered by your voices.[33]

Arnaud[34] and Du Roullet[35] also lent weight to this view in many of their writings.

The idea of the union of literature, music, architecture, painting, and choreography in an operatic *Gesamtkunstwerk* had exercised an important influence on practical realization since the time of Lully. The famous four lines of verse in which it was formulated by Voltaire[36] became increasingly familiar after the Querelle des Bouffons and were still often quoted well into the nineteenth century. According to De Rochemont, French opera-goers were interested principally in the libretto, while the music "has no other purpose than to enhance the poetic beauties. French musicians have been obliged to employ melody and harmony to augment the impression that the words they have sung would have made with the aid of declamation alone.

---

33 Dorat, *La déclamation théatrale*, 117.

34 "In most of our operas the members of the chorus, nearly always idle, scarcely have a function beyond that of the pipes which enable a learned piece of organ music to be heard, but here all the choruses are in action." *Œuvres complettes de l'abbé Arnaud*, vol. II, 370.

35 "Habit alone can no doubt breed tolerance of these superfluous characters who, planted on the stage like so many organ pipes, are brought on for no other reason than to utter empty noises." *Lettre sur les Drames-opera*, 29–30.

36 "Il faut se rendre à ce palais magique / où les beaux vers, la Danse, la Musique, / L'art de tromper les yeux par les couleurs, / L'art plus heureux de séduire les cœurs, / De cent plaisirs font un plaisir unique" ("Come, let us hasten to the magic palace / where poetry, dance, music, / colours that deceive the eye, / the happier skill of stealing hearts/ form a unique pleasure from a hundred"). From *Le Mondain* by Voltaire, quoted in Marmontel's *Poétique françoise* (Paris, Lesclapart, 1763), vol. II, *De l'opéra*, 329; in the French edition of Algarotti's *Saggio, Essai sur l'opéra* (Paris, 1773), 101; on the title-page of Dom Arteaga's *Les révolutions du théâtre musical en Italie* (London, 1802); in Castil-Blaze's *Dictionnaire de Musique moderne* (Paris, 1825), vol. II, 96–97; in the *Chroniques secrètes et galantes de l'Opéra 1667–1845* by G. Touchard-Lafosse, (Paris: Gabriel Roux et Cassanet, 1846), 107.

Such is the law imposed on them in France and the principle by which the public has judged them. These musicians have done admirable things in this line of work – by the exactness of their feeling, by the truth of the expression."[37] Later he remarks that the composer "unites the pleasures of the heart, the ears and the eyes. It is an assemblage of all that is most enchanting in the Arts."[38] Similar thoughts are expressed in an open letter about *Iphigénie en Aulide*, in which the author refers to the Muses' decision to join forces in creating a work of art – the opera – which is bestowed on mankind by Apollo's decree. "What means to seduce, to please, to enchant! What resources in the hands of a skilful man! He knows how to take hold of our senses, to stir them in passing! What daring flights! But also what genius it takes not to stay on the beaten track! This, Madame, is what our opera should be like. The union of all the arts, the blending of all sensations: this is what distinguishes it from all other spectacles in the world; this is what was envisaged by Quinault, the inimitable creator of the genre."[39] Similar views were expressed by Antonio Planelli, who listed "poetry, music, declamation, and décor" as the essential elements of opera, and dance as non-essential.[40] "Our spectacle will be perfect, when all the skills of which it is compounded contribute to the end, which is the *melodramma*."[41]

37 "n'a eu d'autre but que de faire valoir les beautés poëtiques. Les Musiciens François ont été obligés d'augmenter à l'aide de la mélodie & de l'harmonie l'impression que les vers qu'ils ont chantés auroient faite par le secours de la seule déclamation. Telle est la loi qu'on leur a imposée en France, & le principe sur lequel le public les a jugés. Ces Musiciens ont exécuté dans ce genre de travail des choses admirables. Par la justesse de leur sentiment, par la vérité de leur expression." De Rochemont, *Réflexions d'un patriote sur l'opéra françois, et sur l'opéra italien*, 3rd Proposition (Paris, 1754), 24–25.
38 *Ibid.*, 6th Proposition, 42.
39 "Que de moyens de séduire, de plaire, d'enchanter! que de ressorts dans la main d'un homme habile! Il peut s'emparer de toutes nos sensations, en agiter à parcourir! quel essor à prendre! quel génie il faut pour ne pas demeurer en chemin! / Voilà, Madame, ce que doit être notre Opéra. La réunion de tous les Arts, l'ensemble de toutes les sensations; voilà ce qui le distingue de tous les Spectacles du monde; voilà comme l'a envisagé Quinault, le créateur inimitable de ce genre." *Lettre à Madame de*** sur l'opéra d'Iphigénie en Aulide* (Lausanne, 1774) in *Querelle des Gluckistes et des Piccinistes*, ed. F. Lesure (Geneva, 1984), vol. II, 13–14.
40 "la Poesia, la Musica, la Pronunziazione, e la Decorazione." PlanelliO, 16.
41 "Allora dunque il nostro Spettacolo sarà perfetto, quando tutte le Discipline, che lo compongono, concorreranno al fine del Melodramma." *Ibid.*, 18.

Declamation and recitative: some issues

In Lullian *tragédie en musique*, word-setting in the form of recitative was the acid test for the composer. Where Lully and Quinault had achieved a balance of text and music, Rameau, in his first such work, had tilted the balance in favor of music and thus found himself embroiled for decades in a dispute with the Lullistes,[42] although he himself regarded Lully's word-setting in recitative as exemplary. He showed himself conciliatory toward the Lullistes in the conception of the first version of *Castor et Pollux*, giving recitative a more prominent role. But recitative remained a bone of contention even after the Querelle des Bouffons, and became a regular topic of discussion in Italian writing on operatic reform. As Metastasian opera reached France, Italian secco recitative received more and more attention and was compared with French recitative. The two camps of Gluckists and Piccinnists once again gave the arguments about recitative and the proper balance between music and the dramatic element a central place in their reviews of Gluck.

In 1754, shortly after the Querelle des Bouffons had ended, Blainville drew up a systematic table of four types of declamation (conversational tone, declamation for the law-courts, dramatic declamation, and musical declamation), and distinguished strictly between Italian and French recitative.[43] The negative value he gave to the former is apparent immediately in the first sentence of his comparison: "The first time I heard Italian recitative, it made on me the same impression as a legal submission: I found there a spirit of truth, but a stiff and uncouth manner such as good taste would never have directed."[44] Blainville thought the conversational tone appropriate only in simple dialogue or *récit*, "but as soon as some passion, some imagery enters, the musical tone should again assert its superiority." There was no place in the theatre for the kind of speech heard from the pulpit or in a court of law but only for "the effects of nature rendered musically." Like other authors he acknowledged one advantage of Italian recitative, namely that it made arietta more effective: "Our recitative, through its more flexible, more agreeable intervals, as far as may be from the lawyer's

---

42 See R. Klingsporn, *Jean-Philippe Rameaus Opern im ästhetischen Diskurs ihrer Zeit* (Stuttgart: Metzler, 1996).

43 BlainvilleE; see the chapter "Du récitatif," 47–58.

44 "La premiere fois que j'ai entendu le Recitatif Italien, il fit sur moi la même impression qu'un playdoyer; j'y trouvois un esprit de vérité, mais un air roide & sauvage que le bon goût n'a jamais dicté." *Ibid.*, 50–51.

tone, has something of the character of dramatic declamation; it does not cut clearly enough, some will say, the periods are not sufficiently well marked; in a word, our recitative sings too much, or else our airs do not sing enough." (This was a reproach that would be raised again later, against Gluck.) The aim should be a "recitative full of charms, where feelings and their expression would march in step," and where the adoption of a "simple" or "elevated" tone should be governed by the meaning of the text. It was particularly hard, in Blainville's view, to strike the appropriate note in recitative in the "heroic genre," and there Lully's recitatives provided a model. Inevitably Lully's ornamentation came in for criticism: "the ornaments achieve nothing but to slow the art of gesture and the action of both the sung and the declaimed text." Yet Blainville found French recitative superior to Italian, as he demonstrated by his comparison of Italian recitative to the speech of sailors on a Venetian dockside and French to the declamation of heroes, poets or musicians. Blainville's ideal manner of declamation contained an "animated character" and a "spirit of nobility and majesty," and he found it in Armide's monologue. He thought his age would do well, however, while preserving decorum, to learn from the Italians "the simple tone of pure declamation, the bold characteristics that paint violent passions so vividly, the chords of unexpected modulations, the silences, the reduced accompaniments."[45]

De Rochemont thought that French opera composers were confronted by especially many difficulties, which he laid at the door of the dramatic quality of the operas and understanding of the text. "It is the national character, which has laid down laws for French opera, and demanded that music should express words with the most scrupulous exactitude. And so the French artist has been obliged to overcome in his work many difficulties that the Italians have not had at all. He has had to deal with two genres, singing a less musical language, composing without daring to allow himself any license, and unable to expect the least mercy from the spectators for his

---

45 "mais pour peu qu'il entre quelque passion, quelqu'image, le ton musical doit reprendre ses avantages," "Notre Recitatif, par des intervalles plus lians, plus agréables, tout à fait éloignés du ton du barreau, tient au genre de la déclamation dramatique: il ne tranche point assez, dira-t'on; les passages n'en sont point assez marqués; enfin, notre Recitatif chante trop, ou nos airs pas assez," "ton simple de la pure déclamation, ces traits hardis qui peignent si bien les passions violentes, ces cordes de modulations inattendues, ces silences, ces accompagnemens coupés." See *ibid.*, 51–57.

very smallest slips."[46] All attempts to escape from the "French system" had failed: "It is founded on the incontrovertible principle that the interest one takes in a theatrical action is the most agreeable of all the stirrings of the soul, the most acute of all pleasures, the most accessible of all amusements to the greatest number of spectators; at the same time, [it is] that which, in the nature of things, lasts longest and wears out less quickly than all others . . . Interest is the soul of French theatre, and for us there is no interest without good words."[47] So it was necessary for music to yield pride of place to the dramatic element and this had the direct consequence that a special weight fell upon recitative.

De Rochemont's reflections were the product of a comparison of *tragédie lyrique* and *dramma per musica*. He stressed that Italians were accustomed to write recitative "which renders the meaning of the words exactly, adding very little to the poetic expression. This very monotonous recitative is scarcely endurable except to those who understand the language well and are used to hearing it spoken." How the "madrigals" (the aria texts) were set was what mattered most to Italians. "And so the Italian musician begins by neglecting the true beauties of his poem in order to bestow value on a superfluous afterthought that has little connection with the subject . . . It has been said that recitative, when it is good, does no more than render the poet's words and thoughts exactly without adding much to the expression of the verses or to the energy of the style."[48] For this reason the Italians also often preferred spoken verse to secco recitative, while the regrettably rare *récitatif obligé* (accompanied recitative) was often regarded

46 "C'est le caractère national qui a donné des loix à l'Opera François, & qui a exigé que la Musique exprimât les paroles avec la plus scrupuleuse exactitude. Ainsi l'artiste François a été obligé de vaincre dans cet ouvrage bien des difficultés que n'ont point eu les Italiens. Il a traité les deux genres, il a chanté une langue moins musicale; il a composé sans oser se permettre aucune licence, & sans pouvoir espérer des Spectateurs la moindre grace sur les plus petites négligences." De Rochemont, 51.
47 "Il est fondé sur ce principe incontestable, que l'intérêt qu'on prend à l'action théatrale est de tous les mouvemens de l'âme le plus agréable, de tous les plaisirs le plus vif, de tous les amusemens celui qui est constamment à la portée du plus grand nombre des Spectateurs; en même tems celui, qui par la nature des choses, a plus de tenue, & s'use moins vite que tous les autres . . . L'intérêt est l'âme du spectacle François, & pour nous point d'intérêt sans de bonnes paroles." *Ibid.*, 33.
48 "qui rend avec exactitude le sens des paroles, en ajoutant peu de chose à l'expression poétique. Ce récitatif très-monotone n'est gueres supportable qu'à

as superior to the most beautiful arias. For De Rochemont, Lully's recitative was still "the model of the good sung declamation of the French."[49]

Algarotti, in his *Saggio sopra l'opera in musica* (1755), which was known to the French from 1757 but not published in translation in full until 1773, wrote of recitative as a weak spot in Italian opera. "We do not hesitate to say that it is the most neglected part of opera. Now more than ever, it appears that composers pay little attention to the recitatives, regarding them as contributing little to the giving of pleasure, and, consequently, they do not deign to work at them." After a historical excursus in which he discusses tempo variation in delivery, according to the content of the words, and "these outbursts incised into expression by violence of emotion and the transports unrivalled by the most beautiful ariettas of our time,"[50] he turned to the effectiveness of contemporary *récitatif obligé* and urged that it should be used instead of secco recitative. It was his conviction that it not only gave Italian recitative greater expressive force but also bridged the gap between recitative and aria. The anonymous person who translated Algarotti's essay into French added an illuminating footnote, indicating what recitative meant from a French point of view: "There is nothing in music which connoisseurs esteem more highly than recitative, and nothing in which they are harder to please. If an artist excels in this, however poor he may be in everything else, it is enough to raise him, for the connoisseurs, to the ranks of the most illustrious: and the celebrated Porpora was immortalized for no other reason."[51] Like several

ceux qui connoissent bien la Langue, & qui sont dans l'habitude de l'entendre parler. / Ainsi le Musicien Italien débute par négliger les véritables beautés de son Poëme, pour faire valoir une pensée peu liée au sujet & postiche [...] On a dit que le récitatif n'a d'autre effet, quand il est bon, que de rendre avec exactitude les pensées & les paroles du Poëte, sans ajouter beaucoup à l'expression des Vers & à l'énergie du style." *Ibid.*, 11–12.

49 "le modèle de la bonne déclamation chantante des François," De Rochement, 62.

50 "Nous ne craignons pas de dire que c'est la partie la plus négligée de l'Opéra. Il paroit actuellement plus que jamais, que les Compositeurs ne font pas grand cas des récitatifs, qu'ils regardent comme très-peu propres à causer du plaisir, & qu'en conséquence ils ne daignent pas les travailler ... ces éclats que la violence des passions grave dans l'expression und les transports que les plus belles Ariettes de nos jours n'ont jamais pu obtenir," Algarotti, 31–34.

51 "Il n'y a point de partie dans la Musique dont les Connoisseurs fassent autant de cas, que du Récitatif, & sur laquelle ils soient aussi difficiles. Il suffit même d'exceller dans cette seule partie, fût-on médiocre dans tous les autres, pour s'élever chez eux au rang des plus illustres Artistes; & le célèbre Porpora ne s'est imortalisé que par-là." Algarotti, 181.

French writers, Algarotti found fault with arias for "ostentatious ornamentation,"[52] excessive length, and excessively long ritornellos. The "grand and magnificent spectacle"[53] of operas with mythological subject matter demanded ambitious recitative, to live up to the "vivid image of Greek tragedy."[54]

Dorat, who has already been quoted here, showed himself to be an adherent of Italian opera, in his strictures on recitative and even more in his defense of the aria:

> Our taste, more justly proud,
> Complains of the melancholy of our recitatives;
> These modulations, whose chilled refrain
> Is like a funeral hymn addressed to sleep.
> True recitative, without frivolous trimmings,
> Should walk, should fly, as words themselves do.
> This text is formed to bind the action,
> And should be sung rather than declaimed.
> So why all these cries, these ponderous inflexions,
> These prolonged emphases on dull syllables,
> This cold yapping you take such delight in stretching out?
> Cease to stun me when you should be talking to me.
> Give up this paraphernalia, this insipid emphasis,
> Not the basis but the stumbling block of our singing,
> And cease to pride yourselves on your mad obsession
> With melodiously sending the audience to sleep.[55]

52 "grands ornemens." *Ibid.*, 35.
53 "Spectacle grand & magnifique." *Ibid.*, 12.
54 "vive image de la Tragédie Grecque." *Ibid.*, 101.
55 "Notre goût, plus superbe avec plus de justesse, / De nos récitatifs accuse la tristesse; / Ces modulations, dont le refrein glacé [sic] / Semble un hymne funébre au sommeil adressé. / Le vrai récitatif, sans appareil frivole, / Doit marcher, doit voler, ainsi que la parole. / Pour lier l'action ce langage est formé, / Et veut être chanté, bien moins que déclamé. / Pour quoi donc tous ces cris, ces infléxions lourdes, / Ces accens prolongés sur des syllabes sourdes, / Ces froids glapissemens, qu'on se plaît à filer? / Cessez de m'étourdir, quand il faut me parler. / Quittez cet attirail, cette insipide emphase, / L'écueil de notre chant, loin d'en être la base, / Et ne vous piquez plus du fol entêtement / D'endormir le Public mélodieusement." Dorat, *La déclamation théatrale*, 110–111. The most important of the terms he uses about the aria are clearly derived from the Italian da capo aria; cf. also "Keep, oh keep musical pomp / for those appointed pieces where the organ takes flight, / where the soul at last finds release in more impassioned sounds, / and gives free rein to all its feelings. / Then let your inflexions be sustained,/ let them die away on long breaths; / let pedal points and

The position adopted by Laurent Garcin, in his *Traité du mélo-drame*[56] of 1772 (before the composition of *Iphigénie en Aulide*), was highly radical and at the opposite extreme from Dorat. In his opinion, the aria addressed only low feelings and the ear, while "recitative rises above our senses . . . it seeks to touch our soul, it aspires to nothing less than to touch us, move us, transport us out of ourselves: it is thus the most noble, the most expressive, the most varied, the most glorious genre the musician can attempt, but at the same time it is the most difficult." Garcin gave the palm to recitative because it moves the listener most. In company with a number of other theorists he remarked that in Metastasian *dramma per musica* recitative served only to lead from one aria to the next, a wholly subordinate function which led Italian audiences to pay it no attention.

Gluck's apologist Abbé Arnaud derived three categories of recitative from Gluck's French reform operas: "one which is almost *spoken*, one which has more inflexions and moves closer to singing, and finally the *pathetic* recitative, which is flatly called *obligé* . . . It is true that we encounter there [in recitative] harmonic paths unfamiliar as yet to our ears; but we must blame our musicians for that, who, since the celebrated Lully, have always moved in the same circle, and seem to have made a religion of prolonging every modulation once they have tamed it. In recitative above all, where we are deprived of the resource of a constant and fixed tempo, changes of modulation, harmony, and periods should be as rapid as the author's variations of mood."[57] Like others before him, Arnaud laid particular stress on the flow of recitative into singing and back, which Gluck restored to greater prominence than it had had in Rameau and his successors: "*Alceste, Orphée et Eurydice* and *Iphigénie en Aulide*: that recitative connects naturally with singing in regular measures [*chant mésuré*]; that singing in regular measures fades into recitative; that these two procedures enhance each other, when in Italian opera there is no rapport, no analogy between them, in a word, nothing leading from one to

vocal bravura flow in profusion: / the public demands them and will be in ecstasy; / but amid all the twists of a cunning Daedalus / hold on to the melody, let it be your guide" (p. 112).

56 Laurent Garcin, *Traité du mélo-drame, ou réflexion sur la musique dramatique* (Paris, 1771), 424.

57 *Lettre à Madame D'Augny [epouse du fermier-général de ce nom] sur l'Iphigénie en Aulide De M. le chevalier Gluck*, Arnaud, vol. II, 374.

the other. You will admire how these recitatives are more or less felt, more or less involved in the action."[58]

In his letter to Padre Martini, Arnaud defended Gluck's "revolution" and complacently criticized the dramatic failings of Italian opera resulting from the neglect of recitative. "Now for recitative: we cannot disguise the fact that the interest of your dramas does not lie principally in the action and that it is above all on the stage that your music lacks interest. Do your composers neglect recitative because the spectator does not listen to it? . . . For you will agree with me, reverend father, that most of the *couplets* which end your scenes, and which we call *airs* and *ariettes*, are just so many heterogeneous and superfluous passages. Yet these are the very places for which the composer and the poet reserve all their talent and the spectator all his attention."[59] Arnaud's ideal is the melding of recitative and *air* in the operas *Alceste*, *Orphée et Eurydice*, and *Iphigénie en Aulide*.

If the almost imperceptible transition between recitative and aria, a characteristic of Lullian recitative scenes, in which *petits airs* are sung, constituted Arnaud's dramatic ideal, Le Suire took a more critical stance,[60] claiming often scarcely to recognize an aria and accusing Gluck of falling into the old French fault of "psalmody." "Already savoring the foretaste of that exquisite music, one of those days I betook myself to the Théâtre Lyrique, my mouth watering. They were playing Monsieur Gluk's [*sic*] *Alceste*: I was charmed by the overture and the recitative. I waited for the airs: the first passed modestly without my noticing it; I doubled my attention for the second, which is not indicated in the libretto; it escaped

58 "Alceste, Orphée et Eurydice et Iphigénie en Aulide: que le récitatif vient s'y lier naturellement au chant mesuré; que le chant mesuré se perd et se fond dans le récitatif; que ces deux manières de procéder se font valoir réciproquement, quand dans les opéras italiens elles n'ont aucun rapport, aucune analogie, rien en un mot qui conduise de l'une à l'autre. Vous admirerez comment ces récitatifs sont plus ou moins ressentis, plus ou moins intéressés à l'action." Arnaud, vol. II, 410.
59 *Ibid.*, Letter to P. Martini, 409.
60 Le Suire, *Lettre de M. Camille Trillo*, 18–19. He is far more critical of Italian recitative: "This neglected recitative has degenerated into a monotonous cantilena to which no one listens and which makes it hard to enter into the meaning of the piece, separates the airs and destroys the ensemble. The merit of the verses is lost, the finest dramas of Metastasio have no more effect than the word-spinning of an ordinary poet. It is a pleasure for the ear alone; furthermore the affronts to verisimilitude would arouse disgust, if anyone paid attention to what happens on the stage."

me with the same subtlety. In short, I came to the end of the opera almost without having heard anything but recitative. Everyone applauded, and I retired, afflicted, believing that I had lost the faculty of hearing musical airs. I was a little happier at *Orphée*; but on the whole I think that I perceived in this musician's operas the attempt to move out of our former psalmody, with an unhappy tendency to fall back into it; and I saw myself obliged, if I wanted to hear real singing, to visit the Italians to see the *Olympiade*, where I was struck by several ariettas which they parodied felicitously."[61] In another context Le Suire wrote ironically of Gluck's arias passing by "incognito."[62]

Writing in 1779, Boyé, who is not known to have been a partisan supporter of Italian opera, identified recitative as the most important cause of the difficulties the public experienced in accepting Gluck's operas. "It is that the productions of this celebrated man are overloaded with recitatives, and that the normal effect of this genre is to be cold, tedious and unappealing."[63] Understanding arias was a far more spontaneous act than understanding recitatives, as was proved by the universal popularity of Italian arias, which could moreover also be performed to great effect on instruments, which was not the case with recitatives. Italian opera audiences' habit of eating, drinking, talking, and playing cards during recitative was the best proof of his conviction.

61 "Savourant déja l'avant-goût de cette Musique exquise, un de ces jours je me
    rendis tout affriandé au Théatre Lyrique. On donnait Alceste de M. Gluk; je fus
    charmé de l'ouverture & du récitatif. J'attendois les airs; les premier passe
    modestement sans que je m'en apperçoive; je redouble d'attention au second qui
    n'est indiqué sur le livre; il m'échappe avec la même subtilité. Bref, j'arrive à la fin
    de la piece, sans avoir presque rien entendu que du récitatif. Tout le monde
    applaudit, & je me retire affligé, croyant avoir perdu la faculté de saisir les airs. Je
    fus un peu plus heureux à Orphée; mais en général je crus appercevoir dans les
    Opéras de ce Musicien, des prétentions à sortir de notre ancienne Psalmodie,
    avec une malheureuse pente à y retomber; & je me vis obligé, pour entendre
    vraiment du chant, d'aller aux Italiens voir l'Olympiade, où je fus frappé de
    plusieurs Ariettes qu'on a heureusement parodiées." *Ibid.*, 11–12.
62 *Ibid.*, 39: " his airs, though at times they pass by incognito, are nevertheless on
    the whole superior to what we used to have in this genre; indeed, several could
    take their place in Italian operas."
63 "C'est que les productions de cet homme célèbre sont trop surchargées de
    récitatifs, que l'effet ordinaire de ce genre est d'être froid, ennuyeux &
    dégoûtant." Boyé, *L'Expression musicale mis au rang des chimères par M. Boyé*
    (Amsterdam et se trouve à Paris: Esprit, Veuve Duchesne, 1779), 17.

Patricia Howard remarks, apropos of Gluck's reform operas: "In each opera Gluck faces anew the aria–recitative situation and finds different solutions."[64] She says of *Iphigénie en Aulide* that it is "written in a very fluid style, shifting from informal air to accompanied recitative, to dance and chorus, with few full stops in either the music or the action. While this is a very French characteristic, it is also clearly the rational path of development open to Gluck."[65] One must agree with her conclusion: "All that Gluck added to recitative was in the nature of a closer *rapprochement* with the style of aria ... Gluck's development of recitative is possibly the most vital aspect of his reform of opera."[66]

The starting-point for Gluck's development of this variety of solutions to the shaping of recitative was Lully's conception of setting the dramatic element on at least an equal footing with the musical. By this means Gluck opened up perspectives that helped to determine the course of opera in the nineteenth century.

Armide – the paradigm

Writing about *Armide*, Gluck underlines the newness of the conception and prophesies a great future for his opera. In particular, he draws attention to the individual delineation of character: "I have made the music [of the opera] such that it will not go quickly out of date ... *Alceste* is a complete tragedy, and I admit that I believe it falls very little short of perfection; but you cannot imagine the number of nuances and different paths of which music is capable. *Armide* as a whole is so different from *Alceste* that you will think they are not the work of the same composer. Thus I used the little juice remaining to me to finish *Armide*; I tried to be more painter and poet than musician in it ... There is one kind of refinement in *Armide* which is not in *Alceste*, for I found the means to let the characters speak in such a way that you will recognize at once, from their manner of expressing themselves, when it is Armide who speaks or a follower etc. etc."[67] He had already

---

64 HowardG, 62–63.
65 *Ibid.*, 66.
66 *Ibid.*, 71.
67 "J'en [d'Armide] ai fait la Musique de manière qu'elle ne vieillira pas sitôt ... Alceste est une Tragédie complète, & je vous avoue que je crois qu'il manque très-peu de chose à sa perfection; mais vous n'imaginez pas de combien de

written similarly to Du Roullet: "For *Armide* I invented a new method . . . In many scenes it is necessary to trot, or better, gallop with the music so as not to let the cold and tedious elements in the play be perceived . . . if that succeeds as I calculated, your former music is destroyed for ever."[68] Yet it is manifest that, setting aside the polemics for and against *Armide*, in the conception and in individual details it reveals the example of Lully's *tragédie*. Because it uses Quinault's libretto almost unaltered, *Armide* contains longer recitatives than any other of Gluck's reform operas for Paris; they are musically very interesting and dramatically especially effective. Armide, in particular, is characterized by the leaping intervals of her recitatives, in marked contrast to Renaud's "caressing semitones."[69]

Some of the *da capo* forms in Gluck's *Armide*, in both solos and ensembles, are modeled on Lully's. The *da capo* aria "Ah si la liberté" (Act III) follows the model in setting the first stanza only once, but the trio "Au temps heureux" (II, 4) uses reprise in a French manner, to frame a substantial middle section: this form has little in common with the Italian *da capo* aria. The echo effect of the trio is taken up in the chorus that follows (and it also plays a part in the dialogue at the beginning of Act V); this is one of the techniques, comparable to the tendency toward motivic unity in Lully's *Armide*, whereby Gluck creates musical unity within scenes and tableaux. The prominent, dotted, upbeat motive in this chorus, "Ah quelle horreur," is

nuances & de routes différentes la Musique est susceptible; l'ensemble de l'Armide est si différent de celui de l'Alceste, que vous croirez qu'ils ne sont pas du même Compositeur. Aussi ai-je employé le peu de suc qui me restoit pour achever l'Armide; j'ai tâché d'y être plus Peintre & plus Poëte que Musicien . . . Il y a une espèce de délicatesse dans l'Armide qui n'est pas dans l'Alceste: car j'ai trouvé le moyen de faire parler les personnages, de manière que vous connoîtrez d'abord à leur façon de s'exprimer, quand ce sera Armide qui parlera, ou une suivante, &c. &c." Lettre de M. le chevalier Gluck, à M. L.B.D.R., in Lesure, ed., *Querelle des Gluckistes et des Piccinistes*, vol. I, 43–44.

68   "Pour Armide je immaginè une nouvelle methode . . . il faut dans beaucoup de Scènes savoir bien trotter, ou pour mieux dire galopper avec la musique pour ne pas faire apercevoir le froid et l'annayant qui se trouve dans la pièce . . . si cela reussit comme je calculè, votre ancienne Musique est pour toujours anéantie," Letter to Du Roullet, October 14, 1775, "Correspondance inédite de Gluck," ed. J. Tiersot, *La Revue musicale* 10 (1914), 6. Reichardt obviously shared Gluck's opinion, writing "Only Gluck could contrive to take his [Lully's] place among the French" ("Nur Gluck konnte ihn [Lully] bey den Franzosen zu verdrängen anfangen"), *Musikalisches Kunstmagazin*, vol. I, 45.

69   HowardG, 68.

heard again later, in Armide's "Enfin il est en ma puissance," and combined with the echo effect in "Ah quelle cruauté." Other elements used to represent the demonic – rapid, excited triplet motion, note-repetition and the traditional "demonic" scales – form connections between several scenes.

The last confrontation between Armide and Renaud takes place in a highly dramatic recitative, accompanied only by continuo, in which the repetition of individual phrases (a characteristic technique of Lully's) creates an intermediate form, somewhere between through-composed recitative and closed form. The greatest degree of dramatic and expressive intensity is reached in the last scene for Armide, now accompanied by the whole orchestra, with tempo variations, specific rhetoric, and instrumental passages charged with affect all making a contribution. It might be said that Lully's style is developed further here, in a highly accomplished manner, to an acme of perfection.

The through-composed monologue "Enfin il est en ma puissance" is linked to the following *air* by common motivic material, and the *air* to "Venez, secondez mes désirs," which follows it, by a common tonality, E minor. As in several other airs, in "Venez, secondez" the ritornello, constructed in three-bar phrases, is repeated at the vocal entry, and both sections of the text are set twice. In the *air* "Esprit de haine," the text of which consists of two quatrains (7-syllable lines), the second stanza is set as a short middle section, while the first is treated as a ternary text (ab ab cd ab b in the first section; ab ab cd cd ab in the last), resulting in purely textual terms (but not musically) in a kind of *rondeau*. The only element of musical reprise occurs when a four-bar phrase from the first section is repeated in the last – comparable to Lullian technique. A similar procedure underlies Hidraot's "Pour vous quand il vous plaît" in Act I.

Armide's monologue "Venez, venez, Haine implacable" is also remarkable for its form: after the introductory ritornello the first three lines are set once, then the first two lines are set again, to new music, in a form in which they return in reprise, while the first line recurs unchanged as a coda. The music of lines 4–6 appears in the reprise transposed from the dominant to the tonic, like a sonata-form second subject. Making a very strong dramatic point, Gluck repeats the most important line, "Venez, venez, Haine implacable" ("Come, come, implacable Hatred!"), five times, like a litany; this is obviously the fruit of earlier experiments with transferring sonata-form techniques of tonal structuring to the aria. He also encloses the first large-scale section of the opera's closing scene within a musical frame, with the ten bars from the start recurring unchanged after the first ritornello. Renaud's "Allez, éloignez-vous" is also constructed within a similar frame.

Gluck's claim to have provided music specific to the individual characters is confirmed in the dialogue between Armide and Renaud at the beginning of Act V. Each voice keeps to its own melodic/motivic material up until the point at which the scene becomes an actual duet. The attempt at characterization in this scene made less of an impression on Coquéau than the word-setting, which struck him as monotonous, all too French and "Lulliste," hence "bad and contrived." Again and again, contemporary critics alluded to the new function given to the orchestra as a commentator in instrumental interjections and as partner to the singers, reinforcing or undermining the utterances of their characters. The trio for Armide, Phénice, and Sidonie (III, 2) is an especially good example of this: significantly, it is Armide's part which is supported and augmented by the orchestra.

Renaud's most important aria in the opera is "Plus j'observe ces lieux." Ritornello would be too modest a word for its opening sinfonia (Coquéau, like other opponents of Gluck, acknowledged the "delightful accompaniments"), over thirty bars long and constructed in broad spans. It is obviously indebted to the *sommeil* scene in Lully's *Atys*, although it centers on a different conventional topos, the soothing flow of a stream. The two pieces are linked by the use of solo flutes (two recorders in Lully, one flute in Gluck), the music for which recurs periodically during the vocal section with quite long passages from the introduction unchanged.

In the opera's *divertissements*, which even include double chorus, Gluck created immense tableaux in which he followed the Lullian tradition directly and used reprises to shape them as integrated musical structures. The choral da capo "Voici la charmante retraite" in Act IV, after the chorus "Jamais dans ces beaux lieux," is one good example, and the recurrence of the chaconne in Act V is another. Compared with the earlier chaconne, what one notices here is not only the alternation and repetition of components of different lengths, and the irregularly constructed modulating elements, but also the repetition of larger structures such as ten-bar units. The large-scale reprise of the chaconne after the *Air gracieux* consists essentially of a shorter transposed section at the start and a much longer (over seventy bars), unaltered formal section from the later course of the ostinato form. Gluck's integration of the *divertissements* into the dramatic and musical expression of his subject is extraordinarily successful. Admittedly, in view of the subject, their justification purely according to the aspects of drama and content would be questionable.

The extraordinary multiformity of Armide's role is illustrated by the tonalities associated with her. Her principal tonal areas are D minor, the key of her dream narrative in Act I and her self-recognition and self-destruction at the end, A minor, and E minor: these two last are the keys of the famous scenes in Act II, in which the A minor of the monologue "Enfin il est en ma puissance" is expanded to F♯ and C♯, thus associating the demonic with a proliferation of sharps. It is much harder to interpret the F major of the aria "De mes plus doux regards" and the monologue "Venez, venez, Haine implacable," because Act I begins in that same key with Phénice's "Dans un jour de triomphe." The D major of Renaud's "Plus j'observe ces lieux" can be interpreted as a counter to the tragic D minor, for as the magic spell starts to work, so Armide's happiness begins. Gluck follows Lully's lead in giving most monologues and scenes tonal unity, but he abandons the principle at the beginning of Act V: the duet for Armide and Renaud starts in D minor in the dialogue sections, modulates to G minor at "D'une vaine terreur," to C minor at Armide's "La sévère raison," and finally Gluck has them singing together in C major in "Aimons nous, tout nous y convie."

There was no reason, in composing the choruses in *Armide*, to follow the precedents set by Lully when special dramaturgical considerations applied, for Hatred (La Haine) is a female personage in French and therefore her followers are also female. On the other hand the chorus "Dieux infernaux" in *Iphigénie en Aulide* follows Lully's example in comparable pieces in *Atys* in being set in three parts for male voices, to create an especially dark coloration.

Posterity's view of Gluck's relationship to Lully

Jacques Martine praised Gluck's recitative highly: "The *récitatif obligé*, to which Gluck ordinarily gives so much character, has perhaps even more of it here [in *Iphigénie en Tauride*], especially in Iphigénie's dream and the terror of Thoas. The sublime accompaniment of Oreste's monologue expressing his remorse, the vigorous chorus of the Scythians … are tragic beauties of the first order."[70] At the same time Martine acknowledged that Gluck showed a willingness to meet the wishes of adherents of Lully's music and earlier French opera, and thus an opportunism of which Piccinni was innocent. He went on to say, of the setbacks suffered by Piccinni, "he might have been spared them, if he had had more political sense and if, like Gluck, he had shown more consideration for the taste of the partisans of the Lullian tradition by sometimes drawing closer to its style."[71] The importance of recitative to Martine is shown by the fact that in his discussion of *tragédies lyriques* by Gluck, Piccinni, and Sacchini he always mentioned the quality and nature of the recitative.[72]

Liszt's overview of operatic history is not distinguished by profound knowledge of the subject, but even without referring to Gluck's earlier models he is quite right to say that the introduction of a new style of declamation made operatic history: "Gluck lent dramatic music all the splendour, all the majesty and importance of the declamatory style, while Piccini clung to the old faith, the principal dogma of which was that melodic expression suffices for making emotions known."[73] Franz Liszt, however, makes no comment on Lully's music anywhere in his published writings.[74]

70 "Le récitatif obligé, auquel Gluck donne ordinairement tant de caractère, en a ici [in Iphigénie en Tauride] peut-être encore davantage, particulièrement dans le songe d'Iphigénie et dans les terreurs de Thoas. Le sublime accompagnement du monologue d'Oreste qui exprime ses remords, le chœur si énergique des Scythes... sont des beautés tragiques du premier ordre." Jacques Martine, *De la musique dramatique en France* (Paris, 1813), 236.

71 "Il se les [tracasseries] serait peut-être épargnés, s'il eût eu plus de politique, et si, comme Gluck, il avait montré plus de condescendance pour le goût des partisans de l'ancienne musique française, en se rapprochant quelquefois de son style." *Ibid.*, 238.

72 Martine wrote of the recitative in Piccinni's *Iphigénie en Tauride*, for example: "The most vigorous and truest expression characterizes his recitative and his accompaniments" (p. 244), and of those in *Didon*: "The recitative is excellent, and always follows the sense of the words exactly" (p. 245).

73 "Gluck verlieh der dramatischen Musik allen Glanz, alle Majestät und Wichtigkeit des declamatorischen Styls, während Piccini am alten Glauben festhielt, der als Haupt-Lehrsatz aufstellt, daß zur Kundgebung der Gefühle der melodische Ausdruck hinreiche." Franz Liszt, "Scribe's und Meyerbeer's Robert der Teufel," in *Sämtliche Schriften*, vol. V, ed. D. Redepenning and B. Schilling (Wiesbaden: Breitkopf & Härtel, 1989), 31–39.

74 In a footnote of his "Berlioz und seine 'Harold-Symphonie'" (1855), he just mentions the quarrel between the admirers of Lully and of Gluck; see Franz Liszt, *Gesammelte Schriften*, ed. L. Ramann (Leipzig, 1882), vol. IV, p. 14. Another very general remark concerns the opinion that the French from the beginning of the history of opera were accustomed "to place a certain importance on opera texts," see Boyeldieu's "Weisse Dame," vol V, 60.

For Berlioz, Gluck's Paris operas, and the Paris versions of his earlier operas, formed the pinnacle of his achievement. In his discussion of *Alceste*, he gives as much detail about the recitative as about the *airs*, and praises it highly, except for the *récitatif simple*.[75] He observes of the *récitatif obligé* "Apollon est sensible" that it is an example of Gluck's system, "which consists of employing large instrumental forces only in proportion to the degree of interest and passion." In Berlioz's view, the recitative "Il n'est pour moi plus d'espérance" is the equal of the most beautiful *airs*, and he considers that the aesthetic categories of energy and the grandiose are embodied in the recitative "Arbitre du sort des humains," and those of expressive intensity and elevated pathos in Admète's recitative.[76] In his article "*Alceste* d'Euripide" Berlioz repeats the two well-known lines from Boileau's *Art poétique*[77] and comments on them with this insight: "Only he [Boileau] should have said 'Lully chilled', for nothing could be more frigid, vapid, tedious or impoverished than the sounds of this simultaneously antiquated and childish music." He then goes on to a more positive critique of Caron's air, 'Il faut passer tôt ou tard," sung by Adolphe-Joseph-Louis Alizard in Parisian concerts in the nineteenth century:

> The rhythm gave this piece a certain fresh gaiety, which pleased the public and was received with laughter and applause, without one really knowing whether the words or the music prompted the mirth. The expression of the melody is genuine, and the refrain "Sooner or later it befalls one / To board my small boat" fits perfectly the almost grotesque character of Quinault's Caron.[78]

With reference to the performances of Lully's music to *Le Bourgeois gentil-homme* at the Comédie Française during his time, Berlioz states that, in his

75 Berlioz deplores the "stagnant harmony" of the *récitatif simple* with its "effects of torpor and inescapable numbness," a "formidable monotony," the "simplicity of the bass lines" and lacklustre orchestration ("L'Alceste d'Euripide, celles de Quinault et de Calzabigi," 174–175).

76 "qui consiste à n'employer les masses instrumentales qu'en proportion du degré d'intérêt et de passion." See *ibid.*, 163, 167, 181. He also refers there to the recitative as "immense."

77 Hector Berlioz, *Die "Alceste" des Euripides, Musikalische Streifzüge, aus dem Französischen übertragen von Elly Ellès*, in *Literarische Werke* (Leipzig, 1912), vol. VI, 112–175. Quote, p. 123, "Et tous ces lieux communs de morale lubrique / Que Lulli réchauffa des sons de sa musique" (And all these commonplaces of wanton morality / That Lully rekindled with the sounds of his music).

78 *Ibid.*, 123–124.

opinion, the music of *Alceste* has the same "color, tone, and all the attractions" as that of the comédie-ballet. In a more general sense, Berlioz believed that Lully had only "a very limited number of ideas and used in all arias of the work the only process that was known to him."[79] This opinion, like those he held regarding Palestrina, reveal Berlioz's almost total lack of historical understanding before the time of Gluck.

Gustave Bertrand writes, in 1872, identifying Gluck as "the patriarch of *tragédie lyrique*"; he remarks that both Gluck and Spontini returned intermittently to *tragédie lyrique*, and he refers to "the tension of spirit that Gluck's eternal recitatives demand."[80] Reynaldo Hahn, however, probably had the best historical consciousness of the authors cited here, and a far more sophisticated sense of associations than Berlioz. For him, Lully was "the founder of all that is good and admirable in French dramatic music. The Italians of Italy had a feeling for lyricism. Only Lully had an intuition of what French musical declamation was. Gluck wrote *Orfeo* in Italy, but what a distance, in terms of declamation, lies between that work and those he produced subsequently, in France. It is in these that his very verbal genius developed to its most magnificent extent. In sum, what I like about Gluck... is this love uniting the souls of the words and the music; and it was Lully who first revealed it."[81]

79 *Ibid.*, 124.
80 Gustave Bertrand, *Les nationalités musicales étudiées dans le drame lyrique* (Paris, 1872), 44–47.
81 "fondateur de tout ce qui est beau dans la musique dramatique française. Les Italiens d'Italie avaient le sentiment lyrique. Lully seul a eu l'intuition de ce qu'était la déclamation musicale française, Gluck en Italie, a fait Orphée; mais quelle distance, au point de vue de la déclamation, entre cet ouvrage et ceux qu'il produisit par la suite, en France. C'est dans les derniers que son génie si verbal s'est le plus magnifiquement développé. En somme ce qui me plaît dans Gluck... c'est cet amour qui unit l'âme de la parole et celle de la musique; et cela, c'est Lully qui, le premier, l'a fait voir." Reynaldo Hahn, *Notes. Journal d'un musicien* (Paris: Plon et Nourrit, 1933), 111–112.

11 Jules Ecorcheville's genealogical study of the Lully family and its influence on Marcel Proust

MANUEL COUVREUR

"Lully est à la mode," proclaimed Jules Ecorcheville in 1911 at the beginning of a series of articles devoted to the composer.[1] The first indications of a revival of interest had appeared four decades earlier during the 1870s, following Paul Lacroix's re-issue of some libretti. In 1875 Lacombe had published an article titled "Lully, professeur de violon" in the *Chronique musicale*. The following year, as a prelude to the eleven works of Lully that he would re-edit beginning in 1880, Théodore de Lajarte published his anthology of *Airs à danser de Lully à Méhul*. Lajarte had been trained by Charles Truinet, the librarian at the Paris Opéra since 1866. Two decades later, in 1886 under the pseudonym Nuitter, the latter would publish his basic work *Les Origines de l'opéra français* – written in collaboration with Ernest Roquet, known as Thoinan. Lully studies would continue in 1891 with a short contribution by Arthur Pougin and a more substantial work by Emile Radet on *Lully, homme d'affaires, propriétaire et musicien*, which brought a number of archival documents to light. This first salvo of publications must be placed in the context of the profound identity crisis which shook France after the defeat at Sedan. The recognition of Lully's music is one of the manifestations of the return of interest on the part of intellectuals to the time of Louis XIV who, since the time of the highly laudatory homage Voltaire had paid him in 1751, represented an apex of French civilization never again to be attained.[2]

1 EcorchevilleL.
2 As early as this time, however, the interest in Lully was part of a more comprehensive movement focusing above all on the period of the French Baroque, heralded by Pougin's study on Rameau in 1876.

272

It is not until 1906 that we see the flowering of a new series of important works. They were produced by younger researchers who deliberately placed themselves in the lineage of their master, Romain Rolland (1866–1944). The dominant state of mind of this group was profoundly different: certainly the desire to honor the French cultural heritage had not disappeared, but this nationalist aim was conceived in a more general humanistic and European framework. The studies published on the eve of the First World War by Romain Rolland, Lionel de La Laurencie (1861–1933), Jules Ecorcheville (1872–1915), and Henry Prunières (1886–1942) continue, in large measure, to be definitive. First, then, the present article will in a sense pay homage to these pioneers, underscoring their originality and what elements were at stake from their perspective in the personality and music of Lully.

The violence of open opposition that distinguished these young lions from their predecessors goes beyond a simple conflict of generations.[3] It surfaces in a radical break between the former musicology inherited from Fétis, and the new approach to the discipline that was being advanced at that time by Riemann. This new group's goal was to bring musicological research to French universities and to make it an authentic professional specialization. From their education in the German school, these young French musicologists realized their country's terrible deficiencies in this area. The efforts of the "Romain Rolland group" were channeled in three major directions: musicological education, the establishment of learned societies and performance venues, and the creation of means of dissemination. Ultimately, this movement would lead to the formation in 1917 of the "Société française de musicologie," the complex circumstances of which go beyond the focus of our topic.

Romain Rolland, educated at the Ecole normale supérieure and at the Sorbonne, had defended a dissertation in 1895 on "Les origines du théâtre lyrique moderne," published subsequently under the title *Histoire de l'opéra en Europe avant Lully et Scarlatti*. In 1896, Rolland became professor of music history at the Paris Ecole normale supérieure. In 1903, the University of Paris asked him to organize the music department at the Ecole des

---

3 See for example the bitter attack on Pougin by Prunières in his article "Lettres et autographes de Lully," *Revue musicale S.I.M.* 3 (March 15, 1912), 19–20.

Hautes-Etudes sociales. Among his disciples were several of the young musicologists who rallied to Lully's cause. In 1906, Ecorcheville defended a "thèse d'état" devoted to "Vingt suites d'orchestre du XVIIe siècle français," as well as a complementary dissertation titled "De Lully à Rameau (1690–1730): l'esthétique musicale." In 1913, Prunières, one of Rolland's students at the Sorbonne, defended a dissertation devoted to "L'opéra italien en France avant Lully" and a supplementary dissertation titled "Le ballet de cour en France avant Benserade et Lully."

These simultaneous appearances on the French musicological scene necessitated the creation of societies to coordinate and disseminate this work. In 1900 in Paris Romain Rolland and Jules Combarieu organized the first international congress on music history. In October 1901, in collaboration with Pierre Aubry, Maurice Emmanuel, and Louis Laloy, Rolland and Combarieu founded the *Revue d'histoire et critique musicales*, which in 1904 would become the *Revue musicale*. The editorial board of this organ, essentially composed of inheritors of the Ecole Niedermeyer and believers in the Schola Cantorum, would prove itself rather deaf to the new tendencies: they were content to proclaim the singular glory of Saint-Saëns and Massenet.[4] Louis Laloy and Romain Rolland could not subscribe for very long to such a regressive program.

The progressive modernists Louis Laloy and Jean Marnold created the *Mercure musical* in 1905. Among the collaborators, we find several well-known names: along with Romain Rolland appear most of the French musicologists interested either in modern music (Ernest Ansermet, Gustave Samazeuilh) or more particularly in early music (Pierre Aubry, Eugène Borrel, Adolphe Boschot, Michel Brenet, Amédée Gastoué, Lionel de La Laurencie, Paul-Marie Masson, André Pirro, Jacques-Gabriel Prod'homme, Martial Ténéo). The editors could also rely on writers of stature like Rémy de Goncourt and two who inspired Maurice Ravel: Riccioto Canudo and Colette. *La Chronique musicale de Bordeaux*, edited by the very young Jacques Rivière, future secretary of *La Nouvelle Revue française*, launched the career of the most remarkable literary critic of his time: indeed in this capacity Rivière was one of the first to have foreseen the genius of Marcel Proust. Whereas the *Mercure musical* was a periodical

4   See Marnat, 106 and 273.

whose opulent production seemed to address it most particularly to an upper-class readership, the only aristocratic contributor was the composer Armande de Polignac, whose name alone is enough to evoke the most musically gifted noble family of her time. In 1903, Marcel Proust dedicated to the "Salon de la princesse Edmond de Polignac" a famous article in *Le Figaro* whose subtitle "Musique d'aujourd'hui, échos d'autrefois" reveals the two aesthetic trends that she was advancing.

The "secessionists" of the *Revue musicale* were not content merely to create their own journal. Very early on, Ecorcheville announced his intention to establish a society for the study of the history of music. This desire was realized in 1899 when he played an active role in founding the Société internationale de musique. Having done a portion of his musicological training with Riemann, Ecorcheville had naturally subscribed to this German initiative. Noting a perceived lack of independence, Lionel Dauriac, Jacques-Gabriel Prod'homme, and Jules Ecorcheville decided to create a Parisian section on March 28, 1904, of which they were respectively president, secretary, and treasurer. Rolland, always ready to help, accepted the role of official patron.[5] Prod'homme (1871–1956), trained at the Ecole des Hautes-Etudes sociales, had contributed to journals of a clearly leftist orientation (*La Revue socialiste, Droits de l'homme, Messidor*). He, too, had studied in Germany and as early as 1899 had become a militant defender of the internationalist cause and in particular of Franco-German friendship. As for Dauriac (1847–1923), he had taught the psychology of music at the Sorbonne from 1896 to 1903. His internationalist open-mindedness led to works devoted to Rossini (1905) as well as Wagner (1908) and Meyerbeer (1913). In 1907, Charles Malherbe (1853–1911) was elected to the presidency of the Parisian section of the SIM. As the successor of Nuitter at the library of the Paris Opéra, he had overseen the monumental edition of the works of Rameau published by Durand. Upon Malherbe's death in 1911, Ecorcheville succeeded him before taking over the general presidency of the entire society on October 1, 1912.

The Parisian section quickly acquired a means of disseminating its position. Convinced of the necessity to unify their efforts, Laloy and

5 See the notification that appeared in *Sammelbände der Internationalen Musik Gesellschaft* (April–June 1904), 344.

Ecorcheville decided to bring out the first number of the *Mercure musical et Bulletin français de la S.I.M. Société Internationale de Musique (Section de Paris)*, on January 15, 1907.[6] One year later the *Mercure musical* ceased publication. But the *Bulletin français de la S.I.M.* would survive until the declaration of war.[7] In order to reach a broader public, it was produced with a great deal of care but without the more extravagant features of the *Mercure musical*. The Parisian section encouraged the creation of regional sections and in turn promoted their initiatives. Thanks to Ecorcheville's energy the *Bulletin* finally won out. Emile Vuillermoz observed, "The most important musical periodicals, renouncing any rivalry, fused into a new organ. One after the other, *La revue musicale* of M. Combarieu and the *Courrier musical* were brought into its orbit and incorporated into it."[8] Thus the *Bulletin de la S.I.M.* had succeeded in attracting the contributions of d'Indy as well as Debussy. By now it seemed unthinkable that the French government would not subsidize such a publication, and indeed this duly happened.

The spirit of the periodical had two major directions: an international dimension, and an interest in musics of the present as much as of the past. The internationalism of its title was not gratuitous. All Ecorcheville's efforts – the mainspring of the enterprise – were based on the profound conviction that internationalism "is the product of intelligence and reflection, whereas nationalism and originality is based on spontaneity."[9] The declaration of war was not to shake his convictions. A volunteer as early as 1914, Ecorcheville preserved this same credo. On January 15, 1915, he wrote to La Laurencie: "Here at the front we do not share the '*furor antiteutonicus*' that the press is trying to instill in the public."[10] Like Ravel and Proust he refused to reject German culture, setting himself apart from many other French intellectuals, notably Saint-Saëns and Debussy.

The second characteristic tendency of the *Bulletin de la S.I.M.* is the equal attention paid to early and contemporary musicians. Debussy and

---

6 A list of active members of the Parisian Section of the SIM appears in the issue dated February 15, 1907, 212–214.

7 During its seven years of existence, this journal knew no less than six different titles. The list is given in EcorchevilleT, 18, note 1.

8 Emile Vuillermoz, "La revue SIM," in EcorchevilleT, 33.

9 Jules Ecorcheville, "L'internationalisme en musique, conférence prononcée au colloque de Londres" (May 29–June 3, 1911), cited in EcorchevilleT, 29–30.

10 *Ibid.*, 43.

Ravel, while remaining fiercely attached to modernism, composed *hommages* to Rameau and Couperin, published by Durand, who published both of the former as well as Rameau. Romain Rolland conceived his *Musiciens d'autrefois* and *Musiciens d'aujourd'hui* as a diptych. La Laurencie also had a keen interest in Wagner and Chabrier. After publishing a work on Rameau in 1908, Laloy devoted another to Debussy in the following year. According to Laloy, Ecorcheville shared this eclectic taste: "No less than music's past, he was curious about music's future ... He felt it no more remarkable to put Wagner aside for Debussy and Stravinsky than to put Lully aside for Couperin or Rameau."[11] Among its contributors the *Bulletin de la S.I.M.* also included critics who, like Malherbe, Prunières, or Laloy, defended the young Maurice Ravel with passion.[12] For this generation, despite being haunted by the First World War, it was possible to defend French art, modern and *ancien*, without rejecting German art. Such continued to be the attitude of Rolland who, upon receiving the Nobel Prize in 1915, would make the appeal to "raise our sights higher."

One of the most interesting aspects of Ecorcheville's work within the SIM was the interaction he was able to create between purely musicological activities and their more popular counterparts, not only by means of the bulletin, but also through more socially based activities. It was not a simple task at the time to combine concerts and learned colloquia:

> If one of the sessions included listening to examples, the scholars would complain that the society was becoming a venue for concerts: if on the other hand presentations were limited to oral communications, the general public stayed away *en masse*.[13]

In the first year of the new century, Ecorcheville had, as we shall see, looked favorably on the founding of a "Société française des amis de la musique," which attracted a good portion of the capital's wealthy population, as a means of establishing the SIM more firmly. For its contributing benefactors more entertainment was required: concerts had to be presented. Here, too, there was the issue of avoiding the trap of traditionalism observed by the former "Société nationale," founded in 1871 with the goal of presenting

11 Louis Laloy, "Jules Ecorcheville," in EcorchevilleT, 8.
12 See Marnat, 206–207. Laloy's study *La musique retrouvée* provides an excellent account of the concerns of the aesthetic debates of the time.
13 EcorchevilleT, 10.

modern French music to the exclusion of anything old or foreign. A first break arose on November 21, 1886, when Romain Bussine and Saint-Saëns were obliged to cede their place to César Franck, Vincent d'Indy, Ernest Chausson, and Gabriel Fauré.[14] The society underwent a second crisis in 1890 when d'Indy succeeded Franck. To compensate for the general ossification of the Société nationale, Countess Elisabeth Greffulhe, a great admirer of Wagner, ensured the creation of the "Société des grandes auditions," of which she herself held the presidency. In 1903, Ravel's election to the board of the Société nationale would bring about the demise of this institution, which had become a staunch supporter of the Schola Cantorum. It is in this context that we must consider Romain Rolland's group, always partial to Ravel, as we have seen.[15]

An interest in Lully is also quite marked. At the moment when Prunières and La Laurencie were writing their monograph on Lully, a series of articles informed readers about the progress of their research.[16] The composer was so much *à la mode* that he served as the pretext for a hoax, an April Fool's joke announced with much excitement in the April issue of 1912: "A great discovery: Lully was from a French family."[17] Poking fun at the public outcry produced by the publication of documents which confirmed the Italian origins of the musician, our internationalist music scholars, tongues firmly in cheeks, dreamed up a reply by a historian from Amiens, Marie Denizard, who, providing the requisite charts as proof, set out in detail the genealogy of the supposed French ancestors of Lully.[18] The

14 See *Gabriel Fauré, Correspondance*, ed. Jean-Michel Nectoux (Paris: Flammarion), 151–152.

15 On this topic see Michel Duchesneau, *L'avant-garde musicale à Paris de 1871 à 1939* (Liège: Mardaga, 1997). This excellent study appears to overlook the work achieved by the SIM and the Société française des amis de la musique. Yet the tie was real, not just because of the common goals of their aesthetic disputes, but also because of the clear proximity between the SIM and the Société Musicale Indépendante (SMI), and by the presence of common collaborators such as Laloy who was presented in 1909 as a founding member of the SMI, or Vuillermoz, founding member of the SMI and editor of *La revue musicale S.I.M.* from 1911.

16 Besides the three articles by Ecorcheville, see also Romain Rolland, "Notes sur Lully," *Mercure musical et Bulletin français de la S.I.M.*, January 15, 1905; PrunièresJ; and PrunièresL.

17 "Une grande découverte," *Revue musicale S.I.M.* 4 (April 1912), 1.

18 Marie Denizard, "La famille française de Lully," *Revue musicale S.I.M.* 5 (May 1912), 1–14.

issue seemed of such import to the presumed author that she had insisted that a note be added: "Tous droits de reproduction et de traduction réservés." Prunières pretended to believe in the hoax and responded to it with the publication of original documents discovered in Florence.[19]

As a parallel development, an increased desire to hear this music played can be perceived. In June 1906, the SIM put on two performances of the *Triomphe de la Raison sur l'Amour* by Louis Lully at the Bibliothèque Nationale.[20] In the supplement to the May issue of 1914, Leo Staats recounted how he had staged *Psyché* at the Odéon.[21] These events publicized by the SIM had been preceded by a concert entirely devoted to Lully given by Reynaldo Hahn on May 17, 1905, at the Théâtre de l'Athénée.[22] The *Mercure musical* expressed approval, of course, for "Lully is rather unknown today and we can not congratulate M. R. Hahn too enthusiastically for having saved these admirable pages from the catacombs."[23] For Hahn, it was not a temporary flight of fancy, but a mark of profound admiration. The composer envisaged writing a biography of Lully and paid homage to his musical style in the choruses he composed for *Esther*.[24] First heard in the salon of Countess de Guernes, these choruses were performed on April 8,

19 PrunièresF, 57–61.

20 Mentioned by Ecorcheville, "Lully gentilhomme et sa descendance: les fils de Lully," EcorchevilleL, 26, note 2.

21 Leo Staats, "Comment j'ai réglé Psyché à l'Odéon," *Revue musicale S.I.M.*, *supplément* (May 13, 1914), 1–4. See also the account given of a production by André Antoine at the Odéon in *S.I.M. Revue musicale mensuelle* (December 1911), 70–72.

22 *Thésée* (prologue of the old men and the nymphs); *Athys* [sic] (*sommeil* scene, air, metamorphosis scene); *Isis* (scene in the underworld, shivering trio); *Cadmus* (war scene, rustic scene); *Proserpine* (echo chorus); *Armide* (Renaud's air). Mmes Jeanne Raunay, Mathieu d'Ancy, Suzanne Brohly; MM. Jean Périer, Daraux, Plamondon, Fragson et Bernard. On May 23 Hahn gave a second concert devoted entirely to Rameau (Edmond Stoullig, *Les Annales du théâtre et de la musique* [Paris: Ollendorf, 1906], 394, note 2). Hahn's devotion to Rameau's music was to be confirmed by the revised edition of *Naïs* published in 1924 by Durand. On Hahn's relations with Proust see the excellent article by Philippe Blay and Hervé Lacombe, "A l'ombre de Massenet, Proust et Loti: le manuscrit autographe de *L'île du Rêve* de Reynaldo Hahn," *Revue de musicologie* 79 (1993), 83–108.

23 *Mercure musical* 2 (1905), 92.

24 Bernard Gavoty, *Reynaldo Hahn. Le musicien de la Belle Epoque* (Paris: Buchet-Chastel, 1976), 135, note 1. Was it this biography or one of Schumann that Proust had envisioned writing in collaboration with Hahn? See Piroué, 28.

1905, at the Théâtre Sarah-Bernhardt, and again on June 8, under the direction of the author, at a charity concert at the home of Countess René de
Béarn. Although he was a "regular" in this musical salon, Marcel Proust, ill
at that time, was unable to attend either the latter concert or the one devoted
to Lully.[25] His disappointment was great, for in his view *Esther* was "perhaps
the most beautiful music M. Reynaldo Hahn has composed till now, in
which all the grace of the Biblical narrative and the Racinian tragedy are
transposed and, so to speak, exalted."[26] This work, composed in the "neo-
lulliste" style, had a profound effect on Proust, who mentioned *Esther* in his
Contre Sainte-Beuve as well as in *A la recherche du temps perdu*.[27]

Not mentioned in the correspondence, the figure of Lully was invoked
by Proust only one time in *Un amour de Swann*, the second part of *Du côté de
chez Swann*. Completely taken by his love for Odette de Crécy, Charles
Swann can no longer see the world that surrounds him but at a distance:

> he used to enjoy the thought of the smooth efficiency of his household, the
> elegance of his own wardrobe and of his servants' liveries, the soundness of
> his investments, with the same relish as when he read in Saint-Simon, who
> was one of his favorite authors, of the mechanics of daily life at Versailles,
> what Mme de Maintenon ate and drank, of the shrewd avarice and great
> pomp of Lulli.[28]

Now, as Jean-Yves Tadié[29] points out quite correctly, while Saint-Simon
does evoke the etiquette of the court at Versailles and the dinners of the
widow Scarron, he mentions the name of the Florentine composer only

25 Marcel Proust, "Lettre à Robert de Montesquiou" [May 16, 1905], in ProustC,
vol. V, 150–151.
26 Marcel Proust, "La Comtesse de Guerne," *Le Figaro* (May 7, 1905), reprinted in
Clarac, 506.
27 Tadié, 542.
28 Marcel Proust, *Swann's Way*, trans. C. K. Scott Moncrieff and Terence Kilmartin,
rev. D. J. Enright (New York: Modern Library, 1992), 439. In a famous passage
from *La prisonnière*, following the model of Charpentier's *Louise* rather than
that of the Renaissance madrigalists, Proust alludes to the "cris de Paris,"
bringing together an approximate citation from Quinault's *Armide* (ProustRTP,
vol. III, 624). Given that Proust attributes it to Rameau, we do not know if the
first reference is to Lully's *Armide* or Gluck's (Tadié, 273–274): the comparison
between the text of *La prisonnière* and a passage from *Journées de lecture*,
referring to *récitatif*, supports the latter notion. Gluck's *Armide* is likewise
alluded to in his *Portraits of Musicians* (Marcel Proust, *Jean Santeuil*, ed. Pierre
Clarac [Paris: Gallimard, 1971], 82–83).
29 ProustRTP, vol. I, 1227.

once, and then just to specify that Francine is his son-in-law.[30] As another possible source Tadié mentions the correspondence of Mme de Sévigné: yet while the marquise repeatedly refers to both the music and the person of Lully, she mentions neither his parsimoniousness nor his taste for opulence.[31] On the other hand, La Fontaine, in his virulent satire *Le Florentin*, had vituperated the rapaciousness of the composer and had brought hellfire down on him as a sodomite, a detail which could not but pique Proust's curiosity. La Fontaine, however, was silent on "Lully's taste for opulence." Where had Proust picked up this fact? If we remember that *Du côté de chez Swann* was written between 1909 and 1911, we cannot help being struck that these two dates are those of the publication of the first two monographs to be devoted to the composer.

By referring to some concrete facts reported in Radet's study, Rolland, in his *Musiciens d'autrefois*, had sketched a portrait of Lully, torn between his taste for luxury and his miserliness.[32] Both in form and in content, the studies by Prunières and La Laurencie are simply the development of these "Notes sur Lully." In his monograph published in 1909, Prunières also contrasts "Lully the miser" and the financial success of this man: "ennobled, titled, endowed with aristocratic income, possessor of a great fortune, who associates with the highest nobility and has the ear of the king."[33] This same portrait in black and white appears in the *Lully* that La Laurencie published in 1911, which emphasized even more the homosexual debauchery of this man who "even loved women."[34]

How could Hahn and Proust not have had a very special interest in the prodigious life of this homosexual? The pages devoted by Saint-Simon to mordant criticism of the debauchery practiced by Monsieur de Vendôme and other notable sodomites had provoked the novelist's keen interest. Lully's destiny provided another example of social ascendancy based on the innate

30 Saint-Simon, *Mémoires. Additions au journal de Dangeau*, ed. Yves Coirault (Paris: Gallimard, 1983–88), vol. IV, 87.
31 See Lloyd Hibberd, "Mme de Sévigné and the Operas of Lully," in *Essays in Musicology: A Birthday Offering for Willi Apel*, ed. Hans Tischler (Bloomington: Indiana University School of Music, 1968), 153–163.
32 Romain Rolland, "Notes sur Lully," in *Musiciens d'autrefois* (Paris: Hachette, 1908), 108–115.
33 Henry Prunières, *Lully* (Paris: Renouard-Laurens, 1909), 56–57 and 72–77.
34 Lionel de La Laurencie, *Lully* (Paris: Alcan, 1911), 77–88.

weaknesses and the social cohesion of this "cursed race." It is on the basis of this interest that we are suggesting a more fundamental connection. At the conclusion of a series of articles devoted to Lully's descendants, Ecorcheville presented a summary of his genealogical tree. Whoever knows Proust's life and work even a little cannot help being struck by certain coincidences.

The list of the musician's descendants living in 1909 included many of the noble families most in the public eye:

> Let us follow again the genealogical tree and we arrive at the families of the de Larochefoucauld d'Estissac and Greffulhe, direct descendants of the du Moulin de Combreux, and we pass on finally to the families of d'Arenberg, de l'Aigle, de Vogué, Borghèse...the entire armorial of France and Gotha itself are thus descended from J. B. Lully.[35]

Several of these names would serve as Proust's models. This was certainly the case with the countess Elisabeth Greffulhe, *née* Caraman-Chimay, aunt and confidante of Robert de Montesquiou. A writer and a music lover as we have seen, the countess was one of the principal models for the duchess of Guermantes. Also to be seen in the genealogical tree is another close associate of Proust's, Armand de Gramont, the duke de Guiche, son-in-law of the countess.[36]

Further back in the genealogy, there are more surprises; the discovery of two very well-known names, Combreux and Guermanty. The name of the Guermantes was suggested to Proust by a castle near Lagny, a property belonging to the family of his friend François de Paris.[37] This name, which seems to appear in his writing for the first time in July 1908, finally became overwhelmingly important, as is indicated in a letter to Georges de Lauris in which he shows himself anxious to know if this name "has no longer any living heirs and if it is thus available for use in fiction."[38] At the time when

35 EcorchevilleL, 51.
36 Tadié, 386–391 and 498–500.
37 Marcel Proust, "Lettre à Francois de Paris," [July 1908], in ProustC, vol. VIII, 172–173. See also Sandra Beyer, "Une étymologie possible du nom de Guermantes," *Bulletin de la Société des amis de Marcel Proust et des amis de Combray* 31 (1981), 319–322.
38 Marcel Proust, "Lettre à Georges de Lauris," [May 1909], in ProustC, vol. IX, 102. On Proustian onomastics, see Eugène Nicole, "Un modèle de fonctionnement stylistique du nom propre dans la phrase proustienne," *Lingua e stile* (September 1977), 459–480; and "Genèses onomastiques du texte proustien," *Cahiers Marcel Proust* 12, *Etudes proustiennes* 5 (1984), 69–125. The

A la recherche du temps perdu was being written, the name of Guermantes, which at first was simply a place name contrasting with that of Méséglise, was substituted for a former choice, Villebon. This occurred around May 1909. It was only later that the name of Guermantes was used as a patronymic.[39] This name, not included in Saint-Simon's *Mémoires*, is very similar to the Guermanty of the genealogical chart. Moreover, it is in 1909 that the name of Combray definitively replaces that of Etreuille, which was sometimes in *Jean Santeuil* as the fictional name for the real Illiers. The similarity of this place name with the name Combreux, a family linked by marriage to Lully's granddaughter, is thought-provoking. Moreover, it was in the chateau of Combreux in the Loiret region, by then the property of the La Rochefoucauld d'Estissac family, that Ecorcheville found the documents which permitted him to establish the genealogy of the musician.

It may be argued, however, that the possibility of Ecorcheville's articles influencing Proust's choice of names is denied by the irrefutable fact of their publication date of 1911, given that the names Guermantes and Combray had played a fundamental role as early as 1909. If any direct influence must be rejected, is it possible that Proust got wind of this information indirectly?

It seems quite unlikely that the novelist acquired this information from the source. As George Piroué has pointed out, Proust, like all the people of his caste, fled anything that might suggest pedantry and, in this sense, any knowledge of music that might be too technical or historical.[40] Thus, he had nothing but contempt for Romain Rolland, whom he criticizes in the *Contre Saint-Beuve*.[41] As for Prunières, Proust criticizes him sharply for having had the audacity to attack two of his best-loved areas of interest: "One senses his incompetence regarding Vermeer and Debussy, eyes that cannot see, ears that cannot hear."[42] If Proust is numbered among those

latter article includes a specific bibliography (124–125). The psychoanalytical approach of Alain Roger owes nothing to the present study's perspective: see A. Roger, *Les plaisirs et les noms* (Paris: Denoel, 1985).

39 Mireille Marc-Lipiansky, *La naissance du monde proustien dans Jean Santeuil* (Paris: Nizet, 1974), 73.
40 Piroué, 29–30.
41 Marcel Proust, "Romain Rolland," in Clarac, 307–310.
42 Marcel Proust, "Lettre à Jacques Rivière" [April 25, 1920], in ProustC, vol. XIX, 237.

authors who have spoken best about music, his approach, instinctive and full of sensibility, leads him sometimes to write nonsense: a case in point being his comments on an excellent article Prunières devoted to Erik Satie's *Socrate*.[43]

On the other hand several people might have served as intermediaries to describe the tenor of Ecorcheville's work to Proust before its publication. First and foremost was Reynaldo Hahn, whose interest in Lully and his music had appeared as early as 1905 at the time when Rolland, Prunières, Ecorcheville, and La Laurencie were pursuing their work. Although committed to the aesthetics of Gounod, Saint-Saëns, and Massenet, Hahn seems to have maintained close ties with the SIM. In January 1910, the latter organization paid homage to Joseph Haydn, the occasion for which Hahn composed a *Thème varié*. Although no trace of further collaborations has been found, we can infer their regular continuation from an item among the obituaries in which the editors announced the demise of the mothers of "our two collaborators and friends, Messrs. Reynaldo Hahn and Lionel de La Laurencie."[44] As we have already seen, Jacques Rivière contributed regularly to the *Mercure musical*, but it is only after 1914 that he became Proust's close friend.

Another group could also have served as a link with the musicological activities of the SIM. Indeed, Ecorcheville, while aiming at the broader public, had not severed connections with the privileged social classes. Indeed, it was through them that he was able to support his ventures and promote his musical evangelizing. The Société française des amis de la musique aimed to bring together "all those who love music, to help in the broadest possible way in the development of the musical arts in France and in its dissemination abroad; to offer its support and patronage to any musical presentation worthy of interest, so as to create the appropriate means of action to realize, in addition to the artistic program, a social, philanthropic, and utilitarian initiative which will ennoble its efforts and justify its mission."[45]

43 Henry Prunières, "Erik Satie, à propos de *Socrate*," *La nouvelle revue française*, 14 (1920), 605–608.

44 *Revue musicale S.I.M.* 4 (April 1912), 72.

45 *Revue musicale S.I.M.*, supplément (December 1912), 69. In its supplements entitled "Le mois" the SIM routinely listed the names of new members. It is upon these many subscription lists that we rely.

As in his work at the center of the SIM, Ecorcheville, as secretary general of the Société française des amis de la musique, presided over the fortunes of that organization, which brought together a social elite drawn from all parts of the cultural horizon around a presumed common love of music. Even if Proust, already afflicted by his illness, does not seem to have been part of it, a number of his acquaintances participated in its activities, for example, the vice-president (later president) of the administrative board, Prince Auguste d'Arenberg, member of the Institute and president of the Suez company. Proust, who met him in Trouville at the Strausses', seems to have borrowed from him some traits given to Monsieur de Norpois and to the Prince of Guermantes.[46] We find on the advisory board, among the aristocratic members, the names of Countess René of Béarn, the Countess of Haussonville, Countess Paul de Pourtalès, Adhéaume de Chevigné, Princess Bassaraba de Brancovan, the Marquise de Ganay, Baroness Gunsburg, and the Marquis of Polignac. Just as in *A la recherche du temps perdu*, this fringe of the upper aristocracy who took Dreyfus's part in that notorious affair associated with the world of high finance, especially its Jewish members: Baron Zuylen de Nyevelt de Haar, husband of Hélène de Rothschild, Mrs. Alfred Mayrargues, Mrs. Emile Pereire, and Mr. Wiener, son of Louis Stern in whose salon Proust had been a frequent guest. These are the same names that occur in Proust's correspondence and in his literary works.

If Proust, doubtless too ill, seems never to have numbered among the members of the Société des amis de la musique, many of his closest associates did, and one cannot help being struck by the massive presence of his relatives and friends. These include his cousins of the Cruppi family (related through the Crémieux), Ely Rodrigues, father-in-law of Charles Nathan (a distant relative of Proust's mother with whom she had nevertheless remained very close), and especially Mrs. Georges Weil (his aunt, *née* Amélie Oulman, the wife of Mme Proust's brother). Furthermore, they include the Bénacs, the Catusses, and the Finallys, all families most closely related to Proust. One also finds three doctors, Bres, Richelot, and Blondel, all colleagues of Adrien Proust. Among the novelist's close friends, we should mention Michel Ephrussi (related to the Fould family and to

46 ProustRTP, vol. III, 1383; Tadié, 390, note 1.

Charles Ephrussi), Théodore Reinach (brother of Joseph Reinach and a close friend of Mme Strauss), the translator Geneviève Séligman-Lui (related to Reynaldo Hahn), Alice J. Bizet (the wife of Jacques Bizet, ex-wife of Georges Sachs, another member of the society), Mrs. Jules Dietz (whose daughter had been engaged to Francis de Croisset, who instead married the daughter of Madame Laure de Chevigné), and even Jacques Porel, the son of the actress Réjane, the model for Proust's character Berma.

Let us also point out in particular the presence of Baron Otto Bouwens van der Boijen, a fleeting and little known figure in Proust's intimate life.[47] Born in 1872, Otto Bouwens was the son of an architect born into the upper nobility of the Netherlands. Marcel Proust, who met him at the Sciences-Po, collaborated with him between 1890 and 1891 on the journal he directed, *Le mensuel*. Bouwens published several comedies while pursuing a career as dilettante composer. He was also president of the Société des concerts de la Sorbonne. In 1895, he played a role we still do not understand in the correction of the proofs of Albert Lavignac's *La musique et les musiciens* overseen by Reynaldo Hahn.[48]

Among these individuals who might have given Proust information on Lully's genealogy, there were still, of course, direct descendants: Countess Greffulhe and her daughter, Elaine, wife of the duke de Guiche. Clearly, as Ecorcheville recognized, its discovery could not but make a splash in Parisian high society:

> It will not escape the attention of our readers familiar with the musical life of Paris that, on the same genealogical chart of the various descendants of the great musician, one encounters, coming from two different sides, the illustrious names of Riquet de Caraman and Greffulhe, now so felicitously combined in the person of Mme la présidente of the Grandes Auditions de France, Mme the Countess Greffulhe, *née* de Caraman-Chimay. It is as though music had conspired to give us here an ingenious example of musical predestination.[49]

If this generous step up, from a musical point of view, might appear flattering for Countess Greffulhe, we can wager that not a few tattletales were

47 Tadié, 144–145.

48 Marcel Proust, "Lettre à Reynaldo Hahn" [1895], in ProustC, vol. I, 406–407. Note that Madame Dettelbach, in whose house Reynaldo Hahn was then living, was also a member of the Société des amis de la musique.

49 EcorchevilleL, 51–52.

amused to see that she was descended, on both sides, from the Florentine miller.

How could Proust, who made this issue one of the major themes of his masterwork, then already underway, not have been struck by the spectacular social displacement which, in two centuries and only eight generations, had elevated the descendants of a miller to the dignity of the highest French aristocracy? Proust is often compared to Saint-Simon, and like the latter, he kept the chronicle of a given society at a given point in time. To be sure, this comparison is relevant and Proust did everything he could to make the reader aware of it. Nevertheless, by contrast with Saint-Simon, it is the erosion through time of the entire social fabric that is the foundation of *A la recherche du temps perdu*.

From this point on one can assess Proust's full interest in a meditation on the names of family and genealogy:

> Names would retain their beauty now that they were no more than names, now that, disincarnated, they had no more relationships in the talk that one makes of marriages – for it is always with marriages that questions of family relations and heritage find their end – but with other names . . . To be sure, the marriages that I meant to cite in the first instance were for me especially interesting when they concerned M. or Mme de Guermantes. For given its vague nature, unknown to me as it was, the name of their house I kept alive in its own terms, always the same in the past, names of other families into which it had married brought with them various characteristics, often unforeseen, which were hedged in here and there, oriented to a side that I already knew, giving to it a form, describing to me its complexity, allowing me to situate it more exactly . . . Sometimes one of these names coming to me from the eighteenth century to bond with the name of the Guermantes either as one of the Trémoïlle family as a friend of the Guermantes or as some literary or military personality that I found, as a name, either unheard of and nouveau-riche and which inflated itself, as far as I was concerned, to contain within it some marriage with the Trémoïlle family duly noted in history. The name brought with it from the grand exploits that I had learned of under Louis XIV, either from its status or the ranking that it enjoyed in the *Mémoires* of Saint-Simon or in Mme de Sévigné's letters or even simply from the very names Guermantes or Trémoïlle, an effigy which engraved itself on some lackluster, valueless metal to make of it for me a wondrous antique medallion.[50]

50 Marcel Proust, "Esquisse XXXII," ProustRTP, vol. II, 1268–1269.

The example the narrator chooses to illustrate this point is Monsieur de Beaucerfeuil, to whom M. de Norpois wants to offer his daughter's hand in marriage. Mme de Guermantes does not recognize the name, but her husband remembers that the Beaucerfeuils, having since retreated into obscurity, had been related under Louis XIV to a female ancestor of "the Laigle or the Durfort family." In Proust's contemporary reality, this family relationship was that of Charles de Laigle – a descendant of Lully – with Elisabeth Colbert – a descendant of the musician's patron. But what would have been a mismatch in Saint-Simon's time had eventually reversed itself: in *Le Temps retrouvé*, it is in fact the Laigle family which, in marrying into the Colbert family, might fear a similar misalliance:

> Even in that past to which I traced back the Guermantes name in order to give it all its grandeur ... the phenomenon that I was now observing used also to occur. Do we not find them at that time allying themselves by marriage, for example, with the Colbert family, which today seems to us of very noble rank, it is true, since marrying a Colbert is regarded as a fine match for a La Rochefoucauld? But the Guermantes did not ally themselves with the Colberts on account of the latter being noble, for they were simply bourgeois at that time; rather it is through their alliance with the Guermantes that they became noble.[51]

To conclude, if one cannot claim that Ecorcheville's work on Lully's genealogy played a direct role in Proust's archive of names, it would seem difficult to deny that it contributed to some extent to the richness of themes in *A la recherche du temps perdu* because it alerted Proust to the origins of certain contemporaries of his whom he took as models – less glorious by birth than by talent. In their names is inscribed the immense social ferment of Time, henceforth and forever recaptured.

51 Marcel Proust, *The Past Recaptured*, trans. Frederick A. Blossom (New York: Random House, 1927), 1066.

Works cited

Siglum	Citation
Algarotti	Algarotti, Count, *Essai sur l'opéra traduit de l'Italien du comte Algarotti par M.****, Pisa: Ruault, 1773.
AnthonyF	Anthony, James R., *French Baroque Music from Beaujoyeulx to Rameau*, revised edition, New York: W. W. Norton & Co., 1978.
AnthonyF97	*French Baroque Music from Beaujoyeulx to Rameau*, revised and expanded edition, Portland: Amadeus Press, 1997.
AnthonyJ	"Jean-Baptiste Lully," in *The New Grove French Baroque Masters: Lully, Charpentier, Lalande, Couperin, Rameau*, London: Macmillan, 1986.
AnthonyP	"Printed Editions of André Campra's *L'Europe Galante*," *The Musical Quarterly* 56 (1970), 54–73.
Arnaud	Arnaud, François *Œuvres* (reprint of the Paris edition of 1803 [in 12 vols.]), Geneva: Slatkine Reprints, 1972.
Barthélemy	Barthélemy, Maurice, *Catalogue des imprimés musicaux anciens du conservatoire royal de musique de Liège*, Liège: Pierre Mardaga, 1992.
BeaussantL	Beaussant, Philippe, *Lully, ou le musicien soleil*, Paris: Gallimard/Théâtre des Champs-Elysées, 1992.
Becker	Becker, Heinz (ed.), *Quellentexte zur Konzeption der europäischen Oper im 17. Jahrhundert*, Kassel, Basel, and London: Bärenreiter, 1981.
BlainvilleE	Blainville, C. H., *L'Esprit de l'art musical ou Réflexions sur la musique et ses différentes parties*, Geneva: [no publisher], 1754.
BrossardC	Brossard, Yolande de, *La Collection Sébastien de Brossard 1655–1730*, Paris: Bibliothèque nationale de France, 1994.
BrossardY	*Sébastien de Brossard, théoricien et compositeur, 1655–1730*, Paris: Picard, 1987.
BUC	Schnapper, Edith B., *The British Union Catalogue of Early Music Printed Before the Year 1801*, 2 vols., London: Butterworths Scientific Publications, 1957.
Carlson	Carlson, Marvin A., *Places of Performance: The Semiotics of Theatre Architecture*, Ithaca, NY: Cornell University Press, 1989.

CessacCe	Cessac, Catherine, *Marc-Antoine Charpentier*, Portland: Amadeus Press, 1995.
CessacCf	*Marc-Antoine Charpentier*, Paris: Fayard, 1988.
ChampierP	Champier, Victor, *Le Palais Royal d'après des documents inédits (1629–1900)*, ed. G.-Roger Sandoz, Paris: Henri Veyrier, 1990.
Clarac	Proust, Marcel, *Contre Sainte-Beuve, précédé de Pastiches et mélanges, et suivi de Essais et articles*, ed. Pierre Clarac, Paris: Gallimard 1971.
CouvreurL	Couvreur, Manuel, *Jean-Baptiste Lully: musique et dramaturgie au service du Prince*, Brussels: M. Vokar, 1992.
CoeymanO	Coeyman, Barbara, "Opera and Ballet in Seventeenth-Century French Theatres: Case Studies of the Salle des Machines and the Palais Royal Theatre," in *Opera in Context*, ed. Mark Radice, Portland, Oregon: Amadeus Press, 1997.
CPM	*The Catalogue of Printed Music in the British Library to 1980*, vols. XXXII and XXXVI, London: K. G. Saur, 1982 and 1985.
Davidsson	Davidsson, Åke, *Catalogue critique et descriptif des imprimés de musique des XVIᵉ et XVIIᵉ siècles conservés dans les bibliothèques suédoises*, Uppsala: Almquist & Wiksells, 1952.
De Rochemont	De Rochemont, *Réflexions d'un patriote sur l'opéra françois, et sur l'opéra italien*, Paris, 1754.
Ducoin	Ducoin, Pierre-Antoine-Amédée, *Catalogue des livres que renferme la bibliothèque publique de la ville de Grenoble*, vol. II, Grenoble: Baratier frères et fils, 1835.
DucrotR	Ducrot, Ariane, "Les représentations de l'Académie royale de musique à Paris au temps de Louis XIV (1671–1715)," *RMFC* 10 (1970).
Dunning	Dunning, Albert, "Music Publishing in the Dutch Republic: The Present State of Research," in *Le Magasin de l'univers: the Dutch Republic as the Centre of the European Book Trade*, Papers Presented at the International Colloquium Held at Wassenaar July 5–7, 1990, ed. C. Berkvens-Stevelinck, H. G. Buts, P. G. Hoftijzer, and O. S. Lankhorst, Brill's Studies in Intellectual History, XXXI, Leiden: E. J. Brill, 1992, 121–128.
EcorchevilleL	Ecorcheville, Jules, "Lully gentilhomme et sa descendance," " Lully gentilhomme et sa descendance: les fils de Lully," "Les filles de Lully," *S.I.M. Revue musicale mensuelle* (May 15–July 15, 1911), 1–19, 1–27, and 36–52.
EcorchevilleT	Laloy, Louis, Lionel de la Laurencie, and Emile Vuillermoz, in *Le tombeau de Jules Ecorcheville suivi de lettres inédites*, Paris: Dorbon, [1916].

Eeghen   Eeghen, I[sabella] H[enriette] van, *De Amsterdamse Boekhandel* (1680–1725), 5 vols. in 6, Amsterdam: Stadsdrukkerij, 1960–78.

Eitner   Eitner, Robert, *Biographisch-Bibliographisches Quellen-Lexikon*, 10 vols., Leipzig: Breitkopf & Härtel, 1898–1904; reprint Graz: Akademische Druck und Verlagsanstalt, 1969.

EM   *Early Music*, London: Oxford University Press, 1973– .

Fétis   *Catalogue de la bibliothèque de F. J. Fétis acquise par l'état belge*, Paris: Firmin-Didot, 1877; reprint Bologna: Forni, n.d.

Fraenkel   Fraenkel, Gottfried S., *Decorative Music Title Pages: 201 Examples from 1500 to 1800*, New York: Dover, 1968.

Gasperini   Gasperini, Guido, *Catalogo delle opere musicali, teoriche e pratiche, di autori vissuti sino ai primi decenni del XIX secolo, esisenti nelle biblioteche e negli archivi pubblici e privati d'Italia: Città di Bologna*, 3 parts, Parma: Officina grafica Fresching, 1914–39.

GirdlestoneT   Girdlestone, Cuthbert M., *La Tragédie en musique (1673–1750) considérée comme genre littéraire*, Geneva: Droz, 1972.

GML   *Gresham Music Library: A Catalogue of the Printed Books and Manuscripts Deposited in Guildhall Library*, London: Corporation of London, 1965.

GOL   *Gosudarstvennaya Ordena Lenina Biblioteka SSSR imeni V. I. Lenina. Otdel notnykhizdanii i zvukozapisei* [State Order of Lenin Library of the USSR Named for V. I. Lenin. Division of Music Publications and Recordings], Moscow: 1986.

Goovaerts   Goovaerts, Alphonse, *Histoire et bibliographie de la typographie musicale dans les Pays-Bas*, Antwerp and Brussels, 1880; reprint Amsterdam: Frits Knuf, 1963.

GrosQ   Gros, Etienne, *Philippe Quinault, sa vie et son œuvre*, Paris: Champion, 1926; reprint Geneva: Slatkine, 1990.

Guibert   Guibert, A[lbert]-J[ean], *Bibliographie des œuvres de Molière publiées au XVIIe siècle*, 2 vols., Paris: CNRS, 1977 (reprint of the 1961 edn. with the supplements of 1965 and 1973).

GustafsonLI   Gustafson, Bruce, "The Legacy in Instrumental Music of Charles Babel, Prolific Transcriber of Lully's Music," in Heidelberg87, 495–516.

GustafsonLL   "The Lully Labyrinth: Cross References and Misattributions in the *Lully-Werke Verzeichnis*," *Notes: Quarterly Journal of the Music Library Association* 44 (1987), 33–39.

Harman   Harman, R. Alec, *A Catalogue of the Printed Music and Books on Music in Durham Cathedral Library*, London: Oxford University Press, 1968.

Hawkins   Hawkins, Sir John, *A General History of the Science and Practice of Music*, ed. Charles Cudworth, 2 vols., New York: Dover, 1963 (reprint of the Novello edn. of 1853; original edn., 1776).

Heidelberg87   *Jean-Baptiste Lully: Actes du colloque / Kongressbericht Saint-Germain-en-Laye – Heidelberg 1987*, ed. Jérôme de La Gorce and Herbert Schneider, Neue Heidelberger Studien zur Musikwissenschaft, 18, Laaber: Laaber-Verlag, 1990.

HeyerL   Heyer, John Hajdu (ed.), *Jean-Baptiste Lully and the Music of the French Baroque: Essays in Honor of James R. Anthony*, Cambridge: Cambridge University Press, 1989.

Hirsch   Hirsch, Paul, and Kathi Meyer, *Katalog der Musikbibliothek Paul Hirsch, Frankfurt am Main*, 4 vols., Frankfurt am Main and Cambridge: M. Breslauer, 1928–47.

Hortschansky   Hortschansky, Klaus, "Die Datierung der frühen Musikdrucke Etienne Rogers: Ergänzungen und Berichtigungen," *Tijdschrift van de Vereniging voor Nederlandse Muziekgeschiedenis* 22 (1972), 252–286.

HowardG   Howard, Patricia, *Gluck and the Birth of Modern Opera*, London: Barrie and Rockliff, 1963.

Husk   Husk, W. H., *Catalogue of the Library of The Sacred Harmonic Society*, rev. edn., London: The Society, 1872.

Huys   Huys, Bernard, *Catalogue des imprimés musicaux du XVIIIe siècle*, Brussels: Bibliothèque royale Albert Ier, 1974.

JAMS   *Journal of the American Musicological Society*, Richmond, Va.: etc.: American Musicological Society, 1948– .

Kidson *et al.*   Kidson, Frank, William C. Smith, and Peter Ward Jones, "John Walsh (i)," *NG*, vol. XX, 185–186.

Kleerkooper   Kleerkooper, M. M., *De Boekhandel te Amsterdam voornamelijk in de 17^e eeuw: biographische en geschiedkundige aantekeningen*, Bijdragen tot de Geschiedenis van den nederlandschen Boekhandel, vol. X, The Hague: Martinus Nijhoff, 1914–16.

Koole   Koole, Arend, "Roger," *Die Musik in Geschichte und Gegenwart*, ed. Friedrich Blume, vol. XI, Kassel: Bärenreiter, 1960, cols. 630–631.

Laeven   Laeven, A. H., "The Frankfurt and Leipzig Book Fairs and the History of the Dutch Book Trade in the Seventeenth and Eighteenth Centuries," in *Le Magasin de l'univers: the Dutch*

Republic as the Centre of the European Book Trade. Papers Presented at the International Colloquium Held at Wassenaar July 5–7, 1990, ed. C. Berkvens-Stevelinck, H. G. Buts, P. G. Hoftijzer, and O. S. Lankhorst, Brill's Studies in Intellectual History, XXXI, Leiden: E. J. Brill, 1992, 185–197.

La GorceA   La Gorce, Jérôme de, "Une Académie de musique en province au temps du roi-soleil: l'opéra de Rouen," in *La Musique et le rite sacré et profane. Actes du XIIIe congrès de la Société internationale de musicologie, Strasbourg, 29 août–3 septembre 1982*, vol. II, ed. Marc Honegger and Paul Prevost, Strasbourg: Association des publications près les Universités de Strasbourg, 1986, 465–496.

La GorceC   "Contribution des Opéras de Paris et de Hambourg à l'interpretation des ouvrages lyriques donnés à La Haye au début du XVIIIe siècle," in *Aufklärungen: Studien zur deutsch-französischen Musikgeschichte im 18. Jahrhundert – Einflüsse und Wirkungen*, vol. II, ed. Wolfgang Birtel and Christoph-Helmut Mahling, Heidelberg: Carl Winter, Universitätsverlag, 1986, 90–104.

La GorceE   "L'Evolution du décor sur la scène du Palais Royal de 1673 à 1763," *Image et Spectacle: Actes du XXXIIème Colloque International d'Etudes Humanistes* (1989), 405–423.

La GorceO   *L'Opéra à Paris au temps de Louis XIV, Histoire d'un théâtre*, Paris: Desjonquères, 1992.

LagraveT   Lagrave, Henri, *Le théâtre et le public à Paris de 1715 à 1750*, Paris: Librairie C. Klincksiek, 1972.

LajarteB   Lajarte, Théodore de, *Bibliothèque musicale du Théâtre de l'Opéra: Catalogue*, Paris: Librairie des Bibliophiles, 1878; reprint Hildesheim: Olms, 1969.

La Laurencie   La Laurencie, Lionel de, and Amédée Gastoué, *Catalogue des livres de musique (manuscrits et imprimés) de la Bibliothèque de l'Arsenal à Paris*, Paris: Droz, 1936.

LecerfC   Lecerf de la Viéville, Jean-Laurent, sieur de Fresneuse, *Comparaison de la musique italienne et de la musique françoise*, second edition, 1704–06; reprint Geneva: Minkoff Reprints, 1972.

LesureB   Lesure, François, *Bibliographie des éditions musicales publiées par Estienne Roger et Michel-Charles Le Cène, Amsterdam: 1696–1743*, Paris: Heugel, 1969.

LesureC   *Catalogue de la musique imprimée avant 1800 conservée dans les bibliothèques publiques de Paris*, Paris: Bibliothèque Nationale, 1981.

LesureCM	*Collection musicale André Meyer*, Abbeville: n. pub., n.d.
LesureE	"Estienne Roger et Pierre Mortier: Un épisode de la guerre des contrefaçons à Amsterdam," *Revue de Musicologie* 38 (1956), 35–48.
Leuven	Leuven, Lienke Paulina, *De Boekhandel te Amsterdam door katholieken gedreven tijdens de Republiek*, Hooiberg-Epe: N.V. Drukkerij, n.d. [1951?].
Libourne	*Catalogue des œuvres composant la bibliothèque communale de la ville de Libourne*, Libourne: Imprimerie Libournaise, 1897.
LMC	Little, Meredith E., and Carol G. Marsh, *La Danse Noble: An Inventory of Dances and Sources*, Williamstown, New York, Nabburg: Broude Brothers Limited, 1992.
LullyOC	*Œuvres complètes de Jean-Baptiste Lully*, ed. Henry Prunières, Paris: Editions de la Revue Musicale, 1930–39.
Marnat	Marnat, Marcel, *Maurice Ravel*, Paris: Fayard, 1986.
Mélèse	Mélèse, Pierre, *Le Théâtre en France au XVIIᵉ siècle*, Paris: Documentation française, 1957.
Neville	Neville, Don J. (ed.), "Opera 1: Being the Catalogue of the Collection Opera 1600–1750 in Contemporary Editions and Manuscripts now in the Holdings of the Music Library of The University of Western Ontario," *Studies in Music from The University of Western Ontario*, 4 parts (1979).
NG	*The New Grove Dictionary of Music and Musicians*, ed. Stanley Sadie, London: Macmillan, 1980.
Noske	Noske, Frits, "L'Influence de Lully en Hollande (1670–1700)," in Heidelberg87, 591–599.
NUC	*The National Union Catalog Pre-1956 Imprints*, 754 vols., [London]: Mansell, 1968–81.
ParfaictH	Parfaict, Claude, *Histoire de l'Académie Royale de Musique (1645–1742)*, c. 1741. Manuscript, F-Pn, Manuscrits français 12355. Transcription annotated by Renée Girardon-Masson, F-Pn, Département de Musique, Vmb. 47. Manuscript copy by Beffara, F-Po, Rés 536. This work was probably written in collaboration with his brother François.
Parma	*Catalogo generale delle opere musicali, teoriche o pratiche, manoscritte o stampate … Città di Parma*, Parma: Zerbini & Fresching, 1911.
Pincherle	Pincherle, Marc, "Notes sur Estienne Roger et Michel-Charles Le Cène," *Revue Belge de Musicologie* 1 (1946–47), 82–92.
Piroué	Piroué, Georges, *Proust et la musique*, Paris: Denoel, 1960.

PlanelliO   Planelli, Antonio, *Dell'opera in musica trattato*, Naples: Donato Campo, 1777; ed. Francesco Degrada, Fiesole: Discanto, 1981.

PogueB   Pogue, Samuel F., "Ballard, Christophe," *NG*, vol. II, 85–86.

PogueR   "Roger, Estienne," *NG*, vol. XVI, 99–101.

Poole/Krummel   Poole, H. Edmund, and Donald W. Krummel, "Printing and Publishing of Music," *NG*, vol. XV, 232–74.

Primi-Visconti   Primi-Visconti, Jean-Baptiste, *Mémoires sur la cour de Louis XIV, 1673–1681*, ed. Jean-François Solnon, Paris: Perrin, 1988.

ProustC   Proust, Marcel, *Correspondance*, ed. Philippe Kolb, Paris: Plon, 1970–73.

ProustRTP   *A la recherche du temps perdu*, ed. Jean-Yves Tadié, Paris: Gallimard, 1987–89; trans. C. K. Scott Moncrieff and Terence Kilmartin, rev. D. J. Enright as *In Search of Lost Time*, New York: Modern Library, 1992.

PrunièresF   Prunières, Henry, "Lully, fils de meunier," *Revue musicale S.I.M.* 6 (June 15, 1912), 57–61.

PrunièresL   "Lettres et autographes de Lully," *Revue musicale S.I.M.* 3 (March 15, 1912), 19–20.

PrunièresO   *L'Opéra italien en France avant Lulli*, Paris: E. Champion, 1913; reprint New York: Johnson Reprint, 1970.

PrunièresJ   Prunières, Henry and Lionel de La Laurencie, "La jeunesse de Lully (1632–1662)," *S.I.M. Revue musicale mensuelle* 17 (1910), 234–242, 329–353.

Puskas   Puskas, Regula, *The Music Library of Erwin R. Jacobi. Rare Editions and Manuscripts*, 3rd edn., Zurich: Hug, 1973.

Ranum   Ranum, Patricia, "'Mr de Lully en trio': Etienne Loulié, the Foucaults, and the Transcription of the Works of Jean-Baptiste Lully (1673–1702)," in Heidelberg87, 309–330.

RaschD   Rasch, Rudolf, "The Dutch Republic," in *Music and Society: The Late Baroque Era from the 1680s to 1740*, ed. George J. Buelow, Englewood Cliffs, NJ: Prentice Hall, 1994, 393–410.

RaschM   "De muziekoorlog tussen Estienne Roger en Pieter Mortier (1708–1711)," *De zeventiende eeuw* 6 (1990), 89–97.

RISM   *Répertoire international des sources musicales – International Inventory of Musical Sources*, Frankfurt/Main, Germany: *RISM* Zentralredaktion; Cambridge, Mass.: U.S. *RISM* Office at Harvard University, 1977– .

RMFC   *Recherches sur la musique française classique*, Paris: J. Picard, 1960.

Rosow   Rosow, Lois Ann, "Lully's *Armide* at the Paris Opéra: A Performance History: 1686–1766," Ph.D. dissertation, Brandeis University 1981, University Microfilms International 81–26893.

Saint-MardR Rémond de Saint-Mard, *Réflexions sur l'Opéra*, The Hague, 1741; reprint Geneva: Minkoff, 1972.

SauvalH   Henri Sauval, *Histoire et recherches des antiquités de la ville de Paris*, 3 vols., Paris: C. Moette, 1724; reprint Farnborough: Gregg Press, 1969.

ScheurleerA Scheurleer, D[aniel] F[rançois], "Eene Amsterdamsche uitgave van Lully en Colasse. 1690," *Tijdschrift der Vereeniging voor Nederlandsche Muziekgeschiedenis* 9 (1914), 250–251.

ScheurleerM *Muziekhistorische museum van Dr. D. F. Scheurleer. Catalogus van de muziekwerken en de boeken over muziek*, 3 vols., The Hague: Martinus Nijhoff, 1923–25.

SchmidtC   Schmidt, Carl B., *The Livrets of Jean-Baptiste Lully's Tragédies Lyriques: A Catalogue Raisonné*, New York: The Broude Trust for Musicological Publications, 1995.

SchmidtE   "An Episode in the History of Venetian Opera: The *Tito* Commission (1665–66)," *JAMS* 31 (1978), 442–466.

SchmidtG   "The Geographical Spread of Lully's Operas During the Late Seventeenth and Early Eighteenth Centuries: New Evidence from the Livrets," in HeyerL, 183–211.

SchmidtN   "Newly Identified Manuscript Sources for the Music of Jean-Baptiste Lully," *Notes: Quarterly Journal of the Music Library Association* 44 (1987), 7–32.

SchmidtP   "Une Parodie hollandaise peu connue sur la musique de Lully: les *Opwekklyke Zedezangen*," *Dix-septième Siècle* 40 (1988), 371–386.

SchmidtT   "Tito," *The New Grove Dictionary of Opera*, ed. Stanley Sadie, vol. V, London: Macmillan, 1992, 745.

Schmieder   Schmieder, Wolfgang and Gisela Hartwieg, *Musik: alte Drucke bis etwa 1750. Kataloge der Herzog-August-Bibliothek Wolfenbüttel*, vol. XII, Frankfurt am Main: Vittorio Klosterman, 1967.

SchneiderA Schneider, Herbert, "The Amsterdam Editions of Lully's Orchestral Suites," in HeyerL, 113–120.

SchneiderC *Chronologisch-thematisches Verzeichnis sämtlicher Werke von Jean-Baptiste Lully (LWV)*, Tutzing: Hans Schneider, 1981.

SchneiderF "Die französische Kammersuite zwischen 1670 und 1720," in *Jakob Stainer und seine Zeit*, ed. Walter Salmen,

Innsbrucker Beiträge zur Musikwissenschaft, 10, Innsbruck: Hebling, 1984, 163–173.

SchneiderP "La Parodie spirituelle de chansons et d'airs profanes chez Lully et chez ses contemporains," in *La Pensée religieuse dans la littérature et la civilisation du XVIIᵉ siècle en France*, ed. Manfred Tietz and Volker Kapp, Paris, Seattle: Papers on French Seventeenth-Century Literature, 1984, 69–89.

SchneiderR *Die Rezeption der Opern Lullys im Frankreich des Ancien Régime*, ed. Hellmut Federhofer, Mainzer Studien zur Musikwissenschaft, 16, Tutzing: Hans Schneider, 1982.

Schuurman Schuurman, P., "Estienne Roger en de Amsterdamse muziekuitgeverij," *Spiegel historiael* 22 (1987).

Selhof Selhof, Nicolas, *Catalogue of the Music Library, Instruments and Other Property of Nicolas Selhof, Sold in the Hague; 1759*, Auction Catalogues of Music: A Series of Facsimilies, ed. Alec Hyatt King, vol. I, Amsterdam: Frits Knuf, 1973.

Sèvres98 *Quellenstudien zu J. B. Lully/L'œuvre de Lully: Etudes des sources. Hommage à Lionel Sawkins*, ed. J. de La Gorce and Herbert Schneider, Musikwissenschaftliche Publikationen 13, Hildesheim: Georg Olms Verlag 1999.

SmithA Smith, William C., *A Bibliography of the Musical Works Published by John Walsh During the Years 1695–1720*, London: Oxford University Press, 1948.

SmithC *Catalogue of Printed Music Published Before 1801 in the British Museum*, 2nd supplement, London: 1940.

Sonneck Sonneck, Oscar, *Dramatic Music (Class M 1500, 1510, 1520): Catalogue of Full Scores*, Washington: Government Printing Office, 1908; reprint New York: Da Capo, 1969.

Strizich Strizich, Robert, "Derosier [Derozier], Nicolas," *NG*, vol. V, 383.

Swift Swift, Katherine, "Dutch Penetration of the London Market for Books, c. 1690–1730," in *Le Magasin de l'univers: the Dutch Republic as the Centre of the European Book Trade*, Papers Presented at the International Colloquium Held at Wassenaar July 5–7, 1990, ed. C. Berkvens-Stevelinck, H. G. Buts, P. G. Hoftijzer, and O. S. Lankhorst, Brill's Studies in Intellectual History, XXXI, Leiden: E. J. Brill, 1992, 266–279.

Tadié Tadié, Jean-Yves, *Marcel Proust. Biographie*, Paris: Gallimard, 1996.

Trovato Trovato, Robert, *Regestro dei manoscritti in lingua francese esistenti presso il Civico museo bibliografico musicale di Bologna*, Bologna: Patron, 1980.

Vanhulst	Vanhulst, Henri, "Le Chevalier, Amédée," *NG*, vol. X, 584.
Veen	Veen, Henk Th. von, "Pieter Blaeu and Antonio Magliabechi," *Quaerendo* 12/2 (1982), 130–158.
Vlam	Vlam, Christiaan C., "Le Chevalier (Chevallier), Amédée," *Die Musik in Geschichte und Gegenwart*, ed. Friedrich Blume, vol. VIII, Kassel: Bärenreiter, 1960, cols. 426–427.
Walker	Walker, Thomas, "Due apocrifi corelliani," in *Nuovissimi studi corelliani: atti del terzo congresso internazionale (Fusignano, 4–7 settembre 1980)*, ed. Sergio Durante and Pierluigi Petrobelli, Quaderni della Rivista italiana di musicologia, 7, Florence: Leo S. Olschki, 1982, 381–401.
Wood	Wood, David, *Music in Harvard Libraries: A Catalogue of Early Printed Music and Books on Music in the Houghton Library and the Eda Kuhn Loeb Music Library*, Cambridge, Mass.: Harvard University Press, 1980.

Index

Académie de Musique
  (Strasbourg), 200, 201, 204,
  212, 214
Académie Royale de Musique, *see*
  Paris Opéra
Aeschylus, 67, 68
airs/arias, 86, 89, 193, 263, 265
  defining/labeling, 82–83, 88
airs de cour, 83, 87
airs de mouvement, 83, 88, 94
Albicastro, Henricus, 117
Albinoni, Tomaso Giovanni, 117,
  121
Algarotti, Francesco, 247, 248,
  259–260
Alizard, Adolphe-Joseph-Louis,
  270
*Amours d'Apollon et de Daphné,
  Les* (Dassoucy), 167, 182
*Amours de Diane et d'Endymion,
  Les* (Sablières/Guichard), 22
*Amours de Jupiter et de Sémélé,
  Les* (Boyer), 195, 196
Andrian, Gustave W., 189
Angiolini, Gaspero, 252
Ansermet, Ernest, 274
Anthony, James R., 72, 80, 101,
  111, 122, 124, 193, 220
Antoine, André, 279
Ariane (Perrin/Cambert), 21
Arnaud, François, 247–248, 251,
  252, 254, 261–262
arranging/arrangements, 117,
  119, 200, 202–215
Astier, Régine, 42

Astrée, L', 166–167, 170
Aubry, Pierre, 274
audience behavior, 218, 231,
  232–233, 234, 263
Auguste d'Arenberg, Prince, 285
Auld, Louis, 167, 173
Aymard, Maurice, 17

Bach, Johann Sebastian, 32
Bacilly, Bénigne de, 83
Ballard family, 102, 108
Ballard, Christophe, 33, 40, 103,
  110–111, 112, 113, 117, 118,
  119–120, 121–122, 124–125,
  127
Ballard, Jean-Baptiste-
  Christophe, 111
Ballet de la jeunesse, Le
  (Delalande), 28
Ballet des Fragments de Lully, 40
Bapst, Germain, 219, 221, 234,
  239
Baussen, Henri de, 40, 86, 111,
  124, 125
Béarn, René de, 279, 285
Beauchamps, Pierre, 39, 41–42, 43
Beaussant, Philippe, 62, 66
Beethoven, Ludwig van, 244
Beijer, Agne, 236
Bella, Stefano della, 220
Bellinzani, François, 21, 22, 25
Benac family, 285
Benserade, Isaac, 194
Berain, Jean, 224, 236, 237–239,
  240

Berlioz, Hector, 244, 270–271
Bertrand, Gustave, 271
Beys, Charles de, 167, 169
Bizet, Alice J., 286
Blaeu, Pieter and Joan, 107, 110,
    114–117, 123, 125, 145–153
Blainville, Charles-Henri de, 93,
    256–257
Blanchet, Jean, 19
Blay, Philippe, 279
Blondel, Dr., 285
Blondel, Jacques François, 226,
    228, 239
Boileau, Nicolas, 59, 270
Boone, Graeme, 72
Borrel, Eugène, 274
Boschot, Adolphe, 274
Boudet, André, 18, 19, 24
Boudet, Jean, 19
Bouillon, Marie-Anne Mancini,
    Duchesse de, 30
Bouwens van der Boijen, Baron
    Otto, 286
Boyé, Pascal, 263
Boyer, Claude, 195, 196
Brancovan, Princess Bassaraba
    de, 285
branle de Poitou, 34
Brenet, Michel, 274
Bres, Dr., 285
Brooks, William, 194
Brossard, Sébastien de, 30, 83,
    121, 123, 199–200, 201–202,
    204
    and *Alceste*, 200, 202–215
Brossard, Yolande de, 199, 201,
    202, 203, 215
Brunet, xv
Buffequin, Denis, 220
Bulletin de la S.I.M., 276–277
Buschmeier, G., 245
Bussine, Romain, 278

cabales, 30
Cahusac, Louis de, 251
Calzabigi, Raniero, 246
Cambert, Marie-Anne, 29
Cambert, Robert, 15, 16, 20, 21,
    23, 28–29, 221
    Pastorale d'Issy, 16–17, 167,
    169, 188
    Pomone, 21, 22, 187, 195, 221
Campra, André, 83, 111, 122
"canevas," 46
Canova-Green, Marie-Claude, 29
Canudo, Riccioto, 274
Caraman-Chimay, Elisabeth,
    278, 282, 286–287
Carissimi, Giacomo, 203
Carlson, Marvin A., 218
Carter, Tim, 72
Castor et Pollux (Rameau), 246
Cavalli, Francesco, 82
Céphale et Procris (Jacquet de La
    Guerre), 202
Cessac, Catherine, 24, 202, 203
Cesti, Antonio, 116
Chabrier, Emmanuel, 277
chaconnes, 32
Chambonnières, Jacques
    Champion, Sieur de, 121
Champeron, Laurens Bersac de,
    22, 23
Champier, Victor, 219, 220, 221,
    224
Charles II, 29
Charpentier, Denis, 18
Charpentier, Elisabeth, 18
Charpentier, Etiennette, 21
Charpentier, Gilles, 18–19, 23,
    30
Charpentier, Gustave, 280
Charpentier, Jean-Baptiste, 30
Charpentier, Jean-Baptiste-
    Thomas, 30

Charpentier, Marc-Antoine, xiv,
15, 16, 17–18, 19, 20, 21,
23–24, 25–30, 199
Actéon, 27
Arts florissants, Les, 27
Couronne de fleurs, La, 27
*Descente d'Orphée aux enfers,
La*, 26, 27–28
Dispute des bergers, La, 27
Feste de Ruel, La, 27
*Idyle sur le retour de la santé du
Roi, L'*, 28
Médée, 30, 199
Petite pastorale, 26
Plaisirs de Versailles, Les, 27
Charpentier, Nicolle, 19
Charpentier, René, 30
Charpentier, Samuel, 18, 19
Chartres, Duke of, 29–30
Chausson, Ernest, 278
Chevalier, Amédée Le, *see* Le
Chevalier
Chevigné, Adhéaume de, 285
choreography, 37–44, 54, 55, 56,
238, 251, 252–253
Christie, William, x
*Chronique musicale de Bordeaux,
La*, 274
"chute," 85
Cocquis, Agata Amelia, 122
Coe, Ada, 173
Colbert, Jean-Baptiste, 21, 22, 23,
25, 221
Colette, 274
Collasse, Pascal, 108, 109, 115
Colonna, Giovanni Paolo, 202
Coltellini, Marco, 244
Combarieu, Jules, 274, 276
Combreux (name), 282, 283
Comtesse d'Escarbagnas, La, 23
Cone, Edward T., 87
context, perception and, 86–87

Cordeliers, 6, 10
Cordey, Jean, 221, 233
Corelli, Arcangelo, 117, 121, 123
Corneille, Pierre, xiv–xv, 104,
189
Corneille, Thomas, 167
Cosset, François, 200
Couperin, François, 277
Couvreur, Manuel, 16, 93, 94,
172, 187, 189
Coypeau, Charles (Dassoucy),
23, 24, 167, 182
Crecy, Odette de, 280
Croyer family, 20
Cruppi family, 285

Dacier, André, 120
dance, 249, 251, 252–253
dramatic context, 47–49, 55
importance of in opera, 239,
249, 252–253
steps and notations, 33, 34,
37–44, 54, 55, 56
dance music and its relation to
dances, 32–56
texts and, 44–47
dance songs, 94
Dangeau, Philippe de Courcillon,
Marquis de, 28
Daniélis, Daniel, 203
Daphné (La Fontaine), 58
Dassoucy (Charles Coypeau), 23,
24, 167, 182
Dauriac, Lionel, 275
Debussy, Claude, 276–277, 283
de la Coste, G. J., 127
Delalande, Michel-Richard, 28
de Lorme, Jean-Louis, 117, 118,
119–120, 121–122
Denizard, Marie, 278–279
Derosier, Nicolas, 109, 111–112,
113, 114

Des Brosses, Anthoine, 195
des Croix, Chrestien, 166
Desmarets, Henry, 220
des Réaux, Tallement, 166–167
Destouches, André Cardinal, 83
Dettelbach, Madame, 286
De Visé, Jean Donneau, 195
Diaghilev, Sergey, 249
Diderot, Denis, 248, 249
Dietz, Mrs. Jules, 286
Dill, Charles, 88, 89
Dorat, Claude-Joseph, 251–252,
    254, 260
Dreyfus, Alfred, 285
Drinkman, Gerrit, 119, 126
Dubos, Jean-Baptiste, 42, 47
Duchesneau, Michel, 278
Ducrot, Ariane, 217, 224
Durand, 275, 277
Durazzo, Giacomo, 244
Duron, Jean, 72, 203, 204
Du Roullet, Marie-François-
    Louis Lebland, 249, 251,
    253, 254, 265

Eccles, John, 121
Ecorcheville, Jules, xii, 272, 273,
    274, 275–276, 277, 278, 279,
    283, 284, 285, 286, 288
Eeghen, I. van, 109, 114, 115, 117,
    118, 120, 121, 122, 126
elision of scenes, 85
Ellis, Meredith, see Little,
    Meredith
Emmanuel, Maurice, 274
English, 113
engraving, 108, 109, 110, 111,
    118, 119, 124
Ephrussi, Charles, 286
Ephrussi, Michel, 285
Estève, Pierre, 88, 89
Esther (Hahn), 279–280

excerpts, identification of, 116
expression marks and
    annotations to parts, 84,
    88–89

Farinel, Michel, 29
Fauré, Gabriel, 278
Favier, Jean, and Favier notation,
    38–39, 40, 42
Félibien, André, 177
Fend, Michael, 245
Ferrand, Michel, 21
Fétis, François-Joseph, 273
Feuillet, Raoul-Auger, and
    Feuillet notation, 37, 38,
    39–40, 42, 43, 54
Filz, Sieur, 25
Fleck, Stephen, 166, 189
Flothuis, Marius, 252
Foggia, Francesco, 203
form, 83–84, 85–95, 193,
    250–251, 265–268; see also
    dance music
Fossard, François, 115, 203
Foucault, Henri, 108
Fould family, 285
Fourdeaux, Mathieu, 201
Fraenkel, Gottfried S., 111
Francine, Jean-Nicolas de, 224,
    281
Franck, César, 278
Froberger, Johann Jacob, 125
Furetière, Antoine, xi

Ganay, Marquise de, 285
Garcin, Laurent, 261
Gastoué, Amédée, 274
gavottes, 37, 47
Gavoty, Bernard, 279
Gebrauchsmusik, 104
genre labels, 82–83
Gethner, Perry, 166, 167

Gherardi, 126
gigues, 37
Girdlestone, Cuthbert M., 61, 62, 66, 67
Gluck, Christoph Willibald von, 244–246, 261–268
  Berlioz on, 270
  and Lully, 243–246, 250–252, 268–271
  Proust and, 280
  and reform of opera, 246–255
  WORKS
  Alceste, 244, 246–247, 250, 261–263, 264, 270
  Armide, 244, 245, 264–268, 280
  Iphigénie en Aulide, 245, 246, 252, 255, 261–262, 264
  Iphigénie en Tauride, 246, 268–269
  Orfeo/Ophée et Eurydice, 246, 252, 261–262, 263, 271
Gombauld, Jean Ogier de, 167
Goncourt, Rémy de, 274
Goovaerts, Alphonse, 114, 126
Gossec, François-Joseph, 244, 245
Gottlieb, Rebecca, 81, 83
Gounod, Charles, 284
Gourret, Jean, 219, 225
Grabu, Louis, 109
Gramont, Armand de, 282
Grande Mademoiselle, La (Anne Marie Louise d'Orléans, Duchesse de Montpensier), 20, 23, 28
Greffulhe, Elisabeth, 278, 282, 286–287
Grétry, André-Ernest-Modeste, 244
Grimarest, Jean-Léonor Le Gallois, sieur de, 89, 94

Grimm, Friedrich Melchior, Baron von, 248–250, 251
Gros, Etienne, 59, 61–62, 69–70, 93
Guarini, Giovanni Battista, 168
Guermantes (name), 282–283
Guernes, Countess de, 279
Guibert, Albert-Jean, 104, 106
Guichard, Henri, 15, 18–20, 21, 22–23, 26, 28–29
Guiche, Elaine de, 286
Guise family, 23–24
Guise, Elisabeth de, *see* Orléans, Elisabeth d'
Guise, Mlle de, 23, 25, 103
Guise musicians, 26, 27–28, 103
guitar notation, 112
Gunsburg, Baroness, 285
Gustafson, Bruce, 101

Hahn, Reynaldo, 271, 279–280, 281, 284, 286
Harris-Warrick, Rebecca, 37, 38, 43, 44, 100
Haussonville, Countess of, 285
Hawkins, John, 118
Haydn, Joseph, 284
hearing, 86–87
Helfer, Charles d', 200
hemiola, 39, 92–93
Heus, Jean Philip, 107–109, 110, 113, 127, 131–133
Hibberd, Lloyd, 281
Hidemark, Ove, 234, 240
Hilgar, Marie-France, 189
Hitchcock, H. Wiley, 24
homosexuality, 281
Horace, 120, 168
Hortschansky, Klaus, 117
Houle, George, 42
Howard, Patricia, 90, 244, 246, 252, 264, 265

identification of excerpts, 116
Indy, Vincent d', 276, 278
instrumentation, 55
internationalism, 276, 277
Iphigénie (Racine), 59

Jacquet de La Guerre, Elisabeth, 28, 202
Johnson, James, 218, 231, 232–233
Jurgens, Madeleine, 221

Kerman, Joseph, 65
Kidson, Frank, 121
Kintzler, Catherine, 47, 64, 93
Kleerkooper, M. M., 108, 114, 118
Koole, Arend, 117, 126
Krummel, Donald W., 114, 118
Kusser, Johann Sigismund, 199

Lacombe, Hervé, 279
Lacombe, Louis, 272
Lacroix, Paul, 272
Laeven, A. H., 121
La Fontaine, Jean de, 26, 58, 281
La Gorce, Jérôme de, ix, 16, 28, 29, 87, 102, 103, 201, 217, 219, 221, 224, 231, 235, 236, 237
Lagrave, Henri, 217, 219, 225, 228, 229, 230, 231
La Harpe, Jean François de, 59
Lajarte, Théodore de, 217, 272
Lalande, Michel-Richard de, *see* Delalande
La Laurencie, Lionel de, xii, 273, 274, 276, 277, 278, 281, 284
Laloy, Louis, 274, 275–276, 277, 278
Lambert, Michel, 87, 111, 189
Lambranzi, Gregorio, 55
Lancaster, H. Carrington, 189
Launay, Denise, 178, 193

Lavignac, Albert, 286
Lawrenson, T. E., 218
Le Brun, Antoine-Louis, x
Le Cène, Elizabeth, 126
Le Cène, Michel Charles, 107, 118, 119, 121, 124, 125–127, 164–165
Lecerf de la Viéville, Jean-Laurent, sieur de Fresneuse, xv, 6, 10, 42, 46, 57, 89, 94
Le Chevalier, Amédée, 107, 114–117, 127, 145–154
Leclair, Jean-Marie, 110
Legrand, Raphaëlle, 72, 85
le Mercier, Jacques, 220
Leopold, Silke, 243, 244, 245, 250
Les Arts Florissants, x
Lester, Joel, xii
Le Suire, Robert-Martin, 251, 252–253, 262–263
Lesure, François, 110, 117, 118, 120, 121, 122–123, 125
Leuven, Lienke Paulina, 114
Le Vau, Jeanne, 19
Le Vau, Louise, 19
Liger, Françoise, 19
Lindgren, Lowell, 116
listening, 86–87
Liszt, Franz, 269
Little, Meredith Ellis, 33, 36, 37, 39, 40
Loret, Jean, 17
Lorme, Jean-Louis de, 117, 118, 119–120, 121–122
Louis XIV, 16, 17, 22, 24, 100–101, 168, 226
  and Charpentier, 30
  and Lully, 26, 57, 200, 218
  and opera, 26, 28, 57, 68, 200, 218, 224, 233
  and the Palais Royal, 219, 221, 224

Louise (G. Charpentier), 280
Loulié, Etienne, 103
loures, 43
Lucretius, 167
Ludres, Marie-Elisabeth,
    demoiselle de, 57
Lulli, Alessandra, 7, 8, 9, 10
Lulli, Caterina (JBL's mother), 4,
    7
Lulli, Lorenzo di Maldo (JBL's
    father), 1–9, 10
    wills, 7–9, 12–14
Lulli, Raffaello, 11
Lulli, Santi, 9, 10
Lully, Jean-Baptiste
    analysis of music, xi, xii,
        32–56, 175, 177–179,
        182–186
    Berlioz and, 270–271
    character, 9, 11, 15, 218, 281
    as choreographer, 42
    death, xv, 28, 224
    genealogy, 1–11, 278–279,
        282–283, 286–288
    Gluck and, 245–246, 265–271
    handwriting, 6
    later interest in and views of,
        243–244, 249–250, 256, 257,
        272–273, 274, 277, 278–282,
        284
    and librettists, 46, 93–94, 194
    life, 1, 5–6, 9, 10–11, 15–16, 20,
        23, 24–26, 28, 29–30, 58,
        102–103
    Liszt and, 269
    lyrics attributed to, 189
    and the Palais Royal theatre,
        218–219, 221, 224, 233
    and pastorale, 166–196
    privileges, 15–16, 18, 22–31,
        58, 102–103
    Proust and, 280

    Rameau and, 256
    relationship with his father, 7,
        8–9, 10, 11
    shaping of scenes, 72–95
    stage design for operas,
        236–239
    WORKS (*see also* performances
        and publications *at end of
        this entry; see also references
        under librettists*)
    Acis et Galathée, x, 196
    Alceste, xiv, 32, 35–36, 37, 47,
        49, 58, 65, 200–201,
        202–215, 250, 271; analysis
        of passages from, 79, 87–88,
        89; arrangement by
        Brossard, 200, 202–215;
        recordings of, x
    Amadis, x, 54, 93
    Les Amants magnifiques, 167,
        168, 180–187, 193, 194–195
    Armide, x, xii, 34, 49, 60, 67, 94,
        193, 249–250, 257, 268, 280;
        analysis of scene from,
        73–86, 88–89, 90, 92–93;
        Gluck and, 245, 246;
        Rameau on, 72, 89
    Atys, x, 40–1, 49, 57, 58, 59, 60,
        61–62, 65–66, 68, 69–70,
        90–92, 202, 250
    Ballet des Amours déguisez, 178
    Ballet des Arts, 33
    Ballet des ballets (*La Comtesse
        d'Escarbagnas*), 23, 193–194
    Ballet des Muses, 168, 170, 171
    Le Ballet des nations, 194–195
    Bellérophon, 44–45, 49
    Le Bourgeois gentilhomme,
        187–189, 193–194, 195,
        270–271
    Cadmus et Hermione, 37, 42,
        45, 58, 200

Comtesse d'Escarbagnas, La, 23, 193–194

Dies irae, 202

Entr'acte d'Oedipe, 39

Les Fêtes de l'Amour et de Bacchus, 60, 194–198

George Dandin, 177–179, 189, 193, 194, 195

Grand Divertissement Royal de Versailles, 177

Isis, x, xiii, 47, 54, 57–59, 61–71

Mariage forcé, Le, 23

Miserere, 202

O Lachrymae, 215

La Pastorale comique, 167, 170–171, 180, 193, 194

Persée, 38, 51–54, 56, 202

Phaéton, x, 33, 47, 49, 50–51, 67

La Princesse d'Elide, 168, 172–177

Proserpine, xii, xiii, 33, 67

Psyché, (*tragédie-lyrique,* LWV 56), 33

Psyché (*tragédie-ballet,* LWV 45), 189–193, 195

Roland, x, 34–35, 47, 48, 49, 67, 94, 250

Le Sicilien, ou l'Amour peintre, 167, 171–172

Te Deum, 202

Thésée, 45, 58

performances of works, ix–x, 37–38, 40, 54, 58, 101–102, 103–104, 195, 200, 201, 202, 216, 217, 221, 222–223, 224, 279, 280

publications of works, xii, xiv, xvii, 33, 35, 40, 78, 86, 102–105, 107–127 *passim,* 127–165, 201

Lully, Jean-Louis de, 115

Lully, "Laurent de," 9

Lully, Louis de, 115, 279

LWV numbers, 102

Mably, Gabriel Bonnet de, x

Magliabechi, Antonio, 114

Mairet, Jean, 167

Malherbe, Charles, 275, 277

marches, 37

Marc-Lipiansky, Mireille, 283

Mariage de Bacchus et d'Ariane, Le (Des Visé), 195

Mariage de la Grosse Cathos, Le (Philidor *l'aîné*), 38

Marini, Biagio, 121

Marnat, Marcel, 277

Marnold, Jean, 274

Marsh, Carol G., 37, 38, 41

Martine, Jacques, 268–269

Martini, Giovanni Battista, 262

Massenet, Jules, 274, 284

Massip, Catherine, xii

Masson, Paul-Marie, xiii, 88, 90, 274

Mayrargues, Mrs. Alfred, 285

Mazarin, Jules, 16, 17, 220

Melani, Atto, 9

Mélèse, Pierre, 221, 228

menuet(s), 33–37, 38–40, 42, 43

menuet de Poitou, 34

Mercure musical, 274–275, 276, 284

"*mesuré,*" 88–89

Metamorphoses (Ovid), 67, 68

Metastasio, Pietro, 253, 256

Meyerbeer, Giacomo, 275

Mignon, Jacques, 19

Mignon, René, 19

Miller, N., 245

Mithridate (Racine), 59

Mittman, Barbara, 233

modulations, 85

Moetjens, Jacob, 126
Moetjens, James, 126
Molière (Jean-Baptiste
    Poquelin), 15, 18, 20, 23–24,
    104, 166–196 *passim*,
    220–221
death, 221
and Palais Royal theatre, 229,
    232
WORKS
Les Amants magnifiques, 167,
    168, 180–187, 193, 194–195
Ballet des Muses, 168, 170, 171
Le Ballet des nations, 194–195
Le Bourgeois Gentilhomme,
    187–189, 193–194, 195,
    270–271
Comtesse d'Escarbagnas, La 23,
    193–194
George Dandin, 177–179, 189,
    193, 194, 195
*Grand Divertissement Royal de
    Versailles*, 177
Le Malade imaginaire, 181
Mariage forcé, Le, 23
Mélicerte, 168–170, 189
La Pastorale comique, 167,
    170–171, 180, 193, 194
La Princesse d'Elide, 168,
    172–177
Psyché (*tragédie-ballet*, LWV
    45), 189–193, 195
Le Sicilien, ou l'Amour peintre,
    167, 171–172
Tartuffe, 189
Montchrétien, Anthoine, 166
Montespan, Françoise Athénaïs
    de Rochechouart, Marquise
    de, 30, 57, 168
Montesquiou, Robert de, 282
Montpensier, Anne Marie
    Louise, Duchesse de (La
    Grande Mademoiselle), 20,
    23, 28
Montreux, Nicolas de, 166
Moreau, Jean Michel, 232
Moreau-Despreux, 229
Morel, Jacques, 167, 168, 177, 189
Mortier, Pierre, 107, 110, 120,
    121–125, 126–127, 162–164
mouvement, xi–xii
Mozart, Wolfgang Amadeus, 250
Mueller von Asow, H. and E. H.,
    245
music history, first international
    congress on, 274

Nathan, Charles, 285
Newman, Joyce, 72
Nicole, Eugène, 282–283
Norman, Buford, 100
North, Roger, 118
Noske, Frits, 104
Nouvelle revue française, La, 274
Noverre, Jean-Georges, 249, 251,
    252
Nuittier, Charles (Charles
    Truinet), xii, 16, 29, 272, 275

opera
  audience behavior, 218, 231,
    232–233, 234, 263
  choral scenes in, 47, 253–254
  dance in, 47–49, 55, 239
  theories and reforms of,
    246–264
Opéra, Paris, *see* Paris Opéra
orchestras, 233
Orfeo (Rossi), 80–81, 82, 182, 220
Orléans, House of, and network,
    xiv, 15–20, 22–24, 25, 26,
    27–31, 219, 224
Orléans, Elisabeth d', 16, 17–18,
    21, 23, 25, 26, 27–28, 29

Orléans, Gaston d', 16, 17, 19, 20, 22
Orléans, Marie-Louise d', 29
Orléans, Philippe I, Duke of, 16, 20, 22, 24, 25, 26, 29, 220, 224
Orléans, Philippe II, Duke of, 219
Oulman, Amélie, 285
Ovid, 67, 68

Palais Royal theatre, 216–242
    fire in, 242
Palisca, Claude, 80
Parfaict, Claude (and François?), 57, 59, 189, 195
Paris Opéra, 37, 39, 40, 43, 47
    performing materials, 88–89, 200
    theatre in Palais Royal, 216–242
passacailles, 32
pastoral, 55, 166–196
Pastorale d'Issy (Perrin/Cambert), 16–17, 167, 169, 188
Pécour, Guillaume, 37–38, 40, 43, 54
pedagogical repertory, 104
Peines et les plaisirs de l'Amour, Les (Cambert), 23
perception, context and, 86–87
Pereire, Mrs. Emile, 285
performers, 40, 249
    expression marks and annotations to parts, 84, 88–89
    responsibility, 87
    separating singers and actors, 47, 249
Périgny, Président de, 194
Perrault, Charles, ix, x–xi, 46, 65, 166, 233

Perrin, Pierre, 16–17, 18, 20, 21, 22, 23, 25, 28–29, 169, 187, 188, 221
    Lully and, 15
    on opera, xiii
    on words for music, 73
    Pastorale d'Issy, 16–17, 167, 169, 188
    Pomone, 21, 22, 187, 195, 221
Pharo, Carol, 41
Phèdre (Racine), 30, 57, 60
Philidor, André Danican *l'aîné*, 34, 38, 115, 244
    and *Alceste*, 203–204, 209, 210
Piccinni, Niccolò, 269
    Didon, 269
    Iphigénie en Tauride, 269
Pièche, Antoine, 26
Pièche, Pierre, 26
Pierce, Ken, 41
Pincherle, Marc, 119–120, 122, 126
Piroué, George, 283
Pirro, André, 274
Pitou, Spire, 219
Planelli, Antonio, 246–247, 255
Pocquelin family, 18, 23
Pocquelin, Jean-Baptiste, *see* Molière
Pocquelin, Madeleine, 18, 19
Pogue, Samuel F., 111, 118, 120, 126
Pointel, Anne, 109
Pointel, Antoine, 104–105, 107, 108, 109–113, 114, 115–116, 119, 124, 133–145
Polignac, Armande de, 275
Polignac, Marquis de, 285
Pomone (Perrin/Cambert), 21, 22, 187, 195, 221
Poole, H. Edmund, 114, 118
Porel, Jacques, 286

Porpora, Nicola, 259
Pougin, Arthur, 272, 273
Pourtalès, Countess Paul de, 285
privileges/monopolies, 15-31
    passim, 110-111, 147-150
Prod'homme, Jacques-Gabriel,
    244, 274, 275
Prometheus Bound (Aeschylus),
    67, 68
Prosperité des armes de la France,
    La, 220
Proust, Adrien, 285
Proust, Marcel, 274, 275, 276,
    279, 280-288
Prunières, Henry, ix, xii, 1, 41,
    220, 273, 274, 277, 278, 279,
    281, 284
    Proust and, 283, 284
publication and publishers, 104,
    105-128; *see also under*
    Lully
Purcell, Henry, 121
Pure, Michel de, xii
Purkis, Helen, 177

"Quarrel of the Ancients and the
    Moderns," xi, 59-60
"Querelle d'Alceste," 60
"Querelle des Bouffons," 245,
    247, 254, 256
Quinault, Philippe, xiv-xv, 30,
    42, 45, 46, 59-60, 189, 245
    Berlioz and, 244, 270
    later views of opera and,
        249-250, 255
    libretti, 64, 73, 79, 89, 90
    Lully's ways of working with,
        46, 93-94
    WORKS
    Alceste, 60, 65
    Armide, 59, 60, 67, 73-78, 79,
        84, 85, 90, 95, 265, 280

Atys, 57, 59, 60, 61-62, 65-66,
    68, 69-70, 90-92
Les Fêtes de l'Amour et de
    Bacchus, 60, 194, 195-196
Isis, 57, 59, 60-71
Phaéton, 67
Proserpine, 63, 67
Roland, 59, 67
publications of libretti, 103,
    104, 109

Racan, Honoré de Bueil, Marquis
    de, 167
Racine, Jean, 30, 57, 59, 60, 104,
    245
    and Lully/Quinault, x-xi,
        59-60, 65
Racine, Louis, 84
Radet, Emile, xii, 272, 281
Raffman, Diana, 86
Rambour, Jacob, 233
Rameau, Jean-Philippe, 83, 219,
    253, 272, 275, 277
    Gluck and, 244, 245-246, 261
    and Lully, xii, 72, 89, 245, 256
    Proust and, 280
Ranum, Patricia, 45, 102, 103
Rapin, 123
Rasch, Rudolf, 104
Ravel, Maurice, 274, 276-277,
    278
recitative, 256-264, 265
    "récitatif mesuré," 88
Reichardt, Johann Friedrich, 250
Reinach, Joseph, 286
Reinach, Théodore, 286
Revue musicale, 274, 275
Riccoboni, Luigi, xiii, 228, 229,
    239
Richelieu, Armand Jean du
    Plessis, Cardinal, 220
Richelieu, Duke of, 27

Richelot, Gustave, 285
Richer, 111
Riemann, Hugo, 273, 275
Rivière, Jacques, 274, 284
Robert, Pierre, 203
Robethon, Daniel, 115
Robinet, Charles, 194
Rochemont, Ami de, 254–255, 257–259
Rodrigues, Ely, 285
Roger, Alain, 283
Roger, Estienne, xiv, 105–107, 108, 109, 110, 113, 117–123, 126, 127, 154–162
Roger, Françoise, 118, 119, 126
Roger, Jeanne, 118–119, 126
Rolland, Romain, xii, 273–274, 275, 277, 278, 281, 283, 284
Rollin, Monique, 94
Roquet, Ernest, 272; see also Thoinan, Ernest
Rosier, Charles, 116
Rosier, Nicolas de, see Derosier
Rosow, Lois Ann, 103, 124
Rossi, Luigi, 80–81, 82, 182, 220
Rossini, Gioachino, 275
Rothschild, Hélène de, 285
Rouches, Gabriel, 221
Roy, Pierre-Charles, xiv–xv
Ryer, Isaac du, 166

Sablières, Jean Granouilhet, Sieur de, 22–23, 26
Sacchini, Antonio, 269
Sachs, Georges, 286
Saint-Aubin, Gabriel de, 226, 230, 232, 233
Saint-Mard, Toussaint Rémond de, 59, 89
Saint-Saëns, Camille, 274, 278, 284
Saint-Simon, Louis de Rouvroy, Duc de, 280–281, 283, 287, 288

Samazeuilh, Gustave, 274
Satie, Erik, 284
Sauval, Henri, 220, 229, 232
Schérer, Jacques, 85
Scheurleer, D. F., 115
Schmidt, Carl B., 101, 102, 105, 217
Schmidt, Dörte, 245
Schneider, Herbert, ix, 39, 46, 72, 94, 101, 102, 104, 119, 201, 217
Schumann, Robert, 279
Schwartz, Judith, 41
Schwartz, William Leonard, 221, 229
scoring, 55
Scudéry, Madeleine de, 169
Séligman-Lui, Geneviève, 286
Sénecé, Antoine Bauderon de, 166
Sercy, Charles de, 111
Sévigné, Marie de Rabutin-Chantal, Marquise de, 200, 281
Sevin, Pierre, 232, 233
Silvestre, Israel, 226, 227
Simon, Jean, 233
SIM, see Société internationale de musique
Smith, William C., 121
Société des grandes auditions, 278
Société française de musicologie, 273
Société française des amis de la musique, 277–278, 284–286
Société internationale de musique, 275–277, 278, 279, 284
Société musical indépendente, 278
Société nationale, 277–278
Sonrel, Pierre, 234
Sorel, Paul, 167

Soudain, Agnès, 18
Soudain, Geneviève, 18
Sourdéac, Alexandre de Rieux,
	Marquis de, 22, 23, 221
Spontini, Gaspare, 271
Staats, Leo, 279
Stern, Louis, 285
Stichter, Jean, 107, 112, 114, 145
Straus, Geneviève, 286
Stravinsky, Igor, 277
Strizich, Robert, 112
Sutton, Julia, 39
Swift, Katherine, 126

Tadié, Jean-Yves, 280–281
Tasso, Torquato, 78, 167, 168
tempo, xi–xii
Ténéo, Martial, 274
theatres, xiii, 218, 225
	stage seating, 233
	ticket prices, xiii
	see also Palais Royal theatre
Thoinan, Ernest (Ernest
	Roquet), xii, 16, 29, 272
Thorp, Jennifer, 41
Tiersot, Julien, 243, 244
Tito, Il (Cesti), 116
Torelli, Giacomo, 220
Torelli, Giuseppe, 117, 121
Tralage, Jean Nicolas de, 194, 233
Triomphe de l'Amour, Le (Beys),
	167, 169
Triomphe de l'Amour, Le
	(Sablières/Guichard), 22, 23
*Triomphe de la Raison sur
	l'Amour* (Louis Lully), 279
Tristan l'Hermite, 167
Truinet, Charles, 272; *see also*
	Nuittier, Charles

Tunley, David, 45
type, movable, printing from,
	110–113, 115, 120, 124

Urfé, Honoré d', 166–167, 170

Vanhulst, Henri, 115
Veen, Henk Th. von, 114–15
Veracini, Francesco, 117
Vermeer, Jan, 283
vers lyriques, 73
Vigarani, Carlo, 193, 195, 217,
	218, 221–224, 225, 230, 231,
	232, 233, 234–237, 239, 240
Visée, Robert de, 109
Vitali, Giovanni Battista, 108
Vlam, Christiaan C., 115
Voltaire (François Marie
	Arouet), 218, 242, 254, 272
Vuillermoz, Emile, 276, 278

Wagner, Richard, 244, 275, 277,
	278
Walker, Thomas, 110
Walsh, John, 121
Weigert, Roger-Armand, 237
Weil, Emilie, 285
Wiener, Franz, 285
Wolfgang, Abraham, 109
Wood, Caroline, 72
word-setting, 44–45

Young, Bert Edward, 221
Young, Grace Philpott, 221

Zaslaw, Neal, xv
Zuylen de Nyevelt de Haar,
	Baron, 285